I0124598

'A very timely, relevant, and important book – with a compelling explanation of the true nature of Russia's "hybrid warfare", including eye-opening details of the lengths Russia went to orchestrate the 2014 annexation of Crimea, as well as illuminating examinations of earlier actions that offer insights, as well. DeBenedictis establishes convincingly that Russian "hybrid warfare" is best understood as the modern application of traditional Soviet political warfare practices, such as *active measures, maskirovka*, and *disinformation* – and such understanding is critical in the contemporary era of renewed great power rivalries.' *General David Petraeus, US Army (Ret.), former commander of the Surge in Iraq, US Central Command, and Coalition Forces in Afghanistan and former director of the CIA.*

'A brilliant analysis of modern war by a young, yet seasoned, Army leader. Kent DeBenedictis thoughtfully dissects the "hybrid warfare" conducted by the Russians in Ukraine and shows that while it is explosively effective, it is not new to Russian strategy, or to warfare in general. Success, even survival, may depend on our ability to both understand, and to master it.' *General Stan McChrystal, US Army (Ret.), former commander of Coalition Forces in Afghanistan and Joint Special Operations Command.*

'This is a timely and highly relevant analysis that deserves careful consideration by all those who intend to commentate on the threat.' *General Sir Nick Parker, UK advisor to the Ukrainian minister of defence 2016–19.*

'Why does the West keep getting surprised by Russia? Partly, it is because we do not use the past properly to understand the future, and this impressively researched study precisely addresses that, placing the 2014 seizure of Crimea in the context of Moscow's past adventures, an exercise of value to scholars and policy-makers alike.' *Prof Mark Galeotti, author of* We Need to Talk About Putin: How the West Gets Him Wrong.

'This excellent new book makes a valuable contribution to our understanding of Russian political warfare, challenging existing assumptions and prevailing narratives. Extensively researched, it reveals continuities between historical Soviet political warfare practices and Russia's 2014 intervention in Crimea.' *Dr Tracey German, King's College London.*

# Russian 'Hybrid Warfare' and the Annexation of Crimea

*The Modern Application of Soviet Political Warfare*

Kent DeBenedictis

BLOOMSBURY ACADEMIC

LONDON • NEW YORK • OXFORD • NEW DELHI • SYDNEY

BLOOMSBURY ACADEMIC
Bloomsbury Publishing Plc
50 Bedford Square, London, WC1B 3DP, UK
1385 Broadway, New York, NY 10018, USA
29 Earlsfort Terrace, Dublin 2, Ireland

BLOOMSBURY, BLOOMSBURY ACADEMIC and the Diana logo
are trademarks of Bloomsbury Publishing Plc

First published in Great Britain 2022
This paperback edition published in 2022

Copyright © Kent DeBenedictis, 2022

Kent DeBenedictis has asserted his right under the Copyright, Designs and Patents Act, 1988, to be
identified as Author of this work.

For legal purposes the Acknowledgements on p. xiii constitute an extension of this copyright page.

Series design by Adriana Brioso
Cover image © GENYA SAVILOV/AFP/Getty Images

All rights reserved. No part of this publication may be reproduced or transmitted in any form or by any
means, electronic or mechanical, including photocopying, recording, or any information storage or
retrieval system, without prior permission in writing from the publishers.

Bloomsbury Publishing Plc does not have any control over, or responsibility for, any third-party websites
referred to or in this book. All internet addresses given in this book were correct at the time of going
to press. The author and publisher regret any inconvenience caused if addresses have changed or sites
have ceased to exist, but can accept no responsibility for any such changes.

A catalogue record for this book is available from the British Library.

Library of Congress Cataloging Information.

Names: DeBenedictis, Kent, author.
Title: Russian 'hybrid warfare' and the annexation of Crimea : the modern application of
Soviet political warfare / Kent DeBenedictis.
Other titles: Modern application of Soviet political warfare
Description: London ; New York : I.B. Tauris, 2021. | Includes bibliographical references and index.
Identifiers: LCCN 2021025976 (print) | LCCN 2021025977 (ebook) | ISBN 9780755639991 (hardback) |
ISBN 9780755640003 (epub) | ISBN 9780755640010 (pdf) | ISBN 9780755640027 (ebook other)
Subjects: LCSH: Russia (Federation)–Military policy–21st century. | Hybrid warfare–Russia (Federation)–
History–21st century. | Ukraine Conflict, 2014—Case studies. | Hybrid warfare–Ukraine–Crimea–
Case studies. | Crimea (Ukraine)–Annexation to Russia (Federation)
Classification: LCC UA770 .D4378 2021 (print) | LCC UA770 (ebook) | DDC 947.708/6–dc23
LC record available at https://lccn.loc.gov/2021025976
LC ebook record available at https://lccn.loc.gov/2021025977

ISBN: HB: 978-0-7556-3999-1
PB: 978-0-7556-4003-4
ePDF: 978-0-7556-4001-0
eBook: 978-0-7556-4000-3

Typeset by Deanta Global Publishing Services, Chennai, India

To find out more about our authors and books visit www.bloomsbury.com and
sign up for our newsletters

*The views expressed in this book are those of the author and do not necessarily represent the views of the US Army, the Department of Defense or the US government.*
*To my Brothers and Sisters in Arms*

# Contents

# Figures

# Foreword

When I was appointed to serve as the US Senior Defence Advisor to Ukraine in 2016 by Secretary of Defence Ash Carter, I read everything I could about the country. I studied Ukraine's rich history to understand how historical shifts in this 'borderland' state impacted politics, culture and the economy in the present. But I was especially interested in studying Russia's annexation of Crimea and its support to separatists in Ukraine's eastern oblasts of Donetsk and Luhansk, collectively referred to as the Donbas.

Ukraine's military had atrophied since the end of the Cold War. What had once been one of the largest militaries in the world was a shell of its former self by 2014. Considering an attack by Russia unfathomable, Ukraine was completely unprepared for Russia's seizure of Crimea and its support to separatists in its east. Ukraine recognized that it needed to overhaul its military, prompting Ukrainian president Petro Poroshenko to ask for senior defence advisors from the United States, the United Kingdom, Canada, Lithuania, Poland and Germany to help his country reform its defence establishment. I was the first to arrive in October 2016 with my counterparts arriving over the next several months. Together with this remarkable team – the Defence Reform Advisory Board – we worked to provide the young nation with a more effective defence establishment.

Over the next two years, beyond many meetings with President Poroshenko, Minister of Defence Stepan Poltorak and Chief of Defence Viktor Muzhenko, we met with hundreds of officers, ranging from senior generals within their ministry to young officers at the front, conducting training for their Army's second Special Forces Qualification Course and at their national training centre in Yavoriv. We also met with elected officials from the Verkhovna Rada; officials from the defence sector, United Nations and the Organization for Security Co-operation in Europe; volunteers; and other government and non-government officials.

From our first trip to see the troops in their defensive positions in the Donbas, it was clear to see the enormity of the task at hand. Ukraine was attempting to conduct a massive defence reform, in short order, while fighting a war with a large number of forces in defensive positions along the front. As the commander of US Central Command, I witnessed my own military attempt reform on a much smaller scale while fighting wars in Afghanistan and Iraq, so I appreciated their challenge.

To help support and advise our Ukrainian partners, we strove to understand the nature of the 2014 Russian invasion. The world was shocked by Russia's bold and illegal, although brilliantly executed, seizure of Crimea. Less than thirty days after Ukrainian president Viktor Yanukovych fled Ukraine, Russia had successfully annexed Crimea with almost no blood shed and with little real opposition from the international community. In its immediate aftermath, the military operation was studied in great detail by militaries around the world. Many attributed Russia's success to a new model of war, termed 'Russian new-generation warfare' by some and 'Russian hybrid warfare' by others. While these accounts were useful in my preparation as senior defence advisor, they often failed to truly explain what we were seeing or the context of Russia's actions.

I wish that this book, with its insightful study of 'Russian hybrid warfare' and the 2014 annexation, would have been written prior to my experience in Ukraine. Kent DeBenedictis takes an entirely new approach to analysing Russia's seizure of Crimea. Despite being an Army Officer, he analyses the operation not strictly from a military lens but instead through the lens of Soviet political warfare. This unique perspective offers some interesting insights. When comparing Crimea to previous Soviet invasions, DeBenedictis finds that rather than being part of a new form of warfare, instead, it is more of a replay, or twenty-first-century version, of what the Soviet Union did throughout its history, especially in Czechoslovakia in 1968 and Afghanistan in 1979.

While Russia's strategy of political warfare may not be new, a study of its tactics in the Donbas sheds light on what war with a modern state in the twenty-first century might look like. Just as studies of Israel's Six-Day War in 1967 contributed to the development of the US Army's AirLand Battle doctrine that was so effective in the 1991 Gulf War, this conflict needs to be studied to develop the best doctrine given current technologies. Russia's use of drones, electronic warfare, proxy warfare, information warfare and cyber warfare combined with lethal measures of massed artillery, armour and anti-tanks capabilities offer important lessons.

The importance of understanding the true nature of Russian hybrid warfare and its links to the Soviet past is to allow us to prepare for Russia's future actions. As unlikely as it may seem in 2021, Russia's history would indicate that it will attempt a similar invasion in the future. One way to prevent such an invasion is to ensure the preconditions for it do not exist. As such, this book provides a useful understanding of Russia's political warfare tools and hence ways to counter them.

As one of the US Army's Wayne A. Downing Scholars, DeBenedictis was able to use his graduate studies to produce a book of immense value to military, diplomatic and other policy officials. Thus, beyond the useful contribution that this book makes to the understanding of Russian hybrid warfare and countering those practices, it is also a testament to the benefits that the military can reap by investing in the education of its officers.

John Abizaid
Former commander, US Central Command
Former US senior defence advisor to Ukraine

# Acknowledgements

First and foremost, I thank my wife for her support, patience, valuable critiques and reality checks as I completed this work on top of everything else in our lives. I thank my parents for a lifetime of support in all that I have chosen to pursue. I thank the Combating Terrorism Center at West Point and Mr and Mrs Vinnie Viola for their tremendous generosity with the General Wayne A. Downing Scholarship Program, which allowed for the research behind this book. I thank Ruth Deyermond for her encouragement throughout my time working on this project. I thank Mark Galeotti, Tracey German, David Betz, Thomas Rid and the staff and faculty of King's College London for their invaluable feedback on earlier versions. I thank Theo Farrell, JK, GL, GS, JT, DG and the staff of US Embassy Kyiv for the support they gave me to start on the path that has led to this book. I thank AS and MM for the initial inspiration to pursue this topic further. I thank Liam Collins for his tremendous editing and outreach support while putting together this book. I thank the military officers who have gone before me and set the example to pursue PhD-level research for the betterment of our profession. Last and certainly not least, I thank the overwhelming support I received from the Ukrainian military and government, the Fulbright network in Ukraine and the Ukrainian academics, activists, journalists and researchers for their willingness to meet with me and share their experiences and expertise. With this book I hope to help share their story.

# Notes on the text

I have used British spelling throughout the book, including within quotations, in order to standardize the language. I have also used the standard BGN/PCGN romanization of Cyrillic words and names. For Ukrainian proper names and place names, I have used the transliteration from the Ukrainian language. I have used Russian-language transliteration for Russian names. Foreign-language sources are noted as such in the References. All translations into English are my own, either through my own work, the assistance of an interpreter or, in a few cases, through the assistance of machine translation. Any text in square brackets within quotations is my own editing; in all cases, I did not change the meaning or context of the quotation but merely abridged it for clarity or length. Ellipses not in square brackets are from the original source. I am solely responsible for any errors or omissions in the work.

# Abbreviations

| | |
|---|---|
| CIA | US Central Intelligence Agency |
| CIA FBIS | US Central Intelligence Agency Foreign Broadcast Information Service |
| CIS | Commonwealth of Independent States |
| CPCz | Communist Party of Czechoslovakia |
| CPCz CC | Central Committee of the Communist Party of Czechoslovakia |
| CPSU | Communist Party of the Soviet Union |
| CPSU CC | Central Committee of the Communist Party of the Soviet Union |
| ČSSR | Czechoslovak Socialist Republic |
| CSTO | Collective Security Treaty Organization |
| CzPA | Czechoslovak People's Army |
| EU | European Union |
| FRG | Federal Republic of Germany (former West Germany) |
| FSB | Federal Security Service of the Russian Federation |
| GRU | Main Intelligence Directorate of the Soviet Union/of the Russian Federation |
| KGB | Committee for State Security of the Soviet Union |
| MFA USSR | Ministry of Foreign Affairs of the Soviet Union |
| NATO | North Atlantic Treaty Organization |
| NGO | Non-governmental Organization |
| NKVD | People's Commissariat for Internal Affairs of the Soviet Union |
| NSDC | Ukrainian National Security and Defence Council |

PDPA     People's Democratic Party of Afghanistan

SBU      Security Service of Ukraine

StB      State Security of the Czechoslovak Socialist Republic

USAID    US Agency for International Development

USSR     Union of Soviet Socialist Republics

VDV      Russian Airborne Forces

# Map of Crimea with key locations

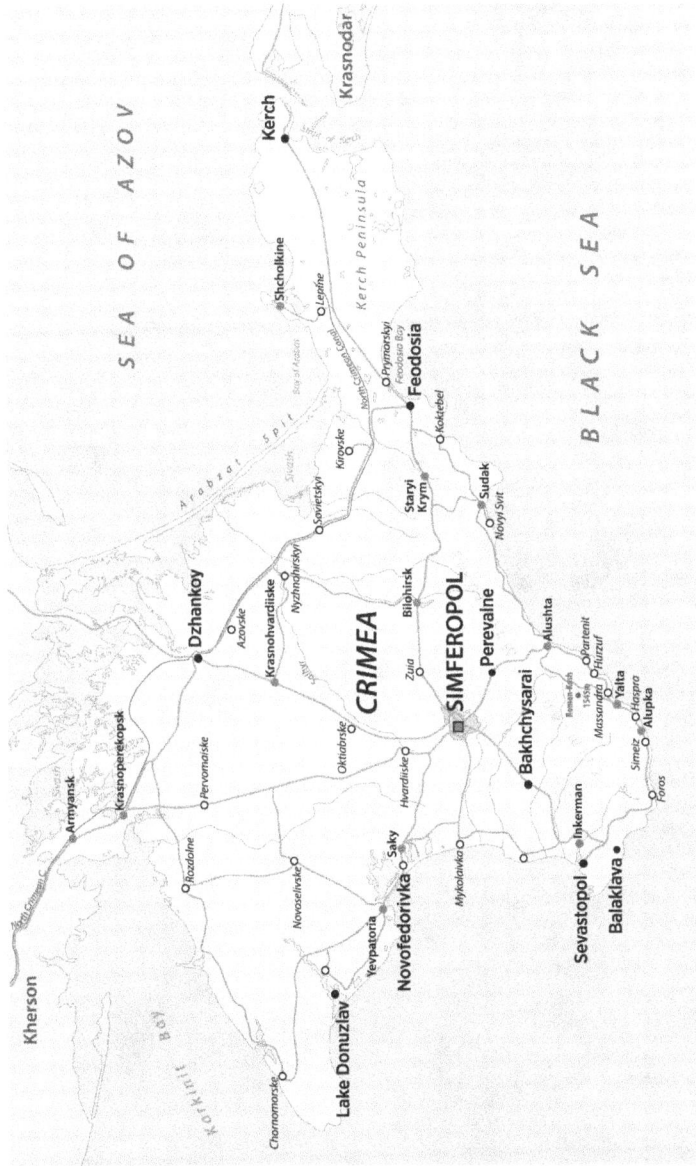

Credit: iStock.com/Rainer Lesniewski, edited by Alison DeBenedictis.

1

# Introduction

In February and March 2014, in the wake of the pro-Western Euromaidan protests that swept over Ukraine and led to the fall of President Viktor Yanukovych's government, the Russian Federation invaded its neighbour and annexed the Crimean Peninsula. The swiftness and decisiveness of the annexation operation sparked an intense wave of literature on the nature of Russia's modern warfare practices. Most commonly, Western academics, politicians and military leaders alike labelled Russia's actions in Crimea and its follow-on operations in Eastern Ukraine as a new form of 'hybrid warfare'. Anders Fogh Rasmussen, the secretary general of the North Atlantic Treaty Organization (NATO) at the outbreak of hostilities in Ukraine, defined 'hybrid warfare' as a combination of military action, covert operations, and a disinformation campaign (Landler and Gordon 2014). General Philip Breedlove, NATO's supreme allied commander at the time, made a similar prognosis, claiming, 'What we see in Russia now, in this hybrid approach to war, is to use all the tools they have [. . .] to stir up problems they can then begin to exploit through their military tool' (Vandiver 2014). The head of Britain's Secret Intelligence Service (MI6) warned that one of his nation's top security threats was 'the increasingly dangerous phenomenon of hybrid warfare', which Russia accomplishes 'through means as varied as cyber-attacks, propaganda, or subversion of democratic process' (Farmer 2016).

Despite these claims, the 2014 Crimean operation was not some new form of warfare but more accurately the Russian Federation's modern application of historical Soviet political warfare practices. The Soviet Union conducted political warfare to attack what it perceived as Western subversion designed to achieve 'counter-revolution' to overturn the communist revolutions in the Soviet sphere. It consisted of overt and covert informational, political and military tools to influence the actions of foreign governments and foreign populations. It involved the use of *active measures*, including propaganda, disinformation, front organizations and forged political processes, as well as *maskirovka*, the military's elaborate deception schemes. Two of the most prominent examples of the Soviet government's application of these political warfare techniques were the 1968 Warsaw Pact invasion of Czechoslovakia in response to the 'Prague Spring' political liberalization programmes and the earliest stages of the 1979 Soviet invasion of Afghanistan. The Soviet government was able to capitalize on these techniques in those campaigns because of the close relationships it held with its fellow communist governments in Czechoslovakia and Afghanistan, giving it the political and military access it needed.

When the 2014 Crimean operation is placed in the context of these historical Soviet political warfare practices, it becomes clear that the Russian government employed these same methods at the operational and tactical levels before and during the annexation. Motivated by the fear of 'colour revolutions' that were sweeping through Eastern Europe and the Middle East in the twenty-first century – a new interpretation of the Soviet belief in Western 'counter-revolutions' – Russia appeared to abandon earlier attempts at cooperation with the West and instead re-adopted the same political warfare responses the Soviet Union and its fellow Communist Bloc countries used throughout the Cold War. Its close ties with the Ukrainian government, especially between the Russian Black Sea Fleet and the Ukrainian Navy in Crimea, expanded under Ukrainian president Viktor Yanukovych's regime and provided the Russian government the same 'fraternal' access the Soviet government utilized in Czechoslovakia and Afghanistan. While in many cases the Russian government adapted these tactics to fit the modern informational, media and political landscapes, the historical linkages of the practices are clear upon closer comparison.

Discussions of Russian 'hybrid warfare' in Eastern Ukraine and elsewhere in the former Soviet states are thus better understood if seen through this lens. Such is also the case to greater comprehend the Russian government's ongoing influence operations in the United States and Europe. As the conflict that spawned these discussions, the 2014 Crimean crisis is the most appropriate starting point to analyse the influence of Soviet political warfare on modern Russian military practice and its consequences for the nature of warfare in the contemporary security environment.

## Structure of the book

To demonstrate these points, this book uses two case studies from the Soviet period, the 1968 invasion of Czechoslovakia and the 1979 invasion of Afghanistan, to refine the concept of Soviet political warfare. It draws on more examples of political warfare practices from throughout the Soviet period, but these two conflicts serve as the core of case study comparison. The book then compares the aspects of the 2014 Russian annexation of Crimea side by side to these Soviet political warfare conflicts to demonstrate that they are pulled from the same toolkit. It is these specific political warfare tools used to execute the campaigns, not necessarily the conflicts themselves, that are the focus of comparison.

The chapters are presented thematically across four key categories: security environment theories, informational tools, political tools and military tools. This approach allows for a more direct, side-by-side analysis across the case studies versus a historical, case-study-by-case-study chapter method. As a result, not all subsections describing a particular aspect of Soviet political warfare cover the three case studies evenly. For any particular tactic or technique, one case study may exhibit an abundance of examples, and another may not display it at all. Military conflict, like all international relations and politics, is a human endeavour. As with all military doctrine, Soviet political warfare techniques moulded to the political and operational environment of each conflict. Whenever a specific aspect of Soviet political warfare is not evident in one of the case studies, an explanation is provided of what situational factors contributed to why it was not used.

The first main purpose of this book is to provide an explanation of Russian 'hybrid warfare' and its connections to Soviet political warfare. Its focus is thus on operations and tactics, not on strategy. It does not answer *why* Russia invaded Crimea or *why* the Soviet Union invaded Czechoslovakia or Afghanistan – outside of the impacts that their respective security environment theories had on their threat perceptions. Instead, it provides the details of *how* the operations were conducted to firmly nest Russia's modern military practices with its Soviet antecedents.

The second main purpose of this book is to paint a detailed, compelling picture of the specific features of Russia's 2014 Crimean operation. It provides original research and new insights into how exactly Russia accomplished the annexation. Those new sources include original interviews with Ukrainian military and defence officials involved in the 2014 crisis, declassified Ukrainian government documents and Russian and Ukrainian media sources. The Crimean case study subsections thus go into more thorough detail than those for the historical case studies, whose main purpose is to establish a framework understanding of the aspects of Soviet political warfare. Viewing the historical case studies through the political warfare lens sheds them in a new light, but this book is not attempting to provide original historical research on the Soviet conflicts. As a result, the Crimean subsections are of significant longer length to provide new information into the nature of the Russian operation.

## Case study selection

This book uses the 1968 invasion of Czechoslovakia and the 1979 invasion of Afghanistan as the two historical case studies because they were two of the three most significant political warfare conflicts the Soviet Union fought during the Cold War. Analysts at the time drew strong connections between the tactics and techniques employed in both conflicts, including the use of deception, subversion and special operations forces, and even considered the invasion of Afghanistan to be modelled on the invasion of Czechoslovakia (see Collins 1986). While the conflicts or the political dynamics surrounding them were by no means identical, they lend themselves as a model of Soviet political warfare tactics and techniques.

Soviet responses to the third significant conflict, the 1956 Hungarian Revolution, in many ways led to the development of the political warfare approaches witnessed in the later conflicts. Yuri Andropov, Committee for State Security (KGB) chairman from 1967 to 1982 and Communist Party of the Soviet Union (CPSU) Central Committee general secretary from 1982 to 1984, was one of the most significant figures in the development and refinement of Soviet political warfare tools; his reaction to the Hungarian Revolution was in many ways the catalyst which led to the implementation of several of these practices. For example, the KGB created Department D (*dezinformatsia*, or disinformation) as a reaction to what it believed it witnessed in Hungary (Dziak 1988: 149).

For the Czechoslovakia and Afghanistan case studies, the starting points of analysis are the discussions among the Soviet leadership in the prelude to the conflict about the possibility of intervention. The ending points are the initial political resolutions of the crises: for Czechoslovakia, the signing of the Moscow Protocol and for Afghanistan, the installation of Babrak Karmal as the new leader of Afghanistan. Outside of additional minor details, this book does not include major follow-on developments, including the replacement of reformer Alexander Dubček with hardliner Gustáv Husák as first secretary in Czechoslovakia in 1969 or the decade-long Soviet war in Afghanistan. These events are beyond the scope of the central Soviet political warfare campaigns that are the focus of this comparison.

For its analysis of Russian 'hybrid warfare', this book concentrates on the 2014 annexation of Crimea. However, most scholarly analysis to date on Russian hybrid warfare – including its components, practices and originality – has instead focused on the conflict in the Donbas region of Eastern Ukraine. On 7 April 2014, three weeks after Russia completed its Crimean operation, violent protesters occupied government buildings in the cities of Donetsk, Luhansk and Kharkiv and called for their own independence from Ukraine. Three pro-Russian separatists were killed in Mariupol ten days later as they tried to seize a military installation, meaning that the conflict immediately surpassed Crimea in the number of lives it cost (BBC 2014c). The Ukrainian government responded with a full-fledged military operation, which is still ongoing. Fighting has been intensive, as the separatists have received tremendous amounts of military support from Russia. Despite significant evidence to the contrary, President Vladimir Putin continues to claim 'outright and unequivocally that there are no Russian troops in Ukraine' (Kremlin 2015).[1]

Because of the severity, duration and magnitude of the ongoing conflict in the Donbas, it has attracted the most attention from researchers. However, the 2014 annexation of Crimea is the most appropriate case study to start an analysis of the genesis of Russia's so-called hybrid warfare. Whereas the war in the East wages on, the Crimean operation is complete, allowing for a holistic view of the operation and the identification of a finite period of study. The Russian government continues to deny its presence in the Donbas, but it has admitted its involvement on the Crimean Peninsula, meaning that more commentary from the Russian perspective – including government statements and speeches – is available for analysis. The Crimean operation is a more direct reflection of any doctrinal changes the Russian military may have made in the period before the conflict, and it was the first instance of what commentators perceive as a departure from recent Russian practice. On the other hand, the campaign in Donetsk and Luhansk benefits from the lessons learned on the Crimean Peninsula and likely incorporates them into an updated strategy, which makes it more of an evolution from the Crimean campaign than a significant shift from earlier Russian practice. Even though the Russian operation in Crimea is shorter in duration and provides fewer data points on tactics and techniques, it is the best case study to illuminate the potential sources of Russia's current 'hybrid warfare' practices, including the influence Soviet political warfare has on those practices.

---

[1]  Putin did subsequently concede that that there were military intelligence officers 'who carried out certain tasks including in the military sphere' (Walker 2015a) but continues to deny anything resembling outright support.

For a similar reason, this book does not address the 2008 Russo-Georgian War (see German 2009; Toal 2017; Gahrton 2010; Cornell and Starr 2009). The Russian government's reintroduction of Soviet political warfare tactics relied heavily on its theory of colour revolution, discussed in detail in Chapter 2. While it began to describe this threat in the early 2000s, it was not until the aftermath of the perceived US interference in the 2011 Russian State Duma elections and Putin's return to the presidency in 2012 that these concepts have truly been refined and taken hold. For example, Russian chief of the General Staff General Valery Gerasimov's seminal article, often cited as the source of some of these tactics, appeared in 2013 (Gerasimov 2013). Because the 2008 Russo-Georgian War predates these developments, it can be seen as a predecessor to the shift in Russian military practice – much as the Soviet invasion of Hungary in 1956 largely predated the refinement of Soviet political warfare practices.

This book's analysis of the Crimean case study starts with the Euromaidan protests beginning in November 2013, as they set off the sequence of events that culminated in Russia's annexation of Crimea in February and March 2014. However, the book also addresses key events that occurred in the months and years before the start of crisis that directly contributed to the Russian government's annexation operation, such as the support it gave to pro-Russian Crimean politicians and political organizations. The end point of analysis is the signing of the annexation agreement on 18 March 2014, with some minor discussion on efforts to consolidate Russian control in Crimea over the following year, especially in the media landscape.

A key similarity between the two Soviet case studies and the Crimean case study is the strong relationship between the Soviet or Russian government and the governments of the targeted states. Czechoslovakia and Afghanistan were fellow communist states at the times of the invasions, meaning the Soviet Union not only enjoyed the 'fraternal bonds' it had with these socialist states, but it also had significant connections at the state level, including advisors serving throughout the structures of their governments. Czechoslovakia was a member of the Warsaw Pact military alliance, which was as much about maintaining Soviet influence over the Pact's member states as it was about deterring NATO aggression (see Sakwa 1998). Afghanistan's communist government similarly owed its success to Soviet support, and both Presidents Nur Muhammad Taraki and Babrak Karmal were recruited KGB agents (Andrew and Mitrokhin 2006: 386–7).

Ukraine has had a complicated history with Russia since independence in 1991, but it still maintained close ties for much of the post-Soviet period. While communism no longer serves as a unifying thread, Russia has relied on the two nations' shared cultural and linguistic heritage as well as strong economic and political connections. The Russian government does not benefit from the dominant role the Warsaw Pact or the role of the CPSU in global communism provided the Soviet Union over its 'fraternal states', but it still believes that it has a legitimate claim to a definite sphere of influence in its 'near abroad' – Russia's post-Cold War term for the countries of the former Soviet Union (Frankland 1992) – of which it strongly considers Ukraine a part (Galeotti 1995b; Lo 2003). The closeness of the Ukrainian government to the Russian government has ebbed and flowed between presidential administrations, but the strong connections under the 2010–14 Yanukovych regime, especially between the Russian Black Sea Fleet and the Ukrainian Navy in Crimea, helped create the sort of interconnectedness that the Soviet Union enjoyed in Czechoslovakia and Afghanistan.

As a result of this distinction, this book is not directly addressing modern Russian activities targeting the United States or other NATO countries. While it defines the concept of Soviet political warfare as a whole and includes several examples of activities that the Soviet Union used to target its Western adversaries during the Cold War, the common thread among the major case studies is the application of those political warfare techniques against fraternal states. There is still broader applicability to the findings, including to modern actions targeting the West, but as the following chapters show, those fraternal connections were key to the success of many of these political warfare tactics. The findings are thus most applicable to other former Soviet and communist states in Russia's perceived sphere of influence.

## Brief historical overviews of the case studies

The following section provides a brief historical overview of each of the three main case studies. The intent of this section is to provide a basic understanding of the nature of the conflicts and their respective political crises before the following chapters then conduct a detailed case study comparison of their specific aspects.

### 1968 Warsaw Pact invasion of Czechoslovakia

The Communist Party of Czechoslovakia (CPCz) came to power after its election victory in 1946. With the backing of the Soviet government, it then solidified its one-party rule in 1948 with a coup to purge non-communists from the government. In 1955, the country was a founding member of the Warsaw Pact, the collective security treaty organization led by the Soviet Union. In January 1968, Alexander Dubček mounted a successful challenge to CPCz first secretary Antonín Novotný and replaced him as leader of the country. CPSU general secretary Leonid Brezhnev chose not to intervene in the power struggle and ultimately welcomed Dubček's appointment because of his expected Soviet leanings based on his previous time spent in Russia. However, Dubček soon implemented a series of liberalizing reforms, which became known as the 'Prague Spring'. These included increased freedom of speech and of assembly and a loosening of government management of the economy. Dubček and his fellow reformers within the CPCz remained committed communists, but they considered their plan 'socialism with a human face'.

The Soviet Union saw these reforms as a threat both to its model of communism, which relied on strict centralized control and minimal dissent with party positions, and to its leading role within the socialist world. In response, it conspired with four other member states of the Warsaw Pact – East Germany, Poland, Bulgaria and Hungary – to invade Czechoslovakia and reverse the reforms before they undermined communist rule from within. Warsaw Pact forces crossed the border on the night of 21 August 1968 as the CPCz members secretly collaborating with the Soviets attempted to dismiss Dubček in a special session of the CPCz Presidium, the government's main executive body. The operation did not go to plan; the military forces reached the Presidium before the critical vote was taken, and Dubček remained in power. Nevertheless, the Warsaw Pact forces continued with the occupation of the country and condemned the 'counter-revolutionary forces' and their supposed Western sponsors that they deemed were secretly behind the reform movement. The Soviet Union arrested Dubček and his key officials and brought them to Moscow for negotiations. Under intense pressure, the Czechoslovak officials agreed to sign the Moscow Protocol, which overturned the series of policy changes they had implemented in the past several months. Dubček remained as first secretary but was forced to resign a year later (for more overview, see Bischof et al. 2010; Dawisha 1984; Dubček 1993).

## 1979  Soviet invasion of Afghanistan

In the April 1978 Saur Revolution, the People's Democratic Party of Afghanistan (PDPA) overthrew and killed President Mohammed Daoud Khan, who in turn had staged a coup against King Mohammed Zahir Shah five years previously. As leader of the PDPA, Nur Muhammad Taraki became president and thus brought communist rule to Afghanistan. Taraki was a recruited KGB agent and had the full backing of the Soviet Union. However, his rule was equally plagued by power struggles both internally with members of his own party and externally with the *Mujahideen* Islamic fighters, who were rebelling against the socialist reforms that the PDPA was now implementing throughout the country. In September 1979, Prime Minister Hafizullah Amin deposed Taraki and took control of the country. He ordered Taraki's murder a month later. Fearful of Amin's erratic, forceful rule as well as his suspected Western leanings – despite being a dedicated communist and leading member of the PDPA, Amin was not a KGB agent but had spent time studying in the United States – the Soviet government conspired with Babrak Karmal, an exiled member of the PDPA, to form a new Afghan government. As another KGB agent, Karmal held the confidence of the Soviet leadership that he would maintain the country in the Soviet sphere.

Over the next few months, the Soviet military deployed several units to Afghanistan. Overtly, they were in the country to support Amin's government against the *Mujahideen*. Covertly, they were planning his downfall. On 27 December 1979, Soviet soldiers disguised as Afghans – including the 'Muslim Battalion', a *Spetsnaz* special forces battalion specifically formed of Central Asian Soviet soldiers to pass as an Afghan unit – stormed the Tajbeg Palace and killed President Amin and members of his family. They quickly installed Karmal as his replacement while consolidating power across the country. Throughout the conflict, the Soviet government attempted to portray the invasion and regime change as an organic Afghan movement. What followed was a massive influx of Soviet soldiers and ten years of bloody conflict plagued by political turmoil and continuous action against the *Mujahideen* (for more overview, see Galeotti 1995a; Braithwaite 2012; Feifer 2010).

## 2014 Russian annexation of Crimea

The Russian Empire under Catherine the Great annexed the Crimean Peninsula from the Ottoman Empire in 1783. After the 1917 Bolshevik Revolution, Crimea remained part of the Russian Soviet Federative Socialist Republic within the Soviet Union. In 1954, however, the Presidium of the Supreme Soviet (the collective head of state of the USSR) issued a decree to transfer the peninsula from Russia to the Ukrainian Soviet Socialist Republic. The reason the Soviet government provided at the time was to streamline the economic management of the region.

Nevertheless, Crimea remained within the Soviet Union, so the move was largely administrative. This changed when the Soviet Union collapsed in 1991. Crimea became an autonomous republic in the newly independent Ukrainian state. The Ukrainian government allowed the Russian Navy to maintain its portion of the Black Sea Fleet in the key port city of Sevastopol, which kept its special status but as a city within Ukraine. The prospect of independence or unification with Russia bubbled up in Crimean politics during a few key instances in the 1990s, especially during a 1995 constitutional crisis, but throughout, Crimea remained as an autonomous republic within Ukraine.

These issues came to a head during the pro-Western protest movement that began in Kyiv in the fall of 2013. On 21 November, Ukrainian president Viktor Yanukovych ordered his government to suspend negotiations with the European Union (EU) on the Ukraine-European Union Association Agreement, the treaty designed to converge Ukraine's economic and political policies with those of the EU and its member states. Ukraine and the EU had been intensely negotiating the treaty since 2011; however, the Russian government viewed the agreement as a threat to its interests because it desired Ukraine, a former Soviet state part of its deemed sphere of influence, to instead join its Customs Union with Belarus and Kazakhstan. After the Ukrainian government announced that it planned to sign the agreement during November 2013's Eastern Partnership summit in Lithuania, the Russian government increased its economic and diplomatic pressure. In August 2013, Russian presidential adviser Sergey Glazyev warned, 'We are preparing to tighten customs procedures if Ukraine makes the suicidal step to sign the association agreement with the EU' (Åslund 2013: 1). After the Ukrainian cabinet had unanimously passed the draft of the association agreement on 18 September 2013 (RFE/RL 2013), Glazyev again threatened that if the Ukrainian government chose to sign the EU agreement at the expense of joining the Russian-led Customs Union, then it would head for a default worth '25 or even 35 billion euros' and topple the economy (Spillius 2013). The Russian government's senior leaders issued these threats directly to their Ukrainian counterparts in the week before the planned summit. Yanukovych held a secret meeting with Russian president Vladimir Putin, and Ukrainian prime minister Mykola Azarov met with Russian prime minister Dmitry Medvedev the day before Yanukovych's decree to halt the negotiations (Traynor and Grytsenko 2013).

Yanukovych's decision to stop the negotiations with the EU sparked the start of months of protests centred on Kyiv's Maidan square that pitted the pro-Western and pro-Russian sectors of Ukrainian society against each other. Close to one million demonstrators gathered as Yanukovych and his pro-Russian Party of Regions attempted to pass strict anti-protest laws and hold onto power. Clashes with police and protesters soon turned violent. Despite signing a compromise deal with his political opponents on 21 February 2014, Yanukovych fled Kyiv the next day for Russia. The following week, masked military men with no national insignia seized key government and military facilities throughout Crimea and Sevastopol, the only regions of Ukraine with a majority ethnic Russian population and the strategic home of the Russian Black Sea Fleet. Under the armed watch of these 'little green men', the Verkhovna Rada of Crimea (the republic's legislative body) suspiciously voted to remove the current leadership, select a new prime minister and hold a referendum on the peninsula's future. The referendum occurred under questionable circumstances on 16 March 2014, and 97 per cent of voters allegedly backed unification with Russia. Putin signed a bill to annex Crimea and Sevastopol into the Russian Federation two days later.

Throughout the operation, the Russian government denied any involvement and claimed that the masked men were 'local self-defence units' (Kremlin 2014h). However, Putin conceded on Russian television a month later that Russian soldiers were 'behind the backs of self-defence forces in Crimea' (BBC 2014c), and a year later he admitted that he had ordered his government on the night of 22 February 2014 to begin 'bringing Crimea back to Russia' (BBC 2015a).

# Key sources

This final section offers additional details and context on some of the more critical sources frequently referenced in this book for both the historical case studies and the Crimean case study.

## Historical case studies

One of the main sources this book uses for primary literature from the 1968 Warsaw Pact invasion of Czechoslovakia is *The Prague Spring 1968: A National Security Archive Documents Reader* (Navratil 1998). The volume is the result of the work of the Czechoslovak Government Commission for Analysis of the Events of 1967–70. With the support of scholars from all of the former communist countries of Eastern Europe as well as from the United States, Canada and some Western European countries, the commission assembled 140 primary documents related to the Prague Spring and the Warsaw Pact invasion, relying heavily on the recently opened archives from these former communist states (Skilling 1998).

A source of primary documents for both the Warsaw Pact invasion of Czechoslovakia and the Soviet invasion of Afghanistan is the Cold War International History Project (CWIHP). Housed in the Woodrow Wilson International Centre for Scholars in Washington, D.C., the project consolidates historical records from the Cold War period, especially from governmental archives from the United States and the former communist states (CWIHP 2018). The collection contains documents from 100 different archives. This book takes advantage of the thousands of records that these anthologies provide, most of which were previously classified, to illuminate the Soviet government's use of its political warfare tactics and techniques to execute the invasions.

Another anthology that offers incredible insights into Soviet political warfare activities throughout the Cold War is the two volumes of KGB archives co-authored by Christopher Andrew and Vasili Mitrokhin (Andrew and Mitrokhin 2000, 2006). Similar to Andrew's work with KGB defector Oleg Gordievsky (Andrew and Gordievsky 1990, 1991, 1992), these volumes provide an extraordinary source of insider documents to help understand Soviet activities during the Cold War. From 1972 to 1982, Mitrokhin was the KGB archivist responsible for moving 300,000 files to the new KGB First Chief Directorate (Foreign Operations) archive building. In the process, he hand-copied thousands of the most important documents, smuggled them to his dacha and defected to MI6 with the copies after the fall of the Soviet Union. While the originals remain classified, a British interdepartmental working group at Whitehall reviewed the content to clear for publication in the anthologies (Andrew and Mitrokhin 2006: xxiii).

Andrew, the University of Cambridge history professor and official UK security service (MI5) historian, has received some criticism that he is filling in gaps in the records, since there are few details on the nature of the original documents, which have largely not been publicly released (Hughes-Wilson 2000; Webster et al. 2000; Getty et al. 2001). However, Andrew claims his role was crucial in synthesizing the documents and providing context and validation through outside sources (Harasymiw 2001). He also received support and information from the British security services in writing the anthologies with both Gordievsky and Mitrokhin (Walker 2003). With these factors taken into account, the Mitrokhin archives are a tremendous resource of KGB activities, especially those related to political warfare.

Two similar anthologies appeared while the Cold War was still ongoing, and they likewise provide an exceptional number of examples of Soviet political warfare practices. In the 1970s and 1980s, John Barron published two volumes on KGB activities (Barron 1974, 1983). He said that he and his research team used world press sources to catalogue reports of KGB activity. They also approached numerous Soviet defectors for interviews or relied on various security services to provide an introduction for them (Barron 1974: xi–xii).

However, Barron did not reveal the extent of the assistance he received. He was a graduate of the US Naval Intelligence School and spent two years serving in Berlin in the 1950s as an intelligence officer (Slusser et al. 1974); he likely used these contacts to maintain a close relationship with the American intelligence services. In a now-declassified memorandum from 1973, David Blee, the US Central Intelligence Agency's (CIA's) associate deputy director for operations, described to the director of Central Intelligence the role the CIA and US Federal Bureau of Investigation (FBI) played in providing the material for the books. He explained that Barron's *KGB* was

> [N]ot a CIA project[,] but Barron has been in touch with Agency officers [. . .] for consultation and advice since 1967 when the idea for the book originated. Barron has also been in contact with the FBI, which gave him considerable help, with MI-6 [*sic*] and with other [W]est European services [. . .] Barron has annotated his book with chapter notes citing actual (non-CIA) sources for virtually everything in the book. Nevertheless, the wealth of detail and relative accuracy and currency of the information will lead knowledgeable observers to infer that the CIA and/or the FBI either wrote or were active collaborators in the book. (Blee 1973)

Barron's books, therefore, were at least in part a secret CIA and FBI project to release damaging material about the KGB. In this regard, they can be seen as an extension of American Intelligence Service archives.

Mitrokhin's KGB archives reveal the impact Barron's books had and the accuracy of his reporting. According to the archives, Barron's 1974 book led to 370 KGB damage assessments and other reports on its impact, and the *rezident* (KGB site lead) in Washington received instructions from KGB headquarters ('Centre') to find ways 'to compromise him' (Andrew and Mitrokhin 2000: 25). Despite Soviet efforts at discrediting him, Barron was not forced to retract any of his published findings, including in the years after the Cold War had ended (Schudel 2005).

Various other defectors published their own memoirs in the West during the Cold War (Sejna 1982; Bittman 1972, 1985; Suvorov 1984a, 1984b, 1989), and they likewise provide valuable insider information into Soviet and Warsaw

Pact political warfare operations. While these stories must be handled with care, as the intelligence agencies may have edited or created some of their elements (Epstein 1989: 41), when taken in proper context, they still provide useful insights. One such example that requires caution is *The Penkovsky Papers*. Oleg Penkovsky was a colonel in the GRU (Main Intelligence Directorate), the Soviet military's intelligence and special forces service. He was executed in 1963 for espionage on behalf of the United States and the United Kingdom (Penkovsky 1965: 17). According to now-declassified documents, the CIA then fabricated a story about how Penkovsky smuggled his memoirs out of the Soviet Union in 1962 and secretly published them as *The Penkovsky Papers* (CIA 1964). However, while the origins of the book are false, the material is mostly original, as the CIA 'incorporate[d] whenever possible Penkovskiy's [sic] own words and phrases from the tapes' of their debriefings (CIA 1963). The content can thus be seen as an insider's reflections on Soviet security service activity.

Aside from inside information from defectors, this book also relies heavily on official Soviet military publications. Soviet military literature remained highly constant across time frames and sources, reflecting the centralized control and review process within the Soviet governmental hierarchy (Douglass 1980). One of those key sources was *Soviet Military Strategy*, written by former deputy defence minister and chief of the General Staff Vasily Sokolovskiy and updated by the Soviet military numerous times (Thomas 2015). While some aspects of it are exaggerated – First Secretary Nikita Khrushchev supposedly instructed its authors to frighten the West with its descriptions of Soviet military might (Kokoshin 1998: 50) – it was still considered 'the most significant military writing of the 1960s, and perhaps of the twentieth century' (Scott and Scott 1988). The work was nominated for the 1969 Frunze Prize, which served as an official endorsement of the views it expressed (Sokolovskiy 1975: xvii). Another book of similar importance was *The Officer's Handbook* (Kazlov 1971), written by several prominent Soviet officials and intended to educate all officers of the Soviet Armed Forces, and especially junior officers, in Soviet military theory. It was part of the Soviet 'Officer's Library' series and was published widely throughout the Soviet Union (Kazlov 1971: vii).

Most significant of the Soviet military publications was *Military Thought*, the official journal of the Soviet Ministry of Defence. A 1989 CIA classified report called it 'the most notable forum for Soviet and Warsaw Pact military officers to discuss and debate changes in the military-technical dimension of military doctrine' (CIA 1989: 5). Articles in the journal came from the most important military organizations, including the Academy of the General Staff, the Frunze

Political Academy, the Lenin Military-Political Academy, the Soviet General Staff and the Ministry of Defence (Douglass 1980: xiii). In 1968, Minister of Defence Marshal Rodin Malinovsky attested to *Military Thought*'s significance when he stated that it 'plays an important role in the working out of military-theoretical problems' (Leebaert 1981: 17). In a testament to that validity, the US government began collecting issues in 1963 and declassifying them in 1976. The articles in the journals matched the doctrinal and strategic developments the West had witnessed throughout the previous decade (Dziak 1981: 2).[2]

## Crimean case study

For the Crimean case study, this book relies heavily on news reporting from the crisis, especially from Russian and Ukrainian news sources. Whenever possible, information is corroborated and deconflicted across reporting. Russian reporting that contradicts the official government narratives, especially interviews with key participants in the annexation operation, is weighted more heavily. These shed a more authentic light on the behind-the-scenes actions during the campaign – and avoid some of the bias that may be prevalent in Russian state media or in Ukrainian news sources. These include interviews conducted years after the events, long after the Russian government formally acknowledged it played a role in the annexation. One news source that has conducted several enlightening interviews is *Meduza*, a Riga-based newspaper created by the former staff of the Russian news site *Lenta.ru* that quit after editor-in-chief Galina Timchenko was fired under government pressure in March 2014 (*Lenta.ru* 2014b).

For perspectives on what has influenced Russian military practices, this book relies on the limited official writing available on the subject. The Russian Ministry of Defence still publishes *Military Thought*, which is no longer classified but is now available by subscription. The journal is still a substantial source of thought and influence within the Russian Armed Forces and the Ministry of Defence today (Bolgov 2017), and this book uses several of its articles to demonstrate the formulation of Russian military thought in the years surrounding the Crimean operation. However, aside from these articles and a few other Russian governmental publications, the official literature on Russian military thought is scarce.

This book, therefore, provides an additional source of information that remains largely untapped, especially in the Western literature: the perspective

---

[2] The Library of Congress and the UCL School of Slavonic and East European Studies library both have extensive collections of *Military Thought* volumes.

of the Ukrainian governmental and military leaders who faced the Russian forces during the Crimean campaign. They are able to recount the details of their interactions with the Russian officials operating on the peninsula, of what they witnessed and of their decision-making during the crisis, thus providing an inside perspective into the nature of the conflict. The Ukrainian servicemen who either still serve on active duty or remained in Ukraine after the annexation can speak freely of what they witnessed – something that few if any Russian servicemen or Ukrainian servicemen who defected can do, especially with Western researchers. Furthermore, the Ukrainian government has declassified some key records from meetings that occurred during the conflict. Interviews with these officials and access to these resources provide further insights into the nature of the conflict in Crimea – and of the tactics and techniques the Russian government employed during it.

In March and April 2017, I conducted thirty-three in-person interviews in Kyiv and Odesa, Ukraine. Personnel included several current and former Ukrainian military officers who were serving in Crimea during the time of the invasion, former senior Ukrainian defence officials, journalists, academics, researchers, leaders of non-governmental organizations (NGOs), activists and others who agreed to meet anonymously. All interviewees had personal experiences from the Crimean operation in 2014 or had conducted specific research on the topic. Full details of what the individuals agreed to share of their biographies are included in the References.

Utilizing these Ukrainian resources requires control for bias. The Ukrainian government has understandably not been a neutral party in its handling of the conflicts in Crimea and Eastern Ukraine and the apparent Russian interference. It passed a law targeting Russia that 'prohibits the promotion of aggressor states . . . or [books] that create a positive image of this aggressor state' (Zaks 2016). The Council of Europe has criticized the Ukrainian authorities for some of these reactions, including the biased investigation of the May 2014 clashes at Odesa's Trade Unions House and subsequent fire, which killed forty-eight people, claiming that it 'failed to meet the requirements of the European Convention of Human Rights' (BBC 2015b). The Ukrainian perspective, however, still provides detailed insights into Russia's operations in Crimea. By structuring interview questions appropriately, drawing conclusions independently of the Ukrainian government's findings and corroborating information with other sources, especially interviews with Russian officials that have since appeared, I attempted to control for this likely bias.

# 2

# Security environment theories

The linkages between Soviet political warfare and modern Russian hybrid warfare practices begin with the parallels between the two states' theories to describe their security environments. The Soviet government's sense of insecurity and fear of Western subversion led it to develop 'counter-revolution theory' to account for what it perceived as the West's actions to undermine socialist governments in the Soviet sphere. Yuri Andropov, who served as both chairman of the Committee for State Security (KGB) and leader of the Soviet Union as Communist Party of the Soviet Union (CPSU) general secretary, was one of the theory's biggest proponents and exemplified the influence it had over the Soviet government's threat perceptions. Counter-revolution theory was the Soviet Union's main explanation for the political developments in Czechoslovakia in 1968 and in Afghanistan in 1979 and its primary justification for armed intervention.

This Cold War view of the security environment remained popular in sectors of the Russian government during the 1990s, but pro-Western policies largely prevailed for much of Boris Yeltsin's presidency and the early stages of Vladimir Putin's presidency. However, events since 2003, especially the so-called colour revolutions, have steadily brought about the return of the 'old thinking' threat perceptions as the norm in Russian security policy. The Russian government has developed its own 'colour revolution theory' of Western subversion to explain the 'true cause' of the wave of democratic movements that swept through the former Soviet states, the Middle East and North Africa in the twenty-first century. General Valery Gerasimov, the chief of the General Staff of the Russian Armed Forces, is the most notable author to describe the theory. The Russian Ministry of Defence's official publications have covered the topic extensively. The Russian government used the precepts of the theory to explain the 2014 revolution in Ukraine and to justify its intervention in Crimea.

Comparing the two theories reveals that colour revolution theory seems to have spawned from counter-revolution theory. They share the same foundational basis and make the same predictions. Both accuse Western governments of waging psychological warfare against states to undermine their governments from within. The two theories consider the West's 'democratization' policies to be a cover for its subversive efforts. Along these same lines, they label non-governmental organizations (NGOs) the front organizations for Western governmental interference in foreign states. Under this mindset, both the Soviet and Russian governments have identified what they consider clear evidence of covert Western leadership of these domestic movements in third countries.

While the purpose of both theories was to describe how the Soviet Union and the Russian Federation perceived Western practices, they simultaneously served as a starting point for the states to develop and implement their own parallel tactics and techniques in response. For the Soviet Union, the result was the development of its political warfare practices. For the Russian Federation, the result was what Western analysts have labelled 'hybrid warfare'. However, because both practices originated in response to what is in effect the same theory, Soviet political warfare and Russian hybrid warfare prescribe nearly identical responses – and thus show the same historical linkages.

## Counter-revolution theory

The fear of counter-revolution, sometimes called 'ideological subversion' (Bittman 1972), was a dominant feature of Soviet ideology. It was even part of the Soviet legal framework. The Criminal Code of the Russian Soviet Federative Socialist Republic (the Russian republic of the Soviet Union) defined counter-revolution as

> [A]ny action directed toward the overthrow, subversion, or weakening of the power of [. . . the] government of the USSR, union and autonomous republics, or toward the subversion or weakening of the external security of the USSR and the fundamental economic, political, and national gains of the proletarian revolution. (RSFR 1934)

The Soviet government believed that Western governments were secretly creating rifts within not only the Soviet Union but also its sister socialist societies to set the conditions to bring about capitalism. It believed they were doing so by undermining communist ideology and unity through propaganda disguised as 'openness' and 'democratization', covertly sponsoring groups seeking to challenge the communist leadership and infiltrating agents to organize and lead the movement against the government, including through armed force. According to the central Soviet leadership, the 1956 Hungarian Revolution and the 1968 Prague Spring in Czechoslovakia were not the result of home-grown reform movements but clear evidence of this Western conspiracy that threatened to infect the entire socialist camp (Suvorov 1984b: 25).

This fear of counter-revolution largely affected the Soviet government's understanding of the security dynamics in the Cold War. As early as 1946, George Kennan (then serving as the US deputy chief of mission in Moscow) warned:

> At [the] bottom of [the] Kremlin's neurotic view of world affairs is [the] traditional and instinctive Russian sense of insecurity [. . .] For this reason they have always feared foreign penetration, feared direct contact between the Western world and their own, feared what would happen if Russians learned the truth about the world without or if foreigners learned the truth about the world within. (Kennan 1946)

To defend against that foreign penetration, Joseph Stalin considered it critical for the Soviet Union to have a delineated sphere of influence. After the Second World War, he established the policy of a *cordon sanitaire*, which British prime minister Winston Churchill popularized as the Iron Curtain, to create a buffer against foreign military aggression and the threat of influence. From the 1950s onwards, Soviet military strategy characterized the creation of the North Atlantic Treaty Organization (NATO) and the Marshall Plan as part of these Western efforts at subversion (Glantz 1992: 169–72).

## The role of the security services and the armed forces

In the Cold War, the Soviet government charged the security services and, to a lesser extent, the armed forces with the responsibility to monitor – and counter – these counter-revolutionary techniques. In a 1960s report, KGB headquarters ('Centre') accused Western governments of conducting 'subversive activity in the political and ideological sphere against the socialist countries . . . seeking to persuade the population of the superiority of the Western way of life', listing among its examples the 'propaganda' spread by the BBC World Service and the US-funded Radio Liberty (Andrew and Mitrokhin 2000: 324).[1] The KGB tracked the activities of Western scholars, students, artists and journalists visiting the

---

[1]   The 'propaganda' accusation was not entirely misplaced, as the CIA covertly funded Radio Liberty and Radio Free Europe until 1972 (see Johnson 2010; Puddington 2000).

Soviet Union because it suspected that they were part of this overarching Western government-driven plot (Bittman 1972: 18).

While the KGB was primarily responsible for identifying and countering ideological subversion, the Soviet military also played a significant role. Even though a conventional East–West war was its main focus (see Douglass 1980; Scott and Scott 1988), the military was still a key player in combating this indirect threat, as evidenced by the military invasions in Czechoslovakia in 1968 and Afghanistan in 1979. For this reason, the Soviet Armed Forces similarly described these supposed Western plots in its literature. *The Officer's Handbook* warned that '[t]he whole of the vast system of anti-Communist propaganda is now aimed at weakening the unity of the socialist countries and the international Communist movement, breaking up the progressive forces of our times and undermining socialist society from within' (Kazlov 1971: 32). The ultimate objectives of these subversive efforts were 'counterrevolutionary wars waged by the bourgeoisie against the proletarian revolutionary movement' (Kazlov 1971: 42). *Soviet Military Strategy* likewise condemned the West's 'so-called "policy of liberation" of the countries of Eastern Europe [. . . and] the systematic provocations of military conflicts in various parts of the globe, including the territories of the socialist camp' (Sokolovskiy 1975: 185–6). To provide military weight against these threats, Soviet minister of defence Marshal Andrei Grechko asserted in 1975 that '[t]he USSR actively and purposefully opposes the export of counterrevolution' and promised that '[t]he combat power of the Armed Forces of the fraternal socialist states' would respond (Scott and Scott 1988: 71).

## Yuri Andropov

Yuri Andropov, KGB chairman from 1967 to 1982 and CPSU general secretary from 1982 to 1984, best exemplified the Soviet government's fear of counter-revolution. He suffered from what his staff called the 'Hungarian complex': Andropov was the Soviet ambassador to Hungary during the 1956 revolution, which he directly attributed to Western interference. He made the lasting conclusion that only the Soviet Union's strong response through armed invasion prevented the fall of the threatened communist regime (Andrew and Mitrokhin 2000: 7). In a speech at a KGB conference in 1979, Andropov explained how seemingly innocuous social activity, such as calls for openness or criticism of the regime, was really part of the West's long-term grand plan to pave the way for counter-revolution:

[D]o various anti-social phenomena or the negative activities of an insignificant handful of people really represent a threat to [the socialist state]? [. . .] Of course not, we reply, if one takes each act or politically harmful trick individually. But if one takes them all together, combining their content with their purpose as regards ideological sabotage, then every such act represents a danger. And we cannot ignore it. We simply do not have the right to permit even the smallest miscalculation here, for in the political sphere any kind of which is hostile to our system – to create an underground, to encourage a transition to terrorism and other extreme forms of struggle, and, in the final analysis, to create the conditions for the overthrow of socialism. (Andrew and Mitrokhin 2000: 431)

He went on to blame both the Hungarian Revolution and the Prague Spring on 'the main organizers of ideological sabotage – the intelligence services and subversive centres of the imperialist nations'. Later, as general secretary, Andropov told the CPSU Central Committee that '[t]he future of mankind depends, in no small measure, on the outcome of this ideological struggle' (Rose 1988: 9). To Andropov, one of the Soviet Union's senior leaders for close to three decades, the threat of counter-revolution defined the struggle with the West.

## Czechoslovakia 1968

Counter-revolutionary theory played a dominant role in the Soviet reaction to the Prague Spring. During the 23 March 1968 meeting of Socialist Bloc countries in Dresden, the leaders of the Soviet Union, Bulgaria, Hungary, East Germany and Poland ('the Warsaw Pact Five') attacked the Czechoslovak leadership for 'losing control' and allowing 'counter-revolution' to develop (Dubček 1993: 140–1). Marshal Ivan Yakubovsky, commander-in-chief of the Warsaw Pact, used a 14 May editorial in *Pravda*, the CPSU's official newspaper, to warn that Western imperialism was 'devoting more and more effort toward the subversive political and ideological struggle against the socialist countries' and that the 'unmasking of anti-Marxist and various kinds of antisocialist elements [. . . was] now acquiring primary significance' (CIA FBIS 1968b: 13).[2] After the Warsaw Pact Five invaded Czechoslovakia that summer, the Soviet leadership even mandated that the Soviet press use this terminology when attributing the cause of the intervention. In a September 1968 meeting with leading Soviet editors, Mikhail Suslov, the chief ideologue for the Politburo (the CPSU's executive committee),

[2] The Foreign Broadcast Information Service (FBIS) was the CIA's component responsible for monitoring and translating foreign media outlets. Several of its archived translated articles are available as part of the CIA's Freedom of Information Act Electronic Reading Room.

directed that they were to use 'creeping counter-revolution' when describing the Prague Spring (Tigrid 1971: 124).

The Soviet Union's clearest explanation of the Western governments' supposed counter-revolution 'model' came during the Prague Spring, as well. On 11 July 1968, *Pravda* published an editorial by I. Aleksandrov – the pseudonym for a direct statement from the Soviet leadership (Cynkin 1988: 27) – titled 'Attack on the Socialist Foundations of Czechoslovakia'. Soviet premier Alexei Kosygin announced on behalf of the Politburo that the article 'reflects our assessment of the events now taking place in Czechoslovakia' (Dawisha 1984: 290). The editorial alleged that 'forces in Czechoslovakia and outside' were trying 'to undermine the Czechoslovak people's friendship with the peoples of fraternal socialist states [and] to prepare the way for counterrevolution'. It blamed the United States and its allies for instigating the reform movement, declaring that '[n]o small role is played in this by the support such forces find among the imperialists in the West'. It called the publication of the '2,000 Words', an editorial signed by seventy prominent Czechoslovaks calling for more intensive reforms, 'evidence of the activation of the right-wing and actually counterrevolutionary forces in Czechoslovakia which are evidently associated with imperialist reaction' (Aleksandrov 1968). The Soviet government's explanation for the liberalizing reforms under Communist Party of Czechoslovakia (CPCz) first secretary Alexander Dubček, therefore, was that Western governments attempted to subvert the Communist Party through covertly creating, sponsoring and supporting counter-revolutionary groups within the country. It viewed the Prague Spring as a model of Western counter-revolutionary tactics.

## Afghanistan 1979

Preventing counter-revolution became the justification for the Soviet invasion of Afghanistan, as well. In March 1979 (nine months before the Soviet intervention), units from the Afghan Army in Herat joined the *Mujahideen* militants fighting against the communist government and led a revolt in the city (see Braithwaite 2012; Urban 1990; Feifer 2010). Soviet foreign minister Andrei Gromyko, however, blamed the violence on

> Bands of saboteurs and terrorists, having infiltrated from the territory of Pakistan, trained and armed not only with the participation of Pakistani forces but also of China, the United States of America, and Iran [. . . who] have joined forces with a domestic counterrevolution. (CPSU CC Politburo 1979d)

An article from three days later in *Izvestia*, the official paper of the Presidium of the Supreme Soviet (the collective head of state of the USSR), claimed that 'foreign agents and mercenaries have been put into Afghan territory and have, together with gangs of counter-revolutionaries [. . .] staged an anti-government uprising in Herat', while Radio Moscow reported that 'Afghanistan has found itself the target of subversive acts launched from Pakistan, Iran, and China' (Urban 1990: 32). In November 1979, the Afghanistan Commission (composed of Andropov, Gromyko, Defence Minister Dmitry Ustinov and CPSU Central Committee International Department head Boris Ponomarev) recommended that the Soviet government take action because of 'the necessity of doing everything possible not to allow the victory of counterrevolution in Afghanistan or the political reorientation of [Afghan President] H. Amin towards the West' (CPSU CC 1979). In its official announcement of the deployment of Soviet troops one month later, the state-run news agency TASS condemned the 'long[-]time interference in [Afghanistan's] internal affairs [. . .] taking place from abroad, including the direct use of armed force [. . . aimed at] the overthrow of the democratic system established as a result of the 1978 April Revolution' (TASS 1979). The statement sent to Soviet ambassadors in fellow Bloc nations defended the intervention because 'armed formations and weapons are being sent into Afghanistan for counterrevolutionary elements and groups whose activity is being directed from abroad' (MFA USSR 1979). As in Czechoslovakia, the Soviet government's explanation for the uprisings in Afghanistan was external subversion, ultimately originating from the US government.

## Evolution of Russian security perceptions

The theory of counter-revolution and the security paradigm that defined it largely guided Soviet decision-making during the Cold War. The Russian government's recent responses to the colour revolutions strongly resemble the Soviet Union's reaction to the fear of counter-revolution. However, this security perception has not always dominated Russian policy. Starting with Mikhail Gorbachev, late Soviet and Russian security perspectives often flipped between viewing Western governments as adversaries and as partners in what could be described as the swings of a pendulum (Legvold 2007). Under Gorbachev's programme of *novoe politicheskoe myshlenie* (new political thinking) reforms initiated in the mid-1980s, the Soviet Union began to shift away from these antagonistic perspectives and towards greater cooperation with the West (see Brown 2008; Sakwa 1990; Sallnow 1989; MccGwire 1991; Shevardnadze 1991). For example, in 1989 Gorbachev called for a 'common European home' as part of improved relations with the Soviet Union's European neighbours (Markham 1989; Malcolm 1989).

Once Boris Yeltsin became president of the new Russian Federation, he at first continued the reformist path Gorbachev had started. The Russian government in the early 1990s emphasized greater international cooperation with the West as it formulated its first national security concept in the post-Soviet period (de Haas 2010). For example, Yeltsin's government initially did not oppose NATO enlargement when the alliance first considered it in 1993 because of its generally 'Atlanticist' perspective (Kugler and Kozintseva 1996). Yeltsin's foreign minister, Andrei Kozyrev, even described NATO as a force for stability in Europe (Ponsard 2007: 61). However, Yeltsin quickly developed a 'hot-and-cold' relationship with NATO, especially in reaction to its military interventions in Bosnia and Kosovo in the Balkans (Galeotti 2010). Yeltsin soon warned of a 'cold peace' in Europe despite NATO's planned inclusion of Russia in the North Atlantic Cooperation Council and the Partnership for Peace military-to-military cooperation programme (Allison et al. 2006).

While Yeltsin's security policies started off as generally pro-Western, significant sectors of the Russian government firmly maintained the 'old thinking' of the Cold War period throughout his presidency. The 'neo-Westernizing' approach to Russian security and foreign relations was always in the minority among both the Russian Federation's elite and general public, even when the approach was dominant in state policy (English 2000). Yeltsin's presidency was in many ways defined by this lack of unity among Russian political actors and institutions in the 1990s (Robinson 2000). He was constantly forced to manage challenges to his foreign policy direction from the more conservative elements within the Russian establishment. In his State of the Federation address in April 1999, Yeltsin named 'preventing schisms and discord within the country . . . our number one task' in *foreign* affairs (Goldgeier and McFaul 2003: 266). For example, Yevgeny Primakov, Russian foreign minister from 1996 to 1998 and Yeltsin's compromise selection as prime minister in 1998, argued for an 'active' foreign policy that sought to challenge the United States and prevent a unipolar world (Tsygankov 2016). Communist Party leader Gennady Zyuganov, Yeltsin's main competitor in the 1996 presidential election, consistently condemned his NATO policies, including calling the 1997 Helsinki agreements with US president Bill Clinton that effectively opened the door for NATO expansion a 'crushing defeat' for Russia (Dutkiewicz and Jackson 1998).

The crisis over the 1999 NATO bombing campaign in Kosovo continued the rift in Russia's relations with the West and allowed some of these conservative viewpoints to prevail (Gorodetsky 2003; Latawski and Smith 2003). Russian politicians from both sides of the spectrum condemned NATO's use of force, causing what was arguably the greatest gulf between the West and Russia since the end of the Cold War. Faced with these pressures, Yeltsin likewise shifted towards an adversarial stance with the West, threatening among other things to send in troops to the Balkans to support the Serbs if NATO launched a ground invasion (Karon 1999). By the end of his presidency, Yeltsin felt that the United States had betrayed the trust he had placed in their cooperation and the concessions he had agreed to: NATO was conducting its first-ever military campaign against Russia's wishes, it was expanding its membership to Russia's traditional sphere of influence and Russia had not received more influence over decision-making in the West's international bodies (Stent 2014).

Despite a short warming of relations after the terrorist attacks on 9/11, Vladimir Putin has continued this aggressive posture towards the United States and the West since he became president in 2000. Initially, Putin maintained the more assertive stance that Yeltsin had settled upon by the end of his presidency. However, the way in which the Russian government supported the United States after the 11 September 2001 terrorist attacks led to fresh cooperation and the belief that the new-found partnership would be enduring (Mankoff 2012). For example, at his speech at the May 2002 Rome summit that created the NATO-Russia Council, Putin did not condemn NATO's eastern expansion as the conservatives in Russian politics would have him do but instead focused on how the agreement signalled a new era of cooperation (Melikova and Korotchenko 2002). At the same time, the conservative threat perceptions remained, especially among Russia's senior military leaders. For example, a 2003 Russian Defence Ministry policy paper warned that NATO's 'offensive military doctrine' would 'require a drastic reorganization of the Russian military's planning and principles of development of the armed forces' (Allison et al. 2006: 10).

The brief period of improved relations did not last, and these Cold War viewpoints again prevailed. The deterioration began when the United States invaded Iraq in 2003. Putin called the decision the 'most serious crisis the world has faced since the Cold War' for the way in which it violated United Nations norms on the use of force (Taylor 2014). What followed in the next two years were the first of the 'colour revolutions' in the former Soviet states: the 2003 Rose Revolution in Georgia, in which protests after a controversial parliamentary election led to the removal of President Eduard Shevardnadze, who had been in power since Soviet times, and a turn towards pro-Western policies; and the 2004 Orange Revolution in Ukraine, in which protests against fraud in the presidential election led to a second run-off that saw the result flipped from the pro-Russian Viktor Yanukovych to the pro-Western Viktor Yushchenko. The George W. Bush administration welcomed the changes in government, leading Russia to conclude that the United States was violating what it considered its legitimate sphere of influence (Stent 2014).

Relations continued to deteriorate over the 2008 Russo-Georgian War (Asmus 2010; Cornell and Starr 2009), and despite the temporary 'reset' of relations with the United States under the Barack Obama administration (Roberts 2014; Rachwald 2011), the conservative, confrontational approach to the West steadily dominated Russian security perspectives. It solidified after the protests following the 2011 elections for the Russian State Duma, the lower house of the Federal Assembly. Putin accused US secretary of state Hillary Clinton of sending 'a signal' to 'some actors in the country [. . . who] with the support of the US State Department began active work' to initiate the protests (Herszenhorn and Barry 2011). Whereas Putin once encouraged cooperation with NATO, he now warned that further expansion would be seen 'as an additional threat to Russia and we will think about how to stop these threats' (TASS 2017b). In the 2014 Russian Military Doctrine, the very first listing under 'main external military risks' was the 'build-up of the power potential of the North Atlantic Treaty Organization', especially 'military infrastructure of NATO member countries near the borders of the Russian Federation, including by further expansion of the alliance' (Kremlin 2014g). A 2014 article in *Military Thought*, the official journal of the Russian Ministry of Defence, described NATO as 'brazenly more aggressive and posing a real threat to the rest of the world, particularly to Russia' (Ilyichyov 2014: 149).

Since the start of the colour revolutions in the mid-2000s, the 'old thinking' about Russia's security threats has prevailed in Russian policymaking. This security ideology is not new; it is the traditional, conservative interpretation of Russia's security environment that was dominant during the Cold War. However, there was not a 'straight line' from Yuri Andropov to Vladimir Putin connecting Soviet and Russian security perceptions; instead, the old Soviet perceptions have re-emerged after periods of pro-Western policy in the 1990s and the beginning of the 2000s.

In parallel with this return to an older mindset, Russia has developed a security environment theory with the same apparent linkages to the Soviet past: colour revolution theory.

# Colour revolution theory

In the twenty-first century, Russia has sought to explain the various democratic movements that have swept not only through the former Soviet states but also through the Middle East and North Africa – the so-called colour revolutions. Russia's use of the term is not limited just to movements such as the Rose Revolution in Georgia, the Orange Revolution in Ukraine and the 2005 Tulip Revolution in Kyrgyzstan; it also broadly includes the 2000 Serbian revolution to oust Slobodan Milošević, the 2014 Euromaidan in Ukraine and the entirety of the Arab Spring in the 2010s. The Russian government explains these phenomena through its colour revolution theory. The Russian literature has developed different terms to describe the concept; authors variably call it 'colour revolution' (Gerasimov 2013), 'colour revolution technology' (Karpovich and Manoilo 2015), 'new-generation war' (Chekinov and Bogdanov 2013) and 'hybrid warfare' (Kiselyov and Vorobyov 2015). Despite the discrepancy in terminology, the descriptions significantly overlap in content and address the same core concept – how to explain the colour revolutions. Regardless of the term used, the conclusion is an old one: the movements are the result of Western governments' subversive activities utilizing a variety of military and non-military tools.

## Gerasimov

The best encapsulation of Russia's view of colour revolution theory is a speech titled 'The Value of Science in Foresight" given by General Valery Gerasimov, the chief of the General Staff of the Russian Armed Forces, to the Russian Academy of Military Sciences a year before the start of the 2014 conflict in Ukraine and summarized in an article in the Russian *Military-Industrial Courier* (Gerasimov 2013). As chief of the Russian General Staff, Gerasimov has much more authority than his nearest equivalents in the American or British systems. His position means he is Russia's senior military planner at the operational and strategic levels. Furthermore, his office is also responsible for force structure and capabilities (Bartles 2016). Thus, his statements – including those defining colour revolution theory – hold the weight of his office, which produces long-term planning guidance for the Russian military.

In the article, Gerasimov emphasized the non-military, psychological and covert nature of modern conflict (see Figure 2.1). He stated that the nature of warfare is shifting towards

[T]he widespread use of political, economic, informational, humanitarian, and other non-military measures implemented by taking advantage of the protest potential of the population [. . .] supplemented by military means of a hidden nature, including the implementation of information warfare and special operations forces. (Gerasimov 2013)

He gave special attention to covert action, especially 'the use of special operations forces and internal opposition [. . .] as well as informational actions, devices, and means that are constantly being perfected'. Gerasimov claimed that 'the so-called coloured revolutions' demonstrate that because the West has developed these tools, 'a perfectly thriving state can [. . .] become a victim of foreign intervention,

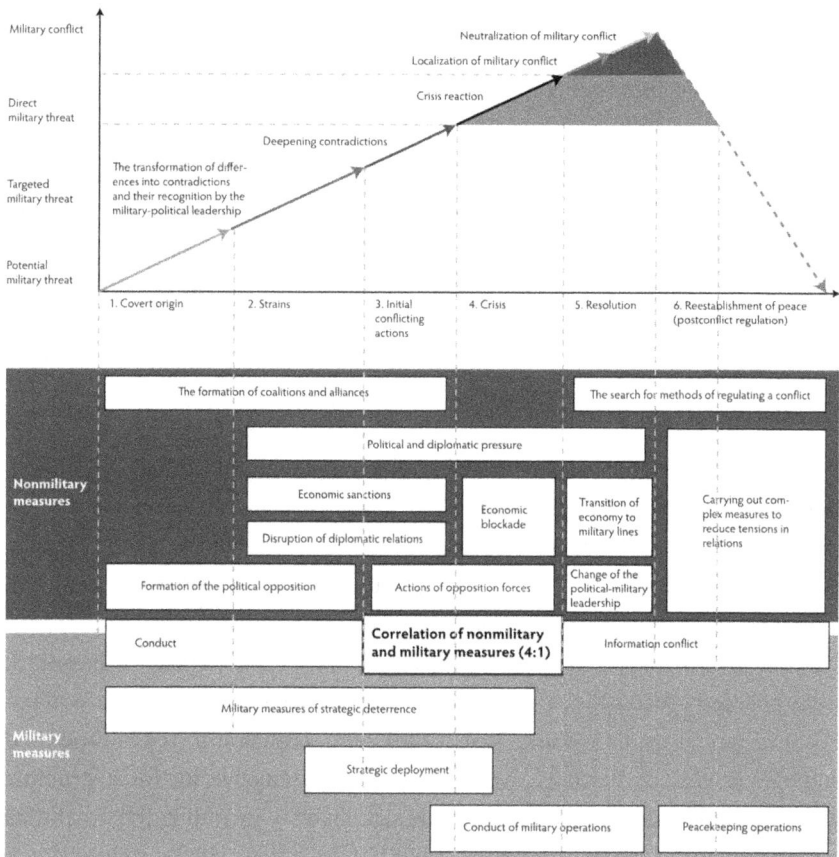

**Figure 2.1** Gerasimov's characterization of the colour revolution model (Gerasimov 2013; graphics recreated by Bartles 2016). This figure is reprinted with the permission of *Military Review*, the Professional Journal of the US Army Combined Arms Center, Fort Leavenworth, Kansas. It was originally published in the January–February 2016 issue of *Military Review*.

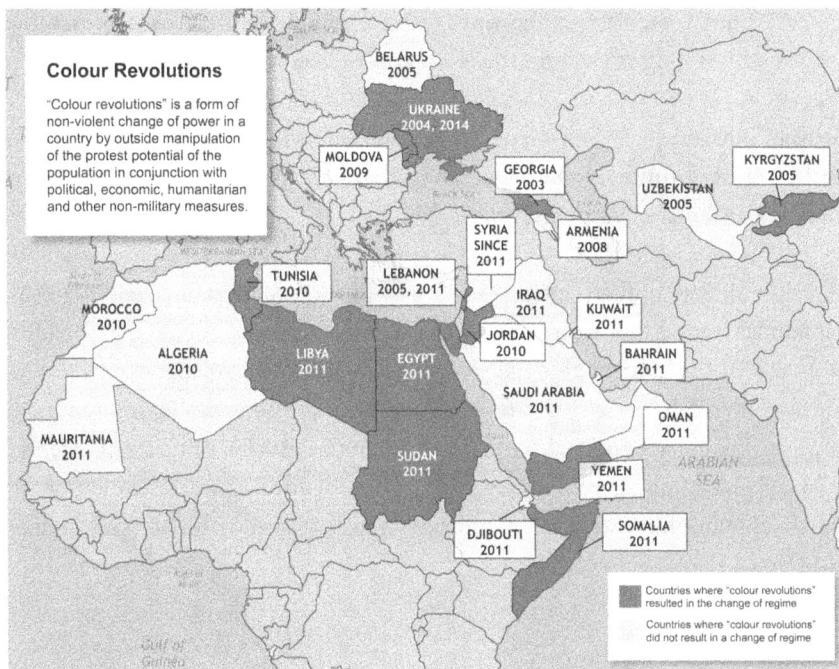

**Figure 2.2** Graphic identifying the 'colour revolutions' from General Gerasimov's presentation at the Russian Ministry of Defence's Third Moscow Conference on International Security, 23 May 2014 (Cordesman 2014). Reprinted with the permission of the Center for Strategic and International Studies. Recreated by A. DeBenedictis.

and sink into a web of chaos, humanitarian catastrophe, and civil war'. He even stressed the importance of refining Russia's understanding of the colour revolution model, pleading for the Academy of Military Sciences to 'create a comprehensive theory of such actions' (Gerasimov 2013).

At the Russian Ministry of Defence's Third Moscow Conference on International Security on 23 May 2014, Gerasimov provided a map identifying all the examples of colour revolutions that the Russian government believes it has witnessed (see Figure 2.2). These included the various colour revolutions in the former Soviet states and the political upheaval during the Arab Spring in North Africa and the Middle East. In his explanation, Gerasimov described these conflicts as evidence of the adaptive approach that the United States and Europe have developed to fight low-cost wars in pursuit of their national interests. He called the 2014 Ukrainian Euromaidan an example of a successful Western operation in the guise of a colour revolution (Cordesman 2014).

Gerasimov – or, at least, the work of his General Staff that he is presenting – has had a lasting impact on the Russian understanding of colour revolution theory. A 2013 *Military Thought* article summarizing the contemporary Russian literature on 'New-Generation War' led with Gerasimov's article and praised it as '[q]uite a standout among them all' (Chekinov and Bogdanov 2013: 12). Gerasimov's definition of this form of warfare is almost verbatim in the 2014 Russian Military Doctrine, which called the chief characteristic of current military conflicts 'integrated employment of military force and political, economic, informational or other non-military measures implemented with a wide use of the protest potential of the population and of special operations forces' (Kremlin 2014g). At the 2014 Moscow Conference on International Security, Lieutenant General Yuri Zhadobin, the Belarusian minister of defence, followed Gerasimov's presentation with a near-identical characterization of the colour revolutions as artificial conflicts driven by outside powers (Cordesman 2014).

## Chekinov and Bogdanov

Other authoritative figures on Russia's colour revolution theory are Colonel Sergey Chekinov and Lieutenant General (retired) Sergey Bogdanov. Chekinov has been chief of the Russian General Staff's Centre for Military Strategic Research since 2009 and has written over eighty academic publications. Bogdanov, a former chief of the centre and now chief research associate, has written over 140 academic papers on military affairs.[3] Together, they have written a significant number of key articles for *Military Thought* over the past few years on the character of conflict. Their range of publications and seniority, as well as the authoritative nature of *Military Thought* as the Russian Ministry of Defence's official journal, make their essays a valid representation of current trends among the Russian General Staff (Giles 2016a: 7). Chekinov and Bogdanov prefer the term 'new-generation war', but their descriptions largely follow colour revolution theory. Like Gerasimov, they write that this form of conflict is defined 'by a combination of political, economic, information, technological, and ecological campaigns in the form of indirect actions and non-military measures' (Chekinov and Bogdanov 2013: 16). While in many ways the concept as they describe it is much broader – for example, they discuss the importance of 'high-precision weapons' and 'high-tech wars' (Chekinov and Bogdanov 2013: 13–14) – many

---

[3] The biographies are from their various publications in *Military Thought*.

of its precepts closely follow the same model as outlined by Gerasimov. The sections that follow draw heavily from their articles on the subject.

## Hybrid warfare

Russian descriptions of 'hybrid warfare' follow the same line. As Colonel (retired) V. A. Kiselyov and Major General (retired) I. N. Vorobyov themselves point out when writing for *Military Thought*, the term is a Western one, which was 'born and gained currency in the West in the early 2010s' (Kiselyov and Vorobyov 2015: 28). In fact, Russian military experts only use the term when discussing Western practices against Russia or its interests, not to describe their own practices (Bartles 2016: 34; see also Fridman 2016; Tsygankov 2015). Despite the difference in terminology, the Russian explanation of hybrid warfare is the same as colour revolution theory: it is the West's chosen means of 'removing regimes unpalatable to the West by launching operations supported by internal opposition and setting the stage for Colour Revolutions to be engineered [. . .] by using a combination of coordinated political, diplomatic, information, propaganda, financial, economic, and military measures' (Kiselyov and Vorobyov 2015: 28–9). As evidenced by these definitions, 'hybrid warfare' when used by Russian authors is a different term for the same theory.

## Parallels between the theories

Both the Soviet Union's counter-revolution theory and Russia's colour revolution theory stem from the same premise – that the West has manufactured regime change in various countries through subversion and the covert use of military and non-military means. As seen from the previous descriptions, they in many respects are characterizing the same phenomenon. When comparing specific aspects of the two theories side by side, colour revolution theory appears even more strongly to be the Russian government's adaptation of the Soviet theory to fit the modern security dynamic. Four key features are essential to both theories: psychological warfare, 'democratization', the use of NGOs and covert Western leadership.

### Psychological warfare

The two theories contend that the West employs a form of psychological warfare to attack societies from within. Soviet writing on counter-revolution focused on how Western governments forced on other states their ideas and values that were unwanted and incompatible with their way of life. It described ideological subversion as 'the attempts by Western powers to impair the unity of the Socialist camp by ideas foreign and inimical to Marxism-Leninism' (Bittman 1972: 18). A *Pravda* editorial from the Prague Spring cautioned that 'the enemy is not concentrating his efforts on a frontal attack, as in [Hungary in] 1956, but on prolonged and sophisticated subversion primarily conducted by methods of psychological warfare' (CIA FBIS 1968a). An editorial from the same period in *Kommunist*, the CPSU Central Committee's official magazine, even accused the West of establishing 'an entire industry of "psychological warfare"' (Demichev 1968: 209).

Russian articles and speeches on colour revolutions make the same accusations about the West's use of psychological warfare. President Putin has denounced the West for imposing an alien ideology through its 'controlled "colour" revolutions'. In 2014, he called the Arab Spring the 'Arab Winter' in which '[s]tandards were imposed on these nations that did not in any way correspond to their way of life, traditions, or these peoples' cultures'; he said that the West's attempt to force 'democracy and freedom' instead led to 'chaos, outbreaks in violence, and a series of upheavals' (Kremlin 2014a). Similarly, Foreign Minister Sergey Lavrov said that the 'United States and Europe use the "colour revolution" to serve their own interests [and] impose their own values' (Cordesman 2014). In describing 'new-generation war', Chekinov and Bogdanov (2013: 16) give the same importance to the psychological side of the conflict, claiming that it 'will be dominated by information and psychological warfare that will seek to [. . .] depress the opponent's armed forces personnel and population morally and psychologically [. . . and] will largely lay the groundwork for victory'. They assert that colour revolutions are driven by '[t]he methodologies of psychologically manipulating and affecting the individual, social institutions, corporations or states [that] were devised and implemented under the supervision of and on commission from the US military and intelligence services' (Chekinov and Bogdanov 2011: 9). Another *Military Thought* article on information warfare applies these tenets directly to the 2014 Ukrainian crisis, claiming that 'information and psychological operations the US conducted in Ukraine [. . .] culminated in the Kyiv Maidan unrest' (Puzenkin and Mikhailov 2015: 3).

Just as the Soviet government warned that the West was avoiding 'a frontal attack' and turning to ideological subversion, these Russian officials contend that the West has developed covert informational and psychological tools to achieve regime change without a conventional military intervention. The defence of

Marxism–Leninism may be gone, but the Russian government is still providing the same attacks on what it sees as Western ideas being forced on the target populations.

## 'Democratization'

Similarly, Soviet counter-revolution theory targeted Western efforts at 'democratization' as code for this counter-revolution. During the Prague Spring, the Warsaw Pact Five clearly defined it as cover for Western subversion in their 15 July open letter to the CPCz leadership (the 'Warsaw Letter'):

> [B]y demagogically using the slogan of 'democratization', reactionary forces have unleashed a campaign against the CPCz and against its honest and dedicated cadres, with the evident intention of destroying the leading role of the party, undermining the socialist system, and setting Czechoslovakia against the other socialist countries [. . . ] Under the guise of praising 'democratization' and 'liberalization' in the ČSSR [Czechoslovak Socialist Republic], the bourgeois press is conducting a subversive campaign against fraternal socialist countries. ('Warsaw Letter' 1968)

In an article in *Kommunist*, the CPSU Central Committee warned that '[h]istorical experience has shown that expatiations concerning democracy and "liberalization" are used by counterrevolutions as a smoke screen for attempts to liquidate the conquests of socialism and socialist democracy' (Demichev 1968: 211). The so-called White Book – the Soviet government's propaganda account of the Prague Spring published and distributed immediately after the Warsaw Pact forces had invaded – chided the Czechoslovak leadership because they 'failed to understand the new devices of counter-revolution; they believed the talks about "democratization" of socialism but did not analyse the activities of those who sought to do away with the socialist system under the pretence of "improving" it' ('White Book' 1968: 49).

Accusations of the West's use of 'democratization' as cover for subversive action reappear virtually unchanged in the Russian literature on colour revolutions. The Russian government views the United States' support for democratization efforts in the former Soviet states as cover for pursuing its national interests at Russia's expense (see Deyermond 2015). After the 2004 Orange Revolution, Putin accused the United States of seeking a 'dictatorship of international affairs' disguised under 'beautiful pseudo-democratic phraseology' (Crowley 2016). One *Military Thought* article contends that the United States through 'non-military measures' overthrew numerous countries 'by waves of colour and velvet revolutions [. . .] under the cover of "defending democratic values and protecting human rights"' (Pavlov et al. 2015: 19). In a June 2014 summit for the Collective Security Treaty Organization (CSTO), the Russian-led military alliance, Russian first deputy defence minister Arkady Bakhin accused Western governments of invading Russia's neighbours 'under "democratizing" slogans to replace the undesirable governments with regimes controlled from abroad' (Allison 2014: 1290). Nikolay Bordyuzha, the Russian general who served as secretary general of the CSTO, called colour revolutions Western subversion disguised 'under the cloak of humanitarian intervention' (Cordesman 2014). These Russian officials view Western democracy promotion in near-identical terms as their Soviet predecessors, with both offering the same subversion explanations for the political changes in their neighbouring states.

## NGOs

The idea that NGOs are merely covert instruments of the West's subversion campaign originated in counter-revolution theory, as well. In the Prague Spring, the Soviet government identified seventy different political action groups, including Club-231, the Club of Non-Party Activists, the Circle of Independent Writers, the Club of Critically-Minded Individuals and the Organization for the Defence of Human Rights, as fronts set up by the 'reactionaries' to challenge the communist regime. Many of these formed under the relaxed restrictions that Dubček's government had instituted. The Warsaw Letter (1968: 152) from the Warsaw Pact Five leadership labelled these various non-governmental groups the vanguard of the West's surreptitious war on Czechoslovakia, claiming that '[t]he political organizations and clubs that have originated in the recent period [. . .] have become in substance the general staff of reactionary forces'.

   Russia's colour revolution theory likewise sees NGOs as secret tools of Western governments. In an interview with *Komsomolskaya Pravda* in May 1999, Putin – who was then still director of the FSB (the Federal Security Service, one of the successor organizations of the KGB) and head of the Russian Security Council – warned that 'foreign intelligence services, besides diplomatic cover, are very active in using in their work various ecological and civil society organizations, the business and charity foundations' (Soldatov and Borogan 2010: 35). As president in 2012, he again asserted that 'the activity of "pseudo-NGOs" [and] other structures which, with outside support, have the aim to destabilize the situation in this or that country, is unacceptable' (Van

Herpen 2016: 28). One *Military Thought* article describes colour revolutions as 'sponsored by foreign non-governmental organizations', especially a 'broad-based coalition of non-governmental organizations' that serve as the 'political mainspring' of the movement; they thus allow Western powers to achieve 'the overthrow of the ruling political regime without foreign countries' military involvement' (Belsky and Klimenko 2014: 21, 25). According to another article from Kiselyov and Vorobyov (2015: 33), 'nonprofit organizations would be the preferred choice for achieving the goals of a hybrid operation' because they can provide a foreign government the means for 'conducting information operations purportedly to protect democracy'. Chekinov and Bogdanov (2013: 17) include in their list of tools of the colour revolutions 'the mass media and religious organizations, cultural institutions, nongovernmental organizations, public movements financed from abroad, and scholars engaged in research on foreign grants'. For these reasons, another *Military Thought* piece lists 'branches of foreign foundations and nongovernmental organizations being established and opened on Russian territory to erode the security of its state and society' as one of the major security threats facing Russia today (Pavlov et al. 2015: 21).

## Covert Western leadership

In the Soviet and Russian mindsets, the foundation of both counter-revolutions and colour revolutions, respectively, was the hidden hand of the West secretly directing the actions to undermine and isolate them and their spheres of influence. As a result, Russian leaders have been just as likely as their Soviet predecessors to identify supposed evidence of Western interference in its many forms. At the 17 July 1968 CPSU Central Committee session held during the Prague Spring, General Secretary Leonid Brezhnev (1968b: 258) concluded, 'We cannot but see a direct link between the tactics of imperialist reactionary forces and the actions of the anti-socialist and counterrevolutionary forces in Czechoslovakia.' In the aftermath of the Warsaw Pact invasion, KGB chairman Yuri Andropov described in a speech to the Komsomol political youth organization how the Czechoslovak reform movement was '[g]raphic confirmation' that the West 'gives direct and indirect support to counterrevolutionary elements, engages in ideological sabotage, establishes all sorts of anti-Socialist, anti-Soviet and other hostile organizations and seeks to fan the flames of nationalism' (Andrew and Gordievsky 1990: 487–8).

The Soviet government drew the same conclusions about Afghanistan. Andropov and Defence Minister Dmitry Ustinov argued in the 8 December

1979 Politburo meeting that Soviet military intervention was necessary because the CIA was attempting to create a 'new Great Ottoman Empire' that would include not only Afghanistan but also the southern republics of the USSR (Lyakhovsky 1995). According to KGB defector Vladimir Kuzichkin, the KGB was convinced that new Afghan president Hafizullah Amin was 'a smooth-talking fascist who was secretly pro-Western [. . . with] links with the CIA', but it 'had no proof' to support those claims (Melville 1982). Amin spoke English and had studied at Columbia University and the University of Wisconsin (Urban 1990: 40). These facts were enough for the KGB to suspect him as a recruited CIA spy, and Andropov was especially keen on such reports (Andrew and Mitrokhin 2000: 508).[4] During the decisive 12 December 1979 meeting in which the Soviet Union decided to invade Afghanistan, Andropov cited the KGB's 'evidence' that Amin had contact with the CIA, including the suggestion that he may have been recruited while a student in the United States in the 1960s. At the end of the session, the Politburo voted unanimously to remove Amin through KGB action and to send Soviet troops into the country (Braithwaite 2012: 79). The morning after the coup occurred, Soviet propaganda labelled Amin 'a bloodthirsty agent of American imperialism' when it had affectionately called him 'Comrade Amin' only the day before (Andrew and Gordievsky 1990: 577).

After the Euromaidan protests culminated with a change in government in Ukraine in February 2014, the Russian leadership drew the same conclusions as their Soviet predecessors – that the hidden US hand was responsible. Foreign Minister Sergey Lavrov claimed US president Barack Obama's remarks that the United States 'had brokered a deal to transition power in Ukraine' were 'proof that from the very beginning, the United States was involved in the anti-government coup' (Sputnik News 2015). Sergey Glazyev, Putin's regional integration advisor whose portfolio included Ukraine, went even further:

> [T]he entire crisis in Ukraine was orchestrated, provoked, and financed by American institutions in cooperation with their European partners [. . .] For fifteen years, the US and Europeans financed neo-Nazis' training, their camps, and preparation [. . .] This work led to the sad situation that now in Ukraine neo-Nazi and neo-fascist ideas prevail [. . . The European Union] engineered their entire coup, human casualties, neo-fascists and all with the explicit purpose of installing in power a puppet to sign the treaty that the EU itself dictated which

---

[4] In the beginning of 1979, US ambassador to Afghanistan Spike Dubs pressed his CIA station chief on whether Amin was an agent, and he assured him that he was not (Braithwaite 2012: 79).

was earlier refused by Yanukovych. As follows, Yanukovych was removed from power, so the EU could make Ukraine its colony. (Simes 2014)

Such rhetoric rivals the most serious accusations against Western subversion levelled during the Soviet period. Sergey Aksyonov, who owes his position as head of the Republic of Crimea to Russian involvement in 2014, continues to avow that 'the Ukrainian leadership is objectively incapacitated and fully operates under the leadership of the *tsereushniks* [American spies]. Nobody hides the fact that the [US] State Department is in charge of the Ukrainian presidential administration today' (Gerasimenko and Galustjan 2014).

### Laboratory experiments

The Soviet authorities further speculated that Western governments had established 'laboratories' to refine their tactics of counter-revolution. In an article from the aftermath of the Prague Spring, *Kommersant* hypothesized:

> In the leading imperialist countries, especially in the United States and West Germany, hundreds of centres, well[-]equipped with modern technology, have been created, including 'scientific' centres which have collected together the most experienced forces of anticommunism and which are developing the strategy and tactics of ideological subversion. (Demichev 1968: 209)

As shown by their statements, Russian officials and authors commenting on the colour revolutions have echoed this characterization but added to it the modern technologies of the twenty-first century. An article from the *Bulletin of the Academy of Military Sciences of the Russian Federation* alleges that in the Arab Spring:

> Revolutionary changes were triggered by information attacks from social networks Facebook and Twitter by sending out messages about planned rallies and protest actions to e-mail and mobile phones of users [. . . from] servers of social networks located in the territory of the US special services. (Kuleshov et al. 2014: 107)

As for video reports 'from the "place of events" about the atrocities of government troops', the authors claim that these were actually '[m]ounted and retouched in special laboratories' in the West (Kuleshov et al. 2014: 107). Chekinov and Bogdanov make the same accusation but are even more specific. They declare that the Americans 'engaged in propaganda from servers of the Facebook and Twitter public networks watched over by the American special services [. . .] controlled from a centre at the US Air Force Base in MacDill, Florida', which is home to US Special Operations Command and US Central Command (Chekinov and Bogdanov 2013: 17). During the Crimean crisis, Putin painted the same picture of American puppeteers working from their laboratory. He lamented, 'I sometimes get the feeling that somewhere across that huge puddle, in America, people sit in a lab and conduct experiments, as if with rats, without actually understanding the consequences of what they are doing' (Kremlin 2014h).

### Foreign agents and undercover operatives

One of the most prominent aspects of both theories is the belief that the United States and its allies not only trained the forces opposing the targeted regime but also deployed troops and spies disguised as members of the domestic movement. The official Soviet account of the Prague Spring asserted that the United States was using secret camps at their bases in West Germany to train the counter-revolutionary forces:

> [T]he forces of counter-revolution had been concentrating in Bad Tölz and Salzburg and had been trained by a subversion expert, the American Colonel Jerry Sage. In August, the number of these tourists from the FRG [West Germany] and Austria had reached eight thousand. Many had had forged documents and had been trained at the tenth special group [i.e. 10th Special Forces Group] of the US Army stationed in the Bad Tölz area [. . .] headed by veteran Nazis and agents of foreign intelligence services. ('White Book' 1968: 120–1)

The 'White Book' propaganda account also accused the Austrian National Democratic Party, which was later banned under anti-Nazi legislation (Constitutional Court of Austria 1988), of sending 'volunteers posing as tourists to Czechoslovakia to carry out subversive activities' ('White Book' 1968: 107).

The Soviet leadership believed that the United States was equally behind the 'counter-revolution' in Afghanistan. During the March 1979 Politburo debate on the uprising in Herat, they accepted the Afghan leaders' excuses that foreign powers – and not their failed domestic policies – were behind the violence. Soviet premier Kosygin recounted how Afghan president Nur Muhammad Taraki had told him that Pakistan had sent 4,000 men 'dressed in Afghan uniforms' including '500 men situated on the airfield in Herat', implying that the revolting Afghan soldiers were actually foreign agents. Similarly, Hafizullah Amin (who at the time was a senior member of Taraki's cabinet) told Defence Minister Ustinov that 'Pakistan and Iran are sending large numbers of saboteurs that are being trained on the territory of Pakistan by Chinese advisors, being equipped with Chinese arms, and are then being sent across the border into Afghanistan'. The Politburo concluded that the United States must ultimately be behind the situation. Foreign Minister Gromyko commented, 'We may assume with full justification that all these events, not only in Afghanistan but in the neighbouring governments, including those in China, are being directed by the hand of the USA' (CPSU CC Politburo 1979d).

In similar fashion, the Russian government draws the same conclusions today that colour revolutions are driven by Western-trained agents and undercover spies. At the 2014 Moscow Conference on International Security, General Vladimir Zarudnitsky, the chief of the Main Operational Directorate of the Russian General Staff, described 'SOF [Special Operations Forces] disguised as rebels' as well as surrogate forces 'like Blackwater' as critical components of the West's colour revolution tactics (Cordesman 2014). Just like the official Soviet propaganda account of the Prague Spring, Kiselyov and Vorobyov (2015: 32) specifically identify the 'US Army's Special Forces [. . . who] are trained to act as mediators and military instructors [and] can each raise a small indigenous army or engineer an insurgency' as the critical military unit for these operations. Yury Abisov, commander of the Crimean *Berkut* special police battalion that defected to Russia after the annexation, claims that the United States used a training exercise with Ukrainian security forces in 2006 to secretly write a manual 'How to Counter *Berkut*' which it then distributed to the far-right group *Pravy Sektor* before Euromaidan (Kondrashov 2015).

Putin's statements about what 'really' occurred in Ukraine strongly echo the words of his Politburo predecessors. On 4 March 2014, he told the press conference to

[L]ook how well trained the people who operated in Kyiv were. As we all know they were trained at special bases in neighbouring states: in Lithuania, Poland and in Ukraine itself too. They were trained by instructors for extended periods. They were divided into dozens and hundreds, their actions were coordinated, they had good communication systems. It was all like clockwork. Did you see them in action? They looked very professional, like special forces. (Kremlin 2014h)

In his speech on 18 March 2014 to mark the signing of the annexation treaty, he reiterated that 'with Ukraine, our Western partners have crossed the line, playing the bear and acting irresponsibly and unprofessionally' by sending into the country 'an organized and well-equipped army of militants' (Kremlin 2014a). In the propaganda documentary produced by Russian state television one year later, *Crimea: The Way Home*, Putin again alleged, '[W]e knew for certain that the real puppeteers pulling the strings were our American partners and friends. They helped to train the nationalists, they helped to train the combat units in western Ukraine, in Poland, and in Lithuania to some extent' (Kondrashov 2015). These statements about interference from Western governments as the hidden source of the colour revolutions parallel the earlier Soviet statements on counter-revolution so closely that they almost appear to have been drafted from them.

### Statements by Western officials as evidence

Driven by this interpretation of events, both the Soviet and Russian governments identified statements from Western officials as evidence of that Western interference. From the Prague Spring, the 'White Book' propaganda account pointed to examples such as a 2 August 1968 speech by US senator Strom Thurmond, when he said that the nature of events made it 'possible to tear the East European socialist countries away from the Soviet Union and win them over to the side of the United States' ('White Book' 1968: 105). To demonstrate that US forces were at work in Czechoslovakia, the account claimed that a 'cynical statement by [US] Congressman John Saylor corresponded completely with the course adopted for a "quiet counter-revolution"'. Saylor had said, 'The time for an uprising has not yet come. The people of Czechoslovakia should not be pushed to open action before the time is ripe.' The 'White Book' proffered this as evidence that the Czechoslovak reformers were waiting on orders and direction from the US government ('White Book' 1968: 105–6).

During the Ukrainian crisis, the Russian government drew the same conclusions about Victoria Nuland, the US assistant secretary of state for European and Eurasian affairs. Nuland had made appearances supporting the Ukrainian protesters at Euromaidan in Kyiv (see Shuster 2013). In a leaked intercepted telephone call from February 2014, she brashly discussed future political leadership in Ukraine with US ambassador Geoffrey Pyatt. For example, she said that she did not think Vitali Klitschko, one of the main Ukrainian opposition leaders, 'should go into the government' and asked Pyatt to arrange a phone call so she could inform the former boxer that they would not support him as deputy prime minister (annotated transcript available from BBC 2014e). However, the most damning evidence of secret US orchestration, according to the Russian officials, was a speech she gave in December 2013 to the US–Ukraine Foundation, a pro-Ukrainian NGO. In it, she stated:

Since Ukraine's independence in 1991, the United States has supported Ukrainians as they build democratic skills and institutions, as they promote civic participation and good governance, all of which are preconditions for Ukraine to achieve its European aspirations [. . .] We have invested over $5 billion to assist Ukraine in these and other goals that will ensure a secure and prosperous and democratic Ukraine. (US–Ukraine Foundation 2013)

The context of the statement was that since the end of the Cold War, the US government had spent approximately $5.1 billion on democracy-building programmes, including military assistance, law enforcement reform and humanitarian aid in Ukraine, much as it has done in states around the globe (Sanders 2014).

This context was lost as the soundbite instead became the Russian government's key evidence that the West was orchestrating a colour revolution in Ukraine. After Nuland and other Western politicians appeared on Euromaidan, the Russian State Duma voted near-unanimously to adopt a resolution accusing Western governments of 'open interference . . . in the internal affairs of the sovereign Ukraine' (Neef and Schepp 2013). In explaining whom was to blame for the Ukraine crisis, Kremlin regional integration advisor Sergey Glazyev argued, 'By US Assistant Secretary of State Victoria Nuland's acknowledgement, the State Department spent $5 billion on the creation of an anti-Russian political and paramilitary elite' (Simes 2014). Secretary of the Russian Security Council Nikolai Patrushev asserted in an interview with Russian state television that the events in Ukraine were 'initiated from the outside' and 'the pressure [on Yanukovych's regime] was mainly organized from the territory of the United States [. . .] because Victoria Nuland claimed that five billion dollars was spent on Ukraine. What was it spent on? Here exactly is the support, including foreign NGOs, in order to carry out their plans' (Patrushev 2014). Just as in Soviet times, the Russian officials bent the American politicians' own words to find the evidence of subversion they were looking for.

## 'Defensive' governmental actions

These same parallels between the Soviet Union's counter-revolution theory and Russia's colour revolution theory appear in the government actions taken to defend against them. According to a defector from the KGB Third Directorate (Military Counterintelligence), the Bolsheviks' very establishment of the Cheka – the first of the Soviet secret police organizations – on 20 December

1917 was to combat 'counter-revolutionary and other criminal elements' (Myagkov 1976: 20). From the 1920s onwards, the main target of the Cheka and its successor organizations was not the capitalist nations but the agents of the 'counter-revolution', initially among the domestic population at home and then among their overseas bases of support (Andrew and Gordievsky 1990: 110).

Once Yuri Andropov took control of the KGB, the assault on the 'counter-revolution' rose to new levels. Two months after he became KGB chairman in 1967, he proposed the establishment of the Fifth Chief Directorate to monitor ideological subversion and dissent (Petrov 2010: 148). In a note to the CPSU Central Committee explaining its purpose, Andropov wrote that 'the newly created fifth sub-units have been called upon to combat ideological subversion inspired by our enemies abroad' (Soldatov and Borogan 2010: 55). The Soviet Bloc countries soon followed suit with parallel departments (Andrew and Gordievsky 1992: 46; Bittman 1972: 19; Freemantle 1982: 48). That same year, Andropov issued KGB Chairman's Order No. 0051, 'On the tasks of State security agencies in combating ideological sabotage by the adversary', in which he called for greater aggression against dissidents at home and their imperialist supporters (Andrew and Mitrokhin 2000: 9). The KGB would later appoint a senior Fifth Chief Directorate officer as a deputy of the First Chief Directorate (Foreign Operations) to synchronize their efforts against ideological subversion. One defector from the Czechoslovak State Security (StB) recounted how a CPSU official travelled to Prague to give mandatory indoctrination sessions to his organization to explain the details of ideological subversion and how to identify it (Bittman 1972: 18).

Counter-revolution and its enablers in the Soviet Union continued to be the focus of the security services throughout the Cold War. In 1982 Vitaly Fedorchuk, then head of the KGB, blamed Soviet citizens who were 'insufficiently hardened ideologically and politically, infected by nationalist prejudices and religious intoxicants or quite simply morally corrupt' for why the West appeared to be succeeding in its subversive activities (Freemantle 1982: 32). The KGB kept statistics on 'harmful attitudes' and 'hostile acts' that contributed to the West's supposed subversion campaign; these included listening to Western pop music or deviating from party-directed political ideology (Andrew and Mitrokhin 2000: 325). The KGB even reported that it had 'taken the necessary measures to identify the instigators [. . . of] a demonstration organized in memory of the English singer, John Lennon' because of the risk they believed it posed to the security of the state (KGB 1980).

The Fifth Chief Directorate did not survive the end of the Cold War – but reappeared once Putin became head of the FSB. Despite an attempt at rebranding, the directorate was abolished in September 1991 after the failed August coup attempt against Mikhail Gorbachev in which KGB chairman Vladimir Kryuchkov had played prominently (Soldatov and Borogan 2010: 56). However, the Russian government revived the directorate in new form in 1998. On 25 July, Yeltsin appointed Putin director of the FSB (Kremlin 1998); two days later, another presidential decree created the FSB Directorate of Constitutional Security (*Nezavisimaya Gazeta* 1998).[5] Based on statements from the chief of the new directorate, Gennady Zotov, it strongly appears to be a reincarnation of its Soviet predecessor. He said that his office would be 'specializing in combating threats to the security of the Russian Federation in the socio-political sphere [. . . including] the attempts of various forces to use the media to conduct anti-state, anti-constitutional propaganda' (*Nezavisimaya Gazeta* 1998). He stated that the directorate was necessary for 'the protection of the country from "internal sedition," for "internal sedition" has always been more terrible for Russia than any military invasion' (Soldatov and Borogan 2010: 56). The new office even faced accusations that it was reinstating *politicheskiy sysk* (political investigation), the Soviet practice of prosecuting political dissidents (*Nezavisimaya Gazeta* 1998).

Public actions the Russian government has taken since Putin returned for his third term as president show similar institutional commitment focused on the threat posed by ideological subversion. In 2012, he signed a decree creating a subdivision in his presidential administration with the explicit responsibility for 'the strengthening of patriotic education and the spiritual-moral foundations of Russian society' to counteract these subversive threats at home (Van Herpen 2016: 78). At the time, one source inside the presidential administration condemned it as an 'attempt to come up with a new name and a new form of a former activity that existed in the past – rigid dictates of ideology from the position of the teacher' (Mikhailov and Samarina 2012). The authors of one *Military Thought* article suggest that the office should 'coordinate information gathering and dissemination on the countrywide scale [. . .] with efforts to counter subversion of every kind and ideological preparation of colour revolutions (velvet, orange, or any other)' (Pavlov et al. 2015: 23).

Also in 2012, Putin signed into law the requirement that NGOs that receive funding from abroad register with the Justice Ministry as foreign agents,

---

[5] The directorate is now the Service for Protection of the Constitutional System and the Fight against Terrorism (Slobodyan 2017).

including annual audits and screening for 'extremist speech' in published materials. The law affected over 1,000 NGOs in Russia (Van Herpen 2016: 40–1). The first organization registered under the new law was the election monitor GOLOS, which the US Agency for International Development (USAID) had openly sponsored for years. Related to this decision, the Russian government expelled USAID, which had spent nearly $3 billion on aid, development and civil society projects in Russia since the end of the Cold War. Despite its claim that the decision was because Russia 'no longer required international assistance', the Russian government ordered the US government agency's operations to close after a series of Russian government statements accused it of fomenting protests after the December 2011 State Duma elections (USAID 2012). These decisions appear to be a direct result of the belief that NGOs are a covert tool of Western colour revolution theory.

The FSB lobbied for changes to the law that made that connection to the fear of colour revolutions explicit. In a presentation to the State Duma, FSB deputy director Yuriy Gorbunov asked the body to include international organizations in its article on High Treason because of 'a change in tactics by foreign intelligence services that actively make use of international organizations in their operations [. . . and] make use of them as cover' (Van Herpen 2016: 42). The State Duma amended the definition of treason to include 'financial, material, technical, advisory or any other support given to a foreign country or to international or foreign organizations engaged in activities against the security of the Russian Federation' (*Rossiskaya Gazeta* 2012). The law strongly echoes Article 58-4 of the Criminal Code of the Russian Soviet Federative Socialist Republic, which criminalized 'whatever kind of aid to that part of the international bourgeoisie [. . .] and likewise to public groups and organizations, being under the influence of or directly organized by that bourgeoisie, in the carrying out of hostile activities toward the USSR' (RSFR 1934; Van Herpen 2016). The Russian government has reacted to the fear of colour revolution with many of the same measures the Soviet Union took to defend against counter-revolution.

## The connection between the theories and state warfare practices

These linkages strongly suggest that the Russian government's colour revolution theory grew out of Soviet counter-revolution theory. However, both the Soviet and Russian authors are describing *Western* practices in their theories.

They should therefore not be taken at face value as characterizations of Soviet or Russian action. Nonetheless, both governments used these theories as a prescription for the development of their own means and methods to keep pace with the West. It has long been a tradition within the Russian military and the Soviet military before it to describe how they perceive the enemy is acting in order to determine what practices they need to adapt (Interview with Mykhailo Gonchar 2017). Soviet authors in official security-sector publications often discussed Western concepts as a cover for disseminating new ideas within their ranks without overtly stating a shift in policy (Douglass 1980: xiv). For example, the American editors of the English translation of *Soviet Military Strategy* identified that much of the chapter on 'Military Strategy of Imperialist Countries and Their Preparation of New Wars' was not an accurate description of Western doctrine; in reality, it was a series of new concepts that the Soviet leadership was considering to implement (Sokolovskiy 1975: 381). The Soviet writing on counter-revolution theory, therefore, largely served as a description of the tactics and techniques the Soviet government wanted to develop in response.

The Russian government appears to have taken the same approach with its descriptions of colour revolution theory. According to the NATO Defence College *Handbook of Russian Information Warfare*, Russia is 'adopting and adapting these "lessons" from the West' based on 'what it believes to be Western practice' (Giles 2016a: 1, 26–7). Through his analysis of the Russian literature and numerous conversations with Russian military officers and observers, Mark Galeotti (2019) finds that they legitimately believe *gibridnaya voina* – a term they have directly translated from the English – to be a Western way of war. Even though Russia presents colour revolution theory as a critique of the West, its recent actions closely follow the characteristics that the Russian authors identify (Bērziņa 2015: 24). The 2014 campaign in Crimea is an example of the culmination of this cycle: Russia perceived new Western techniques and approaches, which it saw applied in Georgia, Ukraine, the Middle East and North Africa; it analysed them, assessed them and developed a model; then it adapted them to its own circumstances and applied them in Crimea (Giles 2016b: 9). In formulating its response to the perceived changing nature of war, the Russian military has effectively used its theory of Western subversion as its own model.

There has been much debate in the Western literature on hybrid warfare on whether the recent Russian publications and statements discussed in the previous sections constitute a doctrinal shift. Since Russia's actions in Ukraine, commentators have reached back to Gerasimov's 2013 article to identify it as evidence of Russia's turning to some new form of warfare as laid out in the article (see Snegovaya 2015; Jonsson and Seely 2015; McKew 2017). When the article was first published, it initially received very little attention, including from within the Ukrainian military; now, however, some senior Ukrainian officers have stated that they see the article as a blueprint for action and that it was directed at them (Interview H 2017). Other authors have taken issue with this characterization. Renz and Smith (2016: 8–9) point out that Gerasimov's article was based on a speech to the Russian Academy of Military Sciences intended to encourage more innovation in Russian military thinking, not to be the basis for some new Russian doctrine. Kofman (2016) argues that Gerasimov was not creating a doctrine of non-linear warfare or hybrid warfare but simply identifying the challenges of the current operating environment. Other experts (Interview E 2016; Bartles 2016) stress that Gerasimov is describing Western practices and in no way offering a prescription for Russian actions in Crimea, especially since it was written before the Euromaidan protests began. Galeotti describes how the term 'Gerasimov Doctrine' – which, he regrets, he himself coined – has developed a life of its own and become accepted by Western scholars and pundits alike as 'a blueprint for a new way of war' (Galeotti 2018a) or 'a supposed dramatic turn in Russian strategic thinking' (Galeotti 2018b). He has even updated his original article, claiming that his use of the term was nothing more than 'going for a snappy title' and pleading others to stop using it because 'there is certainly no expectation that this is the Russian way of war' (Galeotti 2014).

However, as noted previously, Gerasimov's article had a significant impact on other Russian descriptions of colour revolutions. As shown in the following sections, the Russian government adopted and implemented the same techniques it identified in these characterizations. Because of this connection, the colour revolution model appears to have caused such a shift – or, more accurately, a return to historical practices.

## Russian implementation of colour revolution tactics

The Russian government has expressed the need to follow the West's colour revolution tactics for as long as it has been describing them. In discussing the wave of colour revolutions in 2007, then chief of the General Staff Yuri Baluyevsky advised that 'Russian security interests require not only to assess these threats but also to determine appropriate measures to respond to them' (Giles 2016a: 41). The essays in *Military Thought* typically stressed the importance of 'comprehensive research' into these techniques as well as of 'training professionals knowledgeable in the theory and practice of employment of non-military forms of warfare' (Pavlov et al. 2015: 23). Even Gerasimov's article urged his government to gain the lead in developing these tactics, warning that Russia 'must not copy foreign experience and chase after leading countries, but we must outstrip them and occupy leading positions ourselves' (Gerasimov 2013). In their multiple descriptions of the colour revolution trend – both before and after the invasion of Crimea – Chekinov and Bogdanov called for Russia to adopt it for its own purposes. In 2011, they charged Russia 'to map out and eventually also implement a strategy of indirect approach as its state strategy', including the use of 'systemic and comprehensive measures involving political, diplomatic, informational, economic, military and non-military means' (2011: 5, 12). Writing after the start of the Ukrainian crisis, the authors warned that Russia still had not done enough to codify the use of these techniques, pleading that their country *'must start without delay researching the use of non-military measures and indirect actions of confrontation in wars and armed conflicts* [emphasis original]' (2015: 36).

A case in point is the striking similarities between the prescriptions outlined in Chekinov and Bogdanov's 2013 article 'The Nature and Content of a New-Generation War' and Russia's actions during the invasion of Crimea (Chekinov and Bogdanov 2013). The piece arguably 'reads like a how-to manual for the operation that took place in Crimea' based on the numerous parallels (Bruusgaard 2014: 84). Chekinov and Bogdanov predicted that '[h]igh-ranking political and military officers will make public statements for greater effect of the disinformation effort', which will include 'large-scale carefully coordinated measures [. . .] leaking false data, orders, directives, and instructions'. When asked on 4 March 2014 if Russian soldiers were active in the ongoing events in Crimea, President Putin denied it, replying, 'Those were local self-defence units [. . .] There are many uniforms there that are similar. You can go to a store and buy any kind of uniform' (Kremlin 2014h). Chekinov and Bogdanov warned of bribing and blackmailing government and military officers 'to abandon fulfilment of their service duties'. On 20 March 2014, Putin signed a presidential decree that any Ukrainian servicemen who switched allegiances to Russia would be guaranteed recognition of their rank, education credentials and length of service, thus codifying a promise the Russian forces in Crimea had made repeatedly to their Ukrainian counterparts during the crisis. The majority of Ukrainian servicemen in Crimea defected, including the brief commander of the Ukrainian Navy, Rear Admiral Denis Berezovsky (Lavrov 2014: 168, 175). Also key in Chekinov and Bogdanov's 'new-generation war' model was the need to 'impose rigid censorship and constraints on all media'. Russian forces abducted, detained or blocked numerous pro-Ukrainian or Western journalists during the crisis (Bebler 2015: 42). Weeks before the independence referendum, they also seized the main Crimean television transmission centre and replaced Ukrainian channels with state-controlled Russian ones (Chivers and Reevell 2014).[6]

## 'Hybrid warfare': The modern interpretation of Soviet political warfare

The extent of these parallels suggests that the various Russian articles written on colour revolution theory served as much more than merely a description of alleged Western practices. They also served as the starting point for the development of the Russian Federation's own practices to keep pace with the perceived trends in modern conflict. Russian leaders had for years called on its forces to learn from and adopt these 'Western' practices, and the nature of the Crimean campaign is evidence of this decision. However, just as colour revolution theory resembles a modern interpretation of the old Soviet counter-revolution theory, the tactics and techniques Russia has implemented in its reaction to the West also appear to be updated versions of the Soviet government's responses. What has come to be known as Russian 'hybrid warfare' is more accurately described as Soviet political warfare adapted to the twenty-first century. The following section describes the specifics of Soviet political warfare practice and how it evolved in response to counter-revolution theory, and the following chapters then discuss its parallels to Russian hybrid warfare.

## Soviet political warfare

The Soviet Union responded to the counter-revolutionary threat by expanding and refining what are best labelled as its 'political warfare practices'. In its broadest sense, political warfare is the 'vast area of conflict which is neither war nor peace' (Miranda 1985: 4) or 'the third option between diplomacy and open warfare' (Johnson 1989: 260). In the context of the Cold War, George Kennan (1948: 1) – at the time the US State Department's director of policy planning – defined it as the 'employment of all the means at a nation's command, short of war, to achieve its national objectives'. Joseph Kornfeder, the former leader of the

---

[6]   Each of these aspects of the Crimean operation are explored in greater detail in the following chapters.

US Communist Party who later became a vehement anti-communist, similarly described it as 'a form of conflict between states in which a protagonist nation seeks to impose its will upon its opponents without the direct use of armed force [. . . but] frequently backed by the threat of military force' (Kinter and Kornfeder 1962: xiii). Political warfare thus uses the various resources available to the state to achieve its political objectives without resorting to outright warfare while still employing military force and threatening the possibility of open hostilities.

While these Cold War commentators attributed these definitions to the Soviet practices they witnessed, Soviet doctrine does not explicitly use the term 'political warfare'. The closest definition from the Soviet Ministry of Defence's *Dictionary of Basic Military Terms* is of 'war' itself, which it describes as including the use of 'ideological, economic, diplomatic, and other forms and means of strife' (Soviet Ministry of Defence 1965: 48). However, Soviet military doctrine on the conduct of warfare focused almost exclusively on complete thermonuclear war or full-scale conventional war that would inevitably pit the two global ideological camps against each other. From their review of hundreds of Soviet statements on military doctrine, Scott and Scott (1988: 29) found three consistent points: first, doctrine consisted of two sides: political (what types of wars will occur and be supported) and military–technical (how arms and equipment shape the nature of conflict); second, doctrine was relevant to world war – massive war between the 'imperialist' and 'socialist' camps; and third, because war could be short or protracted, the military must prepare both its nuclear weapons and its large armed formations. Similarly, *Soviet Military Strategy* described the essence of modern military strategy itself as 'the strategy of deep nuclear rocket strikes in conjunction with the operations of all services of the armed forces in order to effect a simultaneous defeat and destruction of the economic potential and armed forces throughout the enemy territory' (Sokolovskiy 1975: 11). As seen from these trends, the Soviet military's understanding of war was in effect 'the Third World War'. A survey of *Military Thought* articles from throughout the Cold War finds that the vast majority address the operational and tactical aspects of such a war.

However, several Soviet military conflicts, including the historical Soviet operations discussed in this book, do not meet this threshold. The invasions of Czechoslovakia in 1968 and Afghanistan in 1979 were brief military actions backed by various informational and political tools to protect a communist regime in the Soviet Bloc against 'counter-revolution'. They did not exhibit the use of nuclear weapons or massive conventional formations or pit the forces of the two global ideological camps directly in conflict with one another, all of which the earlier definitions suggest that 'war' should entail. At the same time, these conflicts demonstrated numerous aspects of 'political warfare': the use of informational, political and military tools through both overt and covert means to achieve a political end. While not explicitly identified as such in Soviet writing, political warfare and its specific aspects were described in detail in various Soviet military and security service publications and witnessed frequently in their execution throughout the life of the Soviet Union. Even though *politicheskaya voina* is not a term found in Soviet doctrine, George Kennan's definition of it – the 'employment of all the means at a nation's command, short of war, to achieve its national objectives' – best encapsulates this body of Soviet practice.

## Overt and covert activities

Soviet political warfare could be both overt and covert. Its overt activities were typically within the scope of normal international relations. They included political alliances, economic and developmental aid, public statements and training and equipment support to foreign militaries (Chau 2006: 114). On the other hand, its covert side, which Kennan described in the 'Long Telegram' (1946) as the 'subterranean plane of actions undertaken by agencies for which [the] Soviet Government does not admit responsibility', spanned a range of subversive activities from which the Soviet Union officially distanced itself. These entailed operations including 'black' propaganda (where the originator of the information remained hidden), disinformation, covert sponsorship of foreign political parties and NGOs, support to underground resistance and guerrilla warfare (Miranda 1985: 17; Kennan 1948). When the contemporary literature defines the aspects of modern Russian 'hybrid warfare', it bears a striking resemblance to these covert activities under Soviet political warfare.

The Soviet Union had a long history of employing the covert side of political warfare. After the failed invasion of Poland in 1920, the Bolshevik government changed focus on how it planned on spreading the 'proletariat revolution'. Instead of sending the Red Army to invade foreign countries and expecting spontaneous uprisings among the local populace, the Communist Party placed new emphasis on political warfare, especially propaganda and the creation of trained cadres who could lead political organization, auxiliary movements and subversive activities behind capitalist lines (Atkinson 1966: 20). Vladimir Lenin viewed as irrelevant any delineation between traditional and non-traditional forms of foreign policy – the overt and covert sides of political warfare – and stated that 'the party does not . . . restrict its activities to some preconceived . . . methods of political struggle; it recognizes all methods of struggle as long as they . . . facilitate the achievement of the best possible results under the given conditions' (Atkinson 1966: 4). This 'end-justifies-the-means' approach to state behaviour paved the way for an increased emphasis on covert political warfare. In a speech at the Seventh Congress of the Communist International (Comintern) in 1935, its leader Georgi Dmitrov called for the adoption of 'Trojan Horse tactics':

> Troy was inaccessible to the armies attacking her, thanks to her impregnable walls, and the attacking army, after suffering many sacrifices, was unable to achieve victory until with the aid of the famous Trojan Horse it managed to penetrate to the very heart of the enemies' camp. We revolutionary workers, it appears to me, should not be shy about using the same tactics [. . .] (Davis 1971: 280)

The Soviet Union had soon co-opted several prominent international workers' and students' organizations, established clandestine channels to Communist Parties worldwide and infiltrated media organizations and academic institutions.

## Strategic deception

A key concept behind Soviet political warfare practice was *strategic deception*, 'a political and/or military strategy that conceals its true goals' (Dailey and Parker 1987: xvi). Deceiving its opponents on its true intentions or the truth of its actions was a regular feature of Soviet political warfare practice. Marxist ideology made no conceptual distinction between communications that were factual and those that were purely instrumental – that is, propagandistic (Beichman 1987: 86). Lenin wrote that 'morality is completely subordinated to the class struggle of the proletariat' and suggested that 'everything that is done in the proletarian cause is honest' (Conquest 1987: 124). He stated that to ensure the survival of communism, the Soviet state 'must be prepared to [. . .] resort to all sorts of cunning, schemes, and stratagems to employ illegal methods, to evade and conceal the truth' (Barron 1974: 224). In his notes published posthumously, Lenin opined that 'speaking the truth is a petty-bourgeois prejudice. A lie, on the other hand, is often justified by the end' (Atkinson 1966: 24). Stalin continued this indifference towards the truth in international relations. In his own eloquent analogy, he wrote:

> Words have no relation to action – otherwise what kind of diplomacy is it? Words are one thing; actions another. Good words are a mask for concealment of bad deeds. Sincere diplomacy is no more possible than dry water or wooden iron. (Freemantle 1982: 41–2)

In an editorial in *Pravda* in 1927, Stalin applied this same approach to international treaties, writing, 'War can turn all agreements of any kind upside down' (Suvorov 1989: 167).

In practice, Soviet strategic deception manifested itself in two significant ways: *active measures* and *maskirovka* (Heuer Jr. 1987: 21–2). The former was primarily the domain of the security services, the latter of the military. Both were key to the execution of Soviet political warfare, and both led to the implementation of the tools identified in the writings on counter-revolution theory. The following section discusses *active measures* in more detail, as they are related to the informational and political tools discussed at length in Chapters 3 and 4; Chapter 5 then discusses *maskirovka* before addressing the military tools of Soviet political warfare.

## Active measures

The term 'active measures' came from Service A of the First Chief Directorate of the KGB, known as the Active Measures Service (*Sluzhba Aktivnykh Meropriyatiyl*) (Richelson 1986: 24).[7] Through guidance from the International Department of the CPSU, its responsibilities were to influence political decisions, public opinion, events and behaviours typically through covert, deceptive or illegal means (Kux 1985: 19; Schultz and Godson 1984: 2). Active measures were thus actions taken by the security services on behalf of Soviet foreign policy objectives but often through means intended to offer the Soviet leadership deniability about their role in them (Johnson 1989: 260). Soviet Bloc security services and the CPSU Central Committee used the term to describe these special operations, but the expression was not widely known outside of their circles (Bittman 1972: x). The word 'active' helped differentiate it from the security services' traditional roles, which were the collection of intelligence, espionage and counterintelligence operations (Heuer Jr. 1987: 23). The objectives of active measures – influencing foreign governments and foreign populations to act more favourably to Soviet interests – were not necessarily outside the realm of normal international relations. However, it was the covert, often illegal, and nonattributable nature of these tools used to execute them that brings their legitimacy into question.

---

[7] This book separates *active measures* from *disinformation* because even though the same KGB department at different times held both names, active measures spanned a much wider spectrum of activities, only one of which was disinformation.

Even though active measures were outside of the security services' 'traditional' roles, they quickly became their focus. In 1959, new KGB chairman Alexander Shelepin held a conference with the service's senior leadership, the ministers of defence and internal affairs, and the CPSU Central Committee to announce a newly established department for the official coordination of disinformation/active measures operations. He asked all Soviet ministries to provide it support whenever needed (Dziak 1988: 149). As a result, the directives from KGB Centre to its outstations and the Bloc security services in the 1960s shifted their priority from passive intelligence collection to active measures (Bittman 1972: 19; Kux 1985: 21). Near the end of his tenure as KGB chairman, Yuri Andropov issued Directive No. 0066 instructing that it was the duty of all foreign intelligence officers, no matter which department they served in, to conduct active measures (Andrew and Mitrokhin 2000: 316).

In terms of counter-revolutionary warfare, active measures provided the shaping operations that the Soviet Union needed to create the conditions it considered satisfactory to prevent the success of the 'counter-revolutionaries' or, if necessary, to justify military invasion. Generally, there were five categories of active measures in support of Soviet political warfare:

(1) *Propaganda* was government-sponsored information and themes. It was either 'white' through official government channels, 'grey' through quasi-official sources, or 'black' through covert means, which concealed the origins of the information.

(2) *Disinformation* consisted of false or misleading information that undermined the positions of the Soviet Union's opponents or bolstered its own policies. It often entailed elaborate forgeries that contained some authentic features.

(3) *Collaborators within foreign political parties and foreign governments,* most notably foreign Communist Parties, secretly received funding and direction from the Soviet government to conduct additional active measures and to be a base of support for Soviet policy.

(4) *Front organizations* were ostensibly independent non-governmental organizations, some of whom were recognized by the United Nations, that were secretly funded and directed by the Soviet Union and served as a mouthpiece for its positions.

(5) *Agents of influence* were significant figures in the public and private sectors of the target country who wittingly or unwittingly spread

propaganda from the Soviet government, giving the appearance that the information originated from a domestic source.

These categories of active measures were part of the informational and political tools of Soviet political warfare and are discussed in greater detail as part of the next two chapters – along with the way in which the Russian Federation has adapted them in the twenty-first century.

# 3

# Informational tools

At the awards ceremony for a Russian journalism contest in 2015, Russian defence minister Sergey Shoigu gave a telling description of the importance Russia places on weaponizing information in modern conflicts:

> The day has come when all of us recognize that the word, the camera, the photograph, the internet and information in general have become yet another type of weaponry, another branch of the armed forces. It is a weapon that can be used for good or for evil [. . .] I would like to remind you that the time has come, when mass media encompasses a wide spectrum. And it is indeed a weapon. (Shoigu 2015)

The Russian-led Collective Security Treaty Organization's *Dictionary-Handbook on Information Security* reinforces this view and calls 'information weapons [. . .] comparable in effectiveness to that of weapons of mass destruction' (CSTO 2014: 9).

However, despite Shoigu's message that 'the day has come', the Soviet Union placed this same emphasis on the use of information as a weapon in its political warfare practices. In nearly identical language, Lenin's Decree on the Press from 1917 – which was intended to be a temporary measure during the Bolshevik Revolution but instead remained in effect until 1990 (Richter 1995: 5) – warned that the 'press is one of the most powerful weapons [. . .] no less dangerous than the bullet or the machine-gun' (Lenin 1917). The Soviet government applied this approach to the use of information in its political warfare campaigns.

This Soviet mindset on information and its application in Soviet political warfare have re-emerged in Russia's modern practices. The Soviet government's control of the messaging began with its state control of the media; the Russian government under President Putin has found creative ways to manoeuvre in the modern media landscape and reconsolidate that state control through official and unofficial mechanisms. These measures increased immediately before and during the 2014 Crimean crisis. The Russian government has even reinstituted the Soviet practice of awarding journalists for their pro-government coverage.

The Soviet government next attacked the targeted country's media in its political warfare campaigns. This included seizing key media installations, blocking the domestic signals and media production of those outlets and replacing them with Soviet creations. The Russian government followed this same pattern as it seized the Crimean television and media sites and replaced them with state-run Russian television channels.

The Russian government revived the Soviet use of propaganda, including verbiage from four of the most dominant propaganda themes used during the Cold War: Western aggression, the threat of fascists, the threat of Ukrainian nationalists and the need to protect fellow ethnic Russians – a reinterpretation of the need to protect 'honest communists'. This revival included the adoption of the 'whataboutism' propaganda technique, in which the Soviet government responded to criticism with a 'What about . . .' criticism of the West, and the modification of 'black' propaganda to fit the modern media landscape: instead of recruiting foreign journalists as Committee for State Security (KGB) agents to plant articles in the foreign press, the Russian government simply used 'trolls' to create fake identities and fake websites to traffic propaganda and disinformation on news websites and social media platforms.

Equally significant was the use of *dezinformatsia* (disinformation). These tools included blatant denials from government leaders of their involvement in the ongoing conflicts, despite clear evidence to the contrary; the creation of forgeries to plant false information that supported propaganda themes; and elaborate schemes involving agents to create false events to reinforce those themes. The Russian government used these techniques in Crimea in the same fashion and for the same purposes as the Soviet government employed them in its political warfare conflicts.

These numerous parallels help to demonstrate that the annexation of Crimea was the Russian government's modern adaptation of old Soviet political warfare practices, not the 'dawn of a new day' in terms of the conduct of warfare.

## Control of the domestic media

The foundation that allowed the Soviet Union to execute sophisticated information operations as part of its political warfare campaigns was state control of its own domestic media. In order to frame the information domain, the Soviet government first gained control of the domestic media landscape. This gave it consistency in messaging and the means necessary for it to then apply informational tools as part of a political warfare conflict. The Russian government reasserted control of its own domestic media landscape in the build-up to the Crimean operation, setting the stage for its own political warfare campaign.

## Soviet Union

Control of the domestic information environment was a key facet of Soviet rule from its earliest days. Vladimir Lenin considered the Russian population 'backward', and only through propaganda – or 'political education work' as the Bolsheviks called it – could he and the party teach the population the fundamentals of socialism and the communist message (Kenez 1985; Brandenberger 2011). As a result, the Soviet government created state agencies to manage the media sphere. It designated specially trained cadres to master modern communications techniques and craft messaging to reinforce the Soviet Union's core principles and policy stances (Barghoorn 1964). In the 1920s, the Communist Party of the Soviet Union (CPSU) Central Committee created the Agitation and Propaganda (Agitprop) Department, which had close to thirty sub-departments to focus on various media, including publishing, press, theatre, arts and radio (Van Herpen 2016: 2). In the Cold War, the International Department of the CPSU was responsible for setting the propaganda agenda for all subordinate efforts; from 1978 to 1986, the International Information Department served as an additional level of coordination on foreign messaging programmes (Schultz 1988: 33).

Together with establishing these governmental departments to manage media content, the Soviet government also controlled the media outlets themselves. By the late 1980s, the state was publishing over 8,000 daily newspapers, including approximately 3,000 in non-Russian languages. Journalists were required to belong to the state-controlled Union of Journalists, and the editors-in-chief of the major newspapers came from the members of the CPSU Central Committee (Zickel and Keefe 1991: 378–83). The main state media outlets were so dominant that in 1990, the Moscow-based national publications consisted of only 3 per cent of the total number of newspapers but were 75 per cent of total circulation (Richter 1995: 6). *Pravda*, the official newspaper of the Central Committee, was the most authoritative and reached approximately twenty million people daily. *Izvestia* from the Presidium of the Supreme Soviet was second in importance and reached between eight and ten million. Many of the other state organizations published their own papers, as well; *Trud* from the labour unions, *Komsomolskaya Pravda* from the Komsomol political youth organization, *Krasnaya Zvezda* from the Ministry of Defence and *Literaturnaya Gazeta* from the Union of Writers were the most prominent (Zickel and Keefe 1991: 380–1). However, the diversity in Soviet media was merely in presentation – not in viewpoint (Murray 1994). *Pravda* focused on lengthy official party announcements, *Izvestia* produced shorter articles similar in style to a Western newspaper and *Trud* included pieces on popular culture more interesting to the average reader. Despite this variety in style, their editorial stances on political issues remained consistent across publications.

The government's authority to direct the media was codified in Soviet law, and it held coordination meetings with the media heads to ensure compliance. A directive from 1918 mandated that all newspapers publish the 'decrees and ordinances of the organs of the Soviet power' (Zickel and Keefe 1991: 372). In 1952, the Central Committee of the All-Union Communist Party (or VKP(b), a former name for the CPSU) passed a resolution that gave the Agitprop Department and the Central Committee's Foreign Policy Commission the power 'to conduct a meeting of editors of central newspapers and of social-political and literary-artistic journals, to discuss measures for eliminating shortcomings in the coverage in the press of the struggle for peace' (CC VKP(b) 1952). In other words, the government had the authority to dictate to the various Soviet media sources how to cover events in line with official government positions, especially to draw attention to (in its words) 'the intrigues of imperialist aggressors'.

The government capitalized on this media coordination authority during its political warfare campaigns. As the invasion of Czechoslovakia was underway on 21 August 1968, the Soviet government sent to the country Aleksandr Yakovlev, the first deputy director of the CPSU Central Committee Propaganda Department, with a contingent of Soviet journalists. His mission was to coordinate Soviet media reporting on the situation and ensure that it followed the state's propaganda themes (Petrov 2010: 156). When the Soviet Union invaded Afghanistan in 1979, the Politburo provided TASS, the state-run news agency, with the verbatim announcement it wanted published immediately after hostilities began. The statement condemned interference from abroad as the cause of the country's ills and insisted that the Soviet invasion was the result of the Afghan government's 'urgent request to give aid and assistance in the fight against external aggression' (TASS 1979).

Along with producing its own media, the Soviet government imposed strict censorship on who could publish and what information could be published.

Lenin's Decree on the Press, passed by the Soviet of People's Commissars on 27 October 1917, ordered the closure of all 'bourgeoisie press' that could be considered guilty of 'inciting open opposition to, or disobedience of, the workers' and peasants' government' (Lenin 1917). Even though the decree stated that the censorship measures would be temporary, they remained in effect until the 1990 Law on the Press and Other Mass Media (Richter 1995: 5) – and thus for virtually the entire life of the Soviet Union. From 1922 onwards, the General Directorate for the Protection of State Secrets in the Press (Glavlit), the Soviet Union's official censorship agency, employed 70,000 censors and removed any material deemed harmful to the regime or counter to its messaging (Conquest 1987: 127). Its approval was required for any work to be published in more than nine copies, and a Glavlit representative sat on the editorial staffs of all Soviet press agencies and radio and television stations (Finkel 2007). The Soviet government imposed restrictions on foreign media, as well. It spent on average $150 million per year to jam the radio broadcasts of Voice of America, Radio Free Europe and Radio Liberty – more than it cost the US government annually to run all three stations (Schultz and Godson 1984: 31).

This state control over the media led to the creation of *samizdat*, the self-published or underground press that ran parallel to official channels, especially among dissidents (Skilling 1989). The term came from *samesbyaizdat*, 'publishing house for oneself', and was a parody of *Gosizdat*, the name of an early state publishing house (Johnston 1999: 122). The materials typically passed from reader to reader within controlled, secretive networks to avoid the government censors (Baranczak 1990). Some of the prominent examples which were also published widely in the West were Boris Pasternak's *Doctor Zhivago*, Aleksandr Solzhenitsyn's *The Gulag Archipelago* and Anna Akhmatova's *Requiem* (see Komaromi 2004). A similar system existed for *tamizdat*, materials published abroad and smuggled into the country (see Kind-Kovács and Labov 2013). These banned publications found readership among not only urban intelligentsia but also the industrial and agricultural workers and even members of the government, who ostensibly read them for 'study' (Johnston 1999).

Since these materials circulated outside of the control of the state censors and offered alternative viewpoints to the official narratives, the Soviet government went to great lengths to minimize their impact and target their production – especially since it considered them to be part of the West's counter-revolutionary campaign. In 1966, the KGB helped introduce new articles to the Criminal Code to address the threat from *samizdat*. Article 190-1, for example, targeted 'slander' against the Soviet system and could apply to any literature that questioned socialist principles or the central role of the party (Komaromi 2012: 80). In a 1969 memorandum to the CPSU Central Committee, KGB chairman Yuri Andropov warned that '[i]mperialist reactionaries consider *samizdat* one of the ways in which they can weaken socialist society within our country', blaming outside support for the increased dissemination of such materials (Andropov 1969). The KGB created the Fifth Chief Directorate, whose mission was to monitor ideological subversion, in part to target dissidents and the propagation of these banned media. While some Soviet citizens had access to these unofficial, unapproved media sources, the Soviet government actively sought to limit their exposure and criminalize their content. As a result of these collective measures, the Soviet domestic media landscape was firmly within the control of the state.

## Russian Federation

The foundational basis for Russia's ability to apply informational tools in its modern political warfare campaigns is likewise its control of the domestic media. However, the way in which it asserts that control differs from the Soviet Union's approach to match the changes in legal, political and economic dynamics. After a relaxation of state control over the media in the late twentieth century, the Russian government under President Vladimir Putin has taken measures to reassert a new form of dominance in the domestic media landscape. As with the shift in security perspectives, the loosening – but not the complete removal – of state control of the media began towards the end of the Soviet period. Under General Secretary Mikhail Gorbachev's glasnost (openness and transparency) policies, Soviet media editors received greater freedom to publish on sensitive subjects, including crime, security and morale issues in the armed forces (Zickel and Keefe 1991: 379). In August 1990, the Soviet Law on the Press and Other Means of Mass Communication came into effect. It made it illegal to interfere with the activities of journalists or to deny them information. It also allowed any citizen or organization – including other political parties – to set up a newspaper as long as it did not incite violence, promote racial or religious persecution or reveal state secrets (Murray 1994: 74). The state thus no longer had a monopoly over the media or the messaging. Despite the relaxed restrictions, however, the Soviet government still maintained some control. In addition to the state's continued ownership of its numerous media outlets, Gorbachev personally appointed to these state publications editors who were loyal to his reforms and would use their platforms to endorse his policies (Richter 1995: 7).

These trends – greater protections but still some measures of government control – continued in the Russian Federation under President Boris Yeltsin. The Russian Federation Law on Mass Media from 27 December 1991 provided general legal guarantees of media practice, including ownership rights and freedom to produce information (Russian Federation 1991). However, Yeltsin still used the power of his position to sway media reporting at critical events, including elections (Price et al. 2002). For example, in the lead-up to the election to choose Yeltsin's successor, he issued presidential decrees consolidating many of the state-owned media companies, including VGTRK (the All-Russia State Television and Radio Broadcasting Company). He also created the Ministry for the Press, Television and Radio Broadcasting and Mass Communications to unify state management of the media (Belin 2002: 276). At the same time, the media landscape in the Russian Federation was plural in its ownership – the state had divested of several of its holdings – but it was not necessarily independent. The oligarch owners of Russia's private media outlets used them as a platform to influence the government and public opinion. The media were political actors in their own right, not objective reporters of the government's successes and failures. Some of the oligarchs were supporters of Yeltsin's policies or used their media platforms to gain favour with the government, thus blurring the divide between state-controlled and private media (Fadin 1997).

Since Putin rose to the presidency in 2000, the Russian government has heightened its influence in the domestic media landscape, bringing it closer to the levels of state control of the media that the Soviet Union enjoyed. Even though the number of media outlets in Russia has since increased, the plurality of opinion has sharply decreased – giving it more in common with the Soviet media model than a Western one (Oates and McCormack 2010). Just as the Soviet media existed to educate the public on the CPSU's governing policies, Putin's government sees the contemporary Russian media as a tool of the state, to include privately owned outlets. The roles established in Yeltsin's presidency have reversed: whereas Russian oligarchs held sway over Yeltsin's policymaking by the influence they wielded through their media companies, media oligarchs during Putin's tenure only maintain their wealth and power if they closely align themselves with the government (Shinar 2015). Those that have run afoul of the administration – such as Boris Berezovsky, the one-time owner of the television station *Perviy Kanal* – have faced questionable criminal charges, causing them to lose their money and influence (see Mohiuddin 2007; Beumers et al. 2008; Hutchings and Rulyova 2009). The Putin government also found new ways to exert a form of censorship by passing the Information Security Doctrine, a concept developed but not passed in 1995 under Yeltsin. Citing the need to balance individual rights to information access with the security needs of the state, the administration used the doctrine to increase the number of officials who could classify information and changed licencing requirements for media outlets (Belin 2002: 293–6).

In addition to applying pressure on media oligarchs, the Russian government has increased the number of state-owned publications and consolidated the state's management of them. Within a few years of Putin's rise to power, state agencies controlled over 70 per cent of electronic media outlets, 80 per cent of the regional press and 20 per cent of the national press (Khvostunova 2013). Just as the crisis in Ukraine was worsening in December 2013, the Russian government dissolved the RIA *Novosti* news agency, which had gained a reputation for objectivity since the end of the Cold War (Van Herpen 2016: 76). Putin issued a presidential decree that closed both the news agency and the Russian government's international radio station, Voice of Russia, and replaced them with *Rossiya Segodnya* (*Russia Today*, but not to be confused with the state-run foreign-language television network *RT*). The government then appointed one of its allies as the new head of *Rossiya Segodnya*: Dmitry Kiselyov, the popular, flamboyant, nationalist television host (Gornin 2013). In the first staff meeting at the new media company, Kiselyov instructed his employees that the most important characteristic they needed for their work was not objectivity but 'love for Russia' (Neef and Schepp 2013). Anna Kachkayeva, dean of media and communications at Moscow's Higher School of Economics, called the media changes a return to the 'Soviet and propagandistic past' (Ennis 2013).

At the same time, several outlets that remained outside direct government control have received new pro-government ownership and thus fallen under indirect control. By 2010, half of the national television channels were under the control of three entities: the state itself, the media subsidiary of the state gas company Gazprom or business structures controlled by Yuri Kovalchuk, a member of Putin's inner circle (Horbyk 2015; Lipman et al. 2018). NTV, the only privately owned nationwide television network, was highly critical of Putin during the 2000 presidential election. Owner Vladimir Gusinsky and his Media-Most company soon found themselves facing tax evasion and fraud charges. In 2001, Gazprom acquired a controlling stake in the television channel and then forcibly replaced its managerial staff (see Mickiewicz 2008; Lipman and McFaul 2001; Hoffman 2011). *Izvestia*, the former Soviet newspaper that was privatized in the early 1990s, changed ownership from the state-owned Gazprom-Media to the National Media Group in 2008. Despite the private ownership, part-owner and editor-in-chief Aram Gabrelyanov has stated that the paper is forbidden to write critically about the president, the prime minister or the patriarch (Khvostunova 2013).

Since 2000, the Russian government has established steering meetings with the Russian media to direct coverage in much the same fashion that the Soviet government did previously. After NTV joined the ranks of state-controlled television networks, the heads of these television stations started meeting weekly with Vladislav Surkov, the political strategist from the presidential administration, to discuss content (Ioffe 2010). Putin's deputy chief of staff Alexey Gromov – who previously served simultaneously as the president's press secretary and member of the board of *Perviy Kanal* (*Economist* 2007) – became responsible for coordinating messaging among Russia's mainstream media. Former employees of VGTRK have also attested that the Russian Presidential Administration coordinates content across Russian television channels. Gromov or presidential spokesman Dmitry Peskov have held meetings at the Kremlin with the editors-in-chief of the different networks and given them booklets with directives on what to cover, how to cover it and what approved experts to invite (Sidorov and Orlov 2015). In much the same way that Soviet propaganda could be traced from *Pravda* to TASS to other media outlets, it is possible to track new government talking points from official statements to Russian media published shortly afterwards, suggesting that such coordination is regularly occurring. Furthermore, the top fifteen major Russian news outlets carry strikingly similar editorial positions and perspectives on current events (Interview with Yevhen Fedchenko 2017). While the Russian government does not enjoy the same oversight authority codified in law that the Soviet government did, in practice, it appears to achieve the same effect. In the words of Russian State Duma deputy Ilya Ponomarev, Gromov's orders on what is to be covered in the media 'are as strict as any in the army' (Powell 2014) – leaving little doubt to the authority of these 'coordination' meetings. While this coordination appears to apply only to the state-owned or state-controlled channels, the Russian government under Putin has vastly increased that span of control.

The Soviet government achieved domination of the domestic media landscape by creating numerous state-controlled outlets, prohibiting materials not approved by the state and targeting through legal measures and the security services *samizdat* and *tamizdat* published outside of government control. Because of the Law on Mass Media and other liberalizing measures that limit its centralized role, the Russian government does not have the ability to assert itself in the domestic media landscape in the same direct way that the Soviet government did. Instead, the government under Putin has grown the number of state publications to increase plurality but maintain unified messaging and has assisted pro-government oligarchs – sometimes through trumped-up legal charges against the government's critics – in taking over private publications and aligning their editorial stances with the state's. As a result, the Russian government has achieved a similar level of domination in the domestic media landscape that the Soviet government enjoyed.

The end result of these media consolidation efforts was that by the time the crisis in Ukraine began in the fall of 2013, government-controlled (or government-aligned) media dominated the Russian-language news market. In June 2013, 70 per cent of Russian respondents said they received their news from Russian state TV channels, and 65 per cent believed that the news was 'absolutely' or 'mostly' objectively reported (Levada Centre 2014: 168–9). The top five channels by audience reach were *Perviy Kanal, Rossiya* 1, NTV, TNT and *Pyatiy Kanal* – all state-owned or state-aligned channels. The majority shareholders of *Perviy Kanal* are *Rosimushchestvo* (the Federal Agency for State Property Management) and two of Putin's oligarch allies, Yuri Kovalchuk and Roman Abramovich. *Rossiya* 1 is part of VGTRK, which is also owned by *Rosimushchestvo*. Gazprom-Media controls both NTV and TNT. Yuri Kovalchuk's National Media Group also runs *Pyatiy Kanal* (Khvostunova 2013).

## Crimea 2014

This control of the media landscape meant that Russian government messaging dominated viewers' perspectives on the Ukraine crisis, just as the Soviet government had coordinated messaging during its conflicts in Czechoslovakia and Afghanistan. In December 2013, 61 per cent of Russian respondents trusted that the Russian television channels' portrayal of the situation in Ukraine was accurate (Levada Centre 2014: 210). In the week leading up to the Crimean referendum (10–16 March 2014), *Perviy Kanal, Rossiya* 1 and NTV had all ten of the highest rated by viewership news programmes, including Dmitry Kiselyov's *Vesti Nedeli* (News of the Week) programme on *Rossiya* 1 (Powell 2014).

The nature of the Russian media landscape is relevant to the 2014 Crimean crisis because during the conflict, the Russian government used its state media to employ its informational tools as part of its annexation operation. On 9 March 2014, Russian forces that had seized the main television tower in Crimea replaced the broadcast signals for the Ukrainian channels with Russian state-owned channels. Crimeans, of whom 96 per cent received their news from television (BBG and Gallup 2014), thus only received Russian state television – and heard its version of events – for the critical week before the referendum.

To increase further its control of the information sphere, the Russian government took additional measures to consolidate the domestic media landscape during the Ukraine crisis. Three smaller television channels had remained independent: Rent TV, *Dozhd* (Rain) and Tomsk TV. As the situation in Ukraine intensified, these channels either came under state control or were forced off of the air after the Russian government placed immense pressure on broadcasters and cable providers (Sanovich 2017: 6). The most prominent example is *Dozhd*. During the week of 4 February 2014, the major television providers in Russia announced that they would no longer carry the channel. The reason put forth was the indignity of the channel's online poll on the anniversary of the siege of Leningrad; it had asked readers if it would have been better to surrender the city during the Second World War if the move would have spared hundreds of thousands of lives. After strong condemnations from the government, including from presidential spokesman Dmitry Peskov and deputy chief of staff Alexey Gromov, providers started to pull *Dozhd* from their broadcasts. The channel lost approximately 90 per cent of its audience reach in a month (Dzyadko 2014). Mikhail Zygar, the channel's editor-in-chief, called it 'conclusively clear that a serious war is being waged against us' (Harding 2014). *Dozhd* was the only remaining opposition cable news channel. According to Ioffe (2014), it was the only channel that fairly represented the motivations of the protesters after the 2011 Duma elections. By in effect censoring the channel, the Russian government prevented *Dozhd* from providing a dissident voice to its narrative of the Ukraine crisis, just as the events were sharply turning against Russia's interests in the country.

Similar developments occurred elsewhere in the media once Russia's Crimean operation had begun. On 10 March 2014 – one week prior to the Crimean referendum – the Russian online newspaper *Lenta.ru* published an interview with Dmytro Yarosh, the leader of the far-right Ukrainian group *Pravy Sektor*. Based on hacked text messages from Timur Prokopenko, deputy head of the internal affairs department of the Russian Presidential Administration, the Russian government began searching for ways to completely eliminate *Lenta.ru* within ninety minutes of the article's appearance and even contacted the Office of the Prosecutor General to discuss ways to bring charges (TSN 2015).[1]

---

[1] TSN is the news service of the Ukrainian television channel 1+1. The quoted article is a summary of leaks provided by Anonymous International, known as *Shaltai Boltai* (Humpty Dumpty) in Russian (see Turovsky 2015). The group hacked the SMS messages of Timur Prokopenko. His exchanges

*Roskomnadzor*, the Russian media regulator, issued a warning to the news site over the 'extremist' content, and even before the interview was published, an official from the Russian Presidential Administration had handed Alexander Mamut, the site's principal stockholder, a folder highlighting all of its coverage that the government disliked (Gorbachev 2015). Two days later, *Lenta.ru* announced that it was replacing its editor-in-chief, Galina Timchenko (*Lenta. ru* 2014b). On the final day before the change, eighty-four staff members at the news site signed a letter of protest addressed to their readers and ran it on the editorial page:

> We believe that this appointment is the result of direct pressure on the editorial board of *Lenta.ru*. The dismissal of an independent editor-in-chief and the appointment of a person managed directly by the Kremlin's offices is a violation of the law on the media, which speaks of the inadmissibility of censorship. Over the past couple of years, the space of free journalism in Russia has dramatically decreased. Some publications are directly managed from the Kremlin, others through curators, and others by editors who are afraid of losing their jobs. Some media have closed; others will close in the coming months. (*Lenta.ru* 2014a)

This sort of indirect censorship occurred immediately after the annexation, as well. On 21 March – three days after Russia formally annexed Crimea and Western governments had responded with sanctions – Dmitry Kiselyov in his role as head of *Rossiya Segodnya* notified the Voice of America, the US government-funded radio station, that the Russian government would not be renewing its contract to operate in the country because the station was 'mere spam on our frequencies' (*RT* 2014c).

During the Crimean crisis, the Russian government also used its Soviet-style steering meetings with the media to coordinate across platforms in line with the government's messaging. Text messages hacked by Anonymous International appear to show that Alexey Gromov, the president's deputy chief of staff, drafted talking points for the propaganda theme repeated in Russian media consistently throughout the crisis that the Euromaidan movement was in reality a US-backed coup led by radicals. Prokopenko, the internal affairs department deputy head, then distributed the talking points to the various Russian media outlets (TSN 2015; Fedchenko 2016: 159). Shortly after the Crimean referendum, the Russian government sent another directive to the media. It listed government-approved

---

with Nikolai Molibog, the director general of the Russian media group RBK, are included in the leaks, and Molibog confirmed their authenticity (TSN 2015).

'experts' whom they could invite to comment on the vote as well as the main themes their coverage needed to communicate – most importantly, that the referendum was 'absolutely legitimate' under international law (TSN 2015). Once the annexation was complete, the Russian government directed that the media outlets run at least one story a day on how life was improving for the people of Crimea (Sidorov and Orlov 2015).

To restrict content that contradicted these talking points, the Russian government achieved a form of censorship by utilizing the same pressure levers it had employed in the years prior. On 3 March 2014, the Ulyanovsk Oblast regional website 73online.ru reported that the GRU (the Main Intelligence Directorate, the Russian military's intelligence and special forces service) and other military units from the local area were mobilizing to deploy to Crimea. According to the hacked text messages, Prokopenko threatened to block the website if the news story was not taken down. The website complied within half an hour (TSN 2015). Pavel Durov, the CEO and creator of the Russian social media website VKontakte, claimed that he received an order from the Federal Security Service (FSB) in December 2013 to provide them with the details of the members of the website's Euromaidan group. He refused, arguing that the FSB's jurisdiction did not extend to Ukrainian users. On 21 April 2014, VKontake's board dismissed Durov as CEO; he soon sold his shares and fled the country (Van Herpen 2016: 92). Three days before the planned Crimean referendum, the Russian prosecutor general's office ordered internet service providers to block access to the websites of two of the Russian government's most prominent critics: Alexey Navalny and Garry Kasparov (Sanovich 2017: 12).

While the censorship system is not as straightforward as it was in the Soviet period, the modern Russian regime has found ways to exert pressure to achieve its desired result. The Soviet Union did not face the same issues with opposition media because virtually all media fell under the governmental umbrella. The Russian government does not have the authority to simply close these publications because it disagrees with their content. However, it has found creative levers to achieve the same result, especially through pressure on investors, advertisers and broadcasters. The result is that before and during the 2014 Crimean crisis, the Russian government achieved a similar level of control over the domestic media that the Soviet Union enjoyed, setting the conditions for it to control the messaging and to apply the same informational tools that the Soviet government did in its political warfare campaigns.

## Awards to media

Yet another Soviet practice to control the media that the Russian government revived in the 2014 Crimean operation was the secret presentation of awards to media outlets for favourable coverage during military conflicts. These awards served to encourage the media to act as an arm of the government's information operations. In 1971, the Presidium of the Supreme Soviet awarded ninety key individuals '[f]or the exemplary fulfilment of duties during the events in Czechoslovakia'. Among those deemed to have done indispensable work were Aleksandr Yakovlev, the first deputy director of the CPSU Central Committee's Propaganda Department who had travelled with Soviet journalists into Czechoslovakia to control the reporting; Georgii Fedyashin, the KGB officer who served under cover as the deputy director of the *Novosti* Press Agency; Aleksandr Alekseev, the senior *Novosti* representative in Czechoslovakia; and a large group of journalists and administrators from the Soviet media. They received their awards in secret, and the directive announcing the awards remained classified (Petrov 2010: 158–9).

These sorts of awards ceased at the end of the Cold War, but the Russian government revived the practice virtually unchanged after the annexation of Crimea. At the end of April 2014, Putin signed Decree No. 269 'On Awarding State Awards to the Russian Federation'. The decree is conspicuously missing from the official Kremlin website; presidential spokesman Dmitry Peskov said he 'can confirm that such a decree was signed', but that the Russian government 'do[es] not plan to add any details about it' (Nechepurenko 2014) – making it secret, just like the Czechoslovak directive. According to sources from the Russian newspaper *Vedemosti*, the awards and honours went to over 300 Russian media representatives, including about ninety correspondents, 'for high professionalism and objectivity in covering the events in the Republic of Crimea'. Employees from VGTRK, *Perviy Kanal*, NTV, *RT* and LifeNews were among those awarded (Kamyshev and Bolletskaya 2014). One of the awardees, *Komsomolskaya Pravda* editor Vladimir Sungorkin, called himself a true 'Soviet man' and said the award was an 'incentive' to remain loyal to the regime (Nechepurenko 2014). Among those not awarded were the *Ekho Moskvy* radio station and the *Dozhd* television channel. Coincidentally, the *politonline.ru* website – part of the pro-government *Pravda.ru* media group – created a ranking of the most 'anti-Russian' domestic media outlets based on the key words they used to describe the Ukraine crisis (e.g. 'Anschluss' and 'little green men' vs 'unification' and 'polite people'). *Ekho Moskvy* and *Dozhd* placed first and second on the list (*Politonline.ru* 2014;

Sindelar 2014). The ranking is not necessarily a direct reflection of the Russian government's position on the different media sources, but it coincides with how the government would interpret 'objectivity in covering the events in the Republic of Crimea'.

## Control of the target country's media

Having tight control of the domestic media allowed both the Soviet and Russian governments to control the information space by aligning their countries' media messaging along government lines. During its political warfare campaigns, the Soviet government then seized control of the target country's media landscape to exert similar dominance over the information space and eliminate conflicting messaging. In these operations, it captured the domestic media outlets, blocked other sources and created false flag publications. The intent behind these measures was to dominate the information sphere and allow the Soviet forces to employ their informational tools uncontested. The Soviet government's efforts in Czechoslovakia and Afghanistan provided some of the templates for action that the Russian Federation appeared to adopt during the Crimean crisis.

### Czechoslovakia 1968

One of the key Soviet objectives during the invasion of Czechoslovakia in 1968 was to seize the Czechoslovak national media. The purpose was twofold: to push the message that the population supported the Warsaw Pact operation to 'save' the country and to deprive the reformers of the means to condemn it. In his speech to the Warsaw Pact Five (the Soviet Union, Bulgaria, Hungary, East Germany and Poland) outlining the Soviet plan for the invasion, General Secretary Leonid Brezhnev emphasized the importance of controlling the media and the messaging:

> [A]fter the presidium meets [the session in which Alois Indra and his co-conspirators would challenge First Secretary Alexander Dubček's leadership – see Chapter 4], the printing house and offices of the paper *Rudé právo* [the Communist Party of Czechoslovakia's official newspaper] will be seized and everything will be made ready for a special edition of the paper to appear. Through one of the most trustworthy activists of their group, radio and television will be shut down, as will all telephone and telegraph communications. (Brezhnev 1968a: 398)

The 'trustworthy activist' was Karel Hoffmann, the pro-Soviet chairman of the Central Board for Communications. After the Soviet Union's allies failed to seize control of the government during the 21 August Presidium session, Dubček led the body in drafting a statement condemning the invasion and sent it to *Rudé právo* and *Československý rozhlas* (the national radio station) for publication. Hoffmann intercepted it and ordered the media outlets to run instead a pre-scripted statement the Soviet Politburo had provided him praising the invasion. Employees from both news organizations passed word to Josef Smrkovský, who invoked his authority as chairman of the National Assembly and ordered the Presidium's statement run instead, so Hoffmann switched off the transmitters (CPCz CC Presidium 1968: 414). Simultaneously, the Soviet forces jammed Western radio broadcasts throughout the country (CIA 1968a).

The invading forces and their allies within the Czechoslovak government not only shut down domestic broadcasts but also replaced them with their own publications. *Zprávy*, a new Czech-language newspaper, appeared immediately after the Warsaw Pact forces entered the country. It was sent to *Rudé právo* subscribers, left in stacks on the streets, and distributed through the mail system. It published articles that condemned the reformers for trying to destroy socialism and praised the Warsaw Pact member states for their fraternal assistance. Four months later, the Czechoslovak Ministry of the Interior revealed that *Zprávy* was actually produced by the editorial council of the Soviet forces (Bittman 1972: 207). The operation's planners applied the same tactic to radio. Once Hoffmann had ordered all domestic radio transmitters switched off, a new station appeared on the airwaves of the national radio station. Radio Vltava began transmission in Czechoslovakia at 5.40 am on 21 August, just hours after the invading Warsaw Pact forces had crossed the border. Even though its programmes were in Czech and Slovak, it secretly originated from Karl-Marx-Stadt (Chemnitz) in East Germany. The station's very first broadcast was the TASS statement justifying the invasion (Windsor and Roberts 1969: 129; Tigrid 1971: 105; Dawisha 1984: 323).

## Afghanistan 1979

As in Czechoslovakia, some of the first, critical targets seized by Soviet forces in the invasion of Afghanistan were Afghan media installations. The intent was the same: to monopolize the Afghan media space to dictate the information environment. A communications centre in the middle of Kabul served as the main waypoint for all Afghan government communications. A special demolitions team from the KGB's *Zenit* (Zenith) strike force destroyed it at

7.30 pm on the night of the invasion (Braithwaite 2012: 94; Grau 2003: 309). Also that night, combined teams composed of KGB from *Zenit* and of Russian Airborne Forces (VDV) from the 345th Separate Parachute Regiment seized the main Afghan radio and television centre as well as the main telegraph building. They then shut them down with the help of Afghan collaborators (Grau 2003: 313–5; Feifer 2010: 80). By seizing the various media outlets in the country, the Soviet forces prevented supporters of President Hafizullah Amin from entering the information space and countering the Soviet narrative about the legitimacy of the invasion.

Once again, the Soviet forces then replaced the domestic broadcasts with their own. At 8.45 pm on 27 December, they began transmitting a fake version of Radio Kabul, the national public radio station, over the airwaves of the actual station. The transmission originated across the border from the Soviet invasion force's headquarters in Termez, a city in the Uzbek Soviet Socialist Republic (Andrew and Mitrokhin 2006: 402). In its initial broadcasts, the station announced that a 'Revolutionary Tribunal' had found President Amin guilty of 'crimes against the people', executed him and requested that the Soviet Union send military assistance to help the new regime. No such tribunal had occurred (Girardet 1985: 15). Babrak Karmal, the Soviet government's chosen successor as president, appeared to give a speech on the radio calling for Afghans to rally behind him as their new leader. In reality, the message was pre-recorded. General Yuri Drozdov, the chief of the KGB's illegals operations (the Russian term for agents under non-official cover), prepared the speech and brought it into the region in a special briefcase more than a week prior. With the assistance of A. M. Watanjar, the former interior minister and one of Karmal's co-conspirators, the Soviet forces also broadcast the statement from the seized radio and television centre in Kabul. Karmal was still at the Bagram Soviet airbase under KGB protection and would not travel to the capital until the next day, and the KGB kept him hidden from public view in the outskirts of the city for several more days (Braithwaite 2012: 90, 104–5). By seizing the Afghan media and broadcasting its own sources, the Soviet forces hid these truths from the population and instead spread its propaganda narratives on the unfolding invasion.

## Crimea 2014

As part of its 2014 campaign in Crimea, the Russian government appeared to adapt these same Soviet tactics to seize control of the Crimean media landscape with the same purpose: to monopolize the information space. Media installations were some of the primary targets in the earliest stages of the operation. On 28 February, armed men without insignia captured the main television tower, from which virtually all channels in Crimea broadcasted, as well as the state television and radio channel GTRK *Krym* in Simferopol. They admitted to the local staff that they were members of the Russian Black Sea Fleet (QHA 2014; UNIAN 2014b; *Economist* 2014). On 3 March, the government-run Crimean radio and television broadcasting centre stopped airing Black Sea Television and Radio, the largest private broadcaster on the peninsula. The following day, electricity to the channel's headquarters was cut (The Institute of Mass Information 2014). Representatives from the Crimean broadcasting authorities stated that they were coerced to shut the channel 'by force' before later changing their story to claim that it was for the safety of the journalists (*Radio Svoboda* 2014).

The Russian operation likewise targeted print media. On 1 March, armed, masked men seized the Simferopol House of Trade Unions, which was the headquarters of the online media outlets Centre for Investigative Journalism and the Information Press Centre. A representative from the armed group said that they had seized the offices because the centres were publishing 'false information'. When questioned about the soldiers without insignia who had conducted the seizure, he stated that 'our friends in masks [. . .] have their own powers' and 'are not authorized to speak with anyone'; he was also sure to point out that '[t]hey came in correctly and politely'. Despite calling themselves the 'Crimean Front', the soldiers spoke Russian without the distinctive Crimean accent (Centre for Investigative Journalism (Ukraine) 2014).

Telephone and internet communications infrastructure were disrupted, as well. Ukrtelecom, the Ukrainian national telephone company, announced on 28 February that armed men seized its Crimean facilities and tampered its fibre optic cable network, causing telephone and internet outages throughout the peninsula (Polityuk and Finkle 2014). Russian forces also seized the Simferopol Internet Exchange Point, allowing them to control or sever connectivity to mainland Ukraine (Giles 2016a: 49, 2016b: 64). By controlling the key communications infrastructure in Crimea, the Russian forces prevented reports from mainland Ukraine or further afield from challenging its dominance of the information environment.

Like the Soviet forces in Czechoslovakia, the Russian forces in Crimea also blocked foreign media. During both the 27 February emergency session of the Crimean Rada legislative assembly – the session that appointed Sergey Aksyonov the new prime minister – and the 6 March session to vote on unification with Russia, the unmarked Russian soldiers guarding the building blocked Ukrainian and Western journalists from entering but allowed Russian media in to observe the proceedings (*Telekritika* 2014c; The Institute of Mass Information 2014). Each morning outside the Ukrainian Navy headquarters in Sevastopol, the leadership of the unmarked Russian military and Crimean militia presence blocking access to the base held a meeting. According to one eyewitness, the leaders explicitly instructed the armed men to prevent Ukrainian and foreign journalists from approaching the base but to allow access to Russian media (Interview H 2017). A checkpoint of irregulars prevented a mission from the Organization for Security and Co-operation in Europe (OSCE) from entering Crimea on 6 March. The mission consisted of fifty-two observers from twenty-eight countries and was formed to monitor and report on the developing situation on the peninsula (Walker 2014a). On 11 March, armed men with black face masks detained three journalists from the Norwegian Broadcasting Corporation, accused them of being 'spies' and confiscated their equipment when they attempted to pass through a checkpoint at the border with mainland Ukraine (Tandstad et al. 2014). On 13 March, unidentified military forces arrested a French Canal+ journalist who had been reporting from a military facility in Simferopol (*Le Figaro.fr* and Reuters 2014). Dozens of similar instances occurred throughout March (see The Institute of Mass Information 2014).

As the Soviet forces had done in Czechoslovakia and Afghanistan, the Russian forces then replaced the shuttered Ukrainian media in Crimea with their own broadcasts. On 9 March, the analogue signals for Ukrainian television channels from the seized television tower were replaced with Russian state-owned channels. Digital signals switched the following day (*Telekritika* 2014a, 2014b).[2] The previously seized GTRK *Krym* remained on the air, but its reporting shifted from a pro-Russian Crimean perspective to a virtual copy of Russian media broadcasts (Interview with Volodymyr Prytula 2017). The only way to still receive Ukrainian channels was through satellite (Interview B 2017). Dmitry Polonsky, who became the Crimean information minister after Aksyonov took power, defended the move, claiming that the Crimean Rada's 6 March vote to unify with Russia meant that 'Crimea was no longer subject to Ukrainian legislation' and that the government had 'the right to protect the residents of

---

[2] NTV *Mir* replaced Inter; *Perviy Kanal* replaced 1+1; TNT replaced Channel 5; *Rossiya* RTR replaced *Pershyi*; *Rossiya* 24/*Krym* 24 replaced Black Sea TV; STRC replaced tvFM; and Star replaced StB (*Telekritika* 2014a, 2014b).

Crimea from the escalation of violence, lies and the flow of untrue information that had been flowing from the screens' (ITAR-TASS 2014b; Dolgov 2014).

The Russian government appears to have made this decision to forcibly broadcast its channels in Crimea because it did not believe the existing market share that Russian state TV enjoyed among Crimea's Russian-speaking population was sufficient to execute its information operations. On 25 February 2014, Russian State Duma deputy Leonid Slutsky, who at the time was the chairman of the Committee for Commonwealth of Independent States (CIS) Affairs, Eurasian Integration, and Ties with Compatriots, was in Simferopol. At a meeting with *Rossotrudnichestvo*, the Russian federal agency responsible for civilian aid in the CIS, he said, 'We assumed our mass media were present here [in Crimea and Sevastopol] on a scale slightly bigger than that of some sporadic landing troops. We are not happy about it' (Voice of Russia 2014). At the time, the Russian television channel with the largest share of the Ukrainian nationwide market was *Perviy Kanal* with only 2.11 per cent, ranking twelfth overall (Television Industry Committee 2013). While most Crimean residents received Russian state channels in their homes, and these channels often provided their programming free of charge to the local Crimean versions of Ukrainian channels, it was these Crimean channels that held the largest market share (Interview with Volodymyr Prytula 2017). In the 25 February meeting, Slutsky made an ambiguous conclusion: 'Tomorrow we shall report to our administration that we need to switch to a completely different way of representation of the Russian mass media in Ukraine, and in particular, the Republic of Crimea' (Voice of Russia 2014). Forces from the Russian Black Sea Fleet seized the main television tower in Crimea three days later. It is not clear if Slutsky's findings were the cause for the operation, but in either case, seizing the domestic media and replacing it with Russian broadcasts was one of the key informational tools of the annexation campaign – just as it was in the Soviet Union's operations in Czechoslovakia and Afghanistan.

By adopting the Soviet tactic of blocking local media and replacing it with its own sources, the Russian forces inserted Russian state media as the primary information source for the Crimean population. In polls taken over the five years prior to the 2014 crisis, over 90 per cent of Crimean residents consistently ranked television news as their main source of political information (International Republican Institute 2009, 2011).[3] According to a

---

[3] The United States Agency for International Development (USAID) assisted with funding for these public opinion surveys (International Republican Institute 2009, 2011). I am selectively reporting

poll taken in April 2014 by Gallup and the Broadcasting Board of Governors (BBG),[4] television was by far the most dominant source of news in Crimea with 96 per cent of residents watching television news programmes at least once per week (BBG and Gallup 2014). If the Crimean population thus sought news on the developments of the crisis via their preferred medium – television – in the critical week before the referendum, the only version of events available to them was that as depicted on the Russian government's state-controlled platforms. In addition, by seizing and disrupting internet and telephone communications on the peninsula, as well as blocking Western and Ukrainian media organizations, access to alternate sources of news became increasingly limited.

After the annexation, the Russian government further removed remaining dissent in the Crimean media. Russian law has in effect consolidated the state's control of the media environment in Crimea by making it a criminal offence to question whether Crimea is Russian territory. Article 280.1 of the Russian Criminal Code, which took effect on 9 May 2014, forbids '[p]ublic provocation to commit acts intended to destroy the territorial integrity of the Russian Federation'. The punishment is up to three years in prison and three hundred thousand roubles or two years of wages, whichever is greater. In a clear targeting of media outlets, if the action includes 'the use of media, including information and telecommunications networks or the Internet', the prison term increases to five years (Luhn 2014; Klymenko 2015a: 7–8). The one remaining television channel that covered events from a pro-Ukrainian perspective during the crisis was ATR, the Crimean Tatar cultural channel. It broadcasted from its own dedicated tower and thus was not affected when Russian forces captured the main broadcast tower (Interview with Volodymyr Prytula 2017). Immediately after the annexation, however, the channel came under immense Russian government pressure, including receiving a warning from the media regulator *Roskomnadzor* for 'extremist activities'. When it failed to receive a new broadcasting licence by 1 April 2015, the channel was forced off the air and left Crimea for Kyiv (Shevchenko 2015). Three weeks later, Sergey Aksyonov signed a governmental decree creating the state-supported 'Public Crimean Tatar Television and Radio Company' with the television channel *Millet* (The Nation) and the radio station *Vetan sedasy* (Voice of the

---

the survey data only on relatively objective questions such as what media sources are the most popular as to avoid any doubts about potential political bias in the responses.

[4] The BBG is a US government agency that manages the Voice of America and RFE/RL (BBG 2018). I am similarly limiting the survey data I am reporting to television consumption rate.

Motherland) to run in ATR's place (Government of the Republic of Crimea 2015). The government allocated 177 million roubles to support the media project, and its coverage has been steadfastly pro-government (*Krym Realii* 2015; for the Russian perspective, see Merenkov 2017). The Russian authorities similarly denied the Crimean Tatar news agency QHA a broadcasting licence after the annexation, and it, too, departed Crimea for Kyiv (Klymenko 2015b). The Russian government thus repeated the Soviet political warfare tactic by removing a dissident media source and creating a replacement for it that followed government lines.

As in both Czechoslovakia and Afghanistan, one of Russia's first moves in the military operation in Crimea was to seize key communications infrastructure, block Ukrainian media and replace them with its own. This followed a series of measures the Russian government took since Putin first became president to vastly increase state control over the domestic media. Once it had control of the media environment both at home and in Crimea, it controlled the information space. The Russian government then developed its narrative of events along synchronized propaganda themes. Just as with the techniques to control the media, both the heavy use of propaganda and the specific themes employed had their roots in Soviet political warfare practice.

# Propaganda

Propaganda was the means by which the Soviet government operationalized information in its political warfare campaigns. Through repetitive messaging on consistent themes, it sought to shape the information space to suit its policy objectives. In the Crimean crisis, the Russian government utilized some of the same propaganda themes dominant in the Soviet operations. It also adapted many of the propaganda tools its Soviet predecessors employed to fit the modern informational domain to maximum effect. Four themes dominated the Russian government's propaganda during the Crimean crisis: the conflict was the result of Western aggression, the protest movement was run by fascists, Ukrainian nationalists were a violent threat to ethnic Russians and Russia was the protector of its ethnic brethren under threat abroad. All four of these themes originated in some fashion in Soviet propaganda and appeared frequently throughout the Cold War. Two key Soviet propaganda techniques, 'whataboutism' and 'black' propaganda, similarly reappeared during the 2014 crisis.

## Western aggression

The most dominant theme in Soviet propaganda was the aggressiveness of the West. The North Atlantic Treaty Organization (NATO) was often the target, but the United States was most frequently identified as the source of various conflicts in the world. According to Czechoslovak State Security (StB) defector Ladislav Bittman, the main theme that officers from the Warsaw Pact security services instructed their agents working in Western media to emphasize was that the United States was 'militaristic' and 'dangerous' to try to create rifts between the United States and its NATO allies (Schultz and Godson 1984: 168).

The Western aggression theme was particularly dominant during Soviet political warfare campaigns. In the Prague Spring, the Soviet government published a propaganda pamphlet ostensibly from the Press Group of Soviet Journalists that provided its official account of the cause of events. Soviet forces widely distributed the pamphlet in Czechoslovakia immediately after the invasion. Titled 'On Events in Czechoslovakia', it soon earned the nickname 'The White Book' because of its white cover and its attempt to 'whitewash' the reasons behind the invasion (Littell 1969). It blamed 'numerous sabotage specialists and spies from the Western countries' for 'spreading anti-Soviet propaganda' and 'bring[ing] arms into Czechoslovakia' ('White Book' 1968: 113). It claimed that the leaders of Club-231, the political prisoner association allowed to form under the Dubček reforms, had been 'exposed as American intelligence agents' and were in 'close contact with the British Embassy' ('White Book' 1968: 76). The *Pravda* editorial written by I. Aleksandrov – the pseudonym for the Soviet senior leadership – blamed 'the unstable situation which has arisen in the country' on 'the support such [counterrevolutionary] forces find among the imperialists in the West' (Aleksandrov 1968: 15).

The Soviet Union reapplied this theme in explaining the need for intervention in Afghanistan. When the violence in the country began to worsen in early 1979, the Soviet government ordered the production of propaganda blaming foreign interference, led by the United States, for the decline. The CPSU Central Committee directed both its foreign propaganda department and the KGB 'to prepare and send to third countries materials about the interference in the internal affairs of Afghanistan by the USA, Pakistan, Iran, China, and other countries'; these materials were in addition to other press, television and radio propaganda separately prepared for domestic consumption (CPSU CC Politburo 1979a). Leonid Zamyatin, the chairman of the International Information Department, informed the Central Committee that his department had 'articles prepared about Afghanistan' to meet the needed 'supply of propaganda' (CPSU CC Politburo 1979d). Soon after the invasion, *Pravda* and TASS both ran articles that Amin was a CIA agent who had received assurances from 'certain circles' in Washington that he would receive US military support (Hammond 1984: 100). These government publications clearly employed the propaganda theme that the West was responsible for aggressive actions and subversion in the targeted countries, thus justifying the Soviet Union's decision to act in the interests of defending a fellow socialist government.

The Russian government and its state media revived the Western aggression theme and used some of the exact same messages from the Soviet period in explaining the Ukraine crisis. In a December 2013 episode of his *Vesti Nedeli* programme on *Rossiya* 1, host Dmitry Kiselyov called the Euromaidan protests a 'co-production' ordered and paid for by the US State Department (*Economist* 2013). Kiselyov even stated that his show 'promotes, or rather propagandizes – I'm not afraid to use this word – healthy values and patriotism' (Yaffa 2014) – thus literally describing its role as a propaganda tool of the state. His comments of this sort during the Ukraine crisis caused a group of Russian academics to write an open letter of complaint to the minister of communications and mass media, arguing that his position as head of *Rossiya Segodnya* was causing 'irreparable damage to Russia's reputation in the world' (Solomina et al. 2014).

Contrary to the Russian academics' denunciation, Kiselyov's rhetoric was fully representative of the messaging in Russian media during the Crimean crisis. State and state-controlled television channels produced a number of 'documentaries' during the crisis to show that the protesters were a 'fifth column' that had conspired with foreign funders to stage a violent revolution (Lipman et al. 2018: 169). On 13 March 2014, NTV ran a report claiming that hacked email messages between US and Ukrainian officials discussed plans to stage an attack on its military aircraft to serve as justification for a US attack on Russia (Leonard 2014). The main theme of Euromaidan coverage on *RT*, the Russian state-run television network broadcast to foreign audiences in various foreign languages, was 'Western involvement', including on-air accusations that the United States and the European Union (EU) were 'directing' the protests, 'muddling and meddling' in Ukraine's affairs, and acting 'politically aggressive' towards Russia and its interests (Miazhevich 2014).

Quantitative analyses demonstrate the prevalence of the Western aggression propaganda theme in both periods. Schultz and Godson (1984: 54–7) conducted an analysis of two major Soviet state publications, *Pravda* and *The New Times* (the weekly political magazine from the trade unions' newspaper *Trud*), from

1960 to 1980. Among the propaganda themes they identified, over half of them focused on the aggressiveness of the West, especially the United States, and its effort to destroy the Soviet Union and its allies. Similarly, the Ukrainian NGO StopFake.org, largely run by journalism professors, analysed over 500 pieces of Russian propaganda published since the start of the Ukrainian crisis. It found the same themes re-emerging: the United States and NATO are secretly conducting the war in Ukraine, the change in government was a coup d'état and the new Ukrainian leadership is a Western-backed junta (Fedchenko 2016: 158). Just as the Soviet media did before it, the Russian media consistently blamed Western interference for a crisis in its periphery.

## Fascists

In addition to reapplying the Soviet propaganda theme that Western aggression was the source of the conflict in Ukraine, the Russian government also reused the 'fascist' propaganda label to discredit its opponents. In Soviet propaganda, one of the most common methods to discount critics or enemies of the Soviet regime was to label them as fascists. The actual political opinions or activities of the targeted groups or individuals were largely irrelevant. As the name of the enemy in the Great Patriotic War – Russia's emotive name for the Second World War – the term 'fascist' or 'Nazi' evoked the strongest negative emotional response in its Soviet audience. It was thus the severest insult to be labelled on the state's opponents, regardless of the colour of their politics. The Soviet government applied the term to dissidents as far ranging as liberal democrats to communists seeking a more state-specific approach. The common feature was not their political leanings but their opposition to Soviet domination in the socialist sphere (Kuzio 2016).

During the Cold War, the Soviet government used the fascist propaganda theme to attack a wide range of its political enemies. To undermine the Vatican's moral authority in Europe and its opposition to communism, First Secretary Nikita Khrushchev approved in 1960 a secret plan code-named 'Seat-12' to use various media to portray Pope Pius XII, who had died two years previously, as an anti-Semitic, fascist sympathizer who supported the rise of Adolf Hitler (Pacepa 2007). KGB propaganda operations in West Germany in the 1950s and 1960s smeared West German politicians who advocated stern policies on East Germany and the Soviet Bloc by labelling them as neo-Nazis. The KGB shared an archive in East Berlin with the HVA (the East German security service) that contained Nazi and *Schutzstaffel* (SS) records seized by the Red Army during the Second

World War. To attack anti-Soviet politicians, the active measures departments fabricated their names onto these authentic documents and secretly released them to the press to slander them as neo-Nazis or war criminals (Andrew and Mitrokhin 2000: 573–4). During the Hungarian Revolution in 1956, KGB chairman General Ivan Serov flew to Budapest to personally oversee his agency's operations in support of the invasion. In a meeting with the Hungarian security services and police officers, he admonished them for not shooting on the protesters, claiming, 'The fascists and imperialists are bringing out their shock troops into the streets of Budapest, and yet there are still comrades in your country's armed forces who hesitate to use arms!' The Budapest police chief reminded him that the protesters were not 'fascists' or other 'imperialists' but university students and 'the handpicked sons and daughters of peasants and workers' (Andrew and Mitrokhin 2000: 323–4).

Soviet propaganda heavily employed the fascism theme in its political warfare campaigns in Czechoslovakia and Afghanistan, as well. During the Prague Spring, the Soviet government attempted to discredit the Czechoslovak reform movement by tying it to fascist and neo-Nazi elements in West Germany, regardless of the validity of the connection. In its letters to the Czechoslovak government, the Soviet Politburo accused its counterparts of appeasing agitators from West Germany, 'the true political heir to Hitlerite Germany' (CPSU CC Politburo 1968b: 195) where 'Fascism is rearing its head' (Prozumenshchikov 2010: 105). The Warsaw Letter from the Warsaw Pact Five leadership warned that in West Germany, 'the forces of neo-fascism are growing and [. . .] are demanding the revision of frontiers' ('Warsaw Letter' 1968: 155). The 'White Book' propaganda account labelled the members of Club-231, the political prisoner association, as 'former Nazis, Henlein fascists, [and] ministers of the puppet, so-called Slovak State set up by the Nazis' ('White Book' 1968: 76).[5] To demonstrate the bloodlust of these 'fascists', the book claimed that Jaromir Brodsky, the general secretary of the club, shouted at a gathering, 'The best communist is a dead communist, and if he is alive, his legs should be torn off' ('White Book' 1968: 77).

Even though Afghanistan did not provide these historical connections to the Nazis in the Second World War, it did not prevent the Soviet government from applying the same 'fascist' propaganda characterizations to discredit its opponents during the 1979 invasion. In its justifications for calling for Hafizullah

---

[5]  Konrad Henlein, a Sudeten German politician and member of the Nazi Party, was a leading figure during the 1938 annexation of the Sudetenland and the 1938–45 German occupation of Czechoslovakia (Robbins 1969).

Amin's downfall as leader of the Afghan regime, the KGB labelled him a 'smooth-talking fascist' (Melville 1982). After the Soviet government installed Babrak Karmal as the next leader of Afghanistan, he likewise denounced his deceased predecessor as a 'fascist' in his first press conference (Urban 1990). Amin was a loyal communist; he had been a full member of the People's Democratic Party of Afghanistan (PDPA) Central Committee since 1967 and a senior member of the communist government since the PDPA seized power in the 1978 Saur Revolution (Rubin 1995). The use of 'fascist' in these circumstances demonstrates that Soviet propaganda used the emotionally charged term more to smear its enemies than it did to identify any ideological underpinnings.

During the Ukraine crisis, the Russian government and its state media revived this Soviet practice of using the 'fascist' propaganda theme to discredit the protesters and the new Ukrainian government as well as to justify its military actions. The 'fascist' and 'Nazi' accusations were prevalent in official Russian governmental discourse; Putin returned to the theme repeatedly in his public speeches on the Crimean crisis. On 4 March 2014, he condemned 'the rampage of reactionary forces, nationalist and anti-Semitic forces going on in certain parts of Ukraine' (Kremlin 2014h). In his 18 March speech, he asserted that '[n]ationalists, neo-Nazis, Russophobes and anti-Semites executed this coup' that led to Yanukovych's dismissal (Kremlin 2014a). That October, he justified the Crimean referendum because 'people were frightened that power was seized by extremists, by nationalists and right-wingers including neo-Nazis' (Putin 2014). Various Russian media sources conveyed the same message. NTV ran a programme in 2014 titled 'Common Fascism: Ukrainian Variant'. It outlined the ways that the US government and Western NGOs were supposedly empowering fascists in Ukraine to undermine Russian influence there. The programme intentionally reused the title of a 1965 Soviet documentary on the rise of Nazism in Germany (NTV 2014; Fedchenko 2016: 161).

One exchange between a reporter from *The Guardian* newspaper and a Simferopol resident in March 2014 demonstrates the psychological impact of the 'fascism' propaganda on the Crimean population. 'What you foreigners don't get is that those people in Maidan, they are fascists', the man told the reporter, referring to the anti-Yanukovych protesters in Kyiv; 'I mean, I am all for the superiority of the white race, and all that stuff, but I don't like fascists' (Walker 2014b). The man admitted to believing in ethnocentrism, one of the main tenets of nationalist and right-wing political parties, and yet he still condemned the Euromaidan protesters as 'fascists'. He showed no true understanding of what fascism is, only that fascists are the enemies of the ethnic Russian people. It appears that the psychological reaction to the label was so strong that as soon as he believed that the protesters were fascists – as the Russian state media and government officials had told him – the protesters became his enemies.

Just as the presence of neo-Nazis in West Germany provided the Soviet propagandists a platform on which to base their 'fascist' accusations, the existence of the far-right group *Pravy Sektor* (Right Sector) in Ukraine presented the Russian government with the same opportunity. *Pravy Sektor* formed in November 2013 as an amalgamation of far-right Ukrainian nationalist groups. Dmytro Yarosh, its leader, claimed in early February 2014 that they had acquired an arsenal of weapons large 'enough [. . .] to defend all of Ukraine from the internal occupiers', a reference to the Yanukovych regime (Shuster 2014). On Maidan square in Kyiv, the Trade Unions Building served as the headquarters of the protest movement; *Pravy Sektor* occupied its fifth floor. The other leaders of the protest movement refused to give Yarosh a seat at the negotiating table with Yanukovych, but his fighters still played a key role in battling government forces at Maidan and in other cities throughout Ukraine (see Sakwa 2016; Wilson 2014).

While *Pravy Sektor* and other nationalist elements were undeniably part of the political landscape during the 2014 crisis, Russian state media grossly overstated their significance. At the end of January 2014, *Pravy Sektor* reportedly had only approximately 300 members (Shekhovtsov and Umland 2014: 59). Much of the Russian propaganda accused the United States of training and enabling the nationalist elements on Maidan. However, the US Department of State condemned the 'increasing violence' of the street protests and explicitly stated that 'the aggressive actions of members of [the] extreme-right group *Pravy Sektor* are not acceptable and are inflaming conditions on the streets and undermining the efforts of peaceful protestors' (Harf 2014).

The right-wing political parties also performed extremely poorly in the elections at the end of the crisis, calling into question the Russian propaganda claim that Ukraine had become overrun by fascists. In the 25 May 2014 presidential election, Yarosh received only 0.70 per cent of the vote. Oleh Tyahnybok, leader since 2004 of *Svoboda* (Freedom), another Ukrainian nationalist party, received only 1.16 per cent (Ukrainian Central Election Commission 2014c). Despite these numbers, the Russian television channel *Perviy Kanal* initially ran a report on the day of the election with falsified graphics from the Ukrainian Central Election Commission that listed Yarosh in the lead with 37 per cent of the vote (RFE/RL 2014a). Ukraine then held follow-up parliamentary elections for the Verkhovna Rada national assembly in October 2014; under the Ukrainian election laws, half of the 450 deputies were elected by proportional representation from nationwide party lists, and half were elected directly by simple majority in single-mandate constituencies (Law of Ukraine No. 4061-VI 2011). *Pravy Sektor* gained only 1.80 per cent of the nationwide vote, and *Svoboda* earned 4.71 per cent – neither thus surpassing the 5 per cent requirement for representation from the national party lists (Ukrainian Central Election Commission 2014b). Among the single-mandate constituencies, Yarosh won *Pravy Sektor*'s only seat with 30.27 per cent of the vote in his native Dnipropetrovsk Oblast. *Svoboda* won six constituencies, but because Tyahnybok was the top candidate on the national list, he was not one of the new deputies (Ukrainian Central Election Commission 2014a). This was a sharp decline from the thirty-seven seats *Svoboda* had earned in the 2012 parliamentary elections, and even then, the party consisted of only 8 per cent of the Verkhovna Rada (Ukrainian Central Election Commission 2012a, 2012b). As in Czechoslovakia and Afghanistan, the actual influence of neo-Nazi and fascist elements in Ukraine – minimal at best – was unimportant. The Russian government exploited their existence to discredit the entire Euromaidan movement and achieve the same negative effects with the 'fascist' label as the Soviet Union had done in the Cold War.

## The threat of Ukrainian nationalists

An additional Soviet propaganda theme that the Russian government used hand in hand with the danger of fascists was the threat posed by Ukrainian nationalists. During the Crimean crisis, Russian propaganda gave new life to 'Banderite', the Soviet pejorative term for Ukrainian nationalists. Stepan Bandera was a Ukrainian nationalist who led a militant faction of the Organization of Ukrainian Nationalists (OUN), which fought against the Soviet Union (and later against Nazi Germany) during the Second World War in an attempt to establish an independent Ukrainian state. His legacy continues to be a divisive issue in Ukrainian and Russian politics (see Rossolinski-Liebe 2014; Marples 2006; Shkandrij 2015). In the Soviet Union, the term 'Banderite' was used not only against Ukrainian nationalists but also against Western Ukrainians as a whole. As late as the 1980s, it was not uncommon for Western Ukrainians visiting Crimea to be called 'Banderites' by the ethnic Russian population (Interview J 2017).

This theme about the dangers of Ukrainian nationalists had other origins in the Soviet period. A Top Secret KGB manual from 1963 on how to target 'Ukrainian Bourgeois Nationalists' clearly demonstrated how the Soviet regime perceived this threat. It described the Western regions of Ukraine as full of 'criminal nationalist authorities' focused on conducting 'subversive activity against the Soviet regime'. The 'crimes' the manual described were mostly publishing handbills and harbouring anti-Soviet thoughts. In an effort to eliminate the Ukrainian nationalist threat, the Presidium of the Supreme Soviet of the Ukrainian SSR published an order in 1956 'forbidding former leaders of the OUN, bandits and terrorists from living in the western regions of the Ukrainian SSR'. In addition, the KGB infiltrated numerous agents into the OUN and other Ukrainian nationalist groups (KGB 1963). The KGB's efforts to root out nationalism – a force that could unravel Russian control over the entire Soviet Union – fixated on Ukraine (Mitrokhin 2007). Because of these fears, the KGB placed extra scrutiny on any Western Ukrainians its officers recruited as agents, for their loyalties were automatically considered suspicious (Myagkov 1976: 63).

Even though Ukraine is now an independent state, Russian propaganda used these same Soviet themes to speak of the dangers of Ukrainian nationalists. In Putin's speeches during the crisis (Kremlin 2014a, 2014h; Putin 2014), he used the terms 'nationalists' and 'neo-Nazis' conjointly when assigning blame for the conflict. On 18 March 2014, he called the new Ukrainian regime the 'ideological heir of Bandera, Hitler's accomplice during World War II' (Kremlin 2014a). As with the 'fascist' label, these characterizations filtered down to the Crimean population, as well. On the day of the referendum, men with loudspeakers outside of polling stations could be heard shouting, 'If today we do not make the right choice, then tomorrow our children and our grandchildren will wear slave collars of the Bandera-fascist junta' (Kliatskin 2016). Just as it had done with the 'fascist' label, Russian propaganda revived the Soviet 'Banderite' epithet to achieve the same emotive effect among the targeted Crimean population.

## Protect honest communists/protect fellow ethnic Russians

The final propaganda theme which Russia appeared to reuse from Soviet political warfare practice is one that it adapted to match the current political environment: the protection of fellow communists became the protection of fellow ethnic Russians. In the Cold War, the bonds that tied together the Soviet Union and its sphere of influence were ideological. Communism was the unifying factor behind its struggle with the West, and the protection of 'honest communists' became a significant propaganda theme and the casus belli for many of its interventions. During the Hungarian Revolution in 1956, for example, a *Pravda* editorial claimed that the majority of the Hungarian population remained 'loyal', 'honest' and 'healthy' and that Soviet troops were necessary to protect the people from the 'counter-revolutionary gangs' (CIA FBIS 1968a).

Soviet propaganda clearly defined the Warsaw Pact states as the protectors of their fellow communists in the Prague Spring. One of the Soviet Politburo letters to the Czechoslovak Presidium insisted that without drastic measures, 'those who are honest and devoted to the cause of socialism will have to face the bores of rifles, unarmed' (CPSU CC Politburo 1968b). The Warsaw Letter (1968) likewise warned that 'reactionary forces have unleashed a campaign against the CPCz and against its honest and dedicated cadres'. After the invasion, the 'White Book' (1968: 76) claimed that the reform movement had 'murdered a large number of guiltless communists and honest Czechoslovak citizens' and that more would have perished without the Warsaw Pact's fraternal assistance. The Soviet press published appeals from 'honest' Czechoslovaks to strengthen these claims and build the case for Soviet intervention. On 21 June 1968, *Pravda* published a letter from the Czechoslovak People's Militia, which was a conservative armed formation that reported directly to the CPCz Central Committee. It expressed concern over the growing 'antisocialist' activity in the country and its threat to Czechoslovak-Soviet relations. In the next few weeks, Soviet radio and press covered numerous letters from Soviet citizens showing their sympathy, and a 7 July *Pravda* editorial guaranteed the Czechoslovak communists that they could rely on the Soviet people's support (CIA FBIS 1968a). A petition appeared in the Soviet press on 30 July 1968, allegedly authored by ninety-nine workers at the Auto-Praha factory in Prague. In it, they appealed for Soviet help in protecting the Czechoslovak communist workers like themselves from the reactionary forces. Brezhnev used their plea for help to castigate Dubček for allowing such a 'witch hunt' in his country (Navratil 1998: 338).

This unifying communist ideology has disappeared along with the Soviet Union and so, too, has the opportunity to defend fellow communists. However, the Russian government has found a new lever to exert control over its perceived sphere of influence: the presence within the borders of its neighbours of significant ethnic Russian populations, whom the Russian government has given itself the right to protect (see MFA Russia 1999; Knott 2017; Laruelle 2009, 2010, 2015; Zevelev 2008; Shevel 2011). The Russian government has thus adapted the Soviet 'protector' propaganda theme from fellow communists to fellow Russians. The use of this rhetoric predates the 2014 crisis in Ukraine. Yeltsin spoke in 1992 about how the '[t]wenty-five million of our compatriots in these countries [on Russia's borders] must not and will not be forgotten by Russia' (Toal 2017:

74). In 2008 Dmitry Rogozin, who at the time was the Russian ambassador to NATO, used international law to justify Russia's military actions in South Ossetia as self-defence to protect its peacekeepers and passport holders in the region (see Cornell and Starr 2009). The Russian government used the fact that 40,000 of the 45,000 South Ossetian residents held Russian passports to defend its military actions against Georgia, and a few weeks after the conflict, President Dmitry Medvedev announced the protection of Russian citizens abroad as a new key tenet of Russia's foreign policy doctrine (Trenin 2011).

The Russian government employed these tactics to full effect during the Crimean crisis. As Ukraine's only region with a majority ethnic Russian population, Crimea gave the Russian government the opportunity to characterize itself as the protector of its fellow Russians abroad. The emotional rhetoric closely paralleled the 'honest communists' propaganda themes employed by the Soviet Union, particularly as seen in the invasion of Czechoslovakia. Vladimir Putin built on the theme in his various speeches. The day of the annexation, he claimed that 'we could not abandon Crimea and its residents in distress. This would have been betrayal on our part' (Kremlin 2014a). In the Russian state-television propaganda documentary *Crimea: The Way Home*, he stated that Russia 'realized that we could not abandon these people just like that and leave them to their own devices', and his obligation to defend his fellow ethnic Russians led to his decision to authorize the military operation in Crimea (Kondrashov 2015). Russian state media similarly shaped the discourse around Russia's need to protect its compatriots. In the rhetoric used during the Crimean crisis on *Perviy Kanal*, *Rossiya* and NTV – the three dominant Russian television networks – one of the most pervasive themes was 'Russia must defend its compatriots in Crimea' (Kudors et al. 2014: 34). Footage of pro-Russian rallies held under Russian flags and pro-Russian slogans in Crimea flooded Russian state media starting in the end of February (Darczewska 2014: 383). On 2 March 2014, Dmitry Kiselyov said on *Vesti Nedeli* that the 'bandit excesses' in Ukraine had brought 'democracy to its knees' and that Russia had to protect the ethnic Russian population there, for it was 'impossible not to respond to this challenge'. The backdrop during his speech was the image of a crowd of Crimeans waving Russian flags with the caption, 'We don't give up our own' (Ennis 2014). Starting in December 2013, Russian media developed the theme that the *Berkut* special police were the true heroes of the Ukraine crisis and the only forces trying to keep public order in the face of radicals (Kudors et al. 2014: 27) – a modern-day version of the 'honest', 'loyal' forces Soviet narrative.

The Russian media, supported by the Russian government, also employed some of the same 'protector' imagery that the Soviet Union had used as part of its propaganda. During the invasion of Czechoslovakia, the Soviet press published a photograph of a Soviet soldier holding a smiling Czechoslovak girl (see Figure 3.1). The photo conveyed the message that the Soviet troops were there as defenders to protect the innocent girl and her brethren from the brutality of the counter-revolutionaries. In the Crimean crisis, a TASS photographer captured a masked Russian soldier without insignia handing a cat to a Crimean boy (Ryumin 2014). The message was the same: the friendly Russian protectors were in Crimea to save the boy and his fellow ethnic Russians from the savagery of the fascists and nationalists of Euromaidan. It became a lasting propaganda image from the conflict. The Russian government unveiled a monument memorializing the action in Belogorsk in May 2015 (see Figure 3.2). A near-identical monument was unveiled in Bakhchysarai in Crimea in March 2016 (Sharkov 2016). Notably, neither of the statues have their faces covered, as does the soldier in the source image and almost all images of Russian soldiers from the time. To display them as such would not fit the theme that the Russian servicemen were friendly protectors, and the enduring monuments glossed over these details.

An outgrowth of this propaganda campaign was the chosen label for the Russian soldiers without insignia: 'polite people' (*vezhlivyye lyudi*). The term did

**Figure 3.1** Photograph of a Soviet soldier with a Czechoslovak girl during the Prague Spring ('White Book' 1968: 169). Photo credit: Press Group of Soviet Journalists.

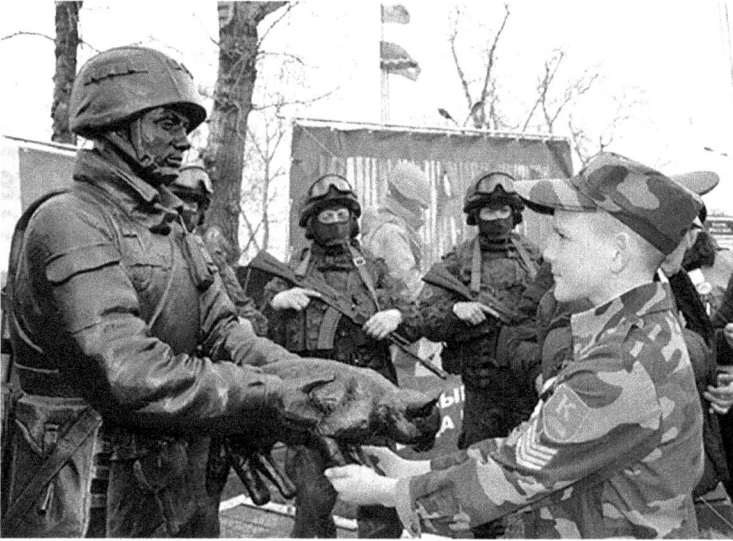

**Figure 3.2** Monument of a Russian soldier debuted in Belogorsk, Russia, on 6 May 2015 (Ministry of Defence of the Russian Federation 2015). Licensed under Creative Commons Attribution 4.0.

not originate with the Russian government, but it soon embraced it and exploited it. On the night of 27–28 February 2014, unmarked Russian forces seized the airport in Simferopol. The airport security chief told a Ukrainian website that his personnel 'were politely asked to leave' (*Meduza* 2015). Boris Rozhin, the editor-in-chief of the internet publication *The Voice of Sevastopol*, then quoted the article on his personal blog and added photos of the soldiers with the tag, 'Polite people have captured two airports in Crimea' (Rozhin 2014). The following day, the Russian pro-government blogger Stanislav Apetian ('Politrash') created a Twitter account for the 'Polite People'. As he stated in a 21 March 2014 interview, 'We realized that a meme about polite people is a gift from the point of view of propaganda [and] information warfare [. . .] We decided to fix this meme by creating an account in which we will give the right propaganda information' (Kashevarova 2014). The account, which quickly gained more than 35,000 followers, posted flattering pictures of the Russian soldiers in Crimea, including some images from photographers specifically contracted by Apetian and his colleagues (Kashevarova 2014).

The Russian government soon seized on the term. Putin first used 'polite people' during a press conference on 21 March 2014 and called them 'the ones in camouflage gear, with semi-automatic rifles strapped to their waists' (Kremlin 2014b). Part of the reason the Russian government adopted the term was to counteract the phrase 'little green men', which had become commonplace in the media surrounding the conflict. During his *Direct Line* call-in show on 21 April 2014, the president implored listeners 'not to use the words "little green men" [. . . because] it is insulting for the people who serve their country' (Kremlin 2014c). 'Polite people' painted the Russian soldiers as the quiet, professional saviours of the ethnic Russians in Crimea, and the Russian government wished to propagate this version of events. The propaganda documentary *Crimea: The Way Home* contains several stories of 'polite people' handing out chocolates, displaying the best of manners and hugging children (Kondrashov 2015). The Russian Defence Ministry soon created branded products with 'Polite People' logos, including T-shirts and other products. On holidays in major Russian cities, the Defence Ministry has set up special pavilions for people to buy the products (RIA *Novosti* 2014b). In September 2014, State Duma deputy Igor Zotov called for 7 October – Putin's birthday – to be commemorated as 'Polite People Day'; in the end, Putin signed a decree to make 27 February – the day of the seizure of the Crimean Rada legislative buildings – as Special Operations Forces Day (Belousov 2015). The Russian government thus did not just adapt the Soviet 'protector' propaganda theme to match its modern circumstances; it brought the operationalization of the message to an entirely new level.

The four dominant propaganda themes the Russian government employed during the Crimean operation – Western aggression was behind the crisis, the protesters were fascists, Ukrainian nationalists were a threat to ethnic Russians and the Russian soldiers were there to protect them – originated in Soviet propaganda. Furthermore, the strong use of such propaganda was a key informational tool of Soviet political warfare. Aside from the themes, the Russian government similarly adapted two significant Soviet propaganda techniques during its 2014 Crimean operation: 'whataboutism' and 'black' propaganda.

## 'Whataboutism'

One such Soviet propaganda technique that Putin and Russian state media implemented in their defence of Russia's actions in Crimea is 'whataboutism'. The West coined the term because of the tendency of Soviet propagandists to respond to every criticism of the Soviet Union with a 'What about . . .' criticism of the West. The technique avoids defending or even addressing the actual criticism levied; it instead seeks to bring both parties onto a level field of moral ambiguity where neither has an advantage. It distracts from the real issue and accuses the accuser of the same (Leonor 2016). Whataboutism even led to a subversive Soviet joke: a caller to a radio programme asks, 'What is the average wage of an American manual worker?' After a long pause, the answer comes: 'Over there they lynch Negroes' (*Economist* 2008).

The Soviet government employed whataboutism as part of its political warfare campaigns to deflect criticism of its military actions. When British foreign secretary Michael Stewart condemned the invasion of Czechoslovakia as a 'challenge to legal norms', a *Pravda* editorial responded not by defending the Soviet actions but instead by attacking the UK with the same accusations:

> [W]hen Labour advocates of British imperialism speak about 'legal norms', one cannot help recalling many things, beginning with the British campaign in Russia, the shooting of the Baku commissars, and ending with the colonial wars of the recent past, the aggression in Egypt, and the present support of the racist [Rhodesian prime minister Ian] Smith in Africa. (Mayevskiy 1968: 20)

The Soviet government applied the same technique in Afghanistan. After the initial Soviet invasion, Soviet foreign minister Andrei Gromyko instructed Afghan foreign minister Shah Mohammad Dost of the new puppet regime on how to employ whataboutism. In a meeting on 4 January 1980, he advised Dost:

> When you are assaulted [with questions] concerning the deployment of a Soviet military contingent in Afghanistan, you can parry this by exposing the aggressive politics of the USA. In Cuba, the USA, despite the constant demands of the Cuban government and people, continues to maintain its military base in Guantanamo. (MFA USSR 1980)

In both conflicts, the Soviet government employed whataboutism to undermine criticisms of its actions by deflecting the accusations.

In the Crimean crisis, the Russian government utilized whataboutism for the same effect. In his October 2014 speech at the Russian think tank Valdai Club, Putin asked 'what about' Kosovo: 'I do not understand why people living in Crimea do not have this right, just like the people living in, say, Kosovo [...] Why is it that in one case white is white, while in another the same is called black?' (Putin 2014). In another 2014 press conference, Putin told a journalist that the United States could not say the annexation was unjust because it took Texas from Mexico (*RT* 2014b). In an *RT America* video from 3 March 2014, the reporter Anastasia Churkina – the daughter of Russia's then permanent representative to the United Nations, Vitaly Churkin (*Moskovskiy Komsomolets* 2014) – responded to multiple US accusations with whataboutism: Russia's use of its Sevastopol military base to launch operations with questions about the thousands of US troops stationed abroad; Russia's invasion of Crimea 'on phoney pretexts' with condemnations of the US invasions of Iraq and Afghanistan; and Russia's rush to use force with denunciations of US military actions in Syria. She concluded, 'The world's top aggressor accuses Moscow of being one, applying double standards upon convenience' (*RT America* 2014). Like in the Soviet conflicts in Czechoslovakia and Afghanistan, the Russian government and its state media avoided addressing the multiple criticisms levied against its actions in Crimea by employing whataboutism to instead attack Russia's critics.

## 'Black' propaganda and 'trolls'

A second Soviet propaganda technique which the Russian government adopted but updated to match the modern media and technology landscape is the use of 'black' or covert propaganda. Depending on its visible association with the government, Soviet propaganda fell into three general categories. The Soviet Union's official channels – such as government policy statements or speeches from governmental leaders – were not hiding the source of the information and could thus be considered 'white' propaganda. Reports from state-run media sources were also evidently government-sponsored positions, but their claims of journalistic autonomy and their overt separation from the Soviet leadership allowed them to espouse independence. These sources could thus be considered 'grey' propaganda. Also in this category were the state media in other Communist Bloc countries and communist publications in third countries. 'Black' propaganda, on the other hand, was the purview of the International Department of the CPSU Central Committee and the security services; through active measures campaigns and agent operations, they concealed the Soviet origins of the information and presented it as authentically originating from outside sources (Bittman 1972: 5; Van Herpen 2016: 67).

During the Soviet era, black propaganda most often required the security services to recruit Western or Third World journalists as agents and to use them to publish articles on their behalf. For instance, during the Prague Spring the KGB used its agents in the foreign press to covertly publish articles that provided the Soviet government with 'evidence' it could publicly cite to back its claims about the counter-revolutionary sources of the crisis. The CPSU Central Committee Propaganda Department (1968: 497) reported that the KGB had successfully 'prepar[ed] and publish[ed] a series of articles in the foreign press about the ties of the anti-socialist underground in Czechoslovakia [. . .] with the intelligence organs of the USA and FRG [West Germany]'. By using its agent networks, the

Soviet government was able to keep the true origins of the propaganda material secret.

Another noteworthy example of the Soviet government's agent approach to black propaganda was the French journalist Pierre-Charles Pathé. The KGB recruited Pathé in the early 1960s. From 1961 to 1967, it paid him 6,000 francs a month to publish the journal *Centre for Scientific, Economic and Political Information*. As his popularity grew, Pathé launched in 1976 the biweekly newsletter *Synthesis* with partial funding from Soviet operatives. Over its seventy issues, the KGB spent 252,000 francs to help publish it. The newsletter soon reached the majority of both the French Chamber of Deputies and the Senate as well as several journalists and ambassadors, thus giving the KGB a significant audience of influential French officials for its propaganda articles. On 5 July 1979, French counterintelligence caught Pathé in Paris in the act of receiving money and documents from his KGB handler, Igor Kuznetsov. In his sentencing, Pathé admitted to holding secret meetings with the KGB and to writing articles on the Soviet government's behalf in exchange for money. The operation cost the KGB in total 974,823 francs in salary and expenses (Andrew and Mitrokhin 2000: 605–14; Schultz and Godson 1984: 134–6; Richelson 1986: 158–9).

The difficulties with this agent approach were the time and resources required. The KGB's agent recruitment process was difficult and time consuming. Recruiting an agent took two to four years, and only a few of the recruited foreign journalists were trusted with propaganda or influence operations; the rest simply passed intelligence. Handlers from the KGB or the CPSU International Department could only provide the journalists with guidelines on what to publish for fear of exposing their connection. They thus did not have complete control over the content (Schultz and Godson 1984: 169–80). Furthermore, as demonstrated in the Pathé case, the arrest of an agent could lead to the collapse of an entire medium through which to publish black propaganda.

To avoid some of these complications, Soviet Bloc governments sometimes created false flag operations and transmitted the black propaganda themselves instead of relying on agents. The CPSU International Department covertly ran two Turkish radio stations, Our Radio and Voice of the Turkish Communist Party. Presenting the stations as genuinely Turkish, the Soviet creators of the stations used the platforms to foment anti-NATO sentiments in the country (Richelson 1986: 153). Hungary's active measures department created a network of fake listeners of Radio Free Europe (RFE), the radio station run by the US government and broadcast into communist countries. Posing as workers, students and housewives, they wrote letters to RFE, asking the station to play more music and entertainment and talk less about politics. Meanwhile, the Hungarian government confiscated around 80 per cent of the genuine letters from real listeners. The goal of the operation was to mislead RFE on its audience and minimize the content it broadcast that could damage the communist regime (Bittman 1972: 148). Due to the nature of the media landscape during the Cold War, however, most Soviet black propaganda operations required the use of agents within existing foreign media. The means to publish information outside of these recognized channels were limited and prevented the more frequent use of such false flag publications.

Conversely, the nature of the *modern* media landscape and of the digital age means that the Russian government has been able to exploit this Soviet propaganda technique to new levels. Intricate agent operations are no longer needed to spread propaganda in the global media; instead, the Russian government can much more easily establish entirely new websites or blogs, create false identities on social media platforms and use them to publish and spread original material. Because of the openness of the internet and the constant growth of news content in the digital age, these alternate sources of information can quickly attract viewership and influence (Giles 2016c: 8). The Soviet Bloc security services preferred targeting print over broadcast media because of its 'permanency' (Bittman 1985: 56). However, online and digital content has largely overcome the dominance of print media in today's media landscape (Choney 2011). Television channels maintain their own websites, providing the same sort of permanency – and ability to quickly spread through the sharing of links – as print media did during the Cold War period.

The key way the Russian government has adapted its approach to black propaganda to these new dynamics is through the use of 'trolls'. In the context of the internet, the term 'troll' refers to a person who posts inflammatory comments or expresses strong opinions, typically with insults, on a news website or social media platform. Most modern news outlets either publish an online version of their content or are entirely digital. They also have a comments section below each article to allow their readers to offer their own opinions, thus giving their consumers a voice on their media platforms. Similarly, social media sites, including Facebook, Twitter, YouTube and Russia's VKontakte, are by their nature a platform for ordinary users to share content and opinions and attract viewers. Each of these media tools require minimal identity verification, meaning users can easily pretend to be someone who they are not, including from a different country. The Russian government and its proxies have exploited these dynamics by establishing 'troll armies', offices full of agents who work to publish online content along established propaganda themes under various personas (Mejias and Vokuev 2017). Whereas Soviet journalist agents took years of KGB cultivation and had to establish themselves as legitimate media sources in their own countries, these Russian trolls are able to artificially list their locations as the United States or Western Europe and adopt new identities by simply changing their profile information (Zannettou et al. 2018). In these modern dynamics, it has become exceedingly difficult to ascertain the true origins of the online content – and much easier for the Russian government to execute false flag information operations, which the Soviet Union attempted to a limited extent.

The 'troll factory' which received the most exposure in both the Western and Russian press during the Ukraine crisis was Internet Research LLC in St. Petersburg, previously registered as the Internet Research Agency LLC. Russian journalists from *Novaya Gazeta* and *Moi Raion* first discovered it in 2013 and managed to infiltrate it by posing as job applicants (Mejias and Vokuev 2017). The owner and general director Mikhail Bystrov was a retired colonel in the *Militsiya* Russian police forces and previously headed the Department of Internal Affairs of the Moskovsky District of St. Petersburg (Butsenko 2014). Trolls typically worked in twelve-hour shifts and had quotas of comments to post on social media platforms each day; targets included Facebook, Twitter, Instagram, LiveJournal, VKontakte and both Western and Russian news websites. Their false accounts contained intentionally deceptive names, like a YouTube page called 'The American Dream' (Hans 2014). One reported directive from the management of Internet Research included mandatory themes for that day's posts, including drawing attention to the Ukrainian Armed Forces' violations of the cease-fire (Soshnikov 2015). Shifts sometimes included 'politology' classes to educate employees on the proper Russian point of view of current events (Chen 2015). The company developed standard practices specific to each platform; for example, because *The Huffington Post* put comments from authors with the most contacts at the top of the feeds, trolls targeting the website were instructed to create 'up to 100 profiles' and connect them (Hans 2014). According to former employees, about half of the staff worked there for the money, not for ideological reasons; they received upwards of 40,000–65,000 roubles in cash (approximately $1,000–2,000) and signed a nondisclosure agreement with no formal contract (Walker 2015b).

Various hacked emails appear to show the linkages between these troll operations and the Russian government. The Concord holding company is owned by oligarch Evgeny Prigozhin, who is known for his friendship with Putin and has been awarded significant government contracts. The emails show Concord approving payments to fund Internet Research operations (Chen 2015). The emails also mention 'Volodin', assumed to be Vyacheslav Volodin, the deputy in Putin's presidential administration responsible for internet policy (Hans 2014). Other alleged hacked emails from Russian prime minister Dmitry Medvedev and Duma deputy Robert Schlegel show apparent coordination for a troll attack on *The New York Times*, CNN, the BBC, *USA Today* and *The Huffington Post* (Turovsky 2015).

During the Ukraine crisis, the Russian government maximized this updated application of Soviet black propaganda techniques. The troll factories reinforced the Russian government's propaganda themes by posting fabricated photographs of Ukrainian teenagers wearing T-shirts with Nazi symbols, sharing pictures of corpses that they claimed were the victims of nationalist Ukrainians and publishing stories of alleged war crimes committed by Ukrainian soldiers (Aro 2016). In an analysis of 27,000 tweets posted by 1,000 Twitter users traced back to the Internet Research Agency, one research study found that these state-sponsored agents were particularly effective in increasing the popularity of news articles originating from *RT*, the Russian state media outlet targeting foreign audiences (Zannettou et al. 2018). The trolls not only followed the Russian government's propaganda themes during the Crimean crisis – such as labelling the Maidan protesters as 'neo-Nazis' and referring to the CIA's supposed control of the new Kyiv government – but they also applied the same propaganda techniques, including 'whataboutism' aimed at achieving moral equivalence between Russia's actions and previous Western campaigns (Gregory 2015).

The Russian black propaganda campaign extended to new false flag publications, as well. Another study used web analytics tools to link together over twenty-seven supposedly anonymous websites that contained pro-Russian, anti-Ukrainian and anti-American content, including whoswho.com. ua, a purportedly Ukrainian website that listed compromising information on Ukrainian officials, and emaidan.com.ua, a website that claimed to be from a disillusioned member of the Maidan protests. The study connected these fake websites to Nikita Podogrny, who was listed as an employee in leaked Internet Research Agency documents (Alexander 2015).

## *Dezinformatsia*

These websites are an example of the other main Soviet political warfare informational tool that the Russian government applied during the Crimean annexation: *dezinformatsia* (disinformation). The Soviet practice of *dezinformatsia* was the dissemination of false or partially false information to deceive political opponents (Kux 1985: 19; Barron 1974: 225; Bittman 1972: 20; Schultz and Godson 1984: 2). The objective was to mislead them into making misdirected conclusions or inhibit their ability to act decisively. Disinformation aimed to influence foreign government decision-making, undermine confidence in the government among its own populace, cause crises and divisions between different states, cast doubt about true Soviet intentions or create confusion when trying to attribute events to Soviet interference. The goal was not only deception but damage to the target's public image (Bittman 1985: 56).

Several Soviet texts described these principles of disinformation and how to implement them. The Great Soviet Encyclopaedia defined *dezinformatsia* as 'the dissemination, in the press, radio, etc., of false information with the intention to deceive public opinion' (Rose 1988: 12). The basic tasks of the KGB were outlined in the Top Secret *Statute of the Committee of State Security attached to the Council of Ministers of the USSR*. Included in its duties was 'to give the enemy misinformation for political and operational purposes'; among its special powers were '[t]o employ operational printing equipment in order to fabricate' (Myagkov 1976: 21). According to one of the security service's publications, 'KGB disinformation operations [. . .] are designed to mislead not the working people but their enemies – the ruling circles of capitalism – in order to induce them to act in a certain way, or abstain from actions contrary to the interests of the USSR' (Andrew and Mitrokhin 2006: 19). Another KGB manual placed responsibility for disinformation operations not only with the security services but across the government, the ministries and the high command of the armed forces (Bittman 1985: 49).

Initially, *dezinformatsia* was the Soviet term for all active measures. In the earliest days of the Soviet Union, the Cheka and its successor security service agencies had a '*Dezinformatsia* Desk' that managed these operations (Barron 1974: 225). As these activities became more significant, the KGB established in 1959 Department D (*Dezinformatsia*) with dedicated responsibility for them. Years later, it was renamed Department A (*Aktivnykh Meropriyatiyl*); as its importance increased, it was elevated to Service A in 1970 (Richelson 1986: 24; Dziak 1988: 149). In conjunction with these changes, *dezinformatsia* came to refer only to disinformation operations within the umbrella of active measures (Schultz and Godson 1984: 37). When the Soviet Union formed a specific department in 1959, Bloc countries East Germany, Czechoslovakia and Hungary followed suit with parallel structures in 1963–4 (Bittman 1972: 16). The issue as discussed here is 'disinformation' in its more limited sense.

Soviet disinformation operations grew in sophistication and scope as the Cold War progressed. James Angleton, the former chief of CIA counterintelligence, even believed that disinformation had become 'the art of the [Soviet] state' (Epstein 1989: 29). Oftentimes the Soviet services would release a variety of discrediting information, as well as ones that contradicted one another, in an attempt 'to keep the West guessing' (Deacon 1972: 512). Techniques included forged documents and photographs, fake news reports, false accusations and intricately staged 'discoveries' of compromising information. These often included large portions of true information augmented by some false details or portrayed in a misconstrued light. A common tactic was to attribute sinister activity occurring on the world stage to the West to introduce the accusation as a plausible explanation and to undermine trust in Western governments' intentions. For example, when the United States created the Peace Corps, its first director, Sargent Shriver, Jr, prevented any connections between his agency and the intelligence community in order not to undermine the programme's efforts. However, within months of its creation, both Radio Moscow and TASS had run stories in Europe on 'Peace Corps Head Shriver CIA Agent' (Wise and Ross 1964: 272). During the Vietnam War, the Soviet press published unfounded articles on how 'Vietnam has been turned into a military testing ground for fifty types of chemical and bacteriological weapons' as a result of the 'war of extermination' the Americans were waging (Schultz 1988: 55). When Iranian Ayatollah Morteza Motahhari, one of the senior figures in the Islamic Revolution, was assassinated in 1979, the Radio Moscow Persian service immediately blamed the CIA for it (Richelson 1986: 147). The Soviet media made a similar claim about CIA involvement in the coup attempt in the Seychelles in 1981; the *Nairobi Nation*, *Lagos Daily Times* and other African newspapers cited these reports when describing the cause of the conflict (Kux 1985: 25).

The Soviet Union also used disinformation to cause confusion over its capabilities, its intentions and its culpability in its own sinister acts. The KGB sent its agent Bogdan Stashinsky to assassinate the Ukrainian dissident Stepan Bandera in Munich in 1959; Stashinsky later turned himself over to Western authorities and revealed the details of the plot. However, at the time of Bandera's death, the *Red Star* and other Soviet media concocted lengthy explanations on how Dr Theodor Oberlander, the West German minister for refugee affairs and a prominent anti-communist, 'decided to liquidate Bandera and obliterate all traces' because of compromising information the Ukrainian supposedly had on him (Barron 1974: 423–6). When the Soviet Union shot down Gary Powers in his CIA U-2 reconnaissance aircraft over its territory in 1960, it fired fourteen missiles and even destroyed one of its own MiG-19 fighters sent to intercept the aircraft; the shockwave is what eventually brought down the U-2. Nevertheless, First Secretary Nikita Khrushchev reported publicly that his military had destroyed it with a direct hit from the first missile and ordered that version to become the official Soviet stance (Penkovsky 1965: 264–6). In 1960, two US National Security Agency (NSA) defectors, Bernon Mitchell and William Martin, revealed that the United States had been decrypting its allies' secret communications, including those of Italy, Turkey, France and Egypt. They sought asylum in the Soviet Union, but Martin then attempted to return to the West. To dissuade him, the KGB produced a forged judgement summary from a closed session of the US Supreme Court that had supposedly sentenced him in absentia to twenty years' hard labour (Andrew and Mitrokhin 2000: 235).

The Crimean crisis saw a return of many of these disinformation techniques. Russian government officials spread disinformation to exaggerate the threat to Crimea's ethnic Russian population and sensationalize the situation. On 1 March 2014 Valentina Matviyenko, the chairwoman of the Federation Council (the upper body of Russian Parliament), announced on state-run *Rossiya-24* that Russian citizens were killed during a storming of the Ministry of Internal Affairs in Crimea. This became one of the main justifications the Federation Council used to give permission to the president to deploy troops to Ukraine (*Lenta.ru* 2014c). During his 4 March 2014 press conference, Putin told a gruesome, emotionally charged story about how radicals had supposedly seized the Party of Regions political headquarters in Crimea, shot one man pleading for his life and burned alive another with Molotov cocktails after locking him in a cellar (Kremlin 2014h). In reality, no Russian citizens were killed in Crimea before the annexation was complete; the one Russian casualty was a member of a Cossack militia, killed on 18 March 2014 during the storming of the 13th Photogrammetric Operational Centre of the Main Directorate of the Armed Forces of Ukraine in Simferopol (RIA *Novosti* 2014a).[6] However, this disinformation about the brutal murder of Russians was a critical tool in the Russian government's information campaign because it provided it with justification for its actions.

The disinformation had the desired effect on the Crimean population, as well. It created such a fear of 'fascists' and 'Banderites' among Crimea's

---

[6] A Ukrainian soldier, Warrant Officer Sergey Kokurin, was also killed in the attack (Ministry of Defence of Ukraine 2014; Bakumenko 2014).

ethnic Russian population that they facilitated the introduction of Russian troops and the annexation operation. According to a citizen of Dzhankoy in northern Crimea, rumours that 'buses with Bandera' were coming to the city 'to demolish the monument to Lenin' and cause other provocations were so prevalent that scores of workers took the day off to protect the public places. When on the same day unmarked Russian soldiers appeared instead, the workers warmly greeted them as 'the "liberators" of Crimea' (Dzhankoets 2016). No 'Banderites' materialized, but the rumours and fear drove the citizens to feel the need for protection, which manifested in the Russian soldiers. The Russian state-television propaganda documentary *Crimea: The Way Home* recounted the story of 'a so-called "friendship train"' full of right-wing *Pravy Sektor* combatants from Kyiv planning a 'punitive operation' in Simferopol on 27 February 2014. In the resulting panic, Crimeans built homemade shields and lined the platform to defend against the impending attack. The train in question was completely empty on arrival, and no signs of the threat materialized, but the Crimeans felt they had narrowly prevented an assault (Kondrashov 2015). By promoting false stories of atrocities caused by the 'fascists' and 'Ukrainian nationalists' behind Euromaidan, the Russian government set the conditions among the Crimean population for the annexation operation.

## Denials

One of the key and most straightforward components of the Soviet disinformation campaign model that the Russian government reapplied during the Crimean crisis was the extensive use of official denials. In times of crisis, Soviet leaders publicly and vocally denied their government's military activities to sow confusion, hinder foreign governments' decision-making and avoid taking responsibility. These denials often occurred even when faced with mounting evidence to the contrary. In 1940, the NKVD (a predecessor of the KGB) executed thousands of Polish prisoners of war near the Katyn Forest. For decades, the Soviet Union angrily and repeatedly denied involvement and blamed the Nazi regime instead. In 1990, Mikhail Gorbachev finally admitted that Soviet forces had committed the atrocity (Cienciala et al. 2007; Zawodny 1971). During the Cuban Missile Crisis in 1962, both the Soviet foreign minister and the ambassador to the United States categorically denied that the Soviet Union was installing missiles on the island, despite clear photographic evidence showing it was (Rose 1988: 13).

## Czechoslovakia 1968

These official denials were a major informational tool in the political warfare campaign in Czechoslovakia. As the Warsaw Pact states prepared for the invasion in the beginning of 1968, senior Soviet military officials vehemently denied that any such preparations were taking place. The French newspaper *Le Monde* published an article in May that alleged the Soviet Army had developed plans to 'save socialism' in Czechoslovakia. General Alexei Yepishev of the Main Political Directorate of the Soviet Army and Navy called the reports 'utterly stupid' and questioned the 'intentions of those who spread such rumours' (Dawisha 1984: 116). In reality, General Margelov of the Soviet Airborne Troops had received a directive on 8 April to begin planning the deployment of his forces to the country (Bischof et al. 2010: 10). Yepishev himself had started lobbying the CPSU Central Committee in April to authorize 'fraternal assistance' against 'counter-revolution' (Valenta 1980: 124).

The Soviet senior political leadership likewise denied the ongoing preparations. In a 14 June meeting between the Soviet and Czechoslovak delegations, Brezhnev tearfully swore that he had no plans to interfere in his neighbour's internal affairs (Dawisha 1984: 147). He had actually discussed military intervention as early as 6–7 March, when Bulgarian leader Todor Zhivkov pledged Brezhnev his country's armed forces if the operation was executed (Bischof et al. 2010: 7). The Soviet Politburo made the final, official decision to intervene during its 15–17 August session, including laying out its plans for its collaborators in the Czechoslovak regime (CPSU CC Politburo 1968e: 379). However, the Soviet government continued to deny for over twenty years that it was directly involved in the political manoeuvring within the CPCz leadership that led up to the invasion (Andrew and Gordievsky 1990: 489). It finally admitted its fault in 1989, stating that 'the entry of the armies of the five socialist countries into Czechoslovakia in 1968 was unjustified' (*Pravda* 1989: 576).

## Afghanistan 1979

Similarly, during the invasion of Afghanistan, the Soviet government's denials over whether it was behind the change in regime were critical to its disinformation campaign. A *Pravda* editorial from 23 December 1979 labelled the claims in Western media that the Soviet troops in Afghanistan were preparing for combat as 'pure fabrications' (Collins 1986: 73). After the invasion, the Soviet government insisted that it played no part in Hafizullah Amin's death and that Babrak Karmal had secretly returned to Afghanistan on his own accord weeks before the coup, despite the fact that both his entry into the country and his rise to power relied entirely on the KGB (Valenta 1980: 135). These Soviet denials continued into the new year. In April 1980, *The New Times* political magazine insisted:

> The fact that the removal of Amin took place concurrently with the beginning of the introduction of the Soviet contingent is a pure coincidence in time and there is no causal relationship between the two events. The Soviet units had nothing to do with the removal of Amin and his accomplices. That was the doing of the Afghans themselves. (Hammond 1984: 100)

The Soviet government ensured that the new Afghan government it installed followed the same public denials. Soviet foreign minister Andrei Gromyko instructed his new Afghan counterpart, Shah Mohammad Dost, that 'one should emphasize that there is no relationship [. . .] between the change in the Afghan leadership and the deployment of the Soviet military contingent in Afghanistan' (MFA USSR 1980).

### Crimea 2014

The Russian government employed these same denial tactics during the Crimean crisis. The Russian senior leadership repeatedly denied any Russian military involvement despite evidence to the contrary. On 4 March 2014, Putin explicitly denied that Russia was 'training Crimean self-defence forces' and claimed there had been no 'deployment of troops' or 'use of armed forces' (Kremlin 2014h). He alleged again on 18 March that 'Russia's Armed Forces never entered Crimea' and cited the 25,000 personnel limit for Russian forces in Crimea under its agreement with Ukraine (Kremlin 2014a) – despite the fact that several of the operation's critical units were not part of the Russian Black Sea Fleet and thus not authorized under the treaty. In an echo of Soviet General Yepishev during the Prague Spring, Russian defence minister Sergey Shoigu on 5 March condemned photographs of military vehicles with Russian licence plates in the media as 'an act of provocation' and swore he did 'not have any idea' about how such modern weaponry could have made it among the so-called self-defence forces (ITAR-TASS 2014d). He also insisted that it was 'absolutely false' that there were Russian soldiers among the armed men without insignia (ITAR-TASS 2014c). Foreign Minister Sergei Lavrov likewise denied that Russia was giving orders to the 'self-defence forces' and maintained that members of the Russian Black Sea Fleet were 'staying at the sites of permanent deployment' (ITAR-TASS 2014a).

On the Crimean Peninsula, Russian government officials and their partners among the Crimean politicians made the same denials. The morning after Russian forces seized the two airports, the Russian Black Sea Fleet spokesman released a statement proclaiming that '[n]o Black Sea Fleet units have moved toward (the airport), let alone taking any part in blockading it' (de Carbonnel 2014a). In a late March 2014 interview, Sergey Glazyev, the Russian presidential advisor who was in Crimea during the crisis to help manage the operation, insisted:

> Russia did not use force in Crimea [. . .] All work on the proclamation of independence of Crimea, all sessions of the Supreme Council and the referendum itself passed without the use of the Russian armed forces, without even the need for their intervention, without any victims or shots fired, which proves that the Crimean population managed everything on its own. (Simes 2014)

On 3 March, the head of the Sevastopol branch of the pro-Russian 'Russian Bloc' political party, Vladimir Tyunin, asked, 'Where are Russian troops here? These are our local self-defence units', while pointing to the unmarked Russian forces blocking the Ukrainian Navy headquarters (Walker 2014c).

The Russian officials continued to issue these denials in the face of mounting evidence of Russia's military presence in Crimea. Journalists from the Norwegian broadcasting network NRK reported that the armed men posted outside of Ukrainian military facilities and manning checkpoints on the peninsula admitted to them that they were Russian servicemen, despite the fact that they had no Russian flags on their uniforms (Tandstad et al. 2014). Outside of the Ukrainian barracks in Bakhchysarai, one armed man told the German *Bild* newspaper, 'I am a Russian soldier; I have come here from Sevastopol days ago. It is a peaceful mission against the extremists in Ukraine.' When pressed on why he did not have insignia on his uniform, he replied, 'The mission is secret' (Ronzheimer and Thelen 2014). Russian servicemen also openly identified themselves to their Ukrainian counterparts. According to the Ukrainian sailors stationed in Lake Donuzlav, they knew from the very beginning that the 'little green men' were Russian servicemen. After the first few days, the Russian servicemen even stopped hiding their identity in conversations and openly displayed their Russian licence plates on vehicles (Interview with Oleksii Kirillov 2017). The 'self-defence forces' outside the Ukrainian Navy headquarters in Sevastopol willingly told the Ukrainian officers barricaded inside that they were Russian VDV Airborne Forces. They said that after the Olympics in Sochi, their phones and documents were confiscated as they were ordered onto landing ships without being told their mission (Interview I 2017). One of the soldiers outside of the base had forgotten to remove a nametag from his kit; a journalist found online his social media VKontakte profile, which showed he was a member of the GRU *Spetsnaz* (Russian Main Intelligence Directorate special forces) and since 27 February had been 'on vacation'. After the story ran, his profile was immediately deleted (*Nasha Niva* 2014). While these lower-level Russian servicemen revealed their true identity, the Russian leadership continued to deny that they were in Crimea.

The heads of the interim Ukrainian government knew from the very beginning of the Crimean crisis that Russian forces were behind the operation. The Ukrainian National Security and Defence Council (NSDC) held an emergency session on 28 February 2014, the day after the Crimean Rada legislative buildings were seized (NSDC 2014).[7] As is evident from these lengthy, then classified discussions between Ukraine's senior leadership, they understood that Russia was the driving force behind the developing crisis. There was no debate about the identity of the so-called self-defence forces or whether the Russian government had deployed additional troops to the peninsula. Instead, they discussed reports about the continued movement of Russian forces; for example, Defence Minister Ihor Tenyukh recounted intelligence reports that there was a 'constant transfer of assault units' from Russia intro Crimea, including GRU *Spetsnaz* (NSDC 2014: 12). The Ukrainian government quickly became certain of Russia's role in its southern territory. However, the Russian government's denials and disinformation operations – despite the clear contradictory evidence – sowed enough doubt on the international stage to hinder a more assertive response. The persistence of that confusion speaks to the power of these disinformation operations, no matter how simple they were to execute.

## Forgeries

In addition to the public denials, the Russian government and its state media also reinstated the most prevalent form of Soviet disinformation: forgeries. In Soviet political warfare practice, forgeries included altered original documents and complete fabrications. Even when proven as false, they often still evoked memories of other similar activities their targets may have done in the past or cast suspicion over the official defence the target provided (Richelson 1986: 139–40). To support the production of forgeries, the Soviet Bloc intelligence services spent a significant amount of time collecting signatures and letterheads from

---

[7]   This source is the since-released minutes from the NSDC session. For more, see Chapter 5.

various governmental and non-governmental agencies as well as their leadership. For example, most KGB residencies in foreign embassies (i.e. its headquarters in that country) or their surrogates sent out hand-signed Christmas cards with the knowledge that Westerners felt obliged to reciprocate, thus providing them with samples for future forgery operations (Bittman 1972: 30). Initially in the 1950s, the Soviet Union published forgeries in its own state-controlled media. However, the results were far less effective, as international audiences often doubted the origins of the questionable information. The Soviet government soon shifted its focus to placing its disinformation in Western or Third World media and letting it spread from there (Richelson 1986: 141). By the 1960s, the disinformation campaign increased to the point that the intelligence services started to call it 'the cold war in forgeries' (Deacon 1972: 521).

The Soviet government typically created forgeries from Western sources and then spread them among various sympathetic media outlets. In 1964, the KGB forged documents showing a CIA plot to assassinate the Indonesian president and a joint US–UK plan to invade his country and gave them to an Indonesian ambassador whom the KGB had already compromised. The resulting outrage led to Indonesian mobs attacking American offices and opened the window for an attempted (but failed) communist coup, which was the Soviet Union's ultimate objective (Barron 1974: 223–4). In 1983, two newspapers in Nigeria printed a supposed internal US embassy memo calling for the assassination of two prominent opposition party figures; the authors unintentionally betrayed it as a Soviet forgery when they left in the words 'wet affairs', the English translation of the Russian term for KGB assassinations (Richelson 1986: 146). The Spanish press anonymously received a forged letter from US president Ronald Reagan to King Juan Carlos in 1981 asking him to destroy 'left-wing opposition' to NATO membership in exchange for US support for the return of Gibraltar (Barron 1983: 16). The Soviet government penned US Field Manual (FM) 30-31B, an offshoot of the legitimate FM 30-31A, that detailed the ways in which US military personnel were instructed to support and incite leftist groups in foreign countries to provoke violent government crackdowns against them. When in 1978 the Italian communist terrorist group Red Brigades murdered Aldo Moro, the president of the Christian Democratic Party, Cuban surrogates delivered a copy of the forged field manual to *El Triunfo*, a Spanish leftist magazine. The publication ran a story citing the manual to show that the United States was behind the Red Brigades murder, and the press in twenty different countries repeated the charge (Kux 1985: 23; Barron 1983: 259–60).

During the Ukraine crisis, the Russian government similarly employed the use of forgeries. However, to adopt their use to the modern media landscape, it forged legitimate-looking news websites and created fake content that it could then quote in its own reporting. BBCCNN.com.ua, an obvious attempt to appear to be a legitimate Western news site, regularly published false information about the crisis that matched the Russian government's propaganda narratives.[8] Russian state-run media would then cite the website's information in its own reporting. Another such news website, Ukraina.ru, was dedicated to reporting on Ukraine and regularly published articles with false or misleading information. Russian state media then quoted its reporting as a legitimate news source. Based on hacked emails from its editor-in-chief, Iskander Khisamov, the website was in reality a secret project of *Rossiya Segodnya*, the Russian state media company (Interview with Yevhen Fedchenko 2017).

One purpose behind Soviet forgeries that the Russian government also reapplied in Crimea was to incite racial violence, especially when the forgeries appeared to be from organizations known to harbour racist views. Prior to the 1984 Olympic Games in Los Angeles, the KGB's Service A fabricated a pamphlet from the Ku Klux Klan that the Washington residency then covertly sent to various African and Asian Olympic committees, attempting to foment racial hatred. Its inciteful language included, 'The highest award for a true American patriot would be the lynching of an African monkey' (Andrew and Mitrokhin 2000: 310–1). Around Christmas 1959–60, the West German police documented 833 anti-Jewish acts, including the desecration of synagogues, the painting of swastikas on Jewish establishments and anonymous threatening phone calls. Those arrested in Cologne were found to have travelled on several occasions to East Germany, and Bernhard Schlottmann, the treasurer of a neo-Nazi organization in West Berlin, confessed after his arrest that he was an East German agent under orders to incite anti-Semitism among West Germany's extremist factions (Barron 1974: 234–6).

During the Crimean crisis, the Russian government appears to have applied the same tactic and targeted *Pravy Sektor* and its anti-Russian views. On 1 March 2014, an appeal appeared on *Pravy Sektor*'s official VKontakte page. In it, its leader Dmitry Yarosh asked Doku Umarov, the infamous Chechen rebel leader,[9] for assistance 'in the fight against Russia'. The Russian media widely reported the

---

[8]  If attempting to visit the website today, the reader is notified that it has been disabled by the server administrator.

[9]  Umarov had been dead since 7 September 2013, but his death was not made public until 18 March 2014 (BBC 2014a).

post, and it even drew a strong condemnation from head of the Chechen Republic Ramzan Kadyrov. However, *Pravy Sektor* – which had unabashedly voiced highly controversial and anti-Russian views in the past – immediately denied making the appeal and accused the Russian government of hacking its account. According to the group's spokesman, 'Our page was blocked for half an hour, and the account of one of the group's administrators was hacked.' Furthermore, the appeal never appeared on the organization's official website (*Komsomolskaya Pravda* 2014; StopFake.org 2014a). What the forged information succeeded in doing was fan the flames of racial tension in support of Russian propaganda themes.

Another approach to forgeries that reappeared in the Crimean crisis was the mischaracterization of actual events to fit propaganda narratives. During the Prague Spring, the East German media reported that American troops with their tanks were already in Czechoslovakia, linking up with counter-revolutionaries, and preparing for the arrival of more American and West German special units. The press from the other Soviet Bloc states repeated the story. In reality, the photographs they ran were from the set of *The Bridge at Remagen*, an American Second World War film shooting at the time with Czechoslovak extras and Czechoslovak equipment (Frolik 1975: 139; Bittman 1972: 193–4). Despite the clear misrepresentation, a retraction or clarification was never published (Andrew and Gordievsky 1990: 489). Russian state media took a similar approach to providing 'evidence' that justified the Russian government's actions in Crimea. In early March 2014, the Russian state-television channel *Perviy Kanal* claimed that 140,000 refugees were fleeing Ukraine for safety in Russia. To substantiate the report, it showed a backlogged Ukrainian border crossing. The footage was actually from a checkpoint between Ukraine and Poland near Shegyni (Ennis 2014). While the Russian propaganda described the scene as Ukrainians seeking protection in Russia, they were actually seeking safety in the EU – one of the supposed aggressors in that propaganda. Similarly, *Vesti.24* used footage of some of the most violent government crackdowns on anti-Yanukovych protesters in Kyiv and labelled it as attacks on ethnic Russians in Simferopol (Sukhov 2014).

## Disinformation through the use of agents

Some Soviet disinformation operations went beyond forged documents or misattributed information. They involved the intricate use of agents to simulate events or to plant disinformation directly. These, too, made a reappearance during the Crimean crisis. In Operation *Trust* from 1921 to 1929, the Soviet Union sent 'defectors' to the West to meet with Western intelligence officials and Russian exile communities. They said they belonged to the Trust, an underground organization that was supposedly conducting an insurgent campaign against the Communist Party from within. In reality, the organization was a false flag front, and the defectors were double agents. The operation allowed the Soviet Union to feed disinformation to Western governments to prevent further interference in its internal affairs and for it to find, discredit and even assassinate exile leadership (Epstein 1989: 22–7). In the 1970s, the US Department of Defence uncovered a KGB plot (which was later abandoned) to disrupt the planned upgrade to Trident nuclear missiles on US submarines. In the plan, KGB agents would secretly leak radioactive material outside of an American nuclear submarine base and then tip off the media. The 'discovery' would cause protests over the damage the base was causing to the environment and lead to calls to scrap the entire programme (Barron 1974: 32).

One extremely intricate plot occurred in Czechoslovakia in May 1964. Operation *Neptune* sought to extend the statute of limitations against war criminals and Nazi collaborators and rekindle anti-German sentiment throughout Europe. The Czechoslovak StB security service with the assistance of the KGB secretly lowered four large cases into the Black Lake in Bohemia. A documentary film crew then found the cases, and when the government recovered and opened them, it announced that they were full of Nazi archive materials. In reality, they contained blank papers; Moscow had in the meantime sent a batch of authentic Nazi documents for the StB to analyse and selectively release as 'discoveries' from the cases. Czechoslovak interior minister Lubomir Strougal stated in his press conference that the find meant he must 'forbid the lapse of criminal prosecution of the most serious criminal acts against peace, war crimes, and criminal acts against humanity perpetrated in the interest of the service of the occupying forces' and reactivated the Commission for the Prosecution of War Crimes. The security service then further spread the 'contents' of the cases through a documentary film (which, ironically, received critical acclaim in the West) and through exposés in the government-controlled Czechoslovak Press Agency (Bittman 1972: 39–78).[10]

These disinformation operations through the use of agents were closely related to the Soviet government's use of disguised forces in its political warfare campaigns (discussed in Chapter 5). Both were false flag operations intended to alter perceptions and misattribute actions to the parties in the conflicts. The major difference between the two techniques was which party of the conflict

---

[10] Bittman was one of Operation *Neptune*'s creators, the diver who buried the cases and the ghostwriter of the press releases.

was targeted; the disinformation operations invented damning evidence against the Soviet Union's enemies, whereas the disguised forces falsely bolstered the supposed strength of the Soviet government's allies. While these two techniques were closely related, their use varied based on the political dynamics of the conflict. The invasion of Czechoslovakia saw the use of agent-driven disinformation operations to discredit the Czechoslovak reformers and incriminate Western governments but not the use of disguised forces; the invasion of Afghanistan saw the use of disguised forces to invent Babrak Karmal's base of power but not the use of any elaborate disinformation agent schemes targeting foreign states.

## Czechoslovakia 1968

These disinformation operations using agents were a critical component of the 1968 invasion of Czechoslovakia. As the Soviet Union increased preparations, KGB chairman Yuri Andropov secretly established a second KGB residency in the embassy in Prague in April 1968. Unlike the first residency, which worked intricately with its Czechoslovak counterpart, the StB, this one remained hidden from the Czechoslovak government. Its mission: manage the illegals network – agents operating under non-official cover and thus without the diplomatic cover of those operating out of the embassy (Andrew and Mitrokhin 2000: 328– 39). The residency ran two major operations. Operation *Progress* infiltrated illegals into Czechoslovakia disguised as Western tourists and businessmen. Their mission was to meet with leaders of the reform movement, whom the KGB believed would be open and frank with sympathetic Westerners, in order to collect intelligence, penetrate the network and develop plans to counter them (Andrew and Gordievsky 1990: 489). In the second operation, code-named *Khodoki* ('go-betweens', a term for peasants who would appeal directly to the Russian leadership), the illegals tried to entrap the reform movement by offering it supposed links to Western intelligence agencies and inciting it to violence. They also attempted to pass articles to the Czechoslovak press that strongly condemned the Soviet Union. They hung posters calling for Czechoslovaks to rise up against communism as Hungary had done twelve years prior (Kramer 1993: 7). They offered the political clubs Western arms through a fictitious underground organization. An *Izvestia* correspondent later recounted how he was given a new assistant whom he had never met before while on assignment in Czechoslovakia. One night, the new assistant – who was most likely an illegal and part of these operations – borrowed their company car; the next day, they discovered a 'weapons arsenal' of handguns and grenades (Petrov 2010: 153).

These operations supported the Soviet propaganda narrative that the reform movement was planning a coup with secret help from the West. They also helped to manufacture the casus belli the Soviet Union needed to justify an invasion. For example, in the Moscow negotiations towards the end of the conflict, Brezhnev pressed the Czechoslovak leaders on the issue of how 'underground cells and ammunition caches have been uncovered' and how it 'prompted the five countries to take extreme but unavoidable measures' (CPSU CC Politburo 1968d: 466). On 12 July 1968, an anonymous call reported one such cache of hidden weapons in a canal under a bridge in Sokolovsko near the West German border. It contained 20 Thompson submachine guns, 35 full magazines, 756 cartridges and 30 Walter pistols in five rucksacks with English lettering and '1968' stamped on them (Bittman 1972: 194–5). The Soviet and Bulgarian press agencies ran sensational stories about the discovery of the cache and the clear attempt to 'arm the counterrevolution', making points like how the 'designations and trademarks, including designations of the military depot and inspectors, belong to the American Army' ('White Book' 1968: 130). These stories suspiciously ran before the Czechoslovak government had announced the cache's discovery (Dubček 1993: 166–7). On 19 July, *Pravda* reported that the weapons cache 'fully conformed to the needs of an insurrection and could be used for actions by small groups of rebels', placing the blame on 'Sudeten revanchists' from West Germany (Dawisha 1984: 223).

Upon further investigation, several issues arose with the supposed cache. Soviet forces had conducted manoeuvres in the area shortly before its discovery (Bittman 1972: 194). The Soviet news stories had quoted several eyewitnesses who claimed they discovered the cache, but the Czechoslovak investigators could not locate any of them (Dawisha 1984: 196). The American weapons were from the Second World War and likely from Soviet Army stockpiles in East Germany. The packing grease was identified as of Soviet origin (Dubček 1993: 167). Some of the rucksacks reportedly still had faint traces of a label in Russian: 'large size rucksacks, top quality, GUM [the Soviet department store]' (Tigrid 1971: 61). After an StB investigation, Interior Minister Josef Pavel concluded that 'the general consensus is that the hidden arms were a provocation aimed at dramatizing the situation in Czechoslovakia' (Bittman 1972: 195). These arms caches, as well as the other aspects of the disinformation operations *Progress* and *Khodoki*, served to feed the Soviet propaganda narrative about the supposed Western sponsorship and radical nature of the reform movement in Czechoslovakia.

## Crimea 2014

During the Crimean crisis, Russian special forces appeared to conduct this same sort of false flag disinformation operation aimed at supporting the Russian propaganda narrative about the risk Ukrainian nationalists posed to the lives of Crimea's ethnic Russian population. On 1 March 2014, heavily armed men in civilian clothes and face masks attacked the Simferopol Council of Ministers building, which was under the control of pro-Russian Crimean politicians and unmarked Russian Armed Forces. Several Russian, Ukrainian and Western television channels ran footage of the assault throughout the day (see, for example, BFMTV 2014). Russian state broadcaster VGTRK reported that their identity was 'unknown' but connected the event to a gathering of 'nationalists from the *Svoboda* and UDAR parties' the day prior (Poddubny 2014).[11] As can be seen in the footage, however, some of the masked men are carrying GM-94 grenade launchers. The weapon was purpose-built for Russian special police and Special Operations Forces, and sightings of it outside of Russian government use are extremely rare (Popenker and Jenzen-Jones 2015). The attackers arrived in a bright yellow bus from the Taigan Lion Park in Yalta, 50 miles south of Simferopol – the opposite direction of the crossings onto the peninsula from where a Ukrainian nationalist militia would enter (StopFake.org 2014b). Yalta is also the location of the Health Resort of the Ministry of Defence of the Russian Federation. Two military vehicles full of armed soldiers without insignia arrived at the resort on 25 February; the resort director admitted that they were Russian servicemen (Skrypnyk and Pechonchyk 2016: 8). While the evidence is not conclusive that the 'assailants' were Russian special forces disguised as violent Ukrainian ultra-nationalists, suspiciously, nothing came of the attack. There were no casualties, no significant exchange of fire and no arrests, and the assailants soon disappeared (Poddubny 2014; StopFake.org 2014b). What did result from the attack was coverage throughout the day on major news channels about an apparent violent attack in Crimea led by Ukrainian radicals.

\* \* \*

The informational tools the Russian government employed as part of its 2014 annexation operation in Crimea originated in Soviet political warfare practice. Under Putin, the Russian government has taken creative measures to

---

[11]   UDAR is Vitali Klitschko's Ukrainian Democratic Alliance for Reform.

reconsolidate government control over the domestic media landscape; while it does not enjoy the same monopoly that the Soviet government possessed, it has still managed to increase state control over media outlets and to coerce other outlets into following government narratives. This control of the domestic media allowed both governments to control the messaging during their military campaigns. The Russian government then followed the model of how the Soviet government seized control of the media and information spaces in Czechoslovakia and Afghanistan: it attacked the main media centres throughout the peninsula, cut off Ukrainian and foreign broadcasting and replaced it with Russian state-controlled media reporting. Once the information space was under control, the Russian government revived four dominant propaganda themes from the Soviet era and the tools used to distribute them. Even though some of these have been adapted to fit the modern operating environment – protecting 'honest communists' has become protecting ethnic Russians, and 'black' propaganda has used 'trolls' and forged websites instead of agents in the foreign media – the roots are still easily traceable to Soviet political warfare practice. These linkages are equally evident with the Russian application of disinformation, including its official denials, use of forgeries and elaborate agent-driven disinformation operations. The following chapter discusses these same Soviet political warfare origins of the political tools used in the Crimean annexation.

# 4

# Political tools

The political aspects of the 2014 annexation of Crimea equally had their roots in Soviet political warfare practices. The Soviet government placed critical emphasis on the appearance of political legitimacy in its political warfare campaigns and used these political actions to legitimize its follow-on military operations, thus minimizing resistance both in the targeted country and on the international stage. While the outward legitimacy of the political process was crucial to the Soviet government, it actively undermined the integrity of the process from within. Its approach to political proceedings in the target country was that they were a tool to manipulate to produce the necessary results that supported Soviet objectives. To this end, the Soviet government secretly conspired with pro-Soviet politicians, with whom it engineered the political process and anointed the new leadership of the country. It deployed senior officials, usually under a cover status, to the target country to organize and arrange the necessary steps. The Soviet government and its collaborators then set the conditions to produce the desired expressions of political will that legitimized a Soviet military invasion. In its campaigns in Czechoslovakia and Afghanistan, these political acts included the removal of the serving government, the instalment of a new regime and the request for a Soviet invasion.

In its operation in Crimea in 2014, the Russian government employed these same political tools to set the conditions for annexation and project legitimacy for its actions. It developed pro-Russian political parties and politicians in support of the future operation in the same way that the Soviet government utilized foreign Communist Parties and recruited Committee for State Security (KGB) agents in foreign governments. Both governments deployed senior officials during the campaigns to identify those collaborators and manage the operations. The political proceedings during the 2014 crisis, including the removal of the serving Crimean government, the installation of Sergey Aksyonov as the new prime minister and the referendum to vote on annexation, mirrored the ways in which the Soviet

Union manufactured the political processes in Czechoslovakia and Afghanistan. To increase the apparent legitimacy of the referendum, the Russian government also employed modern-day versions of Soviet agents of influence and front organizations to observe its proceedings. The Russian government's emphasis on the 'invasion invitation' that former Ukrainian president Viktor Yanukovych supposedly sent it was a virtual replay from similar measures taken by the Soviet government in the invasions of Czechoslovakia and Afghanistan – including the questionable circumstances surrounding how the 'invitation' came about.

# Collaborators within foreign political parties and foreign governments

The Communist Party of the Soviet Union (CPSU) exerted its influence in the politics of foreign countries through the covert sponsorship of fellow Communist Parties. While the 'fraternal bonds' between the parties were overt, the Soviet Union also secretly funded the international parties and provided their leaders with political direction. The Soviet government cultivated politicians within these foreign parties to act as proxies for Soviet policy in their nations, and the KGB recruited several of them as agents and paid them accordingly for their activities in support of Soviet objectives, especially during its political warfare campaigns.

In Crimea, the pro-Russian political parties provided the Russian government with the same means to insert itself into the peninsula's politics. While communism no longer provided the bonds that it did for the CPSU to its sister parties abroad, policies to promote unity among ethnic Russians across national boundaries served a similar purpose for the Russian Federation. In the former Soviet republics, various parties have formed based on these principles, including in Ukraine and especially in Crimea. During the 2014 crisis, Russia capitalized on the infrastructure and leadership of these organizations, as well as pro-Russian politicians among the ruling Party of Regions, to support the annexation operation.

### Foreign Communist Parties

Communist Parties provided the Soviet Union with a direct link into the politics of foreign countries. The parties that were not in power in non-Bloc states technically represented domestic political movements in their own countries; however, in the Cold War, the vast majority of them secretly took direction from the CPSU. The International Department of the CPSU provided the necessary policy directives to the parties, and it along with the KGB clandestinely provided funds to sustain them (Kux 1985: 22). For example, during the Twenty-fourth Congress of the Soviet Communist Party in 1971, senior officials from the KGB First Chief Directorate (Foreign Operations) met with the leadership from over a dozen European and Latin American Communist Parties and tasked them with identifying candidates for recruitment for future Soviet operations (Andrew and Mitrokhin 2000: 367–8). Soviet Main Intelligence Directorate (GRU) defector Oleg Penkovsky (1965: 182) likewise described the ease with which Soviet security service officers could approach members of the French Communist Party: 'It is true that if we approach an ordinary Frenchman and he realises that he is talking to Russians, he will immediately run and report the contact to the police. But French Communists, generally speaking, readily agree to work for us, asking only directions on how and what to do.' The KGB trained some of these members of the French Communist Party in clandestine radio communications and used them to help run operations for its illegals residency, its non-official cover base of operations (Andrew and Mitrokhin 2000: 366).

In these countries where the communists had not seized control, the Soviet government illicitly funded its sister parties to conduct operations in support of Soviet objectives. In 1972, Brazilian police stopped Fued Saad, the leader of the Brazilian Communist Party, on his return flight from Moscow and found $80,000 in cash in his luggage; the KGB had been supplying him $300,000 a year to support his party's activities (Barron 1974: 33). KGB records from the 1970s reveal the trips William Kashtan, the leader of the Canadian Communist Party, made to the Soviet embassy in Ottawa to collect funds from the KGB residency. The KGB also passed him funds through an intermediary organization, the *Ukrainskaya Kniga* Company based in Toronto (Andrew and Mitrokhin 2000: 373–4). Soviet handlers met Filipino communists in Japan throughout the same decade and provided them with false-bottomed suitcases lined with cash (Barron 1983: 266). The New Zealand security services arrested and expelled the Soviet ambassador in 1980 when they caught him passing cash to the Socialist Unity Party in an Auckland hotel room (Kux 1985: 22). As reported in CPSU archives released after the end of the Cold War, the Soviet Union sent over $200 million to sister parties outside of the Communist Bloc in the 1980s alone (Andrew and Mitrokhin 2000: 374). These funds largely sustained these political parties and funded their operations in support of the KGB.

Like other international Communist Parties, the Communist Party USA (CPUSA) was superficially an organic US political party, but it was a de facto arm of the CPSU to alter the American political landscape. The International Department of the CPSU provided it subsidies that grew from $1 million to $3 million per year during the Cold War. KGB officers would deliver the cash in secret 'brush passes' in New York City. As revealed by Jack Childs, CPUSA middleman and secretly a Federal Bureau of Investigation (FBI) informant, the KGB used similar tradecraft – including dead drops, encoded phone calls and messages hidden in undeveloped film – to pass on political instructions from Moscow (Andrew and Mitrokhin 2000: 376–82). Former CPUSA member Dorothy Ray Healey later explained how party leader Gus Hall received instructions in such a manner and then made public statements in line with the directives contained in them. *Pravda*, the official newspaper of the CPSU Central Committee, then reported on his statements, completing the information loop (Healey and Isserman 1990).

In countries with ruling Communist Parties, the CPSU's influence was even stronger. Part of the reason the CPSU was able to exert such strong leverage over the other Communist Parties, especially in Eastern Europe, was that the Soviet Union had achieved the early twentieth century's only successful socialist revolution. The communists in Europe had failed both to prevent the Second World War and to seize power after it, meaning the CPSU emerged as the preeminent model for socialism. The Soviet Union thus used its influence and leadership in the Communist International (Comintern), the international organization advocating for the spread of communism, to impose the *Twenty-One Conditions*, which defined only one acceptable model of party organization – the Soviet model of strict centralized control. Members of the other Communist Parties who tried to defy Moscow's leadership found themselves expelled, further consolidating the CPSU's influence. In 1925, for example, the Comintern ordered the dismissal of the leadership of the Polish Communist Party and hand-picked their replacements (Schoepflin 1993: 47–8, 52). As a result of these dynamics, the European Communist Parties (outside of Yugoslavia and, to a lesser extent, Albania and Romania) owed their rise to power not to domestic forces but to their relationship with the Soviet Union (Fischer-Galati 1979). The Communist Party of Czechoslovakia (CPCz) initially came to power after the Second World War on its own, but when it appeared that it would lose control in the 1948 parliamentary elections, President Edvard Beneš caved to pressure from the party as well as from the Soviet ambassador and allowed for government changes to one-party rule under the Soviet model of socialism (Ulc 1979).

## Czechoslovakia 1968

This measure of control that the CPSU wielded over its fellow Communist Parties, especially those in power, was a critical political tool in its political warfare campaigns. In preparation for the invasion of Czechoslovakia in 1968, the Soviet Union led the Warsaw Pact efforts in identifying and cultivating CPCz members who could serve as their proxies and provide the appearance of legitimacy to the operation. During a meeting in mid-July, the leaders of the Warsaw Pact Five (the Soviet Union, Bulgaria, Hungary, East Germany and Poland) made clear their intent to find collaborators within the Czechoslovak ranks. According to the transcript, they stated:

> If we see that the CPCz leadership does not wish to heed our recommendations, then it will be necessary, obviously, to continue the search for healthy forces in the party and to look for ways of appealing to the forces in the party that might take the lead in initiating a struggle to restore the leading role of the CPCz and normalize the situation in the country. (Polish Modern Records Archive 1968: 227)

In 1968, the main task KGB Centre gave to the Line PR (political and military strategic intelligence) officers stationed in Prague and its liaison officers working at the StB (Czechoslovak state security service) was not coordination with their Czechoslovak counterparts but identification of pro-Soviet CPCz members whom they could trust to lead the government installed after the Soviet invasion. Through their efforts, they identified key members Alois Indra, Vasil Bil'ak, Drahomír Kolder and Jozef Lenárt and brought them to the Soviet embassy for confidential discussions out of the purview of First Secretary Alexander Dubček and his government. The KGB even deployed a female illegal operative disguised as a Swiss citizen to make contact with Rudolf Barák, the former interior minister and another possible co-conspirator (Andrew and Mitrokhin 2000: 329).

The Soviet government secretly worked with its partners in the CPCz to orchestrate the invasion and the change in government. The Politburo (the CPSU's executive committee) privately kept Indra and Bil'ak informed of the content of its negotiations with Dubček, including providing them directly with copies of official correspondence before it reached the first secretary (Ruggenthaler and Knoll 2010: 167). The Politburo also drafted a final warning letter to Dubček and planned to deliver it on 18 August 1968. However, when Soviet ambassador Stepan Chervonenko briefed Indra and Bil'ak on it, they convinced him to delay delivering it until the evening of 19 August to leave

Dubček less than twenty-four hours to react before the planned invasion and 'to avoid sparking off premature actions by the rightist forces' (Chervonenko 1968: 390). The Czechoslovak officials thus helped shape the operation to lessen the chances that Dubček could peacefully resolve it or avoid the introduction of Warsaw Pact troops.

The Czechoslovak collaborators legitimately believed in the supposed dangers of Dubček's liberalization reforms. Indra wrote in April 1968 that the changes had created a 'counter-revolutionary situation' that was leading to 'anarchy . . . and the destruction of the state' (Dawisha 1984: 168). Indra and Kolder presented a policy paper to the CPCz Presidium on how the 'counter-revolutionary forces' were endangering the country in an attempt to win over the rest of the body to their point of view (Mlynář 1980: 201–3). Nevertheless, their secret collaboration with the Soviet Union amounted to conspiracy against their own government and would not have been successful without Soviet intervention and support. They clandestinely passed reports to the Soviet government on the developments in their country, such as informing them that General Václav Prchlík, the head of the CPCz Military Administrative Department, had voiced the need to prepare militarily for a possible invasion (Kramer 1993). These reports significantly improved Soviet operational planning and informed Politburo decision-making. Based on the relationships the Soviet Union had cultivated within the ranks of the CPCz and the leading role the CPSU had within the greater communist community, the Soviet government was able to find collaborators to support its planned invasion.

## Afghanistan 1979

As in Czechoslovakia, the Soviet Union held close ties with senior members of the ruling Afghan Communist Party, the People's Democratic Party of Afghanistan (PDPA), and used those relationships to facilitate the 1979 invasion. Its most trusted associates were recruited KGB agents. The Soviet government relied on these figures to support its violent coup to overthrow Hafizullah Amin in 1979 and then installed them as the heads of the new proxy regime in the country. In effect, the purpose of the invasion was to empower one KGB agent, Babrak Karmal, as head of the country after Amin had deposed another KGB agent, Nur Muhammad Taraki.

Taraki, the first communist president of Afghanistan, was a long-standing KGB agent and held a close relationship with the Soviet government. The KGB recruited Taraki in 1951, and he remained actively in its service for the remainder of his life. While still an underground organization, the PDPA elected Taraki as first secretary in 1965. The International Department of the CPSU brought Taraki to Moscow soon after his election to provide him policy guidance and issue him directives. With Soviet support, he went on to become the first communist president of the country through the 1978 Saur Revolution that deposed President Mohammed Daoud Khan (Andrew and Mitrokhin 2006: 386).

The Soviet government did not have such a relationship with Hafizullah Amin, who deposed Taraki in 1979. Amin was still a committed communist figure; he was a full member of the PDPA Central Committee from 1967 onwards and held senior positions in the communist government since they seized power in 1978, including minister of foreign affairs and deputy prime minister (Urban 1990). The Soviet government thus still had strong connections and contact with Amin as it did with the other Afghan communist leadership. However, Amin was not a recruited KGB agent. Because he spoke English and had studied in the United States, the KGB and the Politburo suspected that he must have been a Central Intelligence Agency (CIA) agent instead. After Amin seized control of the PDPA and assassinated Taraki in the fall of 1979, the Soviet Union feared that he would reorient the country towards the West and pull Afghanistan from the Soviet sphere (CPSU CC 1979). Largely because of these suspicions – and the fear that it could not control Amin as it could control Taraki – the Soviet government orchestrated the rise to power of Babrak Karmal, another strong Soviet loyalist.

Like Taraki, Karmal had been a KGB agent since the 1950s (Andrew and Mitrokhin 2006: 387). The KGB naturally gravitated towards the PDPA's Parcham faction, of which Karmal was the leader, because it was the more urban and cosmopolitan of the party's two factions; it recruited not only Karmal but also several other of its members (Melville 1982). Karmal was another founding member of the PDPA and served in various senior positions within the communist regime, including vice president of the Revolutionary Council and deputy premier. However, he fell out of favour in 1978 when Taraki implicated him in a conspiracy to seize power and revoked his citizenship (Kakar 1995). Once marginalized, Karmal tried to seek asylum in Czechoslovakia, where he was then serving as ambassador (CPCz CC 1978).

After the Soviet government decided to remove Amin from power, it selected Karmal to replace him and set the conditions to do so. KGB Centre sent one of its former officers to meet him in Czechoslovakia in October 1979 to form a government-in-exile. The KGB then brought Karmal, three other exiles and three serving Afghan ministers to Moscow the following month to refine the plan. As discussed in a secret memorandum from KGB chairman Yuri Andropov to General Secretary Leonid Brezhnev, these discussions confirmed for the Soviet leadership that the use of its armed forces would be necessary for 'rendering such assistance' to ensure the success of the coup (Andropov 1979). In December, the Soviet government secretly flew Karmal and his cohort to the Bagram Soviet airbase north of Kabul and kept them under a *Spetsnaz* guard detail from 'Group A' (later renamed *Alfa*) until Soviet forces eliminated Amin (Andrew and Mitrokhin 2006: 398–401; Feifer 2010: 61–3).

## Crimea 2014

Like the Soviet government's sponsorship of foreign communists in its political warfare campaigns, the Russian government capitalized on pro-Russian political parties and pro-Russian Crimean politicians during the 2014 annexation of Crimea. Communism no longer serves as the unifying thread between the Kremlin and foreign political parties. Instead, parties in former Soviet regions have emerged on a platform of Russian culture and identity as well as a desire for closer relations with their eastern neighbour. In place of protecting fellow communists, the Russian government has built ties with these parties on the basis of defending the interests of fellow ethnic Russians (see Knott 2017; Laruelle 2009, 2010, 2015; Zevelev 2008; Shevel 2011). During the 2014 operation, the Russian government utilized the footprint these pro-Russian parties had in Crimean politics to insert itself into the political landscape. It then enlisted the support of pro-Russian Crimean politicians to shape the ensuing operation. Like their Czechoslovak and Afghan predecessors, these Crimean politicians secretly conspired with Kremlin officials against the Ukrainian government and the serving Crimean leadership to set the conditions for the annexation.

### Pro-Russian political parties

Pro-Russian political parties played a frequent role in the political life of Crimea under an independent Ukraine. Several pro-Russian social organizations and political groups formed between 1993 and 1994, and they loosely shared a platform emphasizing Russian nationality and unification (in some form) with the Russian Federation. Their power peaked in 1994, when the political parties forming the Russia Bloc movement won 67 per cent of the popular vote in elections for the Verkhovna Rada of Crimea ('Crimean Rada'), the local legislative body. However, Russia Bloc politician Yuriy Meshkov, the newly elected president of Crimea, followed up the election with a declaration that he would hold a referendum on Crimea's status as part of Ukraine – which led to confrontations with the Kyiv government, a constitutional crisis and the abolishment of the presidential position. By the end of the year, only 5 per cent of Crimeans supported Meshkov, and the Russia Bloc fractured into smaller parties (Sasse 2007). At the time of the 1998 Crimean Rada election, the pro-Russian parties had virtually disappeared from the political landscape.

After the 2004 Orange Revolution that saw pro-Western Viktor Yushchenko become president of Ukraine, however, pro-Russian parties made a resurgence in Crimea with the help of funding from the Russian government. During the 2006 Crimean Rada elections, the Russian Community of Crimea (ROK) and Russian Bloc (not the same as the earlier Russia Bloc) united with Viktor Yanukovych's Party of Regions to form the For Yanukovych! Bloc, which won a plurality of seats. The ROK was one of the social organizations created in 1993 to protect the interests of Crimeans 'who consider the Russian language and Russian culture native' (Russian Unity 2015), and Russian Bloc was a newer pro-Russian political party originally founded in 1999 as the Russian Movement of Ukraine (*Ukrainskaya Pravda* 2014). The financing of these two entities, however, relied heavily on Russian government support. In 2006, the US State Department identified increased Russian political activity in Ukraine and drew special attention to the ROK's 'contacts with Moscow' (de Carbonnel 2014b). The ROK received funding from the Russian Foreign Ministry and State Duma deputy Konstantin Zatulin, who was also the first deputy chairman of the Committee on Affairs of the Commonwealth of Independent States, Eurasian Integration and Relations with Compatriots ('CIS and Compatriots Committee'). One of the biggest backers of Russian Bloc was Yury Luzhkov, who at the time was mayor of Moscow (Kuzio 2010: 13). Both of these Russian benefactors actively sought the reunification of Crimea with Russia. In 2008, Ukraine barred Luzhkov from entering its territory; there was an ongoing money laundering investigation into his activities in Sevastopol, partially related to his political activities, and he had also recently given a speech in which he claimed that the status of Crimea 'remained unresolved, and we will solve it' (UNIAN 2008). Ukraine named Zatulin persona non grata three separate times for making similar statements questioning Crimea's status (*UKRINFORM* 2012). However, in a sign of his own political allegiances, Viktor Yanukovych lifted the ban on both individuals after becoming Ukrainian president in 2010 (Kuzio 2010: 31).

### Russian Unity and Sergey Aksyonov

The next Crimean Rada election in 2010 saw the emergence of a new pro-Russian political actor in Crimea, Sergey Aksyonov. He joined the ROK in 2008, and the following year, he spearheaded the organization's creation of a new political party, Russian Unity (*OGO* 2010; Russian Unity 2015). Its initial manifesto did not explicitly list unification with the Russian Federation as part of its party platform, but it did accuse the Ukrainian government of systemically violating the rights of ethnic Russians in Crimea, claimed that there were no 'sincere and consistent supporter[s] and all[ies] of the Russian people of Crimea among the leaders of the Ukrainian political parties' and described its plan to 'expel from Crimea [. . .] latent Ukrainian nationalists' (Russian Unity 2009). The party registered in time for the 2010 Crimean Rada elections with Aksyonov as its senior candidate.

Over the next four years, however, both Aksyonov and his Russian Unity party made minimal impact on Crimean politics. In the 2010 Crimean Rada election, the party received only 4 per cent of the vote, giving it only three of the 100 seats in the Rada. By comparison, the Qurultai-Rukh, the political party aligned with the Crimean Tatar national congress, received 7 per cent and five seats. The Party of Regions won a massive eighty seats (Interfax-Ukraine 2010). In the 2012 elections for the Verkhovna Rada of Ukraine ('Verkhovna Rada', the national parliament), Russian Unity ran candidates in four districts, all of them in Crimea. It failed to win any of the seats, meaning the party was not represented in Ukraine's national parliament. Aksyonov ran in the Simferopol Central District and finished fourth behind the Party of Regions victor with only 9.12 per cent of the vote. He received half of the votes of Leonid Grach, the former communist leader of Crimea during Soviet times, who ran as an independent (Ukrainian Central Election Commission 2012c). The other three Russian Unity candidates received between only 2 and 4 per cent in their districts (Ukrainian Central Election Commission 2012e, 2012f, 2012d).

What is clear from the results of these elections – conducted only two to four years before the 2014 crisis, during peacetime, and without foreign forces operating throughout the peninsula – is that both the ROK and its political wing, Aksyonov's Russian Unity party, had minimal support from the population of Crimea. What these organizations did provide, however, was a platform for the Russian government to channel funds, exert its influence into Crimean politics and build relationships with Crimean politicians, much as the fellow Communist Parties provided the CPSU the same during the Cold War. They also provided future willing collaborators in its plans for the 2014 annexation. In this regard, the Russian government relied not only on Aksyonov but also on his fellow pro-Russian politicians within the Crimean Party of Regions. Together they served as the core of conspirators who executed the political manoeuvring necessary for the Russian invasion, much like how the CPCz and PDPA members served the Soviet Union before them.

Aksyonov had two main accomplices among the Crimean elite in his associations with Russia: Vladimir Konstantinov and Rustam Temirgaliev. Because of their significance in facilitating the annexation, the three could be labelled as the Crimean *troika* à la the Soviet governing triumvirates (Matsuzato 2016: 242). As the frontmen of Russia's operation in Crimea, they are the parallels of Indra, Bil'ak and Kolder in Czechoslovakia and Karmal and the Taraki-loyalist ministers in Afghanistan. The following sections explain their backgrounds and activities surrounding the annexation.

### Vladimir Konstantinov

Vladimir Konstantinov had been a deputy of the Crimean Rada from the Party of Regions since 1998 and chairman (speaker) of the body since 2010. While he was speaker, he publicly denounced any discussions of Crimea's reunification with Russia. In 2012, Konstantinov called groups calling for reunification 'marginals who don't represent anyone in the republic' and pledged that 'the absurd demands of these political midgets will receive the treatment they deserve in court' (Dobrokhotova and Bigg 2016). In the heat of the Ukraine crisis on 19 February 2014, Crimean deputy Nikolai Kolisnichenko suggested that the Crimean Rada 'should raise the question of the return of Crimea to Russia [. . .] if the situation does not stabilize'. Konstantinov interrupted him to say that such a reaction was 'all emotions' and that their responsibility was to support the government in Kyiv, not discuss secession (*Krym.Kommentarii* 2014a).

Despite these public denunciations, however, Konstantinov was secretly working with Russian officials towards the annexation. He made several visits to Moscow in late 2013 and early 2014. During one trip in early December, he met with Secretary of the Russian Security Council Nikolai Patrushev and reportedly suggested that Crimea would be prepared to leave Ukraine for Russia if the Yanukovych regime were to fall (Zygar 2016; Matsuzato 2016). His public tone quickly shifted, as well. During another visit to Moscow on 20 February, Konstantinov met with various factions of the Russian State Duma, including Speaker Sergey Naryshkin. In a press conference that day, Konstantinov stated that if a new central government were to come to power in Kyiv that challenged Crimea's autonomy, 'then we will have only one way – denunciation of the decision of the Presidium of the CPSU Central Committee of 1954', the Soviet decision to transfer Crimea from Russia to Ukraine (Interfax 2014c). This statement was only one day after Konstantinov had condemned any such talk in the Crimean Rada. Furthermore, it was two days before the Verkhovna Rada removed Yanukovych as president and started the change in government. It is likely that Konstantinov met with Russian officials during the trip to discuss what steps would be necessary for the annexation to succeed should Yanukovych's government fall (Matsuzato 2016: 244). According to Valentyn Nalyvaichenko, the then head of the Security Service of Ukraine (SBU), his organization had evidence as early as 28 February that Konstantinov and Aksyonov were 'engaged in full cooperation, interaction, and planning' with the Russian Black Sea Fleet and the unmarked Russian Armed Forces as they stormed the Crimean government buildings, seized the airports and blocked the Ukrainian military facilities (NSDC 2014: 5).

### Rustam Temirgaliev

The third member of the 'troika', Rustam Temirgaliev, was a member of the Party of Regions, involved in Crimean politics since 2004, and a deputy of the Crimean Rada from 2010. On the one-year anniversary of the referendum, he gave an interview to the Russian newspaper *Vedemosti* that revealed much of the behind-the-scenes political exchanges that occurred before and during the annexation (Kozlov 2015). Temirgaliev described himself and Konstantinov as the 'most pro-Russian Federation politicians' in the Party of Regions' Crimean branch. He said that he 'had very good relations with Moscow' and that he and other Crimean politicians 'always sought support in Moscow' to gain leverage over the central government in Kyiv. He exploited these connections in September 2013, when Crimean prime minister Anatolii Mohyliov relented and made Temirgaliev his deputy, a move that he said 'did not happen without help from Moscow'. Once the Russian government sent representatives to Crimea in 2014 to begin preparing the ground for the annexation, Temirgaliev helped facilitate and participated in many of the meetings. After Aksyonov became Crimean prime minister, he made Temirgaliev his deputy. Several of the following sections use additional details Temirgaliev revealed in his *Vedemosti* interview (Kozlov 2015).[1]

---

[1]   Though he stated that he had 'no regrets' about the course of events in Crimea (Kozlov 2015), perhaps the reason Temirgaliev gave such a frank interview was that he quickly lost his political power:

Like the Czechoslovak and Afghan collaborators before them, these pro-Russian Crimean politicians were an instrumental part to the success of the Russian government's political warfare campaign. They exploited the political system to provide the Russian government the impression of legality and legitimacy for its actions. Also like their Cold War predecessors, the Crimean politicians conspired with Russia against their own government to orchestrate major political upheaval. Aksyonov, Konstantinov and Temirgaliev were afraid to discuss their ongoing meetings with Russian officials in the Crimean Council of Ministers building because they feared that the SBU could be listening. They instead met 'in places where [they] could talk discreetly', such as in a café that Konstantinov owned (Kozlov 2015). Their secrecy suggests that they knew their actions amounted to subversion.

### *Alexey Chaly*

Another Crimean political figure, Alexey Chaly, is not on this list because he did not appear to conspire with Russian government officials to the same extent that Aksyonov, Konstantinov and Temirgaliev did. The swiftness with which he lost his new-found political power also suggests that he was a tangential and not integral part of the Russian plan. Chaly was a Sevastopol resident but a Russian citizen and CEO of Tavrida Electric, a multinational company earning $300 million annually. On 23 February 2014, the day after the Verkhovna Rada removed Yanukovych as president, a crowd of approximately 20,000 people rallied in central Sevastopol against the change in government. During the rally, the crowd 'elected' Chaly as the 'people's mayor'. The actual mayor of the city was Vladimir Yatsuba, who was appointed directly by the president as per Ukrainian law; he resigned the next day (*Gazeta.ru* 2014a).

Unlike the others, evidence has not surfaced that Chaly met with the Russian power brokers before he became Sevastopol's 'people's mayor'. The Ukrainian Prosecutor General's Office has released phone recordings in which Russian officials Sergey Glazyev and Konstantin Zatulin allegedly discuss paying Chaly to mobilize the population, but they are dated from March (Prosecutor General's Office of Ukraine 2016b). Leonid Grach, another Crimean collaborator, witnessed Konstantinov and Aksyonov meeting with senior Russian Ministry of Defence and Federal Security Service (FSB) representatives before the

less than three months after the annexation, the Russian authorities removed him as deputy prime minister of Crimea and instead demoted him to plenipotentiary representative of the Republic of Tatarstan in Kazakhstan. He was also indicted in a criminal case involving stolen gold (Gusakova 2015).

annexation operation began, but he made no mention of Chaly (Zhegulyov 2017). In later interviews, Chaly said that he was skiing in the Alps when the events on Maidan in Kyiv occurred and only returned to Crimea on the night of 22 February (Hobson 2016).

Chaly also did not remain part of the Russian government's plans post-annexation. Chaly, Aksyonov and Konstantinov were the three signatories to the annexation agreement with Vladimir Putin in Moscow on 18 March 2014. However, whereas Aksyonov and Konstantinov remained in their positions under the new Russian administration, Chaly did not. He served for only two weeks as governor of Sevastopol before Putin appointed former deputy commander of the Russian Black Sea Fleet Vice Admiral Sergey Menyailo in his place (Interfax 2014b). Chaly told his colleagues shortly after the change that 'it was not up to him' on whether he would remain as governor (Glukhovsky 2014). He then ran for a seat in the Sevastopol Legislative Assembly in September 2014 and, after winning, was elected speaker. For the next two years, Chaly and Menyailo publicly fought over the policy decisions and direction of the Sevastopol government until Chaly resigned as speaker in 2016 (RIA *Novosti* 2016). Chaly's apparent popularity with the population of Sevastopol – the sort of popularity that Aksyonov never had in earlier elections – suggests that his political rise was a legitimate reflection of public sentiment in the city at the time. However, the way in which he was quickly marginalized while Aksyonov remained in power suggests that the course of political events in Crimea had less to do with popular will and more to do with the Russian government's designs for the peninsula.

## Government officials deployed to the country to manage the process

With these pro-Russian political organizations and politicians in Crimea, the Russian government cultivated key collaborators within the Crimean political system to facilitate its annexation operation, just as the Soviet government had done with the identified 'healthy forces' in the CPCz and PDPA to support its political warfare campaigns. The Russian government then continued this Soviet approach by deploying senior officials to Crimea in the earliest stages of the conflict to manage these relationships. For both the Soviet and Russian leadership, these representatives oversaw their operational plans at the ground level, negotiated with and advised collaborators from the targeted country's regime and set the conditions for follow-on military operations.

In Czechoslovakia, the Soviet Union deployed KGB officers to the country to assess the situation and develop the political plan of action it later implemented during the invasion. KGB chairman Yuri Andropov sent a KGB reserve officer, Mikhail Sagatelyan, as his special envoy to Prague in May 1968 and tasked him with drafting an action plan for the country. Sagatelyan deployed in cover as an assistant editor of the Soviet newspaper *Izvestia*. Two other KGB officers, Georgii Fedyashin and Aleksandr Alekseev, had been working in Prague since April for similar purposes and were also under cover as journalists. Sagatelyan met with a series of Czechoslovak politicians over the next month, including Deputy Prime Minister of Culture and Information Bohuslav Chnoupek, who handed him classified government documents and CPCz plans. Vasil Bil'ak was apparently aware of the meeting, as well, and may have facilitated the handover of documents. Sagatelyan sent his report on 4 June to Andropov, who shared it with the Politburo. The plan: foster a pro-Soviet faction within the Czechoslovak leadership, call a special plenary session of the CPCz Central Committee and use the session to remove Dubček from power and request Soviet assistance (Petrov 2010: 151–2). This plan was exactly what the Soviet government and its Czechoslovak collaborators attempted to execute. During the actual operation, the Soviet government sent a more senior on-the-ground manager. In the Politburo's final directive authorizing the invasion, it ordered one of its members, Kirill Mazurov, 'to perform on-site work' in Czechoslovakia (CPSU CC Politburo 1968e: 378). Mazurov deployed to Prague disguised as 'General Trofimov' with responsibility for managing the political and military aspects of the ensuing operation. He reported directly to the Politburo on the invasion's progress (Navratil 1998: 376).

In Afghanistan, the Soviet Union employed nearly identical tactics. On 28 November 1979, the Politburo sent First Deputy Minister of the Interior Lieutenant General Victor Paputin to Kabul. He was there in an official capacity as President Hafizullah Amin's special advisor for policing matters, and he helped develop strategies to contain the growing insurgency. His real mission from the Politburo, however, was to cultivate an anti-Amin coalition among the Afghan officials in order to prepare for the Soviet invasion. He proceeded to secretly meet with members of both the Parcham and Khalq factions of the PDPA, especially Nur Muhammad Taraki's former supporters, to find potential allies for the upcoming operation. Paputin identified the Afghan ministers whom the Russian government later exfiltrated to Moscow and integrated into the operational plan (Valenta 1980: 131–2; Girardet 1985: 13).

In Crimea, Russian officials from across the government deployed to the peninsula to orchestrate different aspects of the annexation in much the same fashion as their Soviet predecessors. First, members of the Russian parliament conducted the negotiations and on-the-ground assessments in the early stages of the crisis. Dmitry Sablin, a member of the Russian Federation Council (the upper body of the parliament) and its committee on defence and security, was part of the delegation travelling with the patriarch of Moscow (the primate of the Russian Orthodox Church) on his 2013–14 Christmastime tour with the relics of the Gifts of the Magi through Russia, Ukraine and Belarus (*RBTH* 2013). Before September 2013, Sablin was a State Duma deputy and the first deputy chairman of the CIS and Compatriots Committee, thus heavily responsible for affairs with ethnic Russians abroad. In January 2014, the patriarch's delegation made an unscheduled stop at the Belbek military airfield outside of Simferopol in Crimea. Sablin contacted Rustam Temirgaliev and asked him to arrange a meeting with the Crimean leadership. Temirgaliev later stated that he believed Sablin was on the patriarch's trip because he was his long-time friend and 'lobbyist' in Moscow (Kozlov 2015), which meant that Sablin was able to leverage that relationship to gain access to Crimea's senior politicians. Temirgaliev brought Vladimir Konstantinov with him to meet Sablin, who asked them if they were ready 'to raise the banner of an independent or at least absolutely autonomous Crimea' if the situation in Kyiv worsened. Temirgaliev also said that two 'Orthodox priests' oddly sat in on these confidential political discussions. He suggested that they were Russian government officials, likely from the security services, in disguise. Temirgaliev called the meeting 'the first serious conversation [. . .] on the subject of the subsequent events', and Sablin gave him the impression that he was speaking with authority from Moscow (Kozlov 2015). Notably, these discussions occurred over a month before Yanukovych fled from Kyiv, suggesting that the Russian government was already preparing the conditions for the annexation operation before the crisis reached its worst.

Other Russian parliamentarians followed in the next month. On the night of 24 February, a delegation of four Russian State Duma deputies led by Leonid Slutsky, the chairman of the CIS and Compatriots Committee – and thus Sablin's former superior – arrived in Simferopol. While their official purpose was to discuss means for Ukrainian citizens to gain Russian passports, Crimean prime minister Anatolii Mohyliov publicly accused them of meeting with factional Crimean politicians to discuss the future of the peninsula (Matsuzato 2016: 245). Konstantin Zatulin, Slutsky's first deputy chairman in the CIS and Compatriots

Committee, later admitted that he was also in Crimea in this time frame and met with Alexey Chaly (RBK 2016). Vladimir Zhirinovsky, leader of the far-right, nationalist Liberal Democratic Party (to which Slutsky also belongs), was in Crimea 27–28 February. In Sevastopol, he told the gathered crowd, 'I want you to know the position of Moscow is that you will not be left alone or be in trouble' (Salem 2014). Zhirinovsky's fiery rhetoric could be discounted as typical for his politics, especially since he was not in a position to give official Russian government positions. However, hacked text messages from Timur Prokopenko, the deputy head of the internal affairs department of the Russian Presidential Administration, show that Zhirinovsky reported to him with updates on his activities during the trip (TSN 2015).

Two aides from President Putin's personal staff, Vladislav Surkov and Sergey Glazyev (Kremlin 2017), were also instrumental in orchestrating the political operations during the annexation. Surkov is one of Russia's most significant practitioners of 'political technology' – the practice in post-Soviet states of manipulating political results (see Wilson 2014). In his own words, his 'portfolio at the Kremlin and in government has included ideology, media, political parties, religion, modernization, innovation, [and] foreign relations' (Pomerantsev 2014). He is considered one of the architects of the concept of 'sovereign democracy', which calls for strong national leadership, military might, limited foreign investment and economic independence to overcome the chaos Russia experienced in the 1990s (Herd 2010). Under this ideology, Putin's United Russia party has become the dominant force not only in politics but in the various sectors of Russian society (Glikin et al. 2011). Part of Surkov's portfolio was to improve Russia's position in Ukraine, especially starting after the Orange Revolution in 2004. As the situation worsened in 2014, Surkov made numerous trips in early February to both Kyiv and Crimea. Besides meeting with Yanukovych and his loyal politicians and businessmen, Surkov met with the key future collaborators in Crimea – Aksyonov, Konstantinov and Temirgaliev (Marson 2017; Interview C 2017; Kozlov 2015). These trips helped arrange the 20 February meeting in Moscow between Konstantinov and Sergey Naryshkin, his counterpart in the Russian State Duma, after which Konstantinov declared his openness to reunification (Kravtsova 2014).

Glazyev was at one time a critic of Putin before the president co-opted him into the government and made him one of his key operatives. He co-founded the nationalist *Rodina* political party and ran in the 2004 Russian presidential election, but he then quit politics in 2007 after accusing Putin's government of eliminating all political opposition (*Moscow Times* 2012). In 2012, Putin surprisingly appointed him as an aide to manage the development of the Customs Union between Russia, Belarus and Kazakhstan (Kremlin 2012).[2] In late 2013, Putin sent Glazyev to Ukraine to convince its leadership that turning away from the Customs Union in favour of closer ties with the European Union (EU) would lead to economic disaster. After Yanukovych walked away from the November 2013 EU summit in Vilnius without signing the Ukraine-European Union Association Agreement (the treaty designed to converge Ukraine's economic and political policies with those of the EU and its member states), Glazyev was honoured as Russia's 'Person of the Year 2013' at a special ceremony in Moscow's Cathedral of Christ the Saviour for his efforts in 'bringing Ukraine back into the economic union with Russia' (Neef and Schepp 2013). As the situation deteriorated in early 2014, however, Glazyev returned to Ukraine as Russia's plans for the south and east of the country intensified. Konstantin Zatulin admitted that Glazyev was with him in some of his meetings with Crimean officials (RBK 2016). Glazyev remained a key conduit between Moscow and Aksyonov throughout the political crisis, including guiding him on the specifics of the referendum. The Prosecutor General of Ukraine has since brought charges against Glazyev in connection with his activities in February and March 2014 (Prosecutor General's Office of Ukraine 2016a).

The Russian government deployed serving and former Russian military officers as its representatives to manage the operation, as well. Oleg Belaventsev, a retired vice admiral of the Russian Navy, was at the time of the crisis the general director of JSC 'Slavyanka', the company that manages barracks and housing for the Russian Armed Forces. In this role, he was one of Russian defence minister Sergey Shoigu's key deputies. Belaventsev was in Crimea in February 2014 and instrumental in deciding who would become the next prime minister in the new regime. Temirgaliev said that Belaventsev's 'role in the process of reuniting Crimea with Russia [wa]s really very great' (Kozlov 2015). According to Chaly, Menyailo replaced him as governor of Sevastopol because Belaventsev recommended it to Putin (Hobson 2016). Also participating in Belaventsev's meetings in Crimea was Admiral Alexander Fedotenkov, the deputy commander-in-chief of the Russian Navy and the previous commander of the Russian Black Sea Fleet (Zhegulyov 2017). Numerous other Russian military officers and defence officials also travelled to Crimea during the crisis to negotiate directly with the Ukrainian Armed Forces.

---

[2]   The Eurasian Economic Union superseded the Customs Union after Armenia and Kyrgyzstan joined in 2015 (Knobel 2017; Khitakhunov et al. 2017).

As in the Soviet campaigns, the Russian government deployed these officials to manage the annexation operation and direct its allies within Crimea accordingly. They were instrumental in producing the desired political results to legitimize Russia's military operation. The following section discusses how the Russian government achieved those results through the same manufacturing of the political process that the Soviet government employed in its political warfare operations.

# Manufacturing the political process

In its political warfare campaigns, the Soviet government manufactured and falsified the political process in the target country in order to produce results that appeared to legitimize Soviet actions or create regimes favourable to the Soviet Union. The communist ruling elite throughout the Bloc had a similar attitude towards democratic processes as it did towards the 'truth' – they were a tool to be manipulated in pursuit of policy objectives. German communist leader Walter Ulbricht captured it well when he told his inner circle his plans for them to seize power in East Germany after the Second World War: 'it must look democratic, but we must control everything' (Grieder 1999: 14). Even though the results were largely fabricated, the *appearance* of the democratic process was critical because it allowed them to claim that their rise to power was legitimate. In its political warfare conflicts, the Soviet Union heavily manufactured the political processes in the targeted countries in order to claim the legitimacy of its interventions. In Crimea, the Russian government placed the same importance on the appearance of legitimacy and employed some of the same techniques to manipulate the political process to achieve the desired result – but avoided some of the mistakes its Soviet predecessors had made.

## Czechoslovakia 1968

During the Prague Spring, the Soviet Union conspired with its collaborators in the Czechoslovak regime to force a change in leadership. They planned to use the existing CPCz political procedures to install a new government that would request Soviet assistance, thus justifying the Warsaw Pact invasion of the country to remove the 'counter-revolutionary threat'. Leonid Brezhnev summarized the political plan during a meeting with the leaders of the Warsaw Pact Five in Moscow on 18 August 1968. Indra, Bil'ak, Kolder and their fellow collaborators had promised that '[a]t midnight at the [P]residium session they will try to insist on a definitive split and adopt a resolution expressing political no-confidence in the right-wing and take upon themselves the *de facto* leadership of the party and government' (Brezhnev 1968a: 397–8). Indra had passed word through Soviet ambassador Chervonenko that he would get six of the eleven members of the Presidium and an additional fifty members of the CPCz Central Committee to back his resolution by the time the Warsaw Pact troops entered the country, giving the Soviet government the political legitimacy it sought (Kramer 1993). The key conspirators met in Indra's office in the morning of 20 August to finalize the plan previously drafted with their Soviet contacts. The day's Presidium session started at 2.00 pm, and one issue on the agenda was a position paper from Indra and Kolder on the dangers of the 'counter-revolutionary forces' operating in the country. They believed they could convince a majority of the Presidium members to vote to endorse their position. From there, the discussion would lead to a request for 'fraternal assistance' from Moscow and the removal of Dubček to establish a 'revolutionary workers' and peasants' government' in time for the Warsaw Pact forces to enter the country (Mlynář 1980: 201–3).

However, the plan failed. Dubček left Indra and Kolder's discussion until the end of the Presidium session late in the evening; by that time, their debate was interrupted with the news that the Warsaw Pact troops had already crossed the border. Instead of voting on Indra and Kolder's proposals, the Presidium then debated how to respond to the invasion. In another failure for the collaborators, Presidium members Jan Piller and František Barbírek chose to side with Dubček, meaning the body voted seven-to-four to *condemn* the invasion (Tigrid 1971: 104; Dawisha 1984: 322; Navratil 1998: 313). StB officers then accompanied KGB officers into the building to arrest Dubček and his fellow reformers Josef Smrkovský, František Kriegel and Josef Špaček 'in the name of the Workers' and Peasants' Government led by Comrade Indra' (Dubček 1993: 183). They did not realize that Indra's motion had failed. No such revolutionary government had formed; Dubček was still the Czechoslovak leader. The plan's critical sequence of events – the removal of Dubček, the installation of a new government, the request for assistance and then the military invasion – failed because the collaborators did not force the issue in time. Furthermore, they did not have the political support within the Presidium that they claimed. The Soviet plan relied on its co-conspirators in the CPCz to utilize the Presidium's legitimate political processes to bring themselves to power and to invite in the invading forces. It failed because they did not have the levels of support they led their Soviet partners to believe, and they did not have the means to override the political system. While the military invasion continued as planned, it began without its intended cover of political legitimacy.

After the arrest of Dubček and his key lieutenants, the Czechoslovak collaborators were still unable to form a new government. The Czechoslovak population had not reacted as expected; a Soviet Politburo report estimated that the population was initially 50–60 per cent in support of the invasion, but that within a matter of days, 75–90 per cent saw it as 'an act of occupation' (CPSU CC Politburo 1968c: 548–9). Offset by their failure to take control of the government and the negative public reaction, the Czechoslovak collaborators seemingly lost their nerve. Kirill Mazurov, on the ground as the Politburo's special representative, expressed his frustration in a report from 21 August:

> Our friends have gone to pieces, and are not showing the initiative and firmness of purpose that they should have displayed immediately [. . .] We are insisting to our friends that they form a new government without further delay, and that they begin appealing to the people. (Mazurov 1968: 452)

Impatient with their lack of progress, Soviet ambassador Chervonenko called thirteen Czechoslovak officials to the embassy at 5.00 pm on 22 August to push them to form the 'Provisional Revolutionary Workers' and Peasants' Government'. Despite significant jockeying, they could not decide on who would lead the new regime. No one would volunteer to serve as first secretary. Indra, now aware of the strongly negative reaction from the Czechoslovak people, even warned, 'The stigma of treason will be left on everyone who takes over' (Files of Gustáv Husák 1968: 460–3). The high command of the invading Warsaw Pact forces issued an ultimatum that the CPCz form the revolutionary government by 6.00 pm, but the deadline passed without action. After Czechoslovak president Ludvík Svoboda rebuffed Chervonenko's offer for him to lead the revolutionary government in a separate, last-ditch meeting later that night, the Soviet leadership relented and allowed him and a small delegation to fly to Moscow to negotiate for Dubček's release (Tigrid 1971: 110). Despite the Soviet government's efforts in finding and cultivating its collaborators in the ranks of the CPCz and its plans for them to form a new government that backed the invasion, their co-conspirators lost their conviction as the plan began to unravel.

The Soviet plan also failed because it did not effectively seize the different instruments of the Czechoslovak government. The invading forces did not arrive at the CPCz Central Committee building until the morning after Indra and Kolder's key speech in the Presidium, meaning not only could they not ensure that the proceedings went according to their plan, but they also could not prevent the body from subsequently voting to condemn the invasion (Tigrid 1971: 104; Dawisha 1984: 322). The invading forces did not take control of Czechoslovakia's foreign policy structures, either. The Politburo's official after action review faulted the planners for failing 'to provide for the swift occupation of the Ministry of Foreign Affairs to compel them to transmit the appropriate orders' (CPSU CC Politburo 1968c: 547). The Soviet forces had not specifically targeted the ministry; furthermore, Czechoslovak foreign minister Jiří Hájek was abroad at the time of the invasion. As a result, the Dubček regime continued to issue declarations condemning the invasion, undermining the Soviet argument that its forces were invited. Within hours of the invasion, Czechoslovak ambassador to the United Nations Jan Mužík told the Security Council, 'We categorically request the immediate withdrawal of the armed forces of the five states of the Warsaw Treaty and full respect for the state sovereignty of the Czechoslovak Socialist Republic.' Soviet ambassador Jacob Malik tried to retort with the Soviet Union's official propaganda line that '[t]he armed forces of socialist countries, as is well known, entered the territory of the Czechoslovak Socialist Republic on the request of the country's leaders'. As the Security Council continued its deliberations into an unprecedented fourth day, Hájek flew into New York himself to refute the Soviet position and insisted, 'No such demand was ever made' (Vaughan 2012).

In Czechoslovakia, the Soviet government conspired with its Czechoslovak partners to orchestrate the political steps to provide apparent legitimacy to the impending Warsaw Pact invasion. However, it relied on its collaborators to utilize the valid political processes within the Presidium to remove Dubček, take power and request Soviet military assistance. Their efforts failed when they did not get the necessary political support, meaning the invasion awkwardly unfolded as pre-planned, with its forces invoking the authority of a government that did not exist.

## Afghanistan 1979

In the invasion of Afghanistan, the Soviet Union attempted to avoid these mistakes it made in Czechoslovakia: it did not rely on the legitimate political processes in the country but instead simply published the desired results after the military operation was complete. However, because no actual events occurred, the Soviet government and its Afghan partners provided contradictory information and failed to convey a unified narrative. On 27 December 1979, Soviet forces assassinated Hafizullah Amin to clear the way for Babrak Karmal to take power. Brezhnev then sent Karmal a letter in which he wrote, 'I heartily congratulate you on [your] election as General Secretary of the PDPA and high government posts of the Democratic Republic of Afghanistan' (Brezhnev 1979). Those additional positions were chairman of the Revolutionary Council and prime minister, thus consolidating all political power in Afghanistan in the Soviet Union's chosen man. At 2.40 am, the fabricated version of Kabul radio broadcast from the Soviet military headquarters in Termez read an announcement from the alleged Revolutionary Council's secretariat that named Karmal as the new general secretary of the PDPA and president of Afghanistan. Fifteen minutes later, another announcement claimed that the new government 'earnestly demands that the USSR render urgently, political, moral, and economic assistance, including military aid, to Afghanistan' and that the Soviet government had accepted the request. At 3.15 am, a third announcement proclaimed that the 'revolutionary tribunal has sentenced to death Hafizullah Amin for the crimes he has committed against the noble people of Afghanistan' (Hammond 1984: 100; Bradsher 1999: 98–9). This published version of events allowed the Soviet government to claim that its military intervention was legitimate because the government of Afghanistan had legally transferred power to Amin, who then requested the Soviet assistance. It produced the results that the CPCz collaborators in Czechoslovakia had failed to achieve.

Despite these proclamations, no such events occurred. No revolutionary tribunal or any other Afghan political body met that night; some of those who allegedly participated in Karmal's election, including Sultan Ali Keshtmand and Absul Qader, were in prison at the time (Collins 1986: 78). When foreign governments later pointed out that the Soviet military invasion began hours before the new Afghan government's supposed request for assistance was published, Karmal claimed that the meetings to request it had actually occurred earlier that evening (Bradsher 1999: 94). In truth, Karmal himself was not even in Kabul the night of 27 December, let alone part of any extraordinary political sessions; he was still under KGB protection at the Bagram airbase north of the city (Braithwaite 2012: 103). He variously claimed that he had crossed the Pakistan-Afghanistan border in August, October or November and begun to organize support for his rise to power; however, after Soviet forces finally withdrew in 1989, he admitted that he did not learn of the planned Soviet invasion and change in government until '[j]ust before it began' (Bradsher 1999: 94). The public announcements claimed that Karmal and his tribunal had tried and executed Amin, but in reality, Soviet forces disguised as Afghans killed Amin in the Tajbeg Palace. While the Soviet government presented the invasion as a legitimate response to assistance from the newly elected Afghan leader, none of the events the narrative relied upon actually occurred. As a result, the conflicting reports undermined its claims for legitimacy and led to increased condemnation on the international stage.

In 1968, the Soviet government trusted their Czechoslovak allies to successfully navigate the political process and seize power through normal procedure. However, the plan backfired when the collaborators failed to gain the necessary votes to pass their measure, remove Dubček from power and request Soviet assistance before the invading troops arrived. As a result, the Warsaw Pact forces invaded Czechoslovakia without the surrogate government ready to take power, undermining their argument that the operation was at the request of the Czechoslovaks. In 1979, the Soviet government did not attempt to utilize the proper political process in Afghanistan. It used its forces to capture key government facilities, depose Amin and install Karmal. It then acted as if the correct procedures had been followed, announcing that Amin had been tried by a revolutionary tribunal and that the PDPA had elected Karmal its next leader – even though no such events took place. The appearance of political legitimacy was still important to the Soviet government, but it did not risk the failure of the political process as it had in Czechoslovakia. However, the lack of transparency or a unified narrative of events quickly undermined the Soviet Union's argument that the process was valid.

## Crimea 2014

In 2014, the Russian government appeared to reapply the Soviet technique of manufacturing the political process, but it also appeared to have learned from the lessons of both Czechoslovakia and Afghanistan. As its Soviet predecessors had done, the Russian government still fabricated the political process in Crimea to provide the appearance of legitimacy for the annexation. Many of the political tactics and techniques it employed mirrored those in the Soviet operations. Unlike in Czechoslovakia, however, it first asserted control over Crimea's political institutions and then conducted the legal proceedings in questionable circumstances to ensure that they delivered the desired results. The Russian leadership also denied that it had deployed its forces to the peninsula, claiming that its unmarked soldiers were legitimate local-defence forces, thus allowing Russia to deny that it was interfering with the Crimean political process. Unlike in Afghanistan, the Russian government made a public display of the Crimean Rada's decision-making and the referendum on Crimea's status to make the political proceedings appear open. In this way, the Crimean annexation operation applied these Soviet techniques in a manner that achieved a balance between the overt expression of the Crimean political process and the covert control of its results.

The political process that culminated with the annexation was the result of a Russian government plan, not an organic Crimean movement. According to Rustam Temirgaliev, one of the most significant Crimean collaborators, 'Looking back, we can say unequivocally that the entire operation was very seriously analytically thought out. Here, in Moscow, in the Kremlin, someone planned it' (Kozlov 2015). Putin's public statements since the annexation have indirectly confirmed this fact. In 2015, he said that he initiated the active phase of the Russian military operation in Ukraine on the night of 22 February 2014 – the day after Viktor Yanukovych fled Kyiv. He said that he 'invited senior members of our special services and the Defence Ministry to the Kremlin' and gave them two tasks: (1) help Yanukovych out of Ukraine and (2) 'begin working on returning Crimea to Russia' (Kondrashov 2015). On the first point, Putin had revealed a few months prior that Russian forces secretly operating in Ukraine had moved Yanukovych to Crimea and then exfiltrated him to Russia (Putin 2014). On the second point, Putin identified that his decision to begin the annexation process predated any domestic political developments that occurred in Crimea – including the appointment of Sergey Aksyonov as prime minister and the decision to hold a referendum. He is thus suggesting that Russian officials operating on his orders created the conditions for those political developments to occur. In the month after the annexation, presidential spokesman Dmitry Peskov in effect confirmed that Putin was the driver behind the annexation when he stated that the decision 'on the reunification of Crimea with Russia [. . .] was a personal decision of the head of state' (*Korrespondent* 2014).

In February 2015, the Russian newspaper *Novaya Gazeta* published an unverified government policy memorandum that closely paralleled not only Russia's operations in Crimea but its broader plans for Eastern Ukraine. *Novaya Gazeta* is one of the last remaining Russian publications critical of the government; in October 2014, the Russian federal media compliance agency *Roskomnadzor* issued a warning to the paper for 'using mass media to carry out extremist activities' after a series of articles critical of the Russian government (*Roskomnadzor* 2014), and close to a dozen of its journalists have been murdered or survived such attempts since 2000 (DW 2017). The newspaper claimed it received the government policy memorandum from sources in the Russian

Presidential Administration and that it was from sometime between 4 and 12 February 2014 – before the critical sequence of events in Kyiv or Crimea. The document warned that Viktor Yanukovych was 'rapidly losing control of the political process' and that his 'time in power could end at any moment'. It predicted that 'civil war' would soon break out in Ukraine and suggested the strategy excerpted here:

> In these circumstances, it seems appropriate to play along the centrifugal aspirations of the various regions of the country, with a view to initiate the accession of its eastern regions to Russia, in one form or another. Crimea and the Kharkiv region should become the dominant regions for making such efforts, as there already exist reasonably large groups there that support the idea of maximum integration with Russia [. . .] To start the process of a 'pro-Russian drift' of Crimea and the eastern Ukrainian territories, [certain] events should be created beforehand that can support this process with political legitimacy and moral justification [. . . T]he grounds to hold referendums in Crimea and in the Kharkiv region (and then in other regions) should be created, so as to decide on the issue of self-determination and the further possibility of joining the Russian Federation. It is important to organize informal meetings of the leaders or representatives of the eastern regions of Ukraine in Moscow, where they would be supported and given political guarantees (at least, verbal) by an official with sufficient powers [. . .] It is of extreme importance for the 'world community' to have little to no reason to doubt the legitimacy and fairness of these referendums [. . .] (Lipsky 2015)

The memorandum reads like KGB officer Mikhail Sagatelyan's action plan for Czechoslovakia – the plan which the Soviet forces attempted to undertake in 1968. Just as Sagatelyan called for fostering a pro-Soviet faction within the Czechoslovak leadership, the Russian plan called for targeting the pro-Russian population groups in Eastern Ukraine and Crimea. The plan for Czechoslovakia sought to create the conditions for a special plenary session of the CPCz Central Committee to remove Dubček and request Soviet assistance, and the Russian plan sought to create the conditions to hold referendums to break from the central Ukrainian government and request Russian assistance. While the end states of the Czechoslovak and Crimean campaigns were not the same (the establishment of a friendly regime versus the annexation of territory), the political tools implemented to manufacture the political process bear a striking resemblance. Not all aspects of the alleged Russian government document occurred (e.g. it recommended a more gradual Customs Union integration prior to unification), but the different means and objectives it suggested closely followed the Crimean course of events – which in turn appears to have followed previous examples from Soviet political warfare campaigns.

### *Crimean Rada session to change the government and hold the referendum*

Like the 20 August 1968 CPCz Presidium session, an emergency session of the Crimean Rada in which Russia's collaborators could orchestrate a change in government and open the door to Russian involvement was the critical first step in the manufactured political process. On 25 February 2014, around 400 pro-Russian demonstrators rallied outside of the Crimean Rada building and demanded that the parliament take up the issue of Crimea's legal status. Temirgaliev later noted that Aksyonov had a 'mobilization structure' from his time in charge of the Civic Asset of Crimea, the social–political organization that formed half of the Russian Unity party, with which he 'could gather from 500 to 1,000 people – not without costs, of course' (Kozlov 2015). Whether the demonstrators that day were paid participants from Aksyonov's network is unclear. The result, however, was that the Rada agreed to hold an emergency session the following day (The Ukrainian Helsinki Human Rights Union 2017). Speaking to the press before the start of the session on 26 February, Rada chairman Vladimir Konstantinov asserted that 'the agenda does not include the issue of Crimea's separation from Ukraine' and that any suggestion to the contrary was 'a provocation for the purpose of discrediting the Rada [. . . and] depriving it of its legitimacy'. The public denouncement was not unlike his earlier statements insisting there were no plans to discuss independence. In reality, Konstantinov, Temirgaliev and Aksyonov were secretly plotting to put before the Rada that day a motion not only to remove Crimean prime minister Anatolii Mohyliov but to vote on the 'possible' reunification of Crimea with Russia (Matsuzato 2016: 246–7).

The 26 February emergency session, however, failed to materialize. Two massive rallies gathered outside of the building and confronted one another. One crowd, composed mostly of the Russian Unity party, members of the 'Crimean People's Militia' and Cossack organizations, chanted pro-Russian slogans and accused Kyiv of being overrun by 'Nazis' and 'fascism'. The rival crowd, composed heavily of Crimean Tatars as well as some 'Euromaidan-Crimea' Ukrainian activists, shouted that 'Crimea is not Russia' (Kliatskin 2016; The Ukrainian Helsinki Human Rights Union 2017). Because of the unrest outside and the strong emotions surrounding the potential vote on 'reunification', the Rada failed to reach a quorum. Several deputies, especially those from the Crimean

Tatar Qurultai-Rukh faction, refused to leave their offices for the chamber floor. Deputy Leonid Pilunksy claimed that the pro-Russian lawmakers threatened him and his colleagues after they refused to register as present (de Carbonnel 2014b).

The chamber did not reach the required fifty-one deputies; the press had been allowed to witness the session and could see quorum was not met (Kozlov 2015). Konstantinov was therefore forced to call off the session (Matsuzato 2016: 246–7). The plan to follow standard legal procedure had failed. The Russian government's Crimean collaborators could not muster enough deputies to force a vote on removing the existing regime and appealing for direct Russian assistance. Without such a vote, the Russian government could not claim that these moves were the valid wishes of the Crimean people. Any (overt) action on Russia's part without the vote risked undermining its argument of legitimacy – just as the failed vote in the CPCz Presidium had caused such issues in 1968.

The solution was to seize control of the Crimean Rada and force the vote the following day. During the night of 26–27 February, Russian special forces without insignia departed Sevastopol in two Kamaz military trucks. They arrived at the Crimean Rada and Council of Ministers buildings in Simferopol, disarmed the security and took control of the buildings. The soldiers stated that they were local self-defence forces there to guard the Crimean government and to allow an extraordinary session to take place (*Vzglyad Business Newspaper* 2014). However, one eyewitness interviewed early that morning said that he saw men 'armed to their teeth' surrounding the buildings, and when he questioned who they were, they admitted flatly, 'We are Russians' (Kliatskin 2016). According to some sources, the units involved were from FSB *Vympel* and the 45th *Spetsnaz* Regiment. They had arrived in Sevastopol on the landing ships coming from the Sochi Olympics (Interview with Mykhailo Gonchar 2017). Putin later signed a decree designating 27 February as Special Operations Forces Day in Russia (Belousov 2015), thus indirectly confirming that these forces were the ones who seized the Crimean Rada. In control of the parliamentary buildings, the Russian forces could then set the conditions for the vote – and the desired results – that had failed to happen the day before.

For his part, Aksyonov claims that he did not know about the seizure until he received a phone call early the next morning (Kondrashov 2015). That Aksyonov was not aware of Russia's plan to seize the buildings is questionable. However, the picture he is painting is that Russian forces seized the main government buildings of Crimea without the consent, knowledge or request of one of their key collaborators, meaning it would have been a unilateral Russian decision. Unlike his openness on the rest of the operation, Temirgaliev refused to answer questions about the emergence of the 'green men', but he asserted that 'the role of the Crimean elites in these processes [wa]s secondary' to the Russian decision-makers (Kozlov 2015). He thus also presents the situation as such that the Russian leadership, not the Crimean politicians, drove the decision to seize the Rada to ensure the necessary 'vote' was held.

With unmarked Russian forces in control of the parliament building and a Russian flag flying from its roof, the Crimean Rada held the emergency session in the morning of 27 February. At its conclusion, Olga Sulnikova, the head of the information and analytical department of the Crimean Rada, reported to Russian media that the body made three key decisions: of the sixty-four deputies she reported were present, fifty-five passed a motion of no-confidence in the Council of Ministers and ordered Anatolii Mohyliov and his entire cabinet to resign; fifty-three voted for Sergey Aksyonov to replace him as prime minister; and sixty-one voted to hold a referendum on Crimea's 'sovereignty' on 25 May, the day of the planned Ukrainian presidential election (Interfax 2014a, 2014d). The published results of the session gave the Russian government the superficial legitimacy it sought. Mohyliov, whom the Russian officials working in Crimea had failed to court (discussed in next section), had become an impediment to Russian plans for the peninsula and was swept aside, just as was the plan for Dubček and the Czechoslovak reformers before him. Aksyonov, a pro-Russian politician who was already working behind the scenes with Russian officials, took his place. The Crimean Rada took the first critical vote setting the peninsula on course for annexation.

The appearance of the session's legitimacy was critical to the Russian government and its Crimean partners. Olga Sulnikova stressed that the entire process followed legal procedure, including the requirement for the Ukrainian president to concur with the choice for Crimean prime minister (Interfax 2014a). Putin stated a year later that Yanukovych 'approved this appointment' (Kondrashov 2015), and Russia had purportedly sent a fax to the Crimean Rada with Yanukovych's signature (Kozlov 2015). However, the Verkhovna Rada had voted to remove Yanukovych from power on 22 February after he fled the capital (Verkhovna Rada of Ukraine 2014), meaning even if he did somehow approve the appointment, he was no longer in a position to do so. Putin also strongly stressed the legality and legitimacy of the vote, asserting that 'in terms of respecting Ukrainian law, everything was honoured and respected [. . .] From a legal perspective, there is no way you can fault it' (Kondrashov 2015). After he later admitted that Russia used its armed forces during the vote, he insisted that they were only 'to ensure that Crimea's parliament was able to operate, so that it could convene a meeting and carry out the activities prescribed by law' (Kondrashov 2015). In the Russian government's narrative, the Russian military – which Putin and other Russian officials denied was involved on numerous occasions until months later – merely facilitated the legitimate actions of the Crimean Rada.

Despite these public defences, the actual course of the emergency Rada session was far from legitimate. The armed men outside of the building blocked some deputies and Crimean officials from entering, including Mohyliov, even though he was the legitimate prime minister of Crimea and lead representative of the Party of Regions, which controlled 80 of the 100 Crimean Rada seats (de Carbonnel 2014b). Unmarked Russian servicemen and militiamen were in the Rada chamber during the proceedings and confiscated the deputies' mobile phones when they entered, partially to ensure that no images of the Russian servicemen ended up on social media (Kozlov 2015). They also followed deputies to the toilet on their breaks. Deputy Leonid Pilunksy told media that the vote was fixed and occurred behind closed doors without the chance for other members of the Rada to respond. Some Crimean deputies did not show up for the session because the new government in Kyiv had requested that the Crimean Rada suspend its operations. Other deputies, including Nikolay Sumulidi, have claimed that no more than thirty-seven deputies were in attendance, thus falling well below the quorum required to hold a vote (Wilson 2014). Temirgaliev even later reported that only fifty-three deputies were in the chamber, despite the fact that the Rada published that sixty-four members voted (Kozlov 2015). Other deputies have alleged that at least ten of the votes supposedly cast were from members who were not physically present (Kuzio 2015). One such deputy from the Party of Regions told Reuters, 'I wasn't even in Simferopol but my vote was counted [. . .] After the first vote was fabricated, they told us that they would open criminal cases against anyone who spoke out' (de Carbonnel 2014b). He claimed that duplicate voting cards were taken from the Rada's safe and used to cast their votes, but fear of reprisals after a series of threatening phone calls and text messages kept him and the others silent. Ukrainian and Western journalists were not allowed in the chamber, so unlike on 26 February, no independent verification of the number of deputies present occurred (Blockmans 2015).

Russian defence minister Sergey Shoigu admitted a year later that Russia essentially contrived the Crimean Rada session. He said that the 27 February vote 'was a forced measure, because there were a lot of instigators and agitators', referring to the pro-Ukrainian and Crimean Tatar rallies and the Crimean deputies refusing to vote on the issue. He said that Russia's decision to deploy 'polite people' – the preferred Russian term for 'little green men' – to ensure the vote happened was not 'accidental', and that their presence meant that the Rada's 'decision was adopted at that point' (Kondrashov 2015). Shoigu, in effect, stated that the key vote that started Crimea on the path to annexation happened because Russian Armed Forces controlled the process. Igor Girkin, a former Russian security services officer who was by his own admission in Crimea since 21 February, also confirmed that several of the deputies who did vote only did so under military force. He stated that the so-called Crimean self-defence militia, of which he claimed to be one of the commanders, 'collected together the deputies and drove them into their hall so they would make their decision' (*Neuromir TV* 2015).

### Selection of the new Crimean prime minister

With the Crimean Rada building in Russian control and the conditions set to hold the emergency session, the next task for the Russian governmental representatives was to determine who would emerge from it as the next prime minister. The Russian government had first attempted to court the serving prime minister, Anatolii Mohyliov. Mohyliov was a Yanukovych loyalist who had served as head of Crimea since 2011. The January delegation accompanying the Gifts of the Magi contacted Temirgaliev because he had a personal relationship with Dmitry Sablin and was Mohyliov's deputy. They asked Temirgaliev to set up a meeting with Mohyliov, but the prime minister refused. Sablin and his party then met with Temirgaliev and Konstantinov instead. Soon afterwards, Russian presidential aide Vladislav Surkov flew to Simferopol, and this time Mohyliov agreed to meet. However, Surkov left the meeting dissatisfied and returned to Moscow (Kozlov 2015). Mohyliov continued to oppose the secessionist movement. After Konstantinov made his statements on 20 February in Moscow about the possibility of reunification, Mohyliov responded, 'I have repeatedly stated and declared that Crimea is an integral part of Ukraine. This is a historical fact that exists regardless of anyone's desire or unwillingness' (*Krym. Kommentarii* 2014b).

Unable to court the serving prime minister, the Russian officials turned to the last Soviet leader of Crimea, Leonid Grach. A career communist, Grach was the senior party official in Crimea at the collapse of the Soviet Union. He then headed the Communist Party of Crimea as a Ukrainian political party in the following decades. He served from 1998 to 2002 as chairman of the Crimean Rada (the position Konstantinov held at the time of the annexation) and then as a deputy in the national Verkhovna Rada until 2012. At the time of the annexation, he was out of government. A staunch pro-Russian politician, Grach has stated that he maintained contacts with the FSB starting in 2005 in the aftermath of the Orange Revolution. He met his handler, an FSB general, in Moscow and in Kuban, the Russian region directly east of Crimea (Zhegulyov 2017). Like his Afghan predecessors Nur Muhammad Taraki and Babrak Karmal, Grach was thus an agent of the Russian security services, which may have made him the Russian government's preferred target for prime minister.

In an interview three years after the annexation (Zhegulyov 2017), Grach revealed the specifics of Russia's plans to install him as the next leader of Crimea.[3] The details strongly reflect the Soviet Union's negotiations with Karmal in 1979. On 23 February 2014, Grach received a call from an old friend of his, Yuri Khaliullin, who was previously the deputy commander of the Soviet Black Sea Fleet and at that time worked at JSC 'Slavyanka'. He said he was in Crimea and wanted to introduce him to his colleague: Oleg Belaventsev – JSC 'Slavyanka's' general director and one of Russian defence minister Sergey Shoigu's key deputies. They discussed the situation in Crimea and questioned Grach on his thoughts about the future of the peninsula.

In the late evening of 26 February – after that day's failed Crimean Rada session – the men returned to Grach's house, this time with Admiral Alexander Fedotenkov, the deputy commander-in-chief of the Russian Navy. The group set up a special communications system in his house and connected him directly with Shoigu, who told him he would be appointed prime minister of Crimea the following day. Grach happily accepted but warned him that Konstantinov and the Party of Regions would resist his appointment. Shoigu said they would take care of it. Later that night, Grach met near the Cathedral of St. Peter and St. Paul in Simferopol with Fedotenkov, Khaliullin and an FSB officer, who likewise instructed him to accept the role of prime minister the next morning. However, Grach learned at the meeting that both Konstantinov and Aksyonov had met with the contingent before him – about what, he was not sure (Zhegulyov 2017).

On 27 February, Grach was waiting in his office with some of his Russian contacts for the critical phone call. Instead, he received word through his

[3]  It is possible that Grach, like Temirgaliev, was exceptionally frank in the interview because he did not receive the political powers initially promised to him.

channels that the Crimean Rada had voted to appoint Aksyonov as prime minister. The Russian officials shrugged and told him that 'it did not work out', then quietly left (Zhegulyov 2017). During the emergency Rada session, Kremlin officials had in fact proposed that the body elect Grach as the next prime minister. However, as Grach had predicted, Russia's collaborators among the deputies strongly resisted the idea because they disapproved of his authoritarian style of leadership. The Kremlin officials relented, but – in a strong echo of Ambassador Stepan Chervonenko's meetings with his CPCz allies and Politburo representative Kirill Mazurov's urgings for them to 'form a new government without further delay' – they told their allies in the Rada they needed 'to decide quickly, because events were developing rapidly'. Konstantinov convinced Temirgaliev to withdraw his candidacy and back Aksyonov, who became prime minister (Kozlov 2015). Putin later supported this version of events when he claimed that he had 'never heard of' Aksyonov until his lieutenants told him 'that the MPs of the Crimean parliament want him to represent them' (Kondrashov 2015).

Russian officials anointed Leonid Grach as the man who would 'emerge' from the Crimean political process as the next leader. However, it appears that the Russian government's representatives worked through concurrent channels with Konstantinov and Aksyonov and thus accepted Aksyonov as an alternative when Grach ran into resistance. In either case, the emergence of either man as the new prime minister of Crimea relied entirely on Russia's manipulation of the political process. The very session that brought Aksyonov to power would not have occurred had Russia's special forces not seized the Rada building and controlled the proceedings. Both Grach and Aksyonov had secretly met with Russian representatives before the vote occurred, and neither were leading political figures in Crimean politics.

### The referendum

The Russian government's next task in its political operation was the shaping of the Crimean referendum on the peninsula's future. When questioned about the Russian Presidential Administration's involvement in orchestrating the referendum, Temirgaliev confessed that it is 'clear that we were advised by the relevant structures' (Kozlov 2015). Hacked emails from Moscow-based public relations experts and political technologists reveal that Russian firms conducted much of the preparation required to execute the referendum (Hans 2014). Igor Girkin, the former Russian security services officer, stated that he assisted Aksyonov in drafting it (*Neuromir TV* 2015).

This influence is evident in the changes made to the referendum. The Crimean Rada initially announced after the 27 February emergency session that the vote would be held on 25 May, the same day as the expedited Ukrainian presidential election. The original version of the referendum had only one question: 'The Autonomous Republic of Crimea is a sovereign entity and is a part of Ukraine based on agreements and treaties: yes or no' (Verkhovna Rada of Crimea 2014a). The originally planned referendum, therefore, did not mention the possibility of becoming part of Russia. On 3 March, the Presidium of the Crimean Rada decided to move the referendum up to 30 March, but it kept the same question (Verkhovna Rada of Crimea 2014b). That same day, Konstantinov asserted in an interview that he and the new Crimean authorities were 'act[ing] exclusively within the limits of the Ukrainian Constitution and law' (Matsuzato 2016: 249). However, in a press conference the next day, Putin suggested that while he did not at that moment see the possibility of Crimea joining Russia, he emphasized the Crimeans' right to self-determination, the same 'right [that] was granted to the Albanians in Kosovo' (Kremlin 2014h).

Two days later on 6 March, the referendum drastically changed and appeared to take Putin's suggestion into account. The Crimean Rada voted to move the date again to 16 March – merely ten days after the announcement (Verkhovna Rada of Crimea 2014c). The resolution also changed the wording of the referendum. The new version had two questions, which voters were instructed to vote yes to one:

1. Are you for the reunification of Crimea with Russia as a subject of the Russian Federation?
2. Are you for the restoration of the actions of the 1992 Constitution of the Republic of Crimea and for the status of Crimea as a part of Ukraine? (Golos 2014)

Notably, neither of the two options allowed for the status quo, as the 1998 Crimean Constitution was currently law. A 'no' vote was thus not actually possible. The options were joining Russia and reinstating the levels of autonomy under the 1992 constitution that caused the 1994 crisis with Kyiv (Sasse 2007). As with the 27 February session, armed men blocked dissident deputies from entering the building or taking part in the 6 March vote (RFE/RL 2014b). The Rada announced that seventy-eight deputies backed the measure, yet several deputies said they were not present or were not told about the content of the vote beforehand. The Crimean governmental press service released a video from the session of Konstantinov addressing the chamber, but only approximately ten deputies were visible (de Carbonnel 2014b).

Other evidence points directly to Russian involvement in the decision to change the referendum. Temirgaliev stated that he, Konstantinov and Aksyonov decided to move the date to 16 March after consulting with Oleg Belaventsev, the senior Russian Defence Ministry official there to represent the Kremlin (Kozlov 2015). The Ukrainian Prosecutor General's Office also released a recording of a purported phone call between Aksyonov and Sergey Glazyev, the presidential aide, from 6 March. In it, Glazyev told Aksyonov, 'I think that the questions for the referendum are phrased badly. It is not only my point of view; we are thinking over here how to phrase them in a way that they would definitely be understood by the people.' Aksyonov replied that he was working with Russian officials who had brought with them materials 'approved by the State Duma from the viewpoint of it being able to adopt the relevant regulations' for annexation (Prosecutor General's Office of Ukraine 2016b; Makarenko and Shandra 2016).[4] The tape appears to show that the Russian government directed the shift in the planned referendum from one reaffirming Crimea's autonomy within Ukraine to one explicitly calling for reunification with Russia and thus opening the door to annexation, changes passed by the Crimean Rada that same day.

The 6 March Crimean Rada decision also declared that Crimea 'shall be a part of the Russian Federation as its constituent entity' and appealed 'to the President of the Russian Federation and the Federal Assembly of the Russian Federation to commence the procedure on accession to the Russian Federation' (Verkhovna Rada of Crimea 2014c). Temirgaliev announced that the decision came into force immediately (Khimshiashvili and Raybman 2014) – meaning that the referendum was in effect a formality to endorse their resolution. The Russian government instantly backed their decision. The very next day, the key Crimean politicians from the new regime were in Moscow. At a joint conference with Konstantinov, Valentina Matvienko, chairwoman of the Federation Council, announced, 'If the people of Crimea express their will and decide to join Russia [. . . t]he citizens of Crimea will be equal to Russian citizens, with the same salaries, pensions, social benefits and social protection.' At the same time, she condemned the Ukrainian government's decision to hold the presidential election on 25 May because a free and fair election was not possible with 'continuing violence, intimidation, illegal decisions, seizure of buildings,

---

[4]   When the Russian news agency RBK questioned Glazyev on the authenticity of the tapes, he refused to answer (RBK 2016).

humiliation of people, threats to life [. . .] and the repression of political opponents and journalists' (Walker 2014a). She expressed no such concerns about the change of leadership in Crimea or the rushed referendum.

After the referendum was held on 16 March, the publicized results further provided the Russian government with the apparent political legitimacy it sought. According to the final numbers published by Mikhail Malyshev, the head of the Crimean Rada's referendum commission, turnout was 1,274,096 (83.1 per cent), of which 1,233,002 (96.8 per cent) voted to unify with Russia (Malyshev 2014; TASS 2014). The Sevastopol City Council reported that turnout was 274,101 (89.5 per cent) with 262,041 (95.6 per cent) votes for joining Russia (Sevastopol City Council 2014). These numbers were reported widely, not only by Russian officials (Kremlin 2014a) but by the Western media (BBC 2014b; Herszenhorn 2014; Harding and Walker 2014; Withnall 2014). They appeared to show a clear mandate from the people for annexation, which Russia executed immediately. President Putin signed an executive order the following day that read, 'Given the declaration of will by the Crimean people in a nationwide referendum held on March 16, 2014, the Russian Federation is to recognize the Republic of Crimea as a sovereign and independent state, whose city of Sevastopol has a special status' (Kremlin 2014e). The Crimean declaration of independence used similar language and emphasized that it was 'based on the direct expression of the will of the peoples of the Crimea at the referendum' (Verkhovna Rada of Crimea 2014d).

Putin emphasized how the results of the referendum gave Russia's annexation legitimacy and legality in numerous speeches. He said that it was 'in full compliance with democratic procedures and international norms' (Kremlin 2014a) and referenced both Kosovo's declaration of independence and the United Nations court ruling on self-determination as justification (Putin 2014). He claimed that the annexation was 'based only on the people's will, because the people is the ultimate source of all authority' (Kremlin 2014a). Russia, in turn, merely 'answered their call and welcomed the decision of Crimea and Sevastopol' (Kremlin 2014c). The numbers showing the extremely high turnout in which voters almost universally chose to join Russia 'speak for themselves', he asserted (Kremlin 2014a). Putin later said that he would have gone through with the annexation only 'if we were absolutely confident that it was what the people there wanted us to do [. . .] I thought to myself then: whatever the people say they want, let it be so' (Kondrashov 2015). He repeatedly stressed that the referendum was a pure representation of the will of the Crimean people, and the strength of the results validated the annexation.

Upon closer examination, however, the referendum returns were highly unlikely, and various evidence suggests fraud or inflation of the results. Refat Chubarov, the chairman of the Mejlis, the representative body of the Crimean Tatar people, called for a boycott of the referendum because the 'result ha[d] already been decided by Moscow' (Bell 2014). Crimean Tatars consisted of 12 per cent of the population in Crimea. Temirgaliev estimated Crimean Tatar turnout was 40 per cent on the night of the referendum (*Gazeta.ru* 2014b), which to match the published results would mean virtually all of those Crimean Tatar votes were for unification. Based on the feelings of its leaders and the demonstrations outside of the Crimean Rada buildings on 26 February, it is highly unlikely that Crimean Tatar turnout was that high or that a super majority of them backed unification. Furthermore, the only other election in Crimea that came close to the alleged turnout for the referendum was the second round of the 2004 Ukrainian presidential election, but even then, the turnout in Crimea was 73 per cent (Ukrainian Central Election Commission 2004) – 10 per cent lower than that claimed for the referendum.[5] Japanese academic Kimitaka Matsuzato (2016: 249) reported that he spent the entire referendum day in Simferopol and saw queues forming at some polling stations before 8.00 am, suggesting that such a large turnout was possible. On the other hand, journalist Volodymyr Prytula (2017) stated that he visited some of the Simferopol polling stations that in 2004 had long queues in which people waited hours to vote. On the day of the referendum, those same stations had as few as four people. The number of polling stations was also much smaller than in previous elections, meaning such a large turnout would have been difficult to achieve. The Crimean authorities avoided establishing many of the polling stations in the predominantly Crimean Tatar regions because of the community's vocal opposition to the referendum (Charap 2014: 8) – which again calls into question the required near-unanimous yes vote among the Tatar population. The authorities also lacked the time and resources to organize polling stations in the smaller villages – villages that had stations in previous elections – so state-run television asked villagers to head to the closest city to vote. It is unlikely that pensioners living in those villages had the means or ability to make the trip (Interview with Volodymyr Prytula 2017). If they did, then the existing polling stations would have been even more crowded than in previous elections.

Different personal accounts suggest widespread voter fraud in the referendum, as well. The Kyiv government refused to release the most current list of registered

---

[5] In Crimea, 1,159,437 of 1,580,400 eligible voters participated in the second round of the 2004 presidential election (Ukrainian Central Election Commission 2004).

voters to the new Crimean authorities, so they instead relied on the registry from the 2012 parliamentary elections. Officials came to the Ukrainian military bases in the days before the referendum to confirm soldiers' names against the registry. In one instance, the deputy commander of a naval infantry unit started crossing off the names of the conscripts no longer with the unit – in 2012, it had around 50 per cent more men – and the official grew angry and told him to stop. When the Ukrainian officer checked the roster again on the day of the referendum, all of the names were back on the list, and he suspects that votes were cast on their behalf (Interview B 2017). According to the Ukrainian sailors from the corvette *Ternopil*, barricaded inside their ship in Lake Donuzlav on the day of the referendum, their families told them they witnessed numerous buses offloading passengers at their local polling stations. However, the people who disembarked to vote spoke with Russian accents, not the distinctly Crimean accent (Interview with Oleksii Kirillov 2017). Witnesses at polling stations in other cities saw similar buses of voters with Russian licence plates (Interview with Volodymyr Prytula 2017), suggesting that large groups of Russian citizens came to Crimea to vote in the referendum. Another witness was staying with friends in Crimea on the day of the referendum. His friend received a call, telling him to come back to the polling station to vote for a second time and to 'bring your family and friends' (Interview K 2017).

Public opinion surveys taken over the years in Crimea put the referendum results in perspective. Under pro-European president Viktor Yushchenko in 2009, only 2 per cent of Crimean respondents listed 'Crimean annexation to Russia' as the most important issue facing the peninsula, and 63 per cent believed that military conflict in Crimea was not very or not at all likely (International Republican Institute 2009).[6] Under the pro-Russian president Viktor Yanukovych in 2011, only 33 per cent of Crimean respondents believed that Crimea should be separated from Ukraine and become part of Russia. Even among ethnic Russians, the percentage only increased to 39 per cent (International Republican Institute 2011). A Razumkov Centre poll from the same time frame found that the number of respondents who believed violent confrontation between Ukraine's regions – one of the main propaganda themes during the 2014 crisis – was low and statistically the same in Crimea as in the whole of Ukraine (Razumkov Centre 2011: 28). Ten months before the referendum in May 2013, the number of respondents who believed Crimea should become part of Russia dropped to

---

[6] These surveys were conducted by Gallup and the Institute of Polling and Marketing for Baltic Surveys on behalf of the International Republican Institute, which received funding from the US Agency for International Development.

23 per cent (International Republican Institute 2013). In the same poll, 53 per cent of respondents wanted the current autonomous status, and another 14 per cent wanted some other status within Ukraine (i.e. Crimean Tatar autonomy or common oblast). These polls provide a more accurate representation of Crimean public opinion because they were conducted by recognized polling agencies in peacetime (Boltenkov 2014: 145).

In all likelihood, the actual turnout for the referendum was drastically lower than what was reported. A separate report from the Russian government suggested that this was likely the case. Yevgeny Bobrov, a member of the government-run President of Russia's Council on Civil Society and Human Rights, visited Crimea from 16 to 18 April 2014 to assess the social and legal problems the Crimean population may encounter as Russia integrated the peninsula into the federation. In his report, he stated that 'the opinion of almost all of the interviewed experts and citizens' he spoke with was that the actual turnout for the referendum in Crimea was 30–50 per cent with 50–60 per cent of them voting to join Russia, and in Sevastopol, turnout was 50–80 per cent with the vast majority voting in favour (Bobrov 2014). Based on these estimates, only 15–30 per cent of the eligible Crimean population both turned up and voted in favour of unifying with Russia – a far cry from the widely reported 82 per cent. Once Western media (Gregory 2014) found and published Bobrov's report, the Council on Civil Society and Human Rights quickly added a caveat to the report to assert that it was not an official assessment and contained 'only personal observations and opinions of the authors' (Bobrov 2014). However, if a Russian government representative to Crimea in the immediate aftermath of the referendum found that turnout was up to fifty percentage points less than the numbers officially reported, it strongly suggests that the published results were a gross fabrication.

The referendum was the most critical component of the Russian government's claims for the legality and legitimacy of the annexation. Upon closer inspection, its results appear to be as manufactured as the rest of the political process – placing it squarely within the realm of the Soviet political warfare toolkit.

## Agents of influence

The Russian government and its allies in Crimea also controlled which observers were able to 'validate' the referendum. This selective use of observers not only provided additional voices to support Russia's arguments on the referendum's legitimacy and legality, but it also prevented potentially dissenting organizations from discrediting it. To provide that apparent validation, the Russian government sponsored over 100 Western observers to the Crimean referendum – virtually all of whom were members of fringe European political parties (Teper 2016: 117). The way in which the Russian government used these European politicians was the same manner that the Soviet Union employed agents of influence in the Cold War.

Agents of influence were significant figures in the public and private sectors of the target country who wittingly or unwittingly passed propaganda from the Soviet government so as to appear to be originating from a third-party source. The individuals were targeted because of their ability to influence government decision-making or public opinion. Soviet active measures exploited the agents' positions or status as a platform to promote Soviet policies in the foreign country. The intent of the operation was to keep the Soviet connection covert such that it appeared the agent was independently advocating such positions. Agents of influence could be an actual agent recruited by the security services or could simply be an individual sympathetic to the Soviet Union co-opted into unknowingly working with a KGB officer (Bittman 1972: 32, 61; Richelson 1986: 157; Schultz and Godson 1984: 32).

The Cold War saw several significant cases. In 1981, the Danish government arrested Arne Herløv Petersen, a popular writer, who had led the campaign for a 'Nordic Nuclear Weapon Free Zone', had sponsored peace marches and had run a newspaper advertisement signed by 150 Danish artists and intellectuals denouncing the North Atlantic Treaty Organization (NATO) and nuclear weapons. The Danish security services had recorded twenty-three meetings between him and the KGB active measures officer of the Copenhagen residency and found that he had paid for the advertisement with KGB money (Barron 1983: 277). Arne Treholt, the Norwegian Foreign Ministry press spokesman, was arrested in 1984 when departing Oslo to meet his KGB handler in Vienna. Since his recruitment in the 1960s, Treholt had fed classified NATO documents to the KGB and lobbied heavily within the Norwegian government for the Nordic nuclear free zone (Kux 1985: 23). When opened in the 1990s, the archives of the International Department of the CPSU Central Committee revealed that Finnish president Urho Kekkonen, one of the key architects of Finlandization – the Finnish government's policy to maintain good relations with the Soviet Union and avoid criticizing its eastern neighbour – received millions of dollars from the Soviet government during his presidency for his re-election campaigns and for personal use (Van Herpen 2016: 99). The Warsaw Pact security services similarly employed agents of influence. In April 1972, West German chancellor

Willy Brandt faced a vote of no-confidence in the Bundestag over his *Ostpolitik* concessions to East Germany. The HVA (the East German security service) had earlier recruited Julius Steiner, a member of parliament from the opposition Christian Democratic Union. It paid him 50,000 marks to break ranks with his party and vote against removing Brandt, whom both the East German and Soviet governments wished to see remain in power because of his conciliatory policies. The measure failed by only two votes, and Brandt remained chancellor (Andrew and Mitrokhin 2000: 579).

The Russian government used the Western observers to the Crimean referendum in this same fashion as agents of influence. It had first sent its own observers, including twenty members of the State Duma, nine members of the Federation Council and six members of the Civic Chamber, the federal civil society council (Goryashko and Ivanov 2014). However, because of the Russian government's very vocal stance on the fate of Crimea, these officials could not have been presented as neutral observers. Furthermore, most outside election observer organizations were unable or unwilling to participate. The Crimean Central Executive Committee would not grant observer accreditation to the independent Russian voting rights NGO *Golos*. The Organization for Security and Co-operation in Europe (OSCE) boycotted the referendum because, in the words of its chairman Didier Burkhalter, it 'contradict[ed] the Ukrainian constitution and must be considered illegal'. The Russian NGOs Union of Russian Observers ('Sonar') and Citizen Observer did not send representatives for similar reasons. Other independent Russian NGOs, including the Levada Centre polling organization, said that the expedited timeline for the referendum made it impossible for them to send exit poll teams (Goryashko and Ivanov 2014).

The solution was to rely on Western politicians who could provide the appearance of independence and neutrality. According to the Crimean authorities, 135 international observers from twenty-three countries monitored the referendum. These observers provided plenty of quotations to the media, summarized by *RT* (2014a), declaring the fairness and legitimacy of the vote. Aymeric Chauprade, the foreign policy adviser to Marine Le Pen, the leader of France's populist *Front national*, declared that 'the referendum is legitimate'. Former Polish MP Mateus Piskorski said, 'Our observers have not registered any violations of voting rules'. Ewald Stadler, an Austrian member of the European Parliament, claimed, 'I haven't seen anything even resembling pressure' on voters. Pavel Chernev, falsely identified as a member of the Bulgarian Parliament, asserted that the '[o]rganization and procedures [we]re 100 per cent in line with the European standards'. Johannes Hübner, a member of the Austrian Parliament, condemned 'American and European media' for providing a 'very distorted' view of the referendum. Tatjana Ždanoka, a Latvian member of the European Parliament, likewise accused the West of applying 'double standards' by accepting the independence vote in Kosovo and not Crimea. The net result of these statements was that politicians from numerous EU nations reinforced the Russian government's narrative that the referendum was a free and fair representation of the will of the Crimean people.

Upon closer inspection, however, these European observers came from far-right or far-left fringe political parties that were not an honest representation of European governments. They had little impact on their own nations' political scenes, but they shared pro-Russian positions in their party platforms. The Austrian delegates were members of the right-wing, populist Freedom Party of Austria (FPÖ) or its offshoot, the Alliance for the Future of Austria (BZÖ). Stadler formed his own right-wing political party, the Reform Conservatives, after the BZÖ expelled him for behaviour 'demeaning to the party' (Austrian Press Agency 2013). Chernev, founder of the Bulgarian right-wing party Freedom, had not won an election since 2005 but was well known for his opposition to Kosovo's independence and Bulgaria's EU membership (*PIK* 2016). Hübner, the Austrian Freedom Party's foreign policy spokesman, had previously visited the head of the Chechen Republic Ramzan Kadyrov in Grozny. On the trip, which the Austrian Foreign Ministry condemned, he praised Kadyrov for the 'peace and tranquillity' of the region (ORF 2012).

While some of these politicians may have been unwitting 'fellow travellers', evidence has emerged that others may have been paid agents. Piskorski, a former single-term Polish MP for the populist Self-defence Party, has served as an election monitor for numerous post-Soviet states since 2004 and each time supported the Russian government's stance, including endorsing the legitimacy of the 2005 Transnistrian parliamentary elections. In 2007, he founded the European Centre for Geopolitical Analysis to serve as a platform for election observers and headquartered it in Russia (Shekhovtsov 2015a). In February 2015, he then founded a new political party, Change. The Polish counterintelligence agency arrested Piskorski in May 2016 on charges of spying for the Russian intelligence services and secretly receiving funding from the Russian Federation to run his political party (Czuchnowski and Wojciech 2016). Ždanoka is co-chair of the Latvian Russian Union, a pro-Russian, ethnocentric political party similar to the parties formerly in Crimea. In 2014, the Russian Foreign Ministry's Fund for the Support and Protection of the Rights of Compatriots Living Abroad transferred €95,000 to the NGO Latvian Human Rights Committee, which in turn transferred some of the funds to Ždanoka's Latvian Russian Union (LTV 2015). Also in 2014, the Latvian security services investigated Ždanoka over allegations that she was serving as a Russian agent (McGuinness 2014).

The Russian government appears to have in effect paid France's *Front national* for its support for the Crimean referendum, as well. According to hacked text messages from Timur Prokopenko, the Russian Presidential Administration official who coordinated Russian state media during the Crimean crisis, he contacted the *Front national* through interlocutors to ask them to 'take a stand on Crimea' and requested that leader Marine Le Pen head to Crimea for the referendum 'as an observer'. After Le Pen sent her advisor Chauprade, who praised the 'successful' referendum (Morice 2014), the Russian officials wrote that 'it will be necessary to thank the French in one way or another' (*Le Monde* 2015).[7] Le Pen travelled to Moscow the following month and was warmly received by president of the Duma Sergey Naryshkin, head of the Duma's Committee on Foreign Affairs Aleksey Pushkov and deputy prime minister Dmitry Rogozin (Laruelle 2016: 10). Throughout 2014, the *Front national* then received Russian loans totalling €11 million, including €9 million from the now-dissolved First Czech Russian Bank, which had connections to the Russian government. The negotiations for the loan occurred as the Crimean crisis was unfolding (Gatehouse 2017). The net effect of the Russian government's employment of these agents of influence, some of whom it covertly paid for their support, was that even though many of them were not major players in their own domestic politics, the Russian government was still able to assert that over 100 European politicians observed the referendum and 'verified' its openness and fairness. As with the other active measures, the *appearance* of legitimacy was key, regardless of what covert steps were taken to create that appearance.

## Front organizations

The organization that largely arranged for the body of European politicians to serve as observers was the Eurasian Observatory for Democracy and Elections (EODE), a Russia-based NGO founded in 2006 by Belgian right-wing political activist Luc Michel. Based on the publicly available information on this obscure NGO, it is likely the modern-day version of a Soviet front organization. Front

---

[7] Le Pen later backtracked her position and stated that Chauprade would not be 'officially' representing the *Front national* while observing the referendum, but there as a political scientist (AFP 2014).

organizations were described as such because they provided 'a front or façade' for the Soviet Union's activities abroad (see Phelps-Fetherston 1965; Schultz 1988; Richelson 1986; Yost 1987; Atkinson 1966). They allowed for the propagation of the Soviet position on various international matters from sources that could be labelled 'neutral' or 'independent', but in reality, the International Department of the CPSU Central Committee secretly provided them funding and direction. Fronts typically published very few records that shed light on their sources of funding or membership, but in 1979 alone, the Soviet government secretly spent $63 million to run thirteen major front organizations (Richelson 1986: 154).

The most active and well-known front organization in the Cold War was the World Peace Council (WPC). Operating in over 135 countries, its stated aims were 'to mobilise the peoples of the world, if necessary in opposition to their governments, in defence of peace, to expose the "warmongers" and to bring about a peaceful settlement of international differences' (Phelps-Fetherston 1965: 20). In practice, the WPC closely followed the themes of Soviet official propaganda, regardless of their 'peaceful' nature (Schultz 1988: 194). It received directives from the CPSU through the Soviet Committee for the Defence of Peace, of which the vice chairman was an International Department officer (Richelson 1986: 150). When the WPC blamed the Cuban Missile Crisis on the 'aggressive acts' of the United States, it made no mention of the Soviet deployment of missiles to the island (Phelps-Fetherston 1965: 25). It did not make any statements against the Soviet military incursions in Hungary, Czechoslovakia, Angola, Ethiopia or Yemen, and it actually released statements endorsing the Soviet invasion of Afghanistan (Barron 1983: 263). In 1978, US congressmen invited WPC president Romesh Chandra and his staff to a 'Dialogue on Disarmament and Détente' in Washington. Among the members of his entourage was Radomir Bogdanov, ostensibly the deputy of the Moscow Institute of the United States and Canada but in reality a KGB colonel (Barron 1983: 271). After years of refusing to release its financial statements, the WPC finally admitted in 1989 that 90 per cent of its funding came from the Soviet Union (O'Brien 2004: 270).

The EODE strongly resembles these Soviet front organizations. According to its mission statement, the association is committed to 'the unity of Eurasia' and 'achieving a multipolar world' because of 'the activism of Western and American NGOs that seek only to ensure and maintain the domination of the United States and NATO in Eurasia' (Michel 2013). Even though it claims to be a 'non-aligned NGO', it overtly recognizes its alliance with the Russian government, stating that its vision is 'shared by many governmental and political spheres, including the current Russian leadership and V.V. Putin' (EODE 2014). Like the front organizations before it, the EODE reinforced the Russian government's narrative with an endorsement of the Crimean referendum, releasing a press statement declaring that it 'took place in accordance with international election standards' (EODE Press Office 2014).

In addition to its public statements, the EODE also funded the European politicians to serve as referendum observers. How it identified the politicians and how it paid for their trips, however, remains questionable. Frank Creyelman, a Flemish politician from the secessionist Vlaams Belang Party, and Fabrizio Bertot, the former mayor of a northern Italian town who was relieved for his ties to the 'Ndrangheta mafia (*Quotidiano Piemontese* 2012), both stated that the EODE had invited them as observers. However, they said they were largely unfamiliar with the organization, admitting they did not even know what the acronym stood for (Bullough 2014). Austrian Ewald Stadler likewise stated that the EODE had organized his trip to Crimea and that he had received a plane ticket and hotel reservation. However, he said he was unclear on who the actual sponsor that paid for his travel was (*Österreich* 2014). The EODE admits that it receives financial support from some Russian companies, but it asserts that it is independent (Higgins 2014). Nevertheless, it managed to pay for and organize logistical support for over one hundred observers from across Europe on short notice. Piskorski's European Centre for Geopolitical Analysis also helped finance some of the referendum observers (Shekhovtsov 2015b), and as previously mentioned, the Polish government has charged him with receiving illicit funding from the Russian government. The result was that the EODE and the European Centre for Geopolitical Analysis provided the Russian government with ostensibly neutral, independent, foreign NGOs that arranged for politicians from multiple nations to observe and endorse the legitimacy of the annexation in support of its policy objectives – serving as a front, just as their Cold War predecessors had done for the Soviet government.

## Invasion invitation

The last key political tool the Soviet Union utilized to increase the apparent legitimacy of its political warfare campaigns on the international stage was an 'invasion invitation' from the targeted government. It believed that such an overt request for Soviet assistance would not only reduce resistance from the target country's population against the invading Soviet forces but also undercut criticisms of its actions from the international community (Dawisha 1984:

326). As with the political process used to facilitate the invasion, however, the Soviet government manufactured either the request itself, the conditions under which it was submitted, or the intent behind it. During the 2014 Ukraine crisis, the Russian government employed these same tactics to create an invasion invitation, which it then publicized broadly to justify its actions.

## Czechoslovakia 1968

The Soviet Union's collaborators in the CPCz secretly delivered such an invitation in the beginning of August 1968. The 'Letter of Invitation', signed by Alois Indra, Drahomír Kolder, Antonin Kapek, Oldrich Svestka and Vasil Bil'ak, warned the Soviet leadership that 'the very existence of socialism in our country is under threat' and that '[o]nly with your assistance can the Czechoslovak Socialist Republic be extricated from the imminent danger of counterrevolution' (Indra et al. 1968: 324). During the Bratislava conference on 3 August, the conspirators passed the letter in the men's lavatory to Politburo member Petro Shelest, who then handed it to General Secretary Leonid Brezhnev (Navratil 1998: 324). Bil'ak decided it was safer to approach Shelest, who had been acting as an unofficial intermediary with the pro-Soviet members of the CPCz, than to go directly to Brezhnev and risk exposure of their plot, which wholly depended on its concealment from First Secretary Alexander Dubček (Kramer 1993: 12).[8]

However, the letter likely did not have a critical impact on the Soviet Union's decision to invade, as significant planning was already underway. Brezhnev had discussed using military force in Czechoslovakia in a 6–7 March meeting with Bulgarian leader Todor Zhivkov, and the commander of the Soviet Airborne Troops received a planning directive for Czechoslovakia on 8 April (Bischof et al. 2010: 10). Also in March, KGB chairman Yuri Andropov authorized Operation *Progress* – the plan to send KGB illegals into Czechoslovakia to stoke the counter-revolutionary movement (Andrew and Mitrokhin 2000: 328–9). While Brezhnev cited the 3 August letter from the Czechoslovak collaborators during the meeting of the Warsaw Pact Five in Moscow on 18 August (Navratil 1998: 324), it does not appear to be a major turning point in Soviet plans for the country.

---

[8]   Antonin Kapek, a candidate member of the CPCz Presidium, wrote a similar appeal for assistance during the Čierna nad Tisou meeting with the CPSU in July. However, there is no evidence that the letter made it to Brezhnev, presumably because Kapek, a less important figure, was the only signatory (Kramer 1993: 2). The Bratislava appeal is thus here the focus because of the significance of its signatories and the Soviet reaction to it.

Part of the reason the letter did not have more of an impact was that it did not provide the sort of public international legitimacy that a request from the central government would. None of the Czechoslovak signatories were in a position to invoke the mutual defence treaties between their two nations – the Soviet-Czechoslovak Treaty of Friendship, Mutual Assistance and Post-War Cooperation; the Warsaw Pact; or even Article 51 of the UN Charter. Because they were not in the leadership positions that could legally request international military support, their letter was instead conspiracy – a secret plot with a foreign regime to overthrow their own government. Likely for this reason, the Soviet Union staunchly denied that the letter existed. After the invasion, it was stamped 'Top Secret', locked away as Special Dossier No. 255 in the CPSU Politburo archives and labelled with special instructions from the head of the CPSU General Department, Konstantin Chernenko (the future CPSU general secretary): 'To be preserved in the Politburo Archive. Not to be opened without my express permission' (Navratil 1998: 324). After communist rule in Czechoslovakia ended, Vasil Biľak admitted that he and his co-conspirators had drafted a letter in 1968 in which they 'asked the Soviet leadership for assistance [...] if the situation were to deteriorate further and the agreed-on responsibilities were not carried out' (Biľak 1991: 323). However, it was not until President Boris Yeltsin provided a copy of the letter to the Czechoslovak government in 1992 that Russia ended the Soviet Union's denials over its existence (Kramer 1993: 3–4).

Instead of relying on this problematic letter from the Czechoslovak officials, the Soviet Union created an alternate invasion invitation that would satisfy these requirements – one that could be considered a legitimate appeal from the government of Czechoslovakia. On 22 August 1968 (two days after the Warsaw Pact forces invaded), the fabricated letter was published in *Pravda*, the official newspaper of the CPSU Central Committee. It incorporated elements of the real letter from the CPCz collaborators, but it was longer and more detailed in its appeal for Soviet assistance (*Pravda* 1968; Indra et al. 1968). *Pravda* identified it as an 'appeal by a group of members of the CPCz Central Committee, the ČSSR [Czechoslovak Socialist Republic] government, and the ČSSR National Assembly' (*Pravda* 1968) – thus a request from the new Czechoslovak leadership after Dubček's removal from power on the night of 20 August.

This manufactured appeal for support was critical to the Soviet Union's case for legitimizing the invasion. The *Pravda* editorial accompanying the invitation letter used it to defend the military operation because 'the Soviet Union and the other socialist states decided to satisfy the request by [Czechoslovak] party and state figures to render the fraternal Czechoslovak people urgent assistance' (*Pravda* 1968: 14). TASS (1968: 13) reported that 'party and state leaders of the Czechoslovak Socialist Republic have requested the Soviet Union and other allied states to give the fraternal Czechoslovak people immediate assistance'. The Politburo instructed its ambassadors around the world to 'emphasiz[e] that the aid to the Czechoslovak people is being undertaken at the request of the Czechoslovak side' (CPSU CC Politburo 1968a: 409). The note that ambassador to the United States Anatoly Dobrynin sent to President Lyndon Johnson on 20 August stressed the same point (NSC 1968).

However, the failure of the political process to go as planned undermined the supposed legitimacy that the scripted invasion invitation was designed to provide. During the 20 August CPCz Central Committee session, Indra and Kolder were to introduce a measure that condemned the 'counter-revolutionary forces', call for Dubček's removal and invite in Soviet 'fraternal assistance'. The pre-drafted letter was designed to be published the following morning as the culmination of that night's political proceedings. Unfortunately, Indra and Kolder's motion failed to pass, and in the midst of the negative public backlash to the invasion, no Czechoslovak politician would agree to become the new first secretary. The draft letter had left the names of the authors blank, and the plan was to insert the names of the Czechoslovak collaborators who emerged the night of 20 August as the leaders of the new revolutionary government. As a result, the Soviet government was forced to run the letter (a day later than originally planned) without any specific names (Dawisha 1984: 325). *Pravda* did not identify the supposed authors of the letter, nor were they identified at any point in the future. The Soviet government thus had its invasion invitation, but it was largely of its own invention, and the failure of the political proceedings undercut the message behind it.

## Afghanistan 1979

In Afghanistan, the Soviet Union again stressed how the Afghan government had invited its forces into the country. As in Czechoslovakia, however, the origins of that appeal were not as they were portrayed. The Soviet government took the multiple requests from Hafizullah Amin for additional Soviet forces to defend his regime, turned them on their heads and used them to legitimize the invasion and coup to forcibly change the regime instead. Presidents Taraki and Amin made approximately twenty total requests for Soviet forces throughout 1979 to support their fight against the growing *Mujahideen* insurgency in the country.

These included ones for helicopters, paratroopers, a special forces battalion and two entire Soviet divisions (McMichael 1991: 2; Galeotti 1995a: 8; Braithwaite 2012: 54). Lieutenant General Gorelov, the chief of the Soviet military advisory group in Afghanistan, recounted one such request he received on 11 August from Amin, who pleaded that 'the arrival of Soviet troops will significantly raise our moral spirit [and] will inspire even greater confidence and calm' (Gorelov 1979).

Instead, the Soviet Union used these requests to legitimize its military operation that killed Amin and replaced him with Babrak Karmal, the Soviet government's anointed successor – thus twisting these appeals into its 'invasion invitation'. In March, the Politburo stressed to Taraki how important it was for his government to issue formal, written requests for Soviet military support (CPSU CC Politburo 1979d); these requests subsequently served as verifiable evidence with which to legitimize the deployment of troops to Afghanistan. The TASS announcement from 27 December 1979, drafted by the Politburo and published immediately after the invasion, directly referenced these requests: 'In the face of gross foreign interference, including armed interference, the leadership of the Democratic Republic of Afghanistan has repeatedly turned to the Soviet Union in the last two years with a request to help the Afghan people repel aggression' (TASS 1979). The editorial thus stated that those requests justified the invasion. Similarly, Soviet diplomats delivered a note in Western capitals stating that the Soviet government was 'responding to an appeal from the Afghan leadership to repel outside aggression' (Collins 1986: 78). In his response to US president Jimmy Carter's challenge on the legitimacy of sending Soviet troops into Afghanistan, Brezhnev replied, 'For almost two years the government of Afghanistan repeatedly turned to us with this request. Incidentally, one such request was sent to us on 26 December of this year' (CPSU CC Politburo 1979b). Since Amin's 26 December request was for military support, not for Soviet troops to take his life and overthrow his regime, this characterization is hardly honest. Nonetheless, the Soviet leadership still utilized these requests to provide the appearance of international legitimacy to the operation.

## Crimea 2014

The 'invasion invitation' scenario – including its questionable origins – replayed in strikingly similar terms during the Russian operation in Crimea in 2014. At the UN Security Council meeting on 3 March, Russian ambassador Vitaly Churkin held up a letter he said was from Viktor Yanukovych and signed on 1 March.

He said he was 'authorized to say that the President of Russia has received the following request from President Yanukovych' and read it aloud:

> As the legitimately elected President of Ukraine, I wish to inform you that events in my country and capital have placed Ukraine on the brink of civil war. Chaos and anarchy reign throughout the country [. . .] I therefore call on President Vladimir Vladimirovich Putin of Russia to use the armed forces of the Russian Federation to establish legitimacy, peace, law and order, and stability in defence of the people of Ukraine. (UN Security Council 2014a, 2014b)

The date of the letter coincided with the day the Russian Federation Council approved President Putin's request to deploy armed forces to Ukraine, thus giving the impression that Putin's request was in response to Yanukovych's appeal. Putin quickly emphasized the legitimacy for any future Russian actions provided by the letter. The following day, he stated that 'we have a direct appeal from the incumbent and, as I said, legitimate president of Ukraine, Mr. Yanukovych, asking us to use the Armed Forces to protect the lives, freedom and health of the citizens of Ukraine' (Kremlin 2014h).

The timing and origins of the letter, however, raise several questions. On 28 February 2014, Yanukovych reappeared in public in Russia for the first time since fleeing Kyiv a week earlier. At a press conference, he pleaded, 'Russia must use all means at its disposal to end the chaos and terror gripping Ukraine' (de Carbonnel 2014a). However, when asked specifically about the use of armed forces, he stated, 'I think any military action in this situation is unacceptable [. . .] I have no plan to ask for military support' (de Carbonnel 2014c). Additionally, he stated that he believed Crimea should remain part of Ukraine (de Carbonnel 2014c). Despite these statements, the date and content of the 'invasion invitation' letter suggest that Yanukovych requested the very next day for Russia to use its armed forces, but he did not make another public appearance to reinforce the appeal. These issues call into question the veracity of the letter. Moreover, even if the letter is legitimate, it post-dates both when Putin said he made the decision to begin the operation (22 February) and the first use of Russia's Armed Forces (27 February). The appeal thus came after Russia had already invaded Crimea.

The confusion over the invasion invitation increased three years later as the Prosecutor General of Ukraine prepared its treason trial against Yanukovych. On 17 January 2017, the UN Secretariat provided the Ukrainian Permanent Mission with an official copy of the original statement produced by Churkin at the Security Council (Lutsenko 2017). A month later, Yanukovych denied that he had ever sent the letter or requested Russian troops in violation of Ukrainian law. In his words, 'First, this was a statement, not a letter. Second, there are the laws [. . .] I did not betray my people, I tried to protect my people and do this in the framework of my powers' (TASS 2017c). Yanukovych appeared to deny that the 'official' letter presented at the UN was authentic or that he had used any of the specific verbiage Churkin quoted. A month later, the Russian government further complicated the issue. First, the Russian General Prosecutor's Office denied that any such letter existed or that an appeal from Yanukovych had any bearing on governmental decision-making:

Neither the Presidential Administration of the Russian Federation nor the Federation Council of the Federal Assembly of the Russian Federation received any kind of statement from V. F. Yanukovych about a request to use the Armed Forces of the Russian Federation on the territory of Ukraine, and the state bodies did not address these issues. Any statements of the President of Ukraine V. F. Yanukovych were not the basis for the appeal of the President of the Russian Federation to the Federation Council of the Federal Assembly of the Russian Federation for consent on the use of the Armed Forces of the Russian Federation on the territory of Ukraine. (General Prosecutor's Office of the Russian Federation 2017)

Next, presidential spokesman Dmitry Peskov stated that '[n]o letter was officially submitted to the Russian Presidential Administration, [and] no such letter was registered in the administration' (TASS 2017a). Then, Ministry of Foreign Affairs spokeswoman Maria Zakharova claimed that while there was no letter, it was still 'Yanukovych's statement' and that 'Churkin was authorized to quote him in the UN Security Council'. At the same time, she said that the question of how the statement made its way from Yanukovych to Churkin was 'a matter of internal coordination' and not for further discussion (*Govorit Moskva* 2017).

One year later, Yanukovych offered a new version of events. On 2 March 2018, he stated at a press conference in Moscow, 'I wrote an appeal to Putin. In this appeal I referred to the Treaty of Friendship and Mutual Assistance between Ukraine and Russia. I proposed to conduct consultations and suggested to consider the question of introducing a police peacekeeping mission' (Balachuk 2018). Yanukovych thus stated that he did write a letter, but the contents he described do not match what was read by Churkin, implying that the UN letter was an artificial construction – not unlike the Czechoslovak appeal. Furthermore, he said that he suggested consultations about a police mission, thus denying that he requested for Russia to deploy its armed forces.

Now that there are court cases investigating the specifics of the invasion invitation, both Yanukovych and the Russian government have offered multiple, contradicting explanations for it. The intent appears to eliminate the letter as useful evidence. Amid the confusion, however, they have inadvertently revealed that the appeal was not authentic. Additionally, the way in which Putin referenced the request to justify the invasion during the heat of the crisis contradicts the Kremlin's later statements that it was not the basis for his decision-making. What Yanukovych's letter provided was what the appeals in Czechoslovakia and Afghanistan provided: an artificial document that provided a means to claim the legitimacy of the impending military operation.

*    *    *

The Russian government employed the same political tools in the 2014 Crimean annexation as the Soviet government had done in its political warfare campaigns. It supported and relied on pro-Russian politicians within Crimea to serve as its collaborators in the annexation just as the Soviet Union relied on the pro-Soviet members of the foreign Communist Parties. It conspired with the politicians against their own government to facilitate the annexation. Senior Russian officials deployed to the peninsula before and during the crisis to orchestrate the operation in the same fashion that the Soviet government sent key individuals to manage the operations in Czechoslovakia and Afghanistan. The political process that appeared to provide the Russian government with the legality and legitimacy it sought was manufactured in the same way that the changes in government in 1968 and 1979 were – but by finding the proper balance between utilizing the legitimate political processes and guaranteeing the desired results. The tools it employed to enhance that apparent legitimacy included the modern-day interpretations of agents of influence and front organizations. The Russian government reused the Soviet practice of fabricating an 'invasion invitation' from the targeted government to justify its follow-on military actions. As a result, the political aspects of the Crimean annexation operation very clearly link back to Soviet political warfare practice. Little of what occurred could genuinely be considered a new form of conflict or the advent of a new Russian way of war. Instead, it is the reapplication of old methods with slight adaptations to the current operating environment. These same recycled practices appear when examining the military tools, discussed in the next chapter.

# 5

# Military tools

The military side of the Russian operation to annex Crimea utilized the same tools for the same purposes as the Soviet political warfare operations in Czechoslovakia and Afghanistan. The military tools used by the Soviet Union in its political warfare campaigns revolved around the concept of *maskirovka*, a Russian and Soviet principle about the use of deception, camouflage and disinformation in warfare. It was closely related to the security services' use of *active measures*, especially *dezinformatsia*, in that it presented false information in order to affect the opponents' decision-making. In both Czechoslovakia and Afghanistan, the Soviet forces used *maskirovka* to exploit the *bratstvo* (brotherhood) and fraternal bonds with their fellow communist forces to undermine resistance and facilitate the operation. The Russian forces applied this same tactic to their relationship with the Ukrainian servicemen in Crimea, including using some of the same arguments to deceive their counterparts. The Soviet Union similarly used *maskirovka* to disguise its servicemen as Afghan forces in 1979 to support its claim that the rise to power of Babrak Karmal was an indigenous effort for which the Soviet government was not responsible. The 'little green men' in Crimea, the unmarked Russian servicemen whom the Russian government insisted were 'self-defence forces', was the replica of this *maskirovka* tactic. Furthermore, the Russian government disguised Russian soldiers as Ukrainian *Berkut* special police officers during the critical seizure of the Crimean parliamentary buildings on 27 February 2014, giving superficial support to its claims that the change in government was an organic Crimean movement.

Concurrent with these measures to disguise its military efforts, the Soviet government threatened the targeted regime with increased hostilities if it felt conditions warranted it. Soviet leaders warned the Czechoslovak government that if it resisted the Warsaw Pact forces entering the country then they would respond violently and remove the entire government from power. Under this pressure, the Czechoslovak leaders decided that such resistance was futile. The

Russian government made the same threats to the new Ukrainian leadership in 2014, and as is clear from their now-declassified discussions at the time, the Ukrainian political and governmental leaders came to the same conclusions as their Czechoslovak predecessors. Connected to this threat of increased hostilities was the use of military exercises both to serve as a demonstration of force and, in another application of *maskirovka*, to disguise the concentration and movement of forces necessary to conduct the invasion. The intent behind these measures was to minimize the violence required to achieve the operation's objectives and ensure a swift Soviet or Russian victory.

Next, the Russian government applied the same sort of hard-nosed, pressure-laden 'negotiation tactics' during the Crimean crisis that the Soviet government used in its political warfare campaigns. These meetings involved isolating the opponent's representatives from outside sources of information and from each other, offering various 'carrots' and 'sticks' to drive their decision-making and repeating the pressure in multiple sessions until the officials capitulated. The Soviet government used these techniques in the 'negotiations' with the Czechoslovak leadership that led to the Moscow Protocol, which resolved the crisis in the Soviets' favour. The Russian government reused the same approach but applied it to the military domain during the 2014 Crimean crisis. It used these tactics to pressure the Ukrainian servicemen into not resisting and even defecting to the Russian side, thus further facilitating the annexation operation.

## *Maskirovka*

In Soviet political warfare campaigns, strategic deception manifested in the military domain as *maskirovka* (disguise or military deception). The *Military Encyclopaedic Dictionary*, the Soviet General Staff's definitive publication released in 1983 (Jones 2003: 24), defined *maskirovka* as a 'complex of measures for misleading the enemy with regard to the presence and disposition of troops (forces), military objectives (targets), their status, combat readiness and activities, and also the plans of the command' (Trulock III 1987: 279). It comprised four broad categories: camouflage (concealment), simulation (decoy weapons, troops or facilities), feints and demonstrations (decoy manoeuvres), and disinformation (false or misleading information about capabilities or intentions) (Heuer Jr. 1987: 42–3). The *Dictionary* also separated *maskirovka* into three levels: tactical, operational and strategic. It assigned corresponding headquarters the responsibility for planning it; for example, the Soviet General

Staff was responsible for strategic-level *maskirovka* (Jones 2003: 55n42). The importance of *maskirovka* to Soviet military operations was so significant that it could be considered 'woven into the very fabric of Soviet strategy, operational art and tactics' (Glantz 1988). Soviet commanders were not just tasked with concealing their operations; they were required to conduct *aktivnost'* – the active application of deception and disinformation to deceive the enemy and force him to pursue ineffective courses of action, including taking no action (Stevens and Marsh 1982: 27). *Maskirovka* was a military term to describe a military concept. Just as the military (outside of the Soviet Main Intelligence Directorate, the GRU) did not use the term 'active measures', the security services did not use the term *maskirovka* (Heuer Jr. 1987: 42).

From one perspective, there is nothing uniquely Soviet or Russian about *maskirovka*. As two Soviet military authors described in a 1980 editorial, '[M]askirovka has been used since time immemorial as one of the most effective means of defence' (Limny and Gorkin 1980; Reid 1987). If the objectives of *maskirovka* are surprise, the preservation of combat power and survivability (Trulock III 1987: 280), then these same principles are in some form or fashion part of almost any list of the fundamentals of warfare. However, what makes *maskirovka* different from these more general military concepts is its stress on disinformation. The concept of *maskirovka* goes beyond mere 'secrecy' or 'camouflage'; it is more accurately a campaign of 'managed disinformation' (Suvorov 1989: 201). A 1974 Soviet military publication called *Basic Principles of Operational Art and Tactics* instructed its officer audience that the path to victory included 'keeping in strict secrecy all data of interest to the enemy, as well as by using all possible camouflage, and definitely the use of military cunning, [. . . d]emonstrations and misinformation' (Douglass 1980: 47). Soviet planners analysing conflict with the North Atlantic Treaty Organization (NATO) in the 1980s stressed that the '[m]aximum use of cover and deception was essential' (Glantz 1992: 209). This emphasis on spreading false information goes much further than any principle of surprise or secrecy. In these respects, it is the military version of *dezinformatsia*.

*Maskirovka* as a precept of Russian military thought predated the Soviet period but then flourished under it. In 1904, the Tsarist government founded the Higher School of *Maskirovka*, the first time the concept received such a prominent role in the Russian Armed Forces. During the 1904–5 Russo-Japanese War, Russia appeared to apply these principles by denying that its soldiers were operating in Korea and claiming that its citizens identified there were merely 'woodcutters' (Betz 2017). The concepts and manuals from the *maskirovka* school had a lasting impact on Soviet military practice in the decades after the 1917 Bolshevik Revolution (Thomas 2004: 239). For example, the Red Army incorporated many of the same principles into its Draft Field Regulations of 1936 and the Field Regulations of 1940 (Trulock III 1987: 277–8). These practices received institutional support in the Soviet period, as well. In the 1960s, the Soviet General Staff established the Chief Directorate of Strategic *Maskirovka* (GUSM) to oversee and execute its deception operations (Suvorov 1989: 201).

After the dissolution of the Soviet Union, *maskirovka* remained part of Russia's military concepts, but its importance has grown significantly since the warnings surrounding the colour revolutions. Writing for the Russian Ministry of Defence's journal *Military Thought* in 2013, two senior researchers at the Combined Arms Academy of the Russian Armed Forces stressed that 'more time is to be devoted to operational masking [*maskirovka*] as operations are planned and get under way. The local wars fought in the last few decades and aggression by several NATO countries against Libya in 2011 bear this out convincingly' (Orlyansky and Kuznetsov 2013: 11). According to the Russian General Staff, the conflict in Libya that these authors cited was another example of the subversive 'colour revolutions' secretly orchestrated by the West. The authors therefore suggested that the Russian military dedicate a robust staff section at an operational headquarters to developing and managing the *maskirovka* plan (Orlyansky and Kuznetsov 2013: 11–13). Thus, shortly before the events in Crimea, the Russian Ministry of Defence's official journal identified *maskirovka* as a critical part of modern warfare and prescribed significant manpower dedicated to its execution as a key component of future operations.

In its political warfare conflicts targeting states within its sphere of influence, the Soviet military generally focused its *maskirovka* operations around two lines of effort: exploiting the *bratstvo* that the target state's armed forces felt for their Soviet partners to undermine their resistance or deceive them into inadvertently assisting the invasion; and disguising its servicemen as indigenous forces to provide false legitimacy to the Soviet government's claims about the organic nature of the changes in government. These two lines of effort played out in parallel in both the Soviet conflicts and the Russian annexation of Crimea.

## Bratstvo

In its invasions of both Czechoslovakia and Afghanistan, the Soviet Union attacked a state with which it had close fraternal ties. Both were within the Soviet sphere of influence and were in the control of sympathetic Communist

Parties. Their governments significantly shared information, and Soviet advisors worked throughout the partner state's ministries. These connections were especially substantial between the militaries of the countries. The combined training, combined exercises and resident Soviet advisory missions fostered a strong sense of *bratstvo* (brotherhood) between the partner forces. The Soviet military exploited the trust these brotherly ties provided in their *maskirovka* campaigns to deceive their partners on the true nature and intentions of their military operations. In 2014, the Russian and Ukrainian militaries, especially the Russian Black Sea Fleet and the Ukrainian Navy, held similarly close ties not only through shared cultural and linguistic identities but also through shared military experiences and exercises, which increased under President Viktor Yanukovych's government. As part of its *maskirovka* campaign in Crimea, the Russian military likewise manipulated this *bratstvo* to facilitate the annexation.

### Czechoslovakia 1968

The Soviet Union exploited its fraternal connections with Czechoslovakia during the 1968 invasion to undermine Czechoslovak readiness for such an attack and minimize resistance from the Czechoslovak military and population. Prior to the invasion, Soviet officials underscored the bonds between the two countries. In its 4 July 1968 letter to the Communist Party of Czechoslovakia (CPCz) Presidium, the Communist Party of the Soviet Union (CPSU) Politburo (1968b: 198) claimed that 'Soviet [C]ommunists, and all the Soviet people, will always stand shoulder to shoulder with their Czechoslovak brothers'. Soviet premier Alexei Kosygin reinforced this sentiment at a press conference nine days later, stating that '[o]ur country and our party have long marched in struggle and friendship side by side with the Czechoslovak people and the [CPCz]' (Dawisha 1984: 200). As a result, the Czechoslovak leadership largely failed to predict or prepare for the forthcoming invasion. First Secretary Alexander Dubček (1993: 128, 178) later wrote that at no point before 20 August 1968 did he believe that the invasion would happen; he considered a Soviet military operation 'simply unthinkable' because '[i]t ran contrary to my deepest idea of the value system I thought governed the relationships between socialist countries'. He also claimed that when Anton Tazky, the secretary of the Slovak Communist Party Central Committee, saw the invading tanks, he remarked that they must be part of a film shoot; he could not fathom that a Warsaw Pact invasion was underway (Dubček 1993: 173). The Czechoslovak People's Army (CzPA) consisted of 175,000 troops, but because the government did not consider an invasion from the east a possibility, they were all oriented towards NATO on its western borders (Windsor and Roberts 1969: 112).

The Czechoslovak government quickly silenced the few voices who drew attention to a possible Soviet invasion after the Soviet government condemned them for allowing the officials to question these bonds of brotherhood between the two countries. On 15 July 1968, Lieutenant General Václav Prchlík, head of the CPCz department responsible for the military and security services, held a press conference. He asserted that the Warsaw Pact's founding document did not 'give certain partners the right to deploy or station their units arbitrarily on the territory of other members states', and in response, he said he believed that Czechoslovakia had 'only one viable option, which is to insist that we will never allow our state's sovereignty to be violated and will never permit anyone to interfere in our internal affairs' (Prchlík 1968). The outcry from the Soviet government was harsh. Warsaw Pact supreme commander Marshal Ivan Yakubovsky sent a letter to Dubček on 18 July condemning Prchlík's speech and requesting him to 'draw the proper conclusions in this case to which I have drawn your attention in this letter', clearly implying Prchlík's removal (Yakubovsky 1968: 260). Five days later, the Soviet government sent a diplomatic note similarly denouncing Prchlík's statements and stating that it 'expects that the ČSSR [Czechoslovak Socialist Republic] will take the necessary steps to prevent a repetition of matters of this kind' (Kremlin 1968). As a result, the CPCz leadership issued a statement that Prchlík's views 'did not reflect actual facts and do not express an official standpoint' and disbanded his government department (Tigrid 1971: 60). After Prchlík's removal, Czechoslovak defence minister Martin Dzúr refused to allow any mention of a possible military conflict from the east, and his office issued a statement on 26 July strongly denying the rumours that the Czechoslovak military was making any preparations for a Soviet invasion (Dawisha 1984: 247). By feigning insult at the questioning of its fraternal ties with Czechoslovakia, the Soviet government helped remove the minimal readiness the country may have had for the impending invasion.

Once the invasion had begun, the Soviet officials continued to utilize the friendly relationship between their countries to improve the effectiveness of the operation. Most of the key KGB (Committee for State Security) officers in the invasion's initial stages had served as advisors to the StB (Czechoslovak state security service) and the Czechoslovak Ministry of the Interior. They used their intimate knowledge of the structures and personnel of the Czechoslovak organizations to target the most important power centres and to court supporters of the Soviet operation among their ranks (August and Rees 1984: 138). Shortly after midnight on 20 August 1968, Soviet ambassador Stepan Chervonenko handed Czechoslovak president Ludvík Svoboda a letter from the leaders of the Warsaw Pact Five (the Soviet Union, Bulgaria, Hungary, East Germany and Poland) requesting him to 'appeal to the army and people of Czechoslovakia not to resist the troops of the fraternal countries and instead to welcome them as friends' (CPSU CC and Chervonenko 1968: 406). The commander of the Soviet military force occupying Trenčín in Slovakia made a similar appeal to the populace, installing posters throughout the city that argued his forces were restricting movements and enforcing a curfew because they were there 'to help the Czechoslovak people and their institutions of people's power suppress the forces of counterrevolution and save their country from the threat looming over them' (Shmatko 1968: 450). The intent behind these actions was to lead the Czechoslovak people, soldiers and officials to believe that what they were facing was not an armed invasion of their country but some sort of expression of assistance from their brotherly Warsaw Pact nations – and thus undercut any resistance.

The feelings of camaraderie and appeals for calm allowed the Warsaw Pact troops to safely approach the Czechoslovak military and its installations, and they capitalized on this access to then block the Czechoslovak facilities and seize their weapons. Starting on the night of the invasion, the Warsaw Pact forces systematically disarmed the units of the CzPA and confiscated their arms and combat equipment. The seizures continued until 26 August, the day the Czechoslovak leaders signed the Moscow Protocol and submitted to the Soviet demands for political change (Navratil 1998: 443). However, even after the agreement, the Warsaw Pact forces still prohibited the units that retained their arms from using them or manning their equipment. General Karel Rustov, chief of the CzPA General Staff, and General František Bedřich, head of the CzPA Main Political Directorate, briefed the Presidium on 26 August that the Czechoslovak forces were 'not permitted to leave our barracks' because the Warsaw Pact forces continued to block them (Rustov and Bedřich 1968: 485). These restrictions prevented the Czechoslovak military from mounting an armed response, even if its political leaders had called for one.

### Afghanistan 1979

As in Czechoslovakia, the Soviet Union exploited its close relationship with the Afghan government and its armed forces to facilitate the invasion in 1979. By the time of the invasion, Soviet military and security advisors were pervasive throughout Afghanistan. The Afghan government started accepting Soviet military aid in 1956, and by 1972, around 100 Soviet advisors and technical specialists were training the Afghan Armed Forces (Goodson 2001: 59). In the month after the Saur Revolution in April 1978, the new communist government under President Nur Muhammad Taraki signed an additional agreement by which the Soviet Union deployed 400 total advisors to Afghanistan (Russian General Staff 2002: 10). Their numbers steadily grew under the Taraki regime such that by August 1979, there were over 5,000 advisors operating throughout the Afghan government (Urban 1990: 32). The advisors served in all ministries and units of the military down to the battalion and company levels (Grau and Gress 2002: xix; Collins 1986: 66). By the time Hafizullah Amin seized power from Taraki in September, the Afghan military's headquarters could not issue orders for significant operations to their subordinate units without a Soviet advisor co-signing the orders (McMichael 1991: 4). Vladimir Kryuchkov, the head of the KGB's First Chief Directorate (Foreign Operations), and Oleg Kalugin, his deputy for counterintelligence, drafted an intelligence sharing agreement with the Afghan security service after the communists came to power in 1978, providing the KGB with comparable levels of access to its Afghan counterpart (Feifer 2010: 24–6).

To prepare for the invasion, the Soviet government used the false premise that it was assisting its Afghan partners with security at key locations as cover to manoeuvre its elements to the operation's key objectives. In the middle of December 1979, a battalion from the 105th Guards Airborne Division moved from Bagram airbase to the Salang Tunnel, the only year-round passage between Kabul and the north of Afghanistan. The unit said it was to protect the security of the capital, but in reality, it was guaranteeing the movement of forces from Soviet territory to the city during the invasion (Galeotti 1995a: 10). The KGB sent two detachments of its *Spetsnaz* strike forces, code-named *Grom* (Thunder) and *Zenit* (Zenith) and composed of thirty to forty men each, to Kabul in mid-1979 (Feifer 2010: 15). Their overt mission in Afghanistan was to protect the Soviet embassy and its staff and, in response to a request from Amin, to train their Afghan counterparts in counterterrorism tactics. While Amin and his government believed the KGB *Spetsnaz* were there to support them, in December, the units secretly conducted reconnaissance and drew up detailed plans for thirteen key Afghan government objectives which they then seized in the subsequent Soviet operation (Grau 2003: 292; Braithwaite 2012: 56–7).

In the stages immediately before the invasion, the Soviet advisors whom the high command had informed of the pending operation exploited their role to conduct additional preparations. Capitalizing on the expertise their Afghan partners expected them to provide, the Soviet officials convinced the Afghan forces to take a number of measures that were supposedly in their own interests but were actually to minimize resistance during the invasion. The advisors deceived several Afghan units into disarming their tanks before the operation began. They falsely told the unit guarding the central Kabul radio station that the Soviet government was providing them with newer tanks, but they needed the Afghan crews to siphon fuel from their current tanks so they could use it to bring the new ones forward – thus immobilizing the unit. The advisors to the Afghan Seventh and Eighth Mechanized Divisions told their partners to turn in their ammunition for a bogus stock inventory, depriving them of the means to fire upon the invading forces. They also advised the Afghan crews to remove the tank batteries to prepare for the winter weather (McMichael 1991: 5; Galeotti 1995a: 10). The Soviet advisors to the Afghan air defence units used the unfettered access to the Afghans' equipment that their advisory roles gave them to disable the weapons systems by removing the sights or locking them, thus preventing the units from attacking the Soviet air operations soon bringing troops into Kabul (Grau 2003: 295). President Amin's Soviet advisors persuaded him to move from the Arg presidential palace to the Tajbeg Palace on 20 December 1979. The reason they gave him was that they could better provide him security at the new location. In reality, Tajbeg was a more suitable target for the planned raid: it was in the outskirts of Kabul, thus avoiding the dense urban population around the Arg; and it was close to the Soviet embassy, limiting the distance supporting Soviet forces would have to travel (Braithwaite 2012: 90; Andrew and Mitrokhin 2006: 401; Feifer 2010: 68).

Once the Soviet forces had convinced Amin to change residences, they used their advisory role to refine their plan to attack him in it. On 21 December, the senior Soviet advisors joined Amin's Presidential Guard on an inspection of the Tajbeg Palace perimeter and mapped the Afghan defensive positions. Lieutenant General B. S. Ivanov, the senior KGB representative in the country, then instructed his commanders to use that information to plan an attack on the palace instead (Braithwaite 2012: 90–2). Two officers from the *Grom* and *Zenit* KGB strike forces, Majors M. Romanov and Y. Semenov, then visited a restaurant and casino popular with senior Afghan officers on a hill overlooking the palace. They told the staff that they were looking for a location to bring their men to the upcoming new year's celebrations, and from their vantage point in the restaurant, they sketched out the avenues of approach and defensive outposts around the palace in support of their impending operation (Grau 2003: 302).

The Soviet advisors also found ways to celebrate the *bratstvo* between them and their Afghan partners as a means to undercut their military preparedness. They organized a reception for the leadership of the Afghan Presidential Guard on 26 December. The Soviet hosts provided vodka and cognac at the reception, served discreetly in teapots for the sake of the Afghan's Islamic sensibilities. The Soviet officers offered numerous toasts while secretly drinking water from their own glasses. The purpose of the reception was to build the appearance of fraternal bonds between the units but also to disrupt the Afghan units' preparedness for the invasion the following night (Grau 2003: 299; Braithwaite 2012: 93). On 27 December, the Uzbek Soviet Socialist Republic's minister of water resources was visiting the country and held a reception at the Intercontinental Hotel with various Afghan dignitaries. As the invasion began towards the end of the evening, the Soviet forces arrested the guests conveniently gathered in the hotel (Arnold 1985: 94).

Other measures the Soviet partners took were to dispel Afghan suspicions that an attack may be coming. On 29 November, the Afghanistan Commission (composed of KGB chairman Yuri Andropov, Foreign Minister Andrei Gromyko, Defence Minister Dmitry Ustinov and CPSU Central Committee International Department head Boris Ponomarev) suggested to the Central Committee that the Soviet government '[c]ontinue to work actively with [Afghan president Hafizullah] Amin and overall with the current leadership of the PDPA [People's Democratic Party of Afghanistan] and the DRA [Democratic Republic of Afghanistan], not giving Amin grounds to believe that we don't trust him and don't wish to deal with him'. At the same time, the commission suggested that the Soviet government '[h]old off for now on deliveries of heavy weapons and military equipment' to avoid creating 'excess reserves of such weapons and ammunition in Afghanistan' that might be used against Soviet troops during the planned invasion (CPSU CC 1979). The Soviet government thus continued to grant Amin's requests for more general support, including sending some limited military supplies and constructing new radio stations (Andrew and Mitrokhin 2006: 400), but it selectively fulfilled them to undermine the Afghan military's preparedness. In another example, the Soviet forces at the Tajbeg Palace constantly shot flares and left their vehicle engines running on the three days prior to the 27 December assault. They explained that it was part of their normal preparatory procedures, but it was actually to desensitize the Afghan guards to the commotion that would occur during the impending operation (Braithwaite 2012: 92).

The net effect of the persistent, overt support for Amin and his government and the apparent 'brotherly advice' that the Soviet advisors continued to provide to their counterparts was that the Afghan forces were wholly unprepared for the invasion. During Soviet deputy defence minister General Ivan Pavlovsky's visit to Afghanistan on 5 November, he provided the Afghan senior leadership recommendations on addressing their outstanding security issues. Amin responded, 'We are taking all measures to ensure that your recommendations are fulfilled, and we will always work in coordination with Soviet advisers and specialists. Our friendship is unwavering' (Ustinov 1979). He had no evident suspicions that preparations for his overthrow were ongoing. On 26 December, Amin gave an interview to a journalist from an Arab news publication while Soviet military transport planes were landing in the country approximately every ten minutes. He said that the planes must be carrying the aid he had been requesting to help fight the growing insurgency – when they were really part of the invasion force to topple his government (Girardet 1985: 13). The Afghan president was preparing a speech announcing the arrival of the next shipment of arms from the Soviet Union on the same day that the Soviet forces assassinated him (Feifer 2010: 69). As the Tajbeg Palace came under attack, Amin's initial reaction was to order his aide to notify his Soviet military advisors so that they would come to his defence. He was shocked when the aide told him that the Soviet forces were the ones raiding the palace (Grau 2003: 308).

## Crimea 2014

Like in the Soviet conflicts, the Russian military capitalized on the strong feelings of *bratstvo* that the Ukrainian military felt for their counterparts to wage a *maskirovka* campaign that supported the annexation of Crimea. In addition to the historical, cultural and linguistic ties between the Russian and Ukrainian nations, the sister navies had a long, shared history, not least the period in which they jointly controlled the Black Sea Fleet (Deyermond 2008). The senior officers in the Ukrainian military in 2014 had entered service during the Soviet era. For years, they underwent the same training as their peers that were later in the Russian military and served alongside them in the same units. These shared experiences meant that many of them still had a strong affinity for the Russian military and maintained close contacts with its officers (Interview D 2017). The Russian and Ukrainian navies regularly held joint celebrations on Victory Day and Navy Day starting in 1999. For a few years, President Viktor Yushchenko's government stopped the joint parades (Interview H 2017; Interview K 2017), but in 2011, President Viktor Yanukovych moved the date of Ukraine's Navy Day to match Russia's and reinstituted the joint celebrations (Yanukovych 2011). The Russian Black Sea Fleet and the Ukrainian Navy even held a traditional football match between teams of their sailors during the annual new year's celebrations (Interview H 2017). In addition, combined training between the navies drastically increased after Yanukovych became president in 2010, including in the months before the Crimean crisis (Interview A 2017).

The Russian military used these bonds of friendship to undermine the Ukrainian servicemen's resolve and their potential resistance to the annexation. On 23 February 2014, the senior leadership of the Russian Black Sea Fleet, the Ukrainian Navy and the Ukrainian State Border Guard Service (SBGS) in Crimea held a joint party to celebrate Defender of the Fatherland Day (the former Soviet Army and Navy Day) at the Lunacharsky Theatre in Sevastopol. The attendees included Vice Admiral Sergei Yeliseyev, the first deputy commander of the Ukrainian Navy and then Vice Admiral Aleksandr Vitko, the commander of the Russian Black Sea Fleet (Interview G 2017). According to Captain (2nd Rank) Dmytro Glukhov, the commander of the Ukrainian First Surface Ships Brigade, the participants 'radiated with kindness' as they enjoyed the evening together (Kliatskin 2016). Russian president Vladimir Putin, however, had already made the decision to begin the annexation process the previous night, and the Russian military had begun making its preparations for the operation (Kondrashov 2015). The senior Russian officers were thus celebrating their friendships with their Ukrainian peers while their government was planning a military operation against them. The event bears a striking similarity to the KGB's reception for Amin's Presidential Guard the night before the Soviet invasion of Afghanistan.

The efforts of Lieutenant General Igor Turchenyuk exemplify how the Russian forces used this *bratstvo* to influence the Ukrainian servicemen once the military operation had begun. Turchenyuk was the deputy commander of the Russian Southern Military District, to which the Black Sea Fleet belonged. On 3 March 2014, he arrived at the First Separate Naval Infantry Battalion in Feodosia. Based on a recording of the meeting, he told the Ukrainian marines, 'The goal of me coming here . . . is to carry out the task given by the president of the Russian Federation.' Apparently citing the questionable 'invasion invitation' from President Yanukovych that Russian ambassador Vitaly Churkin had read to the UN Security Council that same day, he continued, 'It was a request to Vladimir Vladimirovich Putin to offer help and bring troops in.' Turchenyuk attempted to build rapport with the Ukrainian servicemen, telling them that he had family roots in Ukraine and that he was speaking with them 'as one officer to other officers'. While expressing the outrage at the turn of events, the unidentified Ukrainian marines still responded, 'We have always looked at Russia like an older brother' (*The Guardian* 2014). Like his Soviet predecessors, Turchenyuk used these fraternal ties to attempt to lead the Ukrainian servicemen into believing that Russia's actions were for their support.

As the Warsaw Pact forces had done in Czechoslovakia, the Russian troops used their friendly relations to approach the Ukrainian military facilities, block the forces inside and attempt to confiscate their weapons. The commander of the Ukrainian Fifth Surface Ships Brigade reported that Russian forces appeared at his base at the beginning of March 2014 and demanded that he surrender the entire unit. He said that the Russian officer in charge was a friend of his with whom he had spent the night drinking vodka only one week prior (Interview K 2017).[1] On 1 March, Russian forces arrived at the base of the Ukrainian 501st Separate Naval Infantry Battalion in Kerch. The Russians were from the 382nd Naval Infantry Battalion, a unit part of the Russian Black Sea Fleet stationed in Temyruk on the Russian side of the Kerch Strait. The battalion commander and the commander of the Russian Black Sea Fleet's 810th Naval Infantry Brigade stationed in Sevastopol met with the Ukrainian commander and provided him with various gifts, including vodka and unit flags. The Ukrainian unit was very familiar with the two Russian officers; they had conducted numerous combined training exercises and military parades over the years, especially after 2010. According to one of the Ukrainian officers, 'That's why for us, they were not "little green men" or unknown armed men. We knew them very well' (Interview B 2017). Like the Soviet appeals to the Afghan soldiers in Kabul, the Russian officers insisted that they needed to station their marines on the Ukrainian arms rooms and ammunition depots to protect them from radicals – a veiled attempt at disarming the unit before the Kyiv government potentially ordered armed resistance. The Ukrainian battalion commander rejected the offer, but the Russian servicemen remained with their vehicles outside of the base (Interview B 2017).

Similar to how the Soviet forces in Czechoslovakia and Afghanistan masked the invasions by claiming that their manoeuvres were to support their comrades in defending their own country, the Russian Armed Forces operating in Crimea alleged that they were helping their counterparts defend against radicals. As early as 23 February, armoured personnel carriers from the Russian Black Sea Fleet were staged at key intersections on the outskirts of Sevastopol, giving them control of access to the city if necessary. Their actions were a violation of the bilateral agreements, as any movement outside of their designated bases required

---

[1] A human rights lawyer working in Crimea at the time of the annexation ('Interview K') shared the details of this original interview he conducted.

a Ukrainian police escort, which they had not requested. When questioned, the Russian forces told the Ukrainian Navy that they were merely protecting their installations from violent fascist elements (Interview H 2017). Once disguised Russian soldiers started blockading the Ukrainian Navy headquarters in Sevastopol, they claimed that they were protecting the base from *Pravy Sektor*, the far-right Ukrainian group. However, they used this premise to prevent Ukrainian servicemen from entering the base and thus to disrupt the functions of the headquarters (*Meduza* 2015). Unmarked Russian servicemen arrived at the garrison of the Ukrainian Tenth Naval Aviation Brigade in Novofedorivka. They dismounted their military transport trucks and surrounded the entrance to the base in battle formation. According to Lieutenant Colonel Oleksandr Suraikin, the commander of the brigade's helicopter squadron, the Russian soldiers told them that they were there to prevent the 'angry Tatars' from seizing the base and its arms and using them 'to oppress the Russian-speaking population' (Kliatskin 2016). The commander of the 382nd Naval Infantry Battalion defended how his forces were blockading the Ukrainian naval infantry base in Kerch by warning the Ukrainian servicemen that if the Russians were not there to help, then the Americans would arrive to arm and support the violent radicals. He frequently repeated this claim over the next several days and stated that the lack of any visible American presence on the peninsula was the result of Russia's efforts (Interview B 2017). According to Rostislav Lomtev, the deputy commander of the First Separate Naval Infantry Battalion in Feodosia, the senior Russian military officers who came to their base for 'negotiations' repeatedly referenced the danger of Crimean Tatars storming the base and seizing the weapons and therefore insisted that the Ukrainian unit send their weapons to a storage facility (*Meduza* 2015).

Most of these appeals did not work, and the majority of the Ukrainian units kept their arms. However, while the Russian forces did not successfully confiscate the weapons, their presence outside the gates contributed to the lack of an armed confrontation at any of the Ukrainian bases and in effect neutralized the Ukrainian Armed Forces on the peninsula. It also decreased the threat the Ukrainians may have perceived the Russians posed to them. Their very presence at the Ukrainian military facilities was only possible by the exploitation of the *bratstvo* between the units.

In the same manner of how the Soviet advisors in 1979 deceived their Afghan partners to explain away actions that they were taking as part of the invasion plan, the Russian forces in Crimea provided their Ukrainian counterparts with false reasons to cover up how they were obstructing their ability to defend themselves.

On 28 February, the *Ivanovets*, a missile corvette from the Russian Black Sea Fleet's 41st Missile Boat Brigade, pulled into the Balaklava harbour where the SBGS Sea Guard detachment was based. Under the standing agreements, the ship was not authorized to enter the harbour. When the Sea Guard detachment challenged the *Ivanovets*, it said it was returning from training at sea and could not continue back to Sevastopol because the weather was stormy, which it was not. It then remained parked at the exit to the harbour. It only allowed a Sea Guard ship to pass after demanding to know its purpose (to investigate a passing fishing vessel), but then it followed the Ukrainian ship into the open waters (Interview G 2017). That same day, Captain (2nd Rank) Dmytro Glukhov, the commander of the First Surface Ships Brigade, ordered his command ship *Slavutych* and the corvette *Ternopil* out to sea from Sevastopol Bay. As they were departing, however, the duty officer from the fleet command centre ordered them to halt. The *Slavutych* waited in the middle of the harbour for six hours for further instructions. During this time, a missile boat from the Russian Black Sea Fleet moved to the harbour exit, halted and reported via signal code that it had a fault in the main engine and could not move. There it remained, preventing any Ukrainian ships from leaving the bay (Interview with Oleksii Kirillov 2017; Kliatskin 2016).

The Russian government also exploited the bilateral agreements it had signed with Ukraine authorizing its forces to be deployed in Sevastopol and Crimea. In an interview one year after the annexation, Admiral (retired) Igor Kasatonov, the commander of the Black Sea Fleet in 1991–2, said that the use of the Black Sea Fleet's Sevastopol base as a staging area was critical to the success of the 2014 operation. He said that 'the Black Sea Fleet prepared a foothold; the officers knew what was happening around where the Ukrainian units were located; scenarios for the development of events were worked out on maps' (RIA *Novosti* 2015). His comments suggest that the fleet regularly reviewed operational plans for such a contingency. On 25 February 2014, Russian Black Sea Fleet ships based in Novorossiysk in Russia landed in Sevastopol. Under the existing agreements, such movements were authorized. The ships reported to the SBGS that they were carrying no cargo (Interview F 2017). However, according to Ukrainian military reporting, they were actually carrying close to 1,000 Russian Airborne Troops who had been providing security at the Sochi Olympics (Interview with Yuri Petrovich Fedash 2017). Statements from some Russian soldiers corroborate this claim. The low-ranking Russian soldiers without insignia blocking the Tenth Naval Aviation Brigade in Novofedorivka told the Ukrainian servicemen that they thought they were on their way back to Moscow from the Sochi Olympics when they suddenly found themselves undocking in Crimea (Kliatskin 2016). Oleg Teryushin, a Russian sergeant from the 31st Separate Guards Air Assault Brigade, said that his unit (based in Ulyanovsk in Western Russia) was loaded into the bottom decks of landing ships in Novorossiysk, the Russian port city on the Black Sea, and disembarked for the first time in Sevastopol (*Meduza* 2015). These airborne troops then augmented the Black Sea Fleet forces in forming the bulk of the 'little green men' over the next month. Before 1 March, the number of Russian ships docking in Sevastopol matched the number authorized under the bilateral agreements. However, starting on 1 March – after Russian forces had started to seize control or block key Ukrainian facilities – additional ships began arriving from Russia's Northern and Baltic Fleets, which were not authorized to use the port under the agreements (Interview F 2017). The Russian government therefore took advantage of the friendly agreements it had signed with Ukraine to provide it with the cover to build up its invasion force.

Initially, several of the Ukrainian servicemen believed the rhetoric that their Russian counterparts were telling them. These assertions came not only from the Russian forces but from President Putin himself; during his 4 March press conference, he emphasized the *bratstvo* between the states – just as Kosygin had done in 1968 – and declared, 'I am certain, and I stress, I am certain that the Ukrainian military and the Russian military will not be facing each other; they will be on the same side in a fight' (Kremlin 2014h). According to one senior Ukrainian naval infantry officer, they believed the Russian rhetoric that the real threat would come from armed radicals, whether *Pravy Sektor* or violent factions of the Crimean Tatars, and they did not see the Russian forces as a threat. Many of the Ukrainian servicemen thus initially viewed the Russian forces surrounding their base as legitimately there to help them defend their installations (Interview B 2017). In this regard, the Russian *maskirovka* campaign succeeded in utilizing the *bratstvo* sympathies the Ukrainians shared for their comrades to undercut their defences.

The Ukrainian military partially found itself in this situation because, like its Czechoslovak and Afghan predecessors, it was largely unprepared for a conflict with Russia. The bonds of brotherhood it had developed with the Russian military blinded it to the possibility.[2] According to the former commandant of the Admiral Nakhimov Naval Academy in Sevastopol, the Ukrainian military did not believe Russia would use force against its country because of the long

---

[2]  The degradation of Ukraine's armed forces in the 1990s and 2000s due to that lack of a perceived threat is also to blame (see Lavrov and Nikolsky 2014; Nix 2014).

tradition of friendship and brotherhood between their militaries (Interview with Petr Dmitrievich Goncharenko 2017). A former senior Ukrainian defence official similarly believes that the daily interactions between the forces played a large part in desensitizing Ukraine's military to such a possibility (Interview A 2017). Throughout the 2000s, the Ukrainian Navy's senior staff courses did not highlight any military threats from Russia (Interview F 2017). Once Yanukovych became president, the Ukrainian Navy removed any mention of Russia as the opponent from its various command post exercises and instead used a NATO member state (Interview H 2017). During a 2013 conference of the senior staff of the Ukrainian Navy, the issue of a possible war with Russia was raised. The staff laughed it off as impossible and not worth considering (Interview with Marina Kanaliuk 2017). Less than a year before the invasion, the Ukrainian military appeared completely unprepared for what was to come – just as both Alexander Dubček and Hafizullah Amin were on the eve of the respective Soviet invasions that removed them from power.

The cumulative effect of these decisions, as well as Russia's influence in minimizing that perceived threat, was the Ukrainian government's surprise by the 2014 invasion and its lack of preparedness for such an attack. During the 28 February 2014 National Security and Defence Council session, Ukrainian defence minister Ihor Tenyukh – appointed the day prior after his predecessor fled to Russia – described to his colleagues how their country was 'not ready for a full-scale war'. He said that due to policies under the Yanukovych regime, Ukraine 'd[id] not have an army' and could at most muster 5,000 servicemen for combat operations. Most of Ukraine's soldiers, he claimed, had 'never shot [their weapons] in their lives'. He predicted that deploying them to Crimea would mean that '[t]hey will just die there' (NSDC 2014: 11, 26). In his 11 March report to the Verkhovna Rada, Tenyukh added that only 15 per cent of the Ukrainian Armed Forces' planes and helicopters were mission-capable, and less than 10 per cent of its air defence personnel were trained to combat standards (Galeotti 2016: 70). The head of the SBGS reported to the Verkhovna Rada Committee on National Security and Defence that some of the Ukrainian military units in Crimea had nothing more than wooden sticks for weapons (Zhegulyov et al. 2017).[3] After a month, Ukraine could still mobilize only 10,000 reservists (Navari 2014: 71). The Ukrainian military no longer had standing documents on how to mobilize and employ forces in case of conflict (Interview with Marina Kanaliuk 2017).

---

[3] This resource is a collection of interviews conducted by journalists from *Meduza*, the Riga-based newspaper created by the former staff of *Lenta.ru* that quit after editor-in-chief Galina Timchenko was fired in March 2014 under pressure from the Russian government (*Lenta.ru* 2014b).

This lack of preparedness significantly enhanced the success of the annexation operation. As in the Soviet political warfare campaigns, it was largely the product of Russia's exploitation of the *bratstvo* the Ukrainians felt for their neighbours.

## Disguised forces

Aside from using *bratstvo* to undermine resistance from the Ukrainian Armed Forces, the Russian military also employed disguised forces to sow confusion and weaken criticism on the international stage. The most visible example of *maskirovka* from the Crimean crisis was the use of Russian servicemen disguised as local self-defence forces, coined 'little green men' in the Western and Ukrainian media and 'polite people' in Russian parlance. The masked Russian soldiers without insignia on their uniforms became the lasting image from the conflict (see Figure 5.1). The practice, however, did not originate in the 2014 crisis and was a frequent feature of Soviet *maskirovka* practice.

This sort of deception through disguised forces occurred regularly in Soviet military planning. One of the plans Vladimir Lenin considered during the 1919–21 Polish-Soviet War was to disguise factions of the Red Army as 'greens' – farmers rebelling against Polish rule – thus giving the appearance

**Figure 5.1** 'Little green men' outside the Ukrainian military installation in Perevalne, Crimea on 4 March 2014 (Credit: iStock.com/AndreyKrav).

that local forces were behind the insurrection (Van Herpen 2016: 2). In the Cold War, KGB Centre directed the Bonn residency to acquire the uniforms of Bundeswehr soldiers and government employees working in the railway, forestry and road maintenance sectors. If conflict were to break out with West Germany, the KGB's DRG (Special Group) teams would conduct sabotage operations while wearing the uniforms, providing both the teams access to the critical targets and the Soviet Union deniability about its responsibility (Andrew and Mitrokhin 2000: 474). Before a planned military operation, the GRU would surge several of its intelligence officers and of its *Spetsnaz* soldiers into the target country's Soviet embassy. They would disguise themselves as support staff or even as employees of Soviet firms, such as the Aeroflot airline or TASS news agency, while they awaited execution orders (Suvorov 1989: 169–70, 206). Deception and disinformation over the identity and status of its servicemen operating in a country during a time of conflict was thus the norm in Soviet military practice.

The use of disguised forces was related to the use of agent-driven disinformation operations from the informational toolkit, but the application of the complementary techniques depended on the dynamics of the political warfare campaigns and the intended target: discrediting of opponents or bolstering of allies. The invasion of Czechoslovakia thus saw the disinformation operations to discredit the Czechoslovak reformers and incriminate Western governments but not the use of disguised forces; the invasion of Afghanistan saw the use of disguised forces to pose as Babrak Karmal's base of power but not the use of any agent-led disinformation plans.

### Afghanistan 1979

The use of disguised forces was especially prevalent in the 1979 invasion of Afghanistan. The operation revolved around the central myth that Babrak Karmal and his loyal indigenous forces had led a revolt against Hafizullah Amin and that the Soviet Union was merely responding to a request for assistance from the new regime. To support this narrative, the Soviet government relied heavily on soldiers disguised as Afghan forces to execute the key initial stages of the operation in Kabul. It also disguised some of its forces as technical specialists to hide the fact that they were combat troops in the country to prepare for the invasion. Ironically, the request for Soviet troops in Afghan uniforms originated with the Afghan leadership. After the March 1979 rebellion in Herat, in which some Afghan Army troops mutinied and joined the *Mujahideen* in attacking officials from the Afghan government, Taraki called Soviet prime minister

Alexei Kosygin and pleaded for him to send Soviet troops disguised as Afghans (Andrew and Mitrokhin 2006: 392; Maley 2009: 27; Braithwaite 2012: 50). From the call transcript, he told his Soviet ally:

> I suggest that you place Afghan markings on your tanks and aircraft and no one will be any the wiser [. . .] We want you to send us Tajiks, Uzbeks, and Turkmens. They could drive tanks, because we have all these nationalities in Afghanistan. Let them don Afghan costume and wear Afghan badges and no one will recognize them. (Kosygin and Taraki 1979)

At the time, Kosygin denied Taraki's request, claiming that 'it will not be possible to conceal this. Two hours later the whole world will know' (Kosygin and Taraki 1979).

Despite the initial refusal, the Soviet government soon sent in forces disguised as Afghans. However, it used the request from the Afghan government *not* to support the existing regime but to deploy troops for possible military action in case the situation worsened. Later that month, the Soviet military deployed to Bagram airfield eight Mi-8 helicopters, a squadron of Antonov An-12 transport planes and a field communications centre. The Soviet crews wore Afghan uniforms and painted Afghan markings on their aircraft. Over the next few months, the squadron conducted significant aerial reconnaissance throughout the country – information that was later used to support invasion planning (Grau 2003: 292; Feifer 2010: 16). The senior Soviet officials of the Afghanistan Commission suggested to the Politburo that it use Taraki's requests for additional troops as cover for deploying forces to protect Soviet interests in the country and for keeping its future military options open. It recommended sending around 150 KGB *Spetsnaz* disguised as embassy staff to Kabul to guard the embassy – a standard practice in the prelude to a conflict (Andrew and Mitrokhin 2006: 392–3). For additional combat power, the Soviet government then flew an airborne battalion into Bagram but disguised them as technical specialists there to work on the aircraft. They reported directly to the Soviet senior military advisor in the country (Russian General Staff 2002: 10). The battalion's officers wore sergeants' rank to hide the composition of the unit (Braithwaite 2012: 57).

The Soviet government then capitalized on Taraki's request and stood up a unit of 'Tajiks, Uzbeks, and Turkmens' a month after his appeal. In April 1979, the GRU directed the creation of a special *Spetsnaz* battalion headquartered in Tashkent, the capital of the Uzbek Soviet Socialist Republic in the Soviet Union. The 154th Separate *Spetsnaz* Detachment, commonly known as the 'Muslim Battalion', consisted of 520 Soviet soldiers from the Central Asian Soviet republics. Their Muslim heritage, closely related languages and similar physical features allowed for them to easily pose as Afghan soldiers (Grau 2003: 292–8; Braithwaite 2012: 56, 90–4; Feifer 2010: 58). In December 1979, new president Hafizullah Amin requested additional Soviet forces to help protect him in Kabul. In response, the Politburo sent the Muslim Battalion 'in a uniform which does not reveal its belonging to the Armed Forces of the USSR' to the capital, where it posed as Amin's security detail and guarded the outer perimeter of his residence (CPSU CC Politburo 1979c). Deployed with the Muslim Battalion was a small detachment from the KGB's *Zenit* strike force, disguised as technical advisors; *Grom*, the other KGB strike force, entered the country posing as professional athletes, arrived in Kabul and then also received Afghan uniforms (Grau 2003: 299; Braithwaite 2012: 82, 91).

Amin believed these disguised Soviet soldiers were for his protection, but they were there to conduct the operations resulting in his death and the toppling of his government. The Muslim Battalion and contingents from the *Zenit* and *Grom* strike forces composed most of the Soviet force that attacked the Tajbeg Palace on 27 December in an operation code-named *Storm-333*. The Soviet forces went to great lengths to make it appear as if it was an Afghan contingent overthrowing the palace. They dressed in their Afghan uniforms, tying white strips of bedsheets to their arms for self-identification purposes, and covered their military vehicles with Afghan markings (Feifer 2010: 66; Andrew and Mitrokhin 2006: 402). Before the initiation of the assault, the members of the Muslim Battalion were ordered to hand over their personal documents and identification papers (Braithwaite 2012: 94). If any of them were captured or killed in the battle, their Afghan uniforms, Central Asian features and lack of Soviet identification would allow the Soviet Union to deny involvement. Similarly, the *Zenit* detachment with them had flown from Moscow on a military plane masked with civilian Aeroflot markings and were issued fake documents identifying them as engineers, meteorologists and other technical specialists (Feifer 2010: 16). This gave them the cover of legitimate technical advisors requested by the Afghan government – the unit was Slavic, not Central Asian, meaning they could not pass for Afghans – and hid their identity as an elite KGB strike force.

At the end of the assault on the palace, the Soviet forces had killed Amin, members of his family and several of the Afghan guards and attendants (Andrew and Mitrokhin 2006: 402; Grau 2003: 299). The Soviet government immediately presented the situation as an Afghan operation. That evening, the fake Radio Kabul broadcast originating from the Red Army headquarters in Termez announced that Amin had been tried and found guilty in a 'Revolutionary Tribunal' and executed for 'crimes against the people' and that Babrak Karmal, the new leader, had requested Soviet military assistance. Foreign Minister Andrei Gromyko insisted that there was 'no relationship' linking the deployment of Soviet troops to the country and the change in Afghan leadership (MFA USSR 1980). The use of disguised forces had given the Soviet government the deniability it sought.

### Crimea 2014

Just as the Soviet government sought to support its narrative in 1979 through disguising its servicemen as Afghan forces, the Russian government masked its troops as Crimean self-defence forces to deny its involvement in orchestrating the 2014 annexation. The Russian military began staging its disguised forces on the peninsula even before the key events of 27 February 2014, the date the key Crimean government buildings were seized. Oleg Teryushin, the sergeant from the 31st Separate Guards Air Assault Brigade, said that his unit arrived on landing ships in Sevastopol on 24 February 2014 – three days before the Crimean Rada's decision to hold the referendum and five days before the Russian Federation Council approved the use of the Russian Armed Forces in Ukraine. As soon as they disembarked, their unit's leadership ordered the soldiers to remove all flags and insignia from their uniforms and issued them green balaclavas, sunglasses and knee and elbow pads. They were not allowed to put the patches back on their uniforms until after the referendum (*Meduza* 2015). On 25 February, two Ural military transport vehicles with Russian licence plates arrived at the Health Resort of the Ministry of Defence of the Russian Federation in Yalta, approximately 50 kilometres south of the Crimean capital, Simferopol. Armed soldiers without insignia disembarked the vehicles and entered the resort. While they did not identify themselves, the resort's director Vladimir Klemeshev admitted to local media that they were members of the Russian military (Skrypnyk and Pechonchyk 2016: 8). After some of these unmarked Russian forces seized the Crimean Rada on 27 February, different Russian units – most of whom wore some variant of the 'self-defence forces' uniform – spread throughout the peninsula and blocked the different Ukrainian military units on their installations (*Euromaidan Press* 2015).

The 'little green men' were not the only disguised Russian forces. In the aftermath of the invasion, two different soldiers from the same 31st Separate Guards Air Assault Brigade posted photos of themselves on social media wearing the distinctive blue camouflage uniforms of the Ukrainian *Berkut* special police unit while they were inside the Crimean Rada building. Ukrainian activists from the *Inform Napalm* internet research project identified the soldiers and pieced together their backgrounds (Pavlushko 2015). The photos demonstrate that in addition to the 'green men' outside of the Crimean Rada building, at least some of the police officers from the Crimean *Berkut* unit operating inside of the building were actually Russian servicemen in disguise. In this instance, the Russian forces were wearing not just non-descript uniforms which Russian officials described as 'self-defence forces' but the actual uniforms of a Ukrainian unit based in Crimea – just as the Muslim Battalion had worn the uniforms of their Afghan counterparts. Their appearance seemed to give the Russian officials who denied all involvement further credibility, and these soldiers also facilitated the desired result from the Crimean Rada session.

As in Afghanistan, these denials were persistent throughout the crisis, despite evidence to the contrary. On 4 March, Putin refuted that there were Russian soldiers blocking the Ukrainian facilities by insisting they were 'local self-defence units'. He explained that they merely looked like Russian soldiers because in 'the post-Soviet states [. . . y]ou can go to a store and buy any kind of uniform' (Kremlin 2014h). Nevertheless, the uniform of the 'little green men' betrayed them as Russian servicemen. The green digital pattern on the uniforms worn by the majority of the supposed 'self-defence forces' was the VKBO (*Vsesezonnyy Komplekt Bazovogo Obmundirovaniya*, or 'all-season basic uniform set') camouflage pattern. It was made by the Russian company BTK Group, and the Russian Ministry of Defence began fielding it in 2013. It was not exported for use outside of Russia. Similarly, their military helmet – the 6B27 – was a Russian-military issued item and was not at any point sold to the Ukrainian Armed Forces (*Meduza* 2015).

The Russian government's use of these disguised forces appears to have given its Crimean allies the confidence they needed to support Russia's plans for the annexation. According to some pro-Russian activists in Sevastopol, they were extremely nervous about how the Ukrainian government might respond to the protests and the city's decision to elect the Russian Alexey Chaly as their 'people's mayor'. However, the appearance of the 'polite people' signalled to them that the Russian state had decided to intervene on their behalf and gave them the confidence to become more assertive (Zhegulyov et al. 2017). Rustam Temirgaliev, the Crimean deputy prime minister and one of Russia's key allies who helped orchestrate the political side of the Crimean operation, said that the deployment of the 'little green men' was decisive to the annexation. He believes that the show of force their presence provided prevented the Crimean Tatar community from disrupting the political proceedings or from mobilizing for a more violent response – actions that the Ukrainian government in Kyiv may have taken as a sign to support them and actively resist the annexation (Kozlov 2015).

## Threat of increased hostilities

In addition to *bratstvo* and disguised forces, the next major military tool that Russia implemented in Crimea was the threat of increased hostilities to shape the Ukrainian government's responses. This tool similarly had its roots in Soviet campaigns. The Soviet Union used the same technique to pressure Dubček's government in Czechoslovakia. In Afghanistan, no such threats were necessary since the Soviet forces killed Amin the first night of the invasion, and the Soviet government instead gave him the impression until the last minute that they were partnering with him. In another incorporation of *maskirovka*, both the Soviet and Russian governments loosely disguised these threats of a massive retaliation as normal military exercises, which in some instances – including in their incorporation in the 1979 Afghanistan campaign – masked the build-up of forces, while in other instances served as a visible warning of their intentions.

### Czechoslovakia 1968

After Warsaw Pact forces had entered Czechoslovakia, the Soviet government issued a series of threats to escalate the conflict if the Czechoslovak government resisted them. Soon after the troops had crossed the border, Soviet defence minister Andrei Grechko called his counterpart Martin Dzúr and warned him that if the Czechoslovak forces fired 'even a single shot' in resistance, the Soviet Army would 'crush the resistance mercilessly' and Dzúr would 'be strung up from a telephone pole and shot' (Kramer 2010: 48). Soviet General Ivan Pavlovsky, the operation's commander, soon arrived in Prague and put out the same demand for the Czechoslovak forces to avoid confrontation (*Izvestia* 1989: 432). General Yershov, a member of the Soviet high command, later told Dubček that the Soviet Army was 'only waiting for a sign of active resistance in order to suppress it indiscriminately' (Dubček 1993: 209). As a result, Dubček believed that if he issued an order to resist, it would provide the Soviet government with its *casus belli* – it 'would only result in local fighting, and that would justify Soviet accusations about an organized "counterrevolution"' (Dubček 1993: 180).

The Czechoslovak leadership took the threats seriously and decided to avoid armed confrontation lest they spark a much more violent conflict. Shortly after midnight on 20–21 August, Soviet ambassador Chervonenko visited President Svoboda at his residence to convince him not to resist, and the Czechoslovak president quickly iterated that his first priority was to avoid any bloodshed (CPSU CC and Chervonenko 1968: 405–6). He immediately sent an order to Dzúr instructing as much (Ruggenthaler and Knoll 2010: 165). Dzúr then sent an encrypted order to his military commanders that 'all troops are to remain in their barracks', 'under no circumstances are weapons to be used' and 'Soviet troops who have entered our territory are to be given maximum all-round assistance' (Dzúr 1970: 412). The statement released by the CPCz Presidium in the early hours of 21 August condemned the Warsaw Pact invasion, but at the same time, it called

> [O]n all citizens of the republic to remain calm and to refrain from putting up any resistance against the advancing troops, since it would now be impossible to defend our state borders. Accordingly, units of the Czechoslovak army and the People's Militia have received no orders to defend the republic. (CPCz CC Presidium 1968)

The legitimate Radio Prague broadcast made the same appeal to the populace, pleading with its listeners at 5.30 am, 'Wherever you meet members of the occupation forces do not allow open clashes to arise which might be regarded as provocations' (Windsor and Roberts 1969: 115). At 7.07 am, it warned, '[C]alm and caution and forethought are our only weapons. If you throw a stone, the occupiers may answer with machine guns' (Bittman 1972: 197).

The reason for the capitulation was that based on the Soviet threats, the Czechoslovak leadership feared that resistance would do nothing but lead to scores of casualties and invite a military occupation. General Karel Rustov, the chief of the CzPA General Staff, defended the inaction in testimony to the Czechoslovak Parliament on 26 August 1968. He said that as a result of the decision

> [N]ot to allow bloodshed in our country [. . .] we were able to avoid the awful tragedy that would have occurred had we decided to put up any resistance. Had we done so, the result would have been the annihilation of the entire republic, the routing of the army, the elimination of our sovereignty, and a terrible bloodbath. (Rustov and Bedřich 1968: 484)

During the testimony, Major General František Bedřich, the head of the CzPA Main Political Directorate, drew the same conclusion. He claimed that 'the forces who came to this country are so powerful that we would have been utterly incapable of defending ourselves against them', and the result would have been nothing but 'a fratricidal struggle' (Rustov and Bedřich 1968: 485). Dubček was of the same mindset. He believed that '[p]resenting a military defence would have meant exposing the Czech and Slovak peoples to a senseless bloodbath' (Dubček 1991: x). During the negotiations that led to the Moscow Protocol, Svoboda wanted the Czechoslovak delegation to submit to a solution as soon as possible, for the longer the negotiations carried on, the greater the chance of open hostilities between the Warsaw Pact troops and the Czechoslovak civilians. He warned his countrymen, 'I've seen a lot of dead people in my life, and I will not permit thousands to die just because of your jabbering' (Mlynář 1980: 217). After their return to Prague, Svoboda again asserted that the avoidance of conflict was his guiding principle, telling the CPCz Central Committee on 31 August that he 'did not at any cost want to see blood flowing again and the corpses of my comrades piling up' (Tigrid 1971: 121).

## Crimea 2014

The Russian government issued these same threats of increased hostilities to the Ukrainian government during the 2014 Crimean crisis in order to shape and limit its decision-making. Serhii Kaplin was a deputy in the Verkhovna Rada and the secretary of the Committee on National Security and Defence in 2014. He said that at the time of the crisis, officials from the Russian government openly told the new Ukrainian administration that if it launched military operations against Crimea, then Russia would land its forces in Kyiv and forcibly remove the regime 'as an illegal power' (Zhegulyov et al. 2017). On 28 February 2014, the commander of the Russian Black Sea Fleet warned the commander of the Ukrainian Navy that the Russian Armed Forces were prepared to 'go all the way' and that 'all troops [we]re on full state of alert', thus threatening massive retaliation if the Ukrainian Armed Forces resisted (NSDC 2014: 10). General Dmitry Bulgakov, one of the Russian deputy defence ministers, personally conducted some of the negotiations with the commander of the Ukrainian Navy in Sevastopol in early March. According to a senior Ukrainian staff officer present in the meetings, Bulgakov told then Rear Admiral Serhiy Hayduk that Putin had tasked him and the armed forces to be ready to be in Kyiv in two weeks (Interview with Marina Kanaliuk 2017). Assuming that order from Putin came the night of 22 February, when Putin instructed his staff to 'begin working on returning Crimea to Russia' (Kondrashov 2015), then the Russian government threatened to occupy Kyiv by 8 March; alternatively, two weeks from the quoted negotiations with Hayduk would have been immediately after the planned Crimean referendum on 16 March. In either case, Bulgakov loudly threatened the toppling of the entire Ukrainian government if it resisted.

The words of the senior Ukrainian government officials confirm that the Russian threats severely affected their decision-making. On 28 February 2014, the Ukrainian National Security and Defence Council (NSDC) held an emergency session to discuss the unfolding conflict in Crimea. The new government's senior political leaders and ministers were in attendance. The session was classified, but the Ukrainian government released a transcription of the proceedings in 2016 (NSDC 2014). Their fear of the outbreak of hostilities and their belief in the futility of resistance closely resemble the same despair expressed by their Czechoslovak predecessors.

The members of the council voiced similar concerns that Russia was seeking a casus belli to invade the entire country. Arseniy Yatsenyuk, the new prime minister appointed after Yanukovych was removed as president, believed that Russia was looking to turn the crisis into a 'hot conflict' (NSDC 2014: 15). Viktor Hvozd, the head of the Foreign Intelligence Service, warned that sending troops to fight in Crimea would 'serve as pretext for the invasion into mainland Ukraine, and we will not even have anyone to defend Kyiv' (NSDC 2014: 30). Valentyn Nalyvaichenko, the head of the Security Service of Ukraine (SBU), said that from his intelligence, Russia had

> [E]xpectations that someone from the Ukrainian side – either *Pravy Sektor*, or the Security Service, or the Ministry of Defence – will react to provocations and give a pretext to use weapons by the Russian servicemen. Then their justification will be the protection of Crimean residents from the armed attack of the 'Kyiv junta'. (NSDC 2014: 7)

He also stated that the American and German governments had warned Ukraine that 'active actions' on their part would give Putin the basis 'to launch a large-scale land invasion' (NSDC 2014: 33).

In the middle of the session, the Russian government called and reissued these same threats, confirming the Ukrainians' fears. Sergey Naryshkin, the chairman of the Russian State Duma, called from Moscow and asked to speak with Oleksandr Turchynov, who besides serving as acting president was chairman of the Verkhovna Rada and thus roughly Naryshkin's equivalent. When Turchynov returned to the meeting, he told his colleagues that Naryshkin conveyed 'threats from Putin', including 'Putin's words that if even one Russian dies, they will declare us war criminals and will pursue us around the world', and hinted that they would make a 'decision to send troops not only to Crimea' but throughout Ukraine (NSDC 2014: 31). His phone call strongly echoes not just the threats but even the language Grechko, Pavlovsky and Yershov used to pressure Dzúr and the Czechoslovak government in 1968.

Like their Czechoslovak predecessors, the Ukrainian leaders drew the same conclusions about the futility of resistance. Stepan Kubiv, the chairman of the National Bank of Ukraine, appealed for the government 'to take all measures to prevent bloodshed' – the same term used time and again by the Czechoslovaks – 'and not let us be dragged into the trap [. . .] Today the main thing is not to lose the whole country, which is what they are hoping for' (NSDC 2014: 29). Yulia Tymoshenko, the opposition politician released from prison the week prior, believed that Ukraine had less than 'one chance out of a hundred to win against Putin' militarily and therefore '[n]ot a single tank should leave the barracks, not a single soldier should raise his weapon, because it would mean a loss' (NSDC 2014: 32). Turchynov was convinced that 'Russia's aggression in Crimea can turn into a full-scale war' and warned that '[t]here will be an even bigger panic if there are Russian tanks on the Khreshchatyk', the main street in central Kyiv (NSDC 2014: 19, 34).

The Ukrainian government decided not to resist the Russian forces in Crimea. It did not issue an order authorizing commanders on the peninsula to use force to defend themselves until after Russia had completed the annexation and issued an ultimatum for all Ukrainian units to surrender. By that point, however, the Ukrainian military officers saw little purpose in resisting. Captain (2nd Rank) Dmytro Glukhov, the commander of the First Surface Ships Brigade, believed that if he had then given the order to open fire, 'it would have been "The Navy Heavenly Hundred"', an allusion to the 100 anti-Yanukovych protesters killed on Maidan on 20 February 2014 (Kliatskin 2016). According to then Captain (2nd Rank) Marina Kanaliuk, the assistant to the commander of the Ukrainian Navy for cooperation with the Russian Black Sea Fleet, the senior Ukrainian military leaders believed the best they could muster was a delaying operation. If they could prolong the annexation process in Crimea long enough for Ukraine to consolidate forces in the mainland, then they could prevent the conventional invasion that would overtake the entire country. They believed that Russia would not move on to the eastern parts of the country until the Crimean operation was complete because of the peninsula's strategic importance. They thus found minor ways to extend the negotiations and delay the complete surrender of their ships and installations without providing the Russian government with the casus belli for an all-out invasion (Interview with Marina Kanaliuk 2017).

For example, the *Cherkasy* minesweeper in Lake Donuzlav continued to resist and manoeuvre for five days after the surrender ultimatum (Interview with Yuri Petrovich Fedash 2017). On 26 March, it became the last ship seized by the Russian forces (Reuters 2014). Despite these small measures, however, Russia's frequent threats of massive escalation – just as the Soviet Union had threatened in Czechoslovakia – largely prevented any significant Ukrainian resistance to the annexation operation.

## Military exercises

### Czechoslovakia 1968

Connected to this threat of increased hostilities was another application of *maskirovka*: the use of military exercises to deceptively mass forces for the invasion – either as a thinly veiled demonstration of military might or as cover for the concentration of the forces necessary. As a member of the Warsaw Pact, Czechoslovakia hosted international military exercises regularly, and initial planning for the exercises in 1968 started the year prior. The Soviet Union used the occurrence of these exercises to conduct preparations for the invasion. *Neman* from 23 July to 10 August 1968 was a rear-services exercise and was the largest such exercise ever conducted by the Soviet Union (Navratil 1998: 298). At the time, the CIA considered *Neman* as the greatest indicator that the Soviet Union was preparing to invade Czechoslovakia because it involved the recall of reservists, the military requisition of civilian transportation and the movement of forces from as far away as Latvia to the Czechoslovak border (CIA 2012: 10; Steury 2010: 242). Along with *Skyshield*, an air defence exercise from 11 to 20 August, *Neman* served as cover for the logistical expansion necessary for the impending operation (Dawisha 1984: 251; Valenta 1991: 111). *Horizon*, a separate communications exercise involving Soviet, East German and Polish staffs, began immediately after *Neman* and continued right up to the invasion. The communication networks established in the exercise were what the forces used during the actual operation (Dawisha 1984: 274, 281). Hungary and the Soviet Southern Group of Forces began their own bilateral manoeuvres on 15 August and also continued them up to the invasion (Navratil 1998: 363).

The Soviet Union similarly used *Sumava*, a command post and communications exercise from 20 to 30 June, to shape the invasion. A much larger version of the exercise was initially planned for September, but in April, commander-in-chief of Warsaw Pact forces Marshal Ivan Yakubovsky insisted to the Czechoslovak government that it occur in June (Dawisha 1984: 162).

The Politburo had discussed military intervention for the first time shortly before Yakubovsky's demand. In its 21 March 1968 session, Petro Shelest, first secretary of the Ukrainian Communist Party, stated that the fate of the entire 'socialist camp' was at stake in Czechoslovakia and that only 'military measures' would save it. KGB chairman Yuri Andropov seconded his position and called for 'concrete measures' to start military preparation (Andrew and Mitrokhin 2000: 327). Dubček initially resisted the change in date but relented when Yakubovsky agreed to scale it down to a limited staff exercise. However, the Soviet Armed Forces still brought thousands of more soldiers than what was agreed. When Yakubovsky returned to Prague on 18 June for the start of the exercises, he announced that it would now include the commanders and staffs (including logistics and communications personnel) from the Soviet Union, Czechoslovakia, East Germany, Hungary and Poland (Dawisha 1984: 162). Furthermore, the troops remained on Czechoslovak soil for weeks after the exercise ended and only withdrew after numerous complaints from the Dubček government (Dubček 1993: 158). Still, not all of the troops had withdrawn by the time of the invasion, and those that did regrouped in the neighbouring countries in the posture they would use at the start of the operation (Valenta 1991: 49, 112).

The military exercises were a form of *maskirovka* because they covered the massing and movement of troops before the actual invasion (Valenta 1991: 190). On 24 July, Soviet generals from the Southern Group of Forces travelled to Budapest to meet with chief of the Hungarian People's Army General Staff Károly Csémi. The stated purpose of their visit was to 'prepare for exercises' upcoming in Czechoslovakia, but based on Csémi's notes, they actually conducted an overview of Operation *Danube* (the invasion's codename), including Hungary's designated crossing points and how to handle resistance from the CzPA (Csémi 1968). The Soviet forces also used the exercises as a reconnaissance operation and dress rehearsal for the invasion. After *Sumava*, the Soviet units left up the road signs they had used during the exercise that helped them navigate the Czechoslovak road system (Steury 2010: 243). The Soviet Army communications centre at Ruzyně Airport near Prague also remained operational, and it played a key role in facilitating the landing of Soviet Airborne Forces at the start of the invasion (Dawisha 1984: 186). Czechoslovak citizens reported seeing the same Soviet officers during the invasion and occupation in the same locations they had been during the summers' exercises (Tigrid 1971: 108). In fact, General Semyon Zolotov from the Main Political Directorate of the Soviet Army and Navy reported that the first civilians that the invading columns encountered assumed they were part of yet another exercise (Zolotov 1994: 375).

In addition to using the exercises as cover to posture forces and create infrastructure for the impending invasion, the Soviet Union also used them to serve as a threat to the Czechoslovak government if it did not make the demanded concessions. The Soviet news agency TASS reported that on 13 August, Grechko, Yakubovsky and chief of the Main Political Directorate of the Soviet Army and Navy Alexei Yepishev were in Dresden to witness the ongoing exercises. Western intelligence interpreted the announcement as a public threat to the Dubček government that the Warsaw Pact forces were prepared to intervene if necessary (CIA 1968b). The official Soviet newspaper *Izvestia* had similarly announced the start of the *Neman* exercise on its front page on 23 July (Dawisha 1984: 249). Dzúr warned Dubček on 17 June that the thirty to forty thousand troops planned for the *Sumava* exercise were 'unusually high for an exercise of this nature', implying that he feared more sinister purposes behind it (Dzúr 1968). After the exercise was complete, Dzúr and the senior commanders of the CzPA pointed out the 'certain irregularities' that had occurred, especially the fact that their planners from the CzPA's exercise directorate 'were not invited to consultations or to the start of the exercises and were not kept sufficiently informed about the intended procedures'; furthermore, the Soviet Army extended the exercise without consulting its Czechoslovak hosts (Dzúr et al. 1968: 191–2). Hungarian Generals Olah and Szucs confirmed as much when they reported back to their Politburo that the *Sumava* exercise 'was organized essentially for political reasons and with political objectives', mostly 'to influence the Czechoslovak events in the sense that a show of the strength and determination of the Warsaw Pact states would paralyze and frighten enemies at home' (Olah and Szucs 1968: 199–200).

## Afghanistan 1979

While the Soviet government did not need to threaten increased hostilities in Afghanistan due to the secretive and swift approach it took to removing Amin, it still used mobilization exercises as *maskirovka* to hide its preparations for the invasion. In October 1979, US intelligence noticed an increase in transport aircraft arriving in the Turkmen Military District and the other Soviet military districts adjoining Afghanistan. In November, tens of thousands of reservists from the Central Asian republics were called up to man the Turkmen Military District's five divisions, which were usually maintained at only 10–30 per cent manning but with full equipment (Collins 1986: 71). Additionally, the Soviet forces commandeered 8,000 vehicles and other pieces of heavy equipment from the local economy (Bradsher 1999: 89). When challenged on the sudden influx of forces, the Soviet government insisted that it was part of a routine mobilization exercise, when in reality, it was preparing the invasion force that would cross the border that winter (McMichael 1991: 4). In this regard, the 'exercise' served the same purpose as *Neman* in Czechoslovakia in how it mobilized massive amounts of reserve troops and repurposed the local economy to support the pending operation.

### Crimea 2014

During the 2014 Crimean crisis, the Russian government employed this same tactic of using military exercises to achieve the same effects. The Russian exercises were the largest such drills for its forces to date and clearly demonstrated the force Russia was willing to bring to bear in Ukraine (Renz and Smith 2016: 7). The Russian government announced that the exercises, running from 26 February to 4 March 2014, were 'being conducted as part of a snap inspection of combat readiness of Western and Central Military District forces and a number of armed forces' branches', and – just as TASS had clearly announced that Grechko, Yakubovsky and Yepishev would be observing the exercises in Czechoslovakia – the Kremlin also noted that both President Putin and Defence Minister Sergey Shoigu would personally observe the snap inspections (Kremlin 2014i). The exercises therefore started the day before the Russian forces in Crimea went active – immediately before they seized the Crimean Rada, key airfields and the Kerch crossing and blocked Ukrainian military installations. They involved 150,000 troops, 90 aircraft, 120 helicopters, 880 tanks, 1,200 pieces of military equipment and 80 naval ships (Ministry of Defence of the Russian Federation 2014), thus quickly assembling a force large enough to invade the whole of Ukraine – but maintaining the guise of a normal military exercise. At the same time, the manoeuvres were also a clear demonstration to the Ukrainian government about the risks of taking aggressive action in Crimea. In an apparently veiled threat to the Ukrainian government, the press release from the Russian Ministry of Defence emphasized that military units across the commands were staged and 'ready to deploy to any area to be determined by the General Staff' (Ministry of Defence of the Russian Federation 2014).

Like Dubček's government before them, the Ukrainian government understood the message. Tenyukh, the defence minister, told his colleagues in the NSDC session that within the numbers Russia had mobilized for the 'snap inspection', 38,000 Russian troops, 761 tanks, 2,200 armoured vehicles, 720 artillery and rocket systems, 40 attack helicopters, 90 combat support helicopters, 90 ground attack aircraft and 80 military ships had massed along Ukraine's borders 'under the cover of exercises [. . .] not just [as] a show of force, but real preparation for an incursion in our territory' (NSDC 2014: 10). As these Russian forces massed on Ukraine's border, the central SBGS authorities concentrated their assets and border monitoring forces on the developing situation to the east. Russia's massing of troops thus served to redirect resources from the ongoing crisis in Crimea towards the potentially much larger crisis unfolding on the eastern border (Interview F 2017). The Russian government's use of these exercises thus achieved the same effects as their use had done for the Soviet Union in its political warfare campaigns.

# Negotiations

The third key military tool of Soviet political warfare practice that the Russian government adopted in Crimea was an application of 'negotiations' with the Ukrainian military units to discourage their resistance and compel their defections. In these negotiations, the Russian officials isolated the Ukrainians from each other and from sources of information on what was truly occurring in the country. In its place, they fed them disinformation to shape their thinking and their decision-making. They relied on both 'carrots' and 'sticks' to pressure the Ukrainian servicemen into falling in line behind the annexation. These negotiations were repeated daily during the crisis until the annexation was complete. This Russian approach to 'negotiating' with the Ukrainian military in Crimea mirrored the techniques the Soviet government used to pressure the Czechoslovak officials when drafting the Moscow Protocol in 1968. While these negotiating techniques were a political tool in the Czechoslovak campaign, the Russian government adopted them to use against the Ukrainian military in Crimea. According to Zdeněk Mlynář (1980: 212), who attended the Moscow meetings as secretary of the CPCz, 'the word "negotiations" is hardly appropriate' because the days of meetings were not between official state bodies but 'proposals in the forms of ultimatums' from various Soviet individuals. On 31 August 1968, he called the resulting declaration the result of 'pressure' and 'entirely unsuitable conditions' levied on the Czechoslovak representatives (Tigrid 1971: 116). The Soviet 'negotiations' to compel the Czechoslovak officials to accept the terms of the Moscow Protocol served as a blueprint for the way in which the Russian government applied psychological pressure on the Ukrainian servicemen throughout March 2014.

As with the threat of increased hostilities, this technique did not apply to the Afghanistan campaign because the Soviet government instead chose to mislead Amin until the last minute into believing he had the backing of the Soviet government, then to lead a secret operation with disguised Soviet forces to kill him and remove his government. With the swift removal of Amin and his regime, no strong-armed 'negotiations' were necessary as part of its political warfare campaign.

## Czechoslovakia 1968

The Soviet government treated the Czechoslovak officials as virtual prisoners in Moscow, controlling their interactions with each other, restricting their movements and filtering what information they received in order to extract the desired results from the 'negotiations' (Ruggenthaler and Knoll 2010; Tigrid 1971). In his radio address to the country after their return to Prague, chairman of the National Assembly Josef Smrkovský explained that their decision-making was severely limited by the way in which the Soviet government kept them isolated:

> Under the circumstances, as everyone will agree, deciding what to do was highly problematic. The occupation of the country by the Warsaw Pact armies was a cruel reality. Our contacts with home were limited; at first we had little, indeed almost no, information, and suddenly we had to rely more on our faith in the firm position of our people than on any knowledge of the facts of the situation. (Smrkovský 1968: 489)

During the negotiations, Dubček complained to General Secretary Leonid Brezhnev that he 'and the other comrades were isolated and were brought here [Moscow] without knowing anything' (CPSU CC Politburo 1968d: 467). The Soviet officials controlled the information available to their Czechoslovak counterparts, preventing them from truly understanding the situation on the ground in their country and forcing them to make decisions based only on what was available to them.

Besides isolating the Czechoslovak officials from the outside world, the Soviet government also isolated them from each other during the negotiations. For the majority of the meetings, the Soviet officials met with Dubček alone and then separately with Svoboda alone. According to Dubček (1993: 189), these 'one-on-one interrogations' allowed them to 'find out who stood where, in order to divide us'. In these meetings, the Soviet officials did not inform Dubček that they had also brought Prime Minister Oldřich Černík to Moscow or that Svoboda had arrived to try to secure his release. Their goal was to make him feel isolated and alone in order to force concessions (Navratil 1998: 465). During the 23 August session, Politburo members Brezhnev, Kosygin, Nikolai Podgorny and Gennady Voronov met with Dubček alone for over three hours (CPSU CC Politburo 1968d: 465). This was also the same day that President Svoboda arrived in Moscow. Instead of allowing him to meet with Dubček or the others, the Politburo members pulled him into a meeting by himself soon after he landed and pressured him to form a 'provisional revolutionary government'. Despite the heavy pressure, Svoboda refused (Navratil 1998: 466).

The Soviet Politburo members used a series of 'carrots' and 'sticks' to force the agreement. During the negotiations, Brezhnev threatened Černík, 'Look, you either behave yourself or you'll lose your post as prime minister!' However, he later tempted him, 'Listen, don't you want to become first secretary?' (Černík 1990: 426). The Soviet government made clear to the Czechoslovak politicians that if they refused to sign the declaration, then the Warsaw Pact Five would leave their forces in the country and establish a military dictatorship (Navratil 1998: 477). In his address to the country on 29 August, Smrkovský (1968: 489) said that he and the other Czechoslovak representatives 'considered rejecting any accommodating solution, that sometimes it is better to face bayonets head-on in the interest of the honour and character of one's nation', but they determined that such a stand would have been futile. Similarly, Dubček (1993: 209) wrote that he believed that a 'refusal to sign the "agreement" [in Moscow. . . ] would only lead to a bloodbath'.

The Soviet officials required Dubček to meet with them multiple times per day, often to repeat the same discussions, until he eventually agreed to their terms (Dubček 1993: 202). The other Czechoslovak officials faced the same repetition designed to undermine their resolve. At the end of the four days of intense negotiations, the only one of the twenty-six Czechoslovak representatives who refused to sign the protocol was František Kriegel, a member of the CPCz Presidium and a particularly avid reformer. Even though he was one of the initial five officials forcibly brought to Moscow, the Politburo would not let him participate in the negotiations, probably because of his staunch views. According to Mlynář, the secretary of the CPCz, Kriegel's absence from these repetitive 'negotiations' was why he was not willing to sign like the others: 'Of course, we had all been through this [refusal to sign] ourselves, and he was still in the initial phase of things, just as we had been yesterday. The difference was that Kriegel never advanced to the next phase and held fast to his original refusal' (Mlynář 1980: 236).

At the end of the negotiations, both parties signed the Moscow Protocol, which forced the Czechoslovak officials to accept the Soviet Politburo's demands to undo most of the recent reforms: nullify the ongoing Fourteenth Party Congress in Vysocany, re-emphasize central economic planning, ban political organizations, reimpose censorship, dismiss the most reform-minded officials, disallow repercussions against the officials who had collaborated with the Soviet government, rescind the request to the UN Security Council to consider the situation in Czechoslovakia and avoid a timetable of withdrawal for the Warsaw Pact troops in the country (USSR and ČSSR 1968). Dubček (1993: 204) believed that the protocol allowed the Soviet government to 'legitimize the aggression' by having a document that showed the Czechoslovak officials agreeing with the grounds for the invasion, including its indirect denunciations of the reform plans. While the 'negotiations' hardly allowed for give-and-take between the two parties, the existence of the meetings themselves increased the Soviet Union's claim to legitimacy in how it resolved the conflict.

## Crimea 2014

In the Crimean crisis, the Russian government's meetings with the Ukrainian servicemen used these same techniques in 'negotiating' defections and preventing resistance. First, they isolated the Ukrainians from outside sources of information and from each other. Not only were the Ukrainian television channels replaced with ones from Russian state television, but the internet connections on the Ukrainian ships trapped in their ports also stopped working during the second week of the blockade (Kliatskin 2016). The crew of the ship *Ternopil*, for example, were locked in their ship for twenty-three straight days, all the way from when the alert was issued after forces seized the Crimean Rada to when Russian soldiers forcibly removed them from the ship after the annexation was complete (Interview with Oleksii Kirillov 2017). In this isolation, various high-ranking Ukrainian officers received visits from plain-clothes Russian officials, some of whom admitted or implied that they represented the Federal Security Service (FSB). They fed them spurious information about the 'chaos' in Kyiv and across Ukraine and the consequences that would occur if the Ukrainian servicemen did not join Russia. The Ukrainian officers did not receive clarification or clear guidance from the government in Kyiv to dispel these rumours, and the information quickly spread among the Ukrainian ranks (Interview I 2017). The marines of the First Separate Naval Infantry Battalion in Feodosia reported unmarked Russian armoured personnel carriers surrounding their base with 'loudspeakers blaring disinformation' (Kliatskin 2016). According to one of the marines,

There was much disinformation. We were told things like, 'You are the only unit; all other units have been fighting under the Crimean flag for a long time. They are fighting for the Crimean people.' There was a stadium that bordered on our garrison [. . .] They put acoustic systems on the stadium fence and played back repeatedly Putin's quotes or a list of documents for obtaining Russian passports and things like that. (Kliatskin 2016)

Similarly, the commandant of the Ukrainian Naval Academy said that he 'felt like I was alone' as he attempted to rally support among his staff and cadets to remain loyal to the new authorities in Kyiv (Interview with Petr Dmitrievich Goncharenko 2017).

This isolation occurred in the negotiations, as well. The Russian officials insisted that the commander of the Fifth Surface Ships Brigade attend negotiations by himself. They allowed his subordinate officers to escort him to the meetings, but they were not allowed to participate (Interview with Yuri Petrovich Fedash 2017). Rear Admiral Denis Berezovsky faced a similar situation. On the day that he was named chief of the Ukrainian Navy, he went to the Russian Black Sea Fleet headquarters to negotiate with the Russian officials. He ordered Captain (2nd Rank) Marina Kanaliuk, the assistant to the commander of the Ukrainian Navy for cooperation with the Russian Black Sea Fleet, to join him. She refused, stating that she feared coercion from the FSB, so he went alone. After he returned, Berezovsky declared his allegiance to the 'Crimean people' and independence. The next day, Kanaliuk asked him how many FSB officers he thought were with him at the 'negotiation'. He said that he faced around twenty of them alone (Interview with Marina Kanaliuk 2017). One senior Ukrainian staff officer remembers Berezovsky as generally pro-Ukrainian before that day, and during his public declaration of his allegiance to the Crimean people, Berezovsky did not appear to this officer as his normal, confident self (Interview I 2017). Another senior Ukrainian Navy officer who knew Berezovsky well believes that he had no intention on defecting when he headed to the Russian Black Sea Fleet headquarters, but by the end of the 'negotiation', he was convinced that Crimea was on the path to becoming an independent republic (Interview H 2017). In the end, the Russian government rewarded Berezovsky for his actions; on 24 March 2014, Russian defence minister Shoigu appointed Berezovsky as the deputy commander of the Russian Black Sea Fleet (Interfax-Ukraine 2014).

In the negotiations, the Russian officials offered various such 'carrots' to the Ukrainian servicemen. They swiftly promised to meet whatever demands the Ukrainian officers had. When they pointed out there was no Crimean constitution for them to swear allegiance to, the next day, the negotiators produced a constitution. The Ukrainian Navy's judge advocate identified that Russian law did not allow foreign citizens to join its military; within twenty-four hours, the negotiators showed them that the Russian government had amended the law (Interview H 2017; Interview I 2017). On 20 March 2014, Putin followed up on those promises and signed an executive order that guaranteed that Ukrainian servicemen could transfer their ranks, military education and credit for time served to the Russian Armed Forces as long as they took Russian citizenship and declared themselves part of the 'military formations of the Republic of Crimea' (Kremlin 2014d). On 31 March, he signed a follow-up executive order to increase their wages to match their Russian counterparts (Kremlin 2014f). The negotiators even showed the Ukrainian officers task organization charts to show that they would remain in their same positions on the same bases (Interview B 2017). Some of the Ukrainian officers felt that the Russian officials were simply 'promising the world' and would tell them whatever they wanted to hear to win them over (Interview with Oleksii Kirillov 2017). Vice Admiral Alexander Fedotenkov, the deputy commander-in-chief of the Russian Navy and the previous commander of the Russian Black Sea Fleet, negotiated with Captain (1st Rank) Petr Goncharenko, the commandant of the Naval Academy. He had earlier participated in the meetings to choose the next prime minister of Crimea. Fedotenkov promised Goncharenko that he would reappoint him commandant of the academy once it became part of Russia and would pay him a special bonus for transferring if he defected (Interview with Petr Dmitrievich Goncharenko 2017).

At the same time, however, the Russian negotiators threatened the Ukrainian servicemen with various 'sticks'. One of the rumours that the negotiators spread in the isolated information environment was that the Kyiv government was planning to arrest and charge all remaining Ukrainian service members in Crimea as traitors for not doing more to resist the Russian occupation. At the Naval Academy, the instructors who had already decided to defect to the Russian Navy spread these rumours and used them to try to convince other instructors and the cadets that they had no choice but to defect (Interview with Petr Dmitrievich Goncharenko 2017). Another rumour was that officers would be court-martialled for losing the military equipment they would abandon in Crimea if they withdrew to mainland Ukraine. Under Ukrainian law, unit commanders were responsible for the security of the military property assigned to their units. These rumours persisted even though no officers appeared to have faced such charges in the aftermath (Interview B 2017). The Crimean SBU *Alfa* special operations unit was also based on the grounds of the Naval Academy.

The unit was involved with security operations at the Maidan protests in Kyiv for three weeks before Yanukovych fled. The commandant of the Naval Academy spoke with several of its officers when they returned to their base in late February. Based on their discussions, he learned that the unit was directly responsible for the deaths of at least seven protesters on Maidan, and they believed that if they remained in Ukraine, they would be held accountable for their actions (Interview with Petr Dmitrievich Goncharenko 2017). In the end, approximately 90 per cent of the Crimean SBU *Alfa* unit defected to Russia (Butusov 2017).

The Russian forces issued various ultimatums to try to force the Ukrainians' hands. When Berezovsky returned to the Ukrainian Navy headquarters on 3 March after his defection, he told the staff that they had twenty-four hours to join the 'Crimean Armed Forces' or to leave the peninsula. The deadline passed without action (Interview I 2017). On 9 March – one week before the referendum, and nine days before Putin signed the annexation order – the Russian forces blocking the Second Separate Anti-Aircraft Missile Battalion on their base in Yevpatoria delivered an ultimatum from Yury Zherebtsov, a representative from Sergey Aksyonov's new Crimean government. It gave the unit until 10.00 pm on 10 March to surrender all weapons, including its *Kub* (SA-6) surface-to-air missiles, to a warehouse of the Russian Black Sea Fleet. It also demanded that armed servicemen from the Russian Black Sea Fleet take part in guarding the facility (UNIAN 2014a). However, the deadline also passed without action. Lieutenant Colonel Alexander Lomaka, the commander of the battalion, called it 'psychological pressure' and said it was not the first ultimatum he received (Osborn 2014). Then-Vice Admiral Aleksandr Vitko, the commander of the Russian Black Sea Fleet, personally visited each ship of the Ukrainian Navy to take part in the negotiations (Interview with Oleksii Kirillov 2017). He threatened the ship commanders, stating that he knew the locations of their families and that there would be trouble for them if the servicemen resisted (Interview I 2017). Vitko directly conveyed these threats to the commander of the First Surface Ships Brigade three or four times over two weeks (Kliatskin 2016). The forces guarding the First Separate Naval Infantry Battalion base in Feodosia threw copies of a form over the fence to the Ukrainian servicemen. It was an enlistment form into the 'Crimean Armed Forces' and a pledge of allegiance to the 'people of Crimea'. The attached note insisted that they must complete it before 16 March, the day of the referendum (Kliatskin 2016). The Russian negotiators warned the Ukrainian servicemen that if they did not switch allegiances, then as soon as the annexation was complete, they would be considered illegal forces in Crimea and handled accordingly (Interview with Oleksii Kirillov 2017). During a meeting after the referendum with the officers of the Fifth Surface Ships Brigade, plain-clothed, armed Russian officials told them that if they declared their ship's allegiance to the Russian Navy the following morning, then they would receive a bonus that was bigger than Russian servicemen received at the time, but if they refused, then they would be forcibly removed from the peninsula (Interview with Yuri Petrovich Fedash 2017).

These negotiations were repeated daily throughout the crisis period. Starting 2 March and continuing through the referendum, a constant stream of officials appeared at the Naval Academy to negotiate with Goncharenko, including retired Vice Admiral Sergey Menyailo, the former deputy commander of the Russian Black Sea Fleet who later was appointed the governor of Sevastopol (Interview with Petr Dmitrievich Goncharenko 2017). After then Counter Admiral Serhiy Hayduk was appointed to replace Berezovsky as commander of the Ukrainian Navy, the Russian officials met with him every day, sometimes multiple times per day (Interview with Marina Kanaliuk 2017). The regimental commander of the Russian unit blocking the 36th Coastal Defence Brigade in Perevalne met with the Ukrainian brigade commander several times per day from the day they arrived until after the annexation (Interview with Yuri Valentinovich Golovashenko 2017). Major General Alexander Ostrikov, the commander of the Russian Black Sea Coastal Defence Troops, and Lieutenant General Igor Turchenyuk, deputy commander of the Southern Military District, visited the 501st Separate Naval Infantry Battalion in Kerch every day during the crisis. The commander of the Russian 382nd Naval Infantry Battalion returned to Kerch every few days to join the negotiations. According to one of the Ukrainian deputy commanders of the 501st, the repetition of the negotiations and the bombardment of propaganda reduced their morale day by day (Interview B 2017). The Russian generals also summoned the commander of the First Separate Naval Infantry Battalion daily; one of his deputies, Major Rostislav Lomtev, worried that they were sapping the commander's resolve, and that if they succeeded in winning 'the heart of the commander', that it would 'let the infection in' the entire unit (*Meduza* 2015).

These tactics succeeded in undermining the Ukrainian servicemen's will. According to Lieutenant Colonel Volodymyr Baraniuk from the First Separate Naval Infantry Battalion, the soldiers at first felt that 'something could have been done', but as the standoff continued without resolution or improvement and the negotiations dragged on, 'people started to think, well, why should I' start a war on the territory where my family lives (Kliatskin 2016). After several days of meeting with the Russian negotiators, Colonel Sergei Storozhenko, the brigade commander of the 36th Coastal Defence Brigade at Perevalne, argued to his subordinate commanders that resisting would be 'to send your soldiers to their deaths' and that without clear direction from the government in Kyiv, it was futile to resist the tremendous military potential the Russian forces could bring to bear (Interview with Yuri Valentinovich Golovashenko 2017). Even some of the Ukrainian servicemen who were initially loyal defected as the blockade and information vacuum continued. On the first day of the 'negotiations', one company commander in the 501st Separate Naval Infantry Battalion assembled his men with their weapons in the company common room, nailed the Ukrainian marine oath to the door and refused to discuss the possibility of defection. However, by the time the referendum was complete, he, too, chose to defect. His wife was an ethnic Russian, and he believed the rumours that he would be court-martialled for abandoning his unit's equipment in Crimea. Despite his initial patriotism, the push-and-pull factors presented to him in the 'negotiations' eventually eroded his resolve (Interview B 2017).

As CPCz secretary Zdeněk Mlynář (1980: 236) noted about the Moscow Protocol, these 'negotiations' were successful in wearing down even some of the staunchest patriots. From the isolation to the disinformation to the repetition to the 'carrots' and 'sticks', the Russian government appeared to reapply the same 'negotiating' tactics the Soviet government used to force the Czechoslovak officials to sign the Moscow Protocol. It achieved similar effect. According to some Ukrainian government estimates, up to 75 per cent of the forces serving in Crimea at the time of the crisis defected to Russia (Interview H 2017).

*   *   *

The military tools employed in the 2014 Russian operation to annex Crimea came from the Soviet government's toolkit for its political warfare campaigns. The Russian operation relied on *maskirovka*, the Russian and Soviet military principle of deception and disinformation, and utilized it in the same way as the Soviet operations. The Russian forces exploited the *bratstvo* between them and the Ukrainian servicemen in Crimea, capitalizing on the fraternal bonds that years of combined exercises as well as the sharing of ports and training facilities created, to deceive their counterparts into viewing the invasion as an act of assistance. The Soviet Armed Forces had taken the exact same approach with its communist brothers-in-arms in Czechoslovakia and Afghanistan. Even the apparently novel aspects of the Crimean operation – the deployment of unmarked Russian soldiers and the insistence from the Russian government that these were the native Crimean self-defence forces – were a Soviet *maskirovka* tactic used to near-identical effect in the invasion of Afghanistan. The way in which the Russian government threatened the new Ukrainian regime with an all-out invasion if it resisted its forces in Crimea, including the way in which it used military exercises both to mask the activation of the invasion units and to be a show of force, was likewise a key military tool in the Soviet political warfare campaigns. Even the nature of the 'negotiations' that the Russian forces conducted with the Ukrainian servicemen in Crimea followed the techniques the Soviet Union had used during the Moscow Protocol sessions with the Czechoslovak leadership. As with the informational and political tools, the military tools used by the Russian government in the Crimean annexation operation have clear antecedents in Soviet political warfare practice, especially the invasions of Czechoslovakia and Afghanistan. These linkages suggest that the way the Russian government is waging its modern military campaigns is the modern application of Soviet techniques – spurred by similar perceptions of the security environment – versus the invention of some new type of warfare.

# 6

# Conclusion

Based on the analysis presented in this book, the Russian annexation of Crimea – the operation which inspired discussions about Russian 'hybrid warfare' – was more accurately the modern adaptation of Soviet political warfare practices than it was the invention of a new type of warfare. After a period of hot-and-cold relations with the West from the Gorbachev era through Yeltsin's presidency, the Russian government under Vladimir Putin has once again returned to the Cold War interpretation of the security environment – that which views the United States and NATO as its main adversaries attempting to subvert Russia and its perceived sphere of influence from within. This fear of subversion has been spurred by the wave of 'colour revolutions' that have occurred in the past few decades, leading to the development of Russia's colour revolution theory to explain these alleged Western subversion practices. The theory and the events that inspire it read like the twenty-first-century version of the Soviet counter-revolution theory – the theory that the Soviet leadership used to explain events such as the 1958 Hungarian Revolution and the 1968 Prague Spring. Seeing world events through these similar lenses, the Russian government has thus adopted the same Cold War responses which the Soviet government developed: its political warfare practices.

The Russian government adapted the informational tools of Soviet political warfare to match the modern media and technology environments. Without the state monopoly over information that the Soviet government enjoyed, the Russian government took various steps to consolidate direct and indirect control over the Russian media landscape, including unofficial levers to silence outlets critical of its policies. These efforts increased around the time of the 2014 Crimean crisis and gave the Russian government control of the narrative as it unfolded. In Crimea, the Russian forces repeated the Soviet practice of seizing domestic media and replacing it with their own, including broadcasting Russian state television over the signals of the Ukrainian television channels, thus dominating the information sphere on the peninsula in the critical days before the referendum.

Within the information campaign, the Russian government then applied old Soviet tools, such as the same propaganda themes blaming Western aggression as the cause of the crisis, labelling the pro-Western protesters as 'fascists' regardless of their political motivations, warning of the dangers of Ukrainian nationalists to ethnic Russians and portraying Russian servicemen as the heroic protectors of their innocent victims. It revived the Soviet propaganda practice of 'whataboutism' to deflect criticism of its actions. Instead of relying on journalists recruited as KGB agents to plant information in support of these themes, as the Soviet government had to do, the Russian government adapted this 'black' propaganda technique to the modern era by employing trolls and other false platforms in the internet media space. In the same fashion, the Russian government revived Soviet *dezinformatsia* practices, including consistent government denials despite mounting evidence to the contrary, forgeries to misattribute responsibility for inflammatory actions and elaborate agent schemes to feed the government narrative.

The political tools employed by the Russian government in Crimea played out nearly identically as in the Soviet political warfare campaigns. The Russian government relied on the pro-Russian political parties and its agents within their ranks to facilitate the political actions necessary to move forward with the annexation, just as the Soviet government had used foreign Communist Parties and collaborators within them in its own campaigns. As if learning from the Soviet government's failure to achieve the desired results from the Presidium vote in Czechoslovakia and the lack of overt political proceedings in Afghanistan, the Russian government manufactured the political process in Crimea to bring about the new Crimean leadership and the referendum but found the balance between public displays of political legitimacy and control of the results behind the scenes. It used two more Soviet political warfare tools, agents of influence and front organizations, to add to the appearance of legitimacy for the annexation by employing them as international election observers. The 'invasion invitation' from President Viktor Yanukovych – a key piece of the Russian government's public defence for its actions – was in the same manner directly lifted from Soviet political warfare practice, including the suspicious circumstances under which it came about.

The military tools of the annexation shared these same historical connections. *Maskirovka*, the Russian military tradition of active deception and disinformation in a military operation, manifested in the same fashions in Crimea as it had in earlier Soviet campaigns. The Russian servicemen manipulated the *bratstvo* they enjoyed with their Ukrainian counterparts to undermine their defensive preparations and to deceive them into believing that they were there to support them, not to seize their territory. The Russian government disguised its troops as 'local self-defence forces' much as the Soviet government had created the 'Muslim Battalion' consisting of Central Asian soldiers dressed in Afghan uniforms to give the appearance that local Afghan forces were behind the operation that killed President Hafizullah Amin. The Russian military used exercises both to serve as a show of force and to conceal some of its combat preparations just as the Soviet military had done before Czechoslovakia and Afghanistan. It used some of the same heavy-handed 'negotiation' tactics that the Soviet Politburo had used to coerce the Czechoslovak officials into signing the Moscow Protocol to pressure the Ukrainian servicemen into not offering resistance and even into defecting to the Russian side.

The Russian government applied the informational, political and military tools the Soviet Union employed in its political warfare campaigns, especially the 1968 invasion of Czechoslovakia and the 1979 invasion of Afghanistan, to execute the 2014 annexation of Crimea. It adapted several of these tools to match the modern informational, political and technological environments, but the practices themselves are clearly rooted in the Soviet campaigns – as is the security environment theory leading to the implementation of these tactics. The individual tools are not necessarily unique to Soviet or Russian military history; what is distinctive is the combination of their application into a concerted campaign and the specific ways of their implementation. Modern Russian military practice as witnessed in the annexation of Crimea is, therefore, best understood as the modern application of Soviet political warfare – and not the invention of some new form of 'hybrid warfare'.

\* \* \*

The way in which the Russian government has reintroduced tools from its Soviet past means that its Soviet history offers a useful guide for understanding and predicting its future actions. This is especially true in the 'vast area of conflict which is neither war nor peace' (Miranda 1985: 4) – the realm of Soviet political warfare that equally applies to the modern competition space between Russia and the West. Since Russia has adapted a Soviet mindset of the modern security environment, it is applying the same Soviet tools. To predict Russia's actions, it is necessary to see its perspective to global dynamics through this Cold War lens.

Identifying the nature and origins of the Russian government's military practices is important because Russia has become more assertive in its foreign policy since the start of Putin's third term as president. Because of the significance of fraternal ties for many of the political warfare tools identified in this book, former Soviet or communist states part of Russia's self-deemed sphere of influence are most likely to witness their application. In addition to its ongoing conflict in the Donbas, Russia could potentially pursue further covert or subversive action in the Russian-speaking majority regions of southern Ukraine. The May 2014 clashes at Odesa's Trade Unions House and subsequent fire, which killed forty-eight people, demonstrated the potential for violence between pro-European and pro-Russian groups in the region (BBC 2014d). Similarly, former British defence secretary Michael Fallon has warned that Russia poses a 'real and present danger' to the Baltic States, former Soviet republics with minority ethnic Russian populations within their borders (Farmer 2015). They have already been the targets of interference: in 2015, hackers suspected to be part of the Russian state security organizations attacked a Baltic electricity grid, disrupting its operations (Jewkes and Vukmanovic 2017).

The frozen conflict zones in the former Soviet states could equally see the application of Russia's political warfare techniques. South Ossetia and Abkhazia, two breakaway regions from Georgia, have called for greater recognition and integration with Russia ever since the 2008 Russo-Georgian War. The Russian government has consolidated its already-strong position in Georgia's separatist territories, signing alliance and integration treaties with both of them (German 2016). Transnistria, which has been a de facto independent region of Moldova since the breakup of the Soviet Union, has been another point of constant contention. Shortly after the annexation of Crimea, Transnistria's parliament requested that Russia officially recognize its independence and take similar steps towards unification. Vladimir Putin's special representative in Crimea later pledged that Transnistria would eventually follow the same path (Secrieru 2014: 88).

Former Soviet states that maintain strong relations with Russia but are facing political turmoil – much like Ukraine in 2014, Czechoslovakia in 1968 or Afghanistan in 1979 – also exhibit the conditions that may invite Russia's application of its political warfare tools. Kazakh president Nursultan Nazarbayev resigned in March 2019 after prolonged protests over living conditions in the country. While he still held onto some levers of political power, including serving as chairman of the Security Council, Nazarbayev had been Kazakhstan's only leader since before the fall of the Soviet Union. He has maintained especially close ties with the Kremlin and even called Putin to discuss his resignation before announcing it (Auyezov 2019; RFE/RL 2019). Protests in Kyrgyzstan over alleged fraud and corruption in the October 2020 parliamentary elections led to a political crisis that ended with President Sooronbay Jeenbekov's resignation (Sullivan 2021). In August 2020, Belarus voted in its most recent presidential election, with Alexander Lukashenko again winning with an improbable percentage of the vote. This time, however, Belarusians responded with widescale nationwide protests demanding more openness in their country. Lukashenko was able to hold onto power largely due to continued support from Moscow (IISS 2021). If the Russian government fears that its strong influence over any of these states is under threat as the result of these or future protest movements, it may turn to its political warfare toolkit.

For any of these potential conflict zones, analysts and researchers should look to identify the political warfare tools described in this book. The Russian government is likely to rely on a similar playbook in future conflicts based on the impact historical experiences played on the 2014 Crimean annexation. Identification of these tools, especially the ways they have been adapted to the modern information and political environments, may serve as indicators of a Russian operation.

Viewing Russia's actions through the political warfare lens also lessens the confusion *dezinformatsia* and *maskirovka* are designed to sow, as these practices will be seen for what they are. The Russian government should be expected to make official denials as a matter of policy. 'Whataboutism' will likely follow any criticisms of Russian actions instead of a direct response. False flag media publications, online trolls, forgeries and even fabricated 'findings' of supposed covert Western activity should all be expected to appear. Political parties or political action groups that appear to aid the Russian government and its policies should be monitored closely to confirm they are not acting as its agents or receiving illicit funding. 'Free' expressions of political will by minority groups or 'invasion invitations' asking for Russian assistance should be viewed with additional scrutiny. Russia's intentions behind its troop movements in 'fraternal' states or in connection with its exercises should be taken with caution.

The Cold War mentality has once again found new life in the Russian Federation. While the West has arguably moved on from viewing the world through a Cold War lens, the Russian government, convinced that the same Cold War security dynamics are at play – most significantly in its staunch belief that Western states are on a constant campaign to subvert Russia and its influence abroad, not least through the colour revolutions – has resorted to the same political warfare responses that the Soviet Union employed. Understanding Russian political warfare practices will allow us to identify them and minimize the conditions that support their application. By decreasing the chances of conflict, we increase the chances of peace, meaning we can finally return to the path of cooperation – and leave the Cold War behind us once and for all.

# References

AFP (2014), 'FN Denies Sending Observers to Crimea [in French]', *Libération*, 13 March. Available online: http://www.liberation.fr/france/2014/03/13/le-fn-d ement-envoyer-des-observateurs-en-crimee_986838 (accessed 30 September 2018).

Aleksandrov, I. (1968), 'The Attack Against the Socialist Foundation of Czechoslovakia', *Pravda*, 11 July. Available online: https://www.cia.gov/library/readingroom/docs/ 1980-11-04.pdf (accessed 30 September 2018).

Alexander, L. (2015), 'Open-Source Information Reveals Pro-Kremlin Web Campaign', *Global Voices*, 13 July. Available online: https://globalvoices.org/2015/07/13/open -source-information-reveals-pro-kremlin-web-campaign/ (accessed 30 September 2018).

Allison, R. (2014), 'Russian "Deniable" Intervention in Ukraine: How and Why Russia Broke the Rules', *International Affairs*, 90(6): 1255–97.

Allison, R., M. Light, and S. White (2006), *Putin's Russia and the Enlarged Europe*, London: Royal Institute of International Affairs.

Andrew, C. and O. Gordievsky (1990), *KGB: The Inside Story of Its Foreign Operations from Lenin to Gorbachev*, London: Sceptre.

Andrew, C. and O. Gordievsky (1991), *Instructions from the Centre: Top Secret Files on KGB Foreign Operations, 1975–1985*, London: Hodder & Stoughton.

Andrew, C. and O. Gordievsky (1992), *More 'Instructions from the Centre': Top Secret Files on KGB Global Operations, 1975–1985*, Portland: Frank Cass.

Andrew, C. and V. Mitrokhin (2000), *The Mitrokhin Archive: The KGB in Europe and the West*, London: Penguin.

Andrew, C. and V. Mitrokhin (2006), *The Mitrokhin Archive II: The KGB and the World*, London: Allen Lane.

Andropov, Y. (1969), 'The Birth of Samizdat', *Index on Censorship*, 24(3): 62–3.

Andropov, Y. (1979), 'Personal Memorandum Andropov to Brezhnev', *History and Public Policy Program Digital Archive*, APRF, from notes taken by A. F. Dobrynin and provided to Norwegian Nobel Institute; provided to CWIHP by Odd Arne Westad, Director of Research, Nobel Institute; trans. for CWIHP by Rozas, Daniel, 1 December. Available online: http://digitalarchive.wilsoncenter.org/document/11 3254 (accessed 30 September 2018).

Arnold, A. (1985), *Afghanistan: The Soviet Invasion in Perspective*, Stanford: Hoover Institution Press.

Aro, J. (2016), 'The Cyberspace War: Propaganda and Trolling as Warfare Tools', *European View*, 15(1): 121–32.

Åslund, A. (2013), 'Ukraine's Choice: European Association Agreement or Eurasian Union?', *Peterson Institute of International Economics*, September. Available online: https://piie.com/sites/default/files/publications/pb/pb13-22.pdf (accessed 30 September 2018).

Asmus, R. (2010), *A Little War That Shook the World: Georgia, Russia, and the Future of the West*, New York: Palgrave Macmillan.

Atkinson, J. D. (1966), *The Politics of Struggle: The Communist Front and Political Warfare*, Chicago: Henry Regnery Company.

August, F. and D. Rees (1984), *Red Star over Prague*, London: The Sherwood Press.

Austrian Press Agency (2013), 'Grosz Becomes BZÖ Leader, Stadler Is Excluded [in German]', *Der Standard*, 3 October. Available online: https://derstandard.at/13 79293013914/Gerald-Grosz-soll-neuer-BZOe-Bundesobmann-werden (accessed 30 September 2018).

Auyezov, O. (2019), 'Kazakhstan's Leader Nazarbayev Resigns after Three Decades in Power', *Reuters*, 19 March. Available online: https://www.reuters.com/article/us-kazakhstan-president/president-of-kazakhstan-nursultan-nazarbayev-resigns-i dUSKCN1R01N1 (accessed 18 April 2021).

Bakumenko, R. (2014), 'Weathered Fire [in Ukrainian]', *Narodna Armiya*, 14 April. Available online: http://na.mil.gov.ua/5259-zagartovanij-vognem (accessed 30 September 2018).

Balachuk, I. (2018), 'Yanukovych Changed His Testimony about a Letter to Putin on the Introduction of Troops [in Russian]', *Ukrainskaya Pravda*, 2 March. Available online: https://www.pravda.com.ua/rus/news/2018/03/2/7173389/ (accessed 30 September 2018).

Baranczak, S. (1990), 'Goodbye, Samizdat', *The Wilson Quarterly*, 14(2): 59–66.

Barghoorn, F. (1964), *Soviet Foreign Propaganda*, Princeton: Princeton University Press.

Barron, J. (1974), *KGB: The Secret Work of Soviet Secret Agents*, London: Bantam Books.

Barron, J. (1983), *KGB Today: The Hidden Hand*, London: Hodder & Stoughton.

Bartles, C. K. (2016), 'Getting Gerasimov Right', *Military Review*, 96 (January–February): 30–8.

BBC (2014a), 'Chechen Rebel Leader Doku Umarov "Dead"', 18 March. Available online: http://www.bbc.co.uk/news/world-europe-26634403 (accessed 30 September 2018).

BBC (2014b), 'Crimea Referendum: Voters "Back Russia Union"', 16 March. Available online: http://www.bbc.com/news/world-europe-26606097 (accessed 30 September 2018).

BBC (2014c), 'Deadly Clashes at Ukraine Port Base as Leaders Meet', 17 April. Available online: http://www.bbc.co.uk/news/world-europe-27059321 (accessed 30 September 2018).

BBC (2014d), 'Ukraine Crisis: Dozens Killed in Odessa Fire Amid Clashes', 3 May. Available online: http://www.bbc.co.uk/news/world-europe-27259620 (accessed 30 September 2018).

BBC (2014e), 'Ukraine Crisis: Transcript of Leaked Nuland-Pyatt Call', 7 February. Available online: http://www.bbc.com/news/world-europe-26079957 (accessed 30 September 2018).

BBC (2015a), 'Putin Reveals Secrets of Russia's Crimea Takeover Plot', 9 March. Available online: http://www.bbc.com/news/world-europe-31796226 (accessed 30 September 2018).

BBC (2015b), 'Ukraine's Inquiry into Odessa Fire "Not Independent"', 4 November. Available online: http://www.bbc.co.uk/news/world-europe-34726123 (accessed 30 September 2018).

BBG (2018), 'Mission'. Available online: https://www.bbg.gov/who-we-are/mission/ (accessed 30 September 2018).

BBG and Gallup (2014), 'Contemporary Media Use in Ukraine'. Available online: https ://www.bbg.gov/wp-content/media/2014/06/Ukraine-research-brief.pdf (accessed 30 September 2018).

Bebler, A. (2015), 'Crimea and the Russian-Ukrainian Conflict', *Romanian Journal of European Affairs*, 15(1): 35–54.

Beichman, A. (1987), 'Soviet Active Measures and Democratic Culture'. In: B. D. Dailey and P. J. Parker (eds), *Soviet Strategic Deception*, 77–90, Lexington: D.C. Heath and Company.

Belin, L. (2002), 'The Kremlin Strikes Back: The Reassertion of State Power over the Russian Media'. In: M. E. Price, A. Richter, and P. K. Yu. (eds), *Russian Media Law and Policy in the Yeltsin Decade: Essays and Documents*, 273–301, London: Kluwer Law International.

Bell, Y. (2014), 'Russia "Will Fix" Crimea Referendum, Says Tatar Leader', *Reuters*, 10 March. Available online: https://www.reuters.com/article/us-ukraine-crisis-refer endum-tatars/russia-will-fix-crimea-referendum-says-tatar-leader-idUSBREA29 1BT20140310 (accessed 30 September 2018).

Belousov, S. (2015), 'Putin Establishes New "Polite People" Day in Russia', *Moscow Times*, 27 February. Available online: https://themoscowtimes.com/news/putin-es tablishes-new-polite-people-day-in-russia-44305 (accessed 30 September 2018).

Belsky, A. N. and O. V. Klimenko (2014), 'Political Engineering of Colour Revolutions: Ways to Keep Them in Check', *Voennaia mysl', (Military Thought)*, 23(3): 20–9.

Bērziņa, I. (2015), 'The Russian "Colour Counterrevolution" Model for Containing Geopolitical Expansion by the West', *Journal of Military Operations*, 3(1): 23–6.

Betz, D. (2017), 'Military and Non-Military Means in Modern Warfare'. In: *The Informational Dimension of Hybrid Warfare: Eastern and Western Perspectives on Conflicts in the 21st Century*, 11–12 January, London: King's College London.

Beumers, B., S. Hutchings, and N. Rulyova (eds) (2008), *The Post-Soviet Russian Media*, London: Routledge.

BFMTV (2014), 'Report from Simferopol [in French]', *TV Program*, 1 March. Available online: https://youtu.be/hQ2dbYXmgIw (accessed 30 September 2018).

Bil'ak, V. (1991), 'Vasil Bil'ak's Recollections of the Bratislava Conference'. In: J. Navratil (ed), *The Prague Spring 1968: A National Security Archive Documents Reader*, 320–3, Budapest: Central European University Press.

Bischof, G., S. Karner, and P. Ruggenthaler (eds) (2010), *The Prague Spring and the Warsaw Pact Invasion of Czechoslovakia in 1968*, Plymouth: Lexington Books.

Bittman, L. (1972), *The Deception Game: Czechoslovak Intelligence in Soviet Political Warfare*, Syracuse: Syracuse University Research Corporation.

Bittman, L. (1985), *The KGB and Soviet Disinformation: An Insider's View*, London: Pergamon-Brassey's.

Blee, D. H. (1973), 'Publication of Reader's Digest Book "KGB"', *Library: Central Intelligence Agency*, 9 October. Available online: https://www.cia.gov/library/reading room/docs/CIA-RDP75-00793R000200110004-2.pdf (accessed 30 September 2018).

Blockmans, S. (2015), 'Crimea and the Quest for Energy and Military Hegemony in the Black Sea Region: Governance Gap in a Contested Geostrategic Zone', *Southeast European and Black Sea Studies*, 15(2): 179–89.

Bobrov, Y. (2014), 'The Problems of the Residents of Crimea [in Russian]', *President of Russia's Council on Civil Society and Human Rights*, 22 April. Available online: http://president-sovet.ru/members/blogs/bobrov_e_a/problcmy-zhiteley-kryma-/ (accessed 30 September 2018).

Bolgov, R. (2017), 'The Informational Dimension of Hybrid Warfare'. In: *The Informational Dimension of Hybrid Warfare: Eastern and Western Perspectives on Conflicts in the 21st Century*, 11–12 January, London: King's College London.

Boltenkov, D. (2014), 'Home of the Black Sea Fleet: History and Disposition of Russian Forces in Ukraine'. In: C. Howard and R. Pukhov (eds), *Brothers Armed: Military Aspects of the Crisis in Ukraine*, 135–56, Minneapolis: East View Press.

Bradsher, H. S. (1999), *Afghan Communism and Soviet Intervention*, Oxford: Oxford University Press.

Braithwaite, R. (2012), *Afgantsy: The Russians in Afghanistan 1979–1989*, London: Profile Books.

Brandenberger, D. (2011), *Propaganda State in Crisis: Soviet Ideology, Indoctrination, and Terror under Stalin, 1927–1941*, London: Yale University Press.

Brezhnev, L. (1968a), 'Leonid Brezhnev's Speech at a Meeting of the "Warsaw Five" in Moscow, August 18, 1968 (Excerpts)'. In: J. Navratil (ed), *The Prague Spring 1968: A National Security Archive Documents Reader*, 395–9, Budapest: Central European University Press.

Brezhnev, L. (1968b), 'Speech by Leonid Brezhnev to the CPSU Central Committee on the Proceedings and Results of the Warsaw Meeting, July 17, 1968'. In: J. Navratil (ed), *The Prague Spring 1968: A National Security Archive Documents Reader*, 250–8, Budapest: Central European University Press.

Brezhnev, L. (1979), 'Letter from Leonid Brezhnev to Karmal Babrak, Attachment to CPSU Politburo Protocol #177', *History and Public Policy Program Digital Archive*, TsKhSD, F, 89: 14, D. 32. Translated for CWIHP by Gary Goldberg, 27 December.

Available online: http://digitalarchive.wilsoncenter.org/document/111551 (accessed 30 September 2018).

Brown, A. (2008), *Seven Years That Changed the World: Perestroika in Perspective*, Oxford: Oxford University Press.

Bruusgaard, K. V. (2014), 'Crimea and Russia's Strategic Overhaul', *Parameters*, 44(3): 81–90.

Bullough, O. (2014), 'The Crimean Referendum to Join Russia Was an Unconstitutional Sham', *The New Republic*, 17 March. Available online: https://newrepublic.com/articl e/117044/crimean-referendum-join-russia-was-unconstitutional-sham (accessed 30 September 2018).

Butsenko, A. (2014), 'Trolls from Olgino Moved to a New Four-Story Office at Savushkina [in Russian]', *DP Business Press*, 28 October. Available online: https:/ /www.dp.ru/a/2014/10/27/Borotsja_s_omerzeniem_mo/ (accessed 30 September 2018).

Butusov, Y. (2017), 'Officers of the Crimean Alfa, Who Betrayed Ukraine, Killed in Dagestan, Reports a Journalist [in Russian]', Censor.net, 30 August. Available online: https://censor.net.ua/photo_news/453360/predavshie_ukrainu_ofitsery_krymskoyi _alfy_unichtojeny_v_dagestane_jurnalist_foto (accessed 30 September 2018).

CC VKP(b) (1952), 'Resolution of the Central Committee of the All-Union Communist Party (CC VKP(b))', *History and Public Policy Program Digital Archive*, Khraneniia, Rossiskii Tsentr i Izucheniia Dokumentov Noveishei Istorii (RTsKhIDNI), Fond, 17, op.132, d.507, ll.18-19, obtained and translated by Gould-Davies, Nigel, 1 September. Available online: http://digitalarchive.wilsoncenter.org/document/11 1510 (accessed 30 September 2018).

Centre for Investigative Journalism (Ukraine) (2014), 'The Crimean Front' Wants to Control the "Centre for Investigative Journalism" [in Russian]', 1 March. Available online: https://investigator.org.ua/news/120451/ (accessed 30 September 2018).

Černík, O. (1990), 'Oldřich Černík's Recollections of the Crisis (Excerpts)'. In: J. Navratil (ed), *The Prague Spring 1968: A National Security Archive Documents Reader*, 424–6, Budapest: Central European University Press.

Charap, S. (2014), 'Ukraine: Seeking an Elusive New Normal', *Survival*, 56(3): 85–94.

Chau, D. C. (2006), 'Political Warfare – An Essential Instrument of U. S. Grand Strategy Today', *Comparative Strategy*, 25(2): 109–20.

Chekinov, S. G. and S. A. Bogdanov (2011), 'Strategy of Indirect Approach: Its Impact on Modern Warfare', *Voennaia mysl'*, *(Military Thought)*, 20(3): 1–13.

Chekinov, S. G. and S. A. Bogdanov (2013), 'The Nature and Content of a New-Generation War', *Voennaia mysl'*, *(Military Thought)*, 22(4): 12–23.

Chekinov, S. G. and S. A. Bogdanov (2015), 'The Art of War in the Early 21st Century: Issues and Opinions', *Voennaia mysl'*, *(Military Thought)*, 24(1): 26–38.

Chen, A. (2015), 'The Agency', *The New York Times Magazine*, 2 June. Available online: https://www.nytimes.com/2015/06/07/magazine/the-agency.html (accessed 30 September 2018).

Chervonenko, S. (1968), 'Cable Traffic between the CPSU Politburo and Ambassador Stepan Chervonenko Amending the Text and Delivery Time of the "Letter of Warning", August 17–18, 1968'. In: J. Navratil (ed), *The Prague Spring 1968: A National Security Archive Documents Reader*, 388–90, Budapest: Central European University Press.

Chivers, C. J. and P. Reevell (2014), 'Russia Moves Swiftly to Stifle Dissent Ahead of Secession Vote', *The New York Times*, 14 March. Available online: https://nyti.ms/2D4BKFK (accessed 30 September 2018).

Choney, S. (2011), 'Online News Readership Overtakes Newspapers', *NBC News*, 14 March. Available online: https://www.nbcnews.com/technology/online-news-readership-overtakes-newspapers-124383 (accessed 30 September 2018).

CIA (1963), 'Concerning Penkovskiy Memoirs'. Available online: https://www.cia.gov/library/readingroom/document/0000012426 (accessed 30 September 2018).

CIA (1964), 'Request Approval to Publish the Penkovskiy Memoirs'. Available online: https://www.cia.gov/library/readingroom/document/0000012379 (accessed 30 September 2018).

CIA (1968a), 'Central Intelligence Bulletin', 23 August. Available online: https://www.cia.gov/library/readingroom/docs/1968-08-24b.pdf (accessed 30 September 2018).

CIA (1968b), 'Central Intelligence Bulletin', 16 August. Available online: https://www.cia.gov/library/readingroom/docs/1968-08-16a.pdf (accessed 30 September 2018).

CIA (1989), 'SOV 89–10037CX: The Nature of Soviet Military Doctrine'. Available online: https://www.cia.gov/library/readingroom/docs/DOC_0000499601.pdf (accessed 30 September 2018).

CIA (2012), *Strategic Warning and the Role of Intelligence: Lessons Learned from the 1968 Soviet Invasion of Czechoslovakia*, Washington, DC: CreateSpace Independent Publishing Platform. Available Online: https://www.cia.gov/library/publications/cold-war/czech-invasion/soviet-czech-invasion.pdf (accessed 30 September 2018).

CIA FBIS (1968a), 'Special Report on Communist Propaganda: The I. Aleksandrov Article in Pravda: Inception of a New Stage in Pressure on Czechoslovakia', 18 July. Available online: https://www.cia.gov/library/readingroom/docs/1968-07-18.pdf (accessed 30 September 2018).

CIA FBIS (1968b), 'Special Report on Communist Propaganda', 12 July. Available online: https://www.cia.gov/library/readingroom/docs/1968-07-12a.pdf (accessed 30 September 2018).

Cienciala, A. M., N. S. Lebedeva, and W. Materski (2007), *Katyn: A Crime Without Punishment*, New Haven: Yale University Press.

Collins, J. J. (1986), *The Soviet Invasion of Afghanistan*, Lexington: D.C. Heath and Company.

Conquest, R. (1987), 'Ideology and Deception'. In: B. D. Dailey and P. J. Parker (eds), *Soviet Strategic Deception*, 119–31, Lexington: D.C. Heath and Company.

Constitutional Court of Austria (1988), 'Ruling B999/87 [in German]', 25 June. Available online: https://www.ris.bka.gv.at/Dokumente/Vfgh/JFR_10119375_87B00999_01/JFR_10119375_87B00999_01.pdf (accessed 30 September 2018).

Cordesman, A. (2014), 'Russia and the "Color Revolution": A Russian Military View of a World Destabilized by the US and the West', *Center for Strategic and International Studies*, 28 May. Available online: http://csis.org/publication/russia-and-color-revol ution (accessed 30 September 2018).

Cornell, S. and S. F. Starr (2009), *The Guns of August 2008: Russia's War in Georgia*, Armonk: M.E. Sharpe.

CPCz CC (1978), 'Minutes from Conversation between Babrak Karmal and the Head of the Diplomatic Protocol Tucek', *History and Public Policy Program Digital Archive*, Central State Archive, Archive of the CC CPCz, file Husak, unsorted materials, box Afghanistan, provided by Oldrich Tuma and translated by Francis Raska, 12 September. Available online: http://digitalarchive.wilsoncenter.org/document/11 2467 (accessed 30 September 2018).

CPCz CC Presidium (1968), 'Statement by the CPCz CC Presidium Condemning the Warsaw Pact Invasion, August 21, 1968'. In: J. Navratil (ed), *The Prague Spring 1968: A National Security Archive Documents Reader*, 414–5, Budapest: Central European University Press.

CPSU CC (1979), 'Report on the Situation in Afghanistan, Gromyko, Andropov, Ustinov, and Ponomarev to CPSU CC', *History and Public Policy Program Digital Archive*, APRF, f. 3, op. 82, d. 173, s. 118-127, as cited in A. A. Lyakhovskiy, The Tragedy and Valor of the Afghani (Moscow: GPI 'Iskon', 1995), p. 102, partially published in CWHIP Bulletin 8-9, pp. 157–8 and C. 29 November. Available online: http://digitalarchive.wilsoncenter.org/document/111576 (accessed 30 September 2018).

CPSU CC & Chervonenko, S. (1968), 'Cable to Ambassador Stepan Chervonenko from Moscow with a Message for President Svoboda, August 19, 1968, and Chervonenko's Response, August 21, 1968'. In: J. Navratil (ed), *The Prague Spring 1968: A National Security Archive Documents Reader*, 405–8, Budapest: Central European University Press.

CPSU CC Politburo (1968a), 'Emergency Cable from the CPSU Politburo to Soviet Ambassadors around the World, August 19-20, 1968'. In: J. Navratil (ed), *The Prague Spring 1968: A National Security Archive Documents Reader*, 409, Budapest: Central European University Press.

CPSU CC Politburo (1968b), 'Letter of the CPSU CC Politburo to the CPCz CC Presidium, July 4, 1968'. In: J. Navratil (ed), *The Prague Spring 1968: A National Security Archive Documents Reader*, 194–8, Budapest: Central European University Press.

CPSU CC Politburo (1968c), '"Special Dossier for Oral Presentation" (The Soviet Politburo's Assessment of the Lessons of Operation "Danube" and the Tasks Ahead, November 16, 1968)'. In: J. Navratil (ed), *The Prague Spring 1968: A National Security Archive Documents Reader*, 547–54, Budapest: Central European University Press.

CPSU CC Politburo (1968d), 'Stenographic Account of Alexander Dubček's Talks with Leonid Brezhnev and Other Members of the CPSU CC Politburo, August 23, 1968

(Excerpts)'. In: J. Navratil (ed), *The Prague Spring 1968: A National Security Archive Documents Reader*, 465–8, Budapest: Central European University Press.

CPSU CC Politburo (1968e), 'The Soviet Politburo's Resolution on the Final Decision to Intervene in Czechoslovakia, August 17, 1968, with Attachments'. In: J. Navratil (ed), *The Prague Spring 1968: A National Security Archive Documents Reader*, 376–83, Budapest: Central European University Press.

CPSU CC Politburo (1979a), 'CPSU CC Politburo Decisions on Afghanistan', *History and Public Policy Program Digital Archive*, Archive of the President, Russian Federation (APRF), f. 3 op. 82, d. 137, ll. 121–3, 18 March. Available online: http:// digitalarchive.wilsoncenter.org/document/113261 (accessed 30 September 2018).

CPSU CC Politburo (1979b), 'Excerpt from the Minutes of the CC CPSU Politburo Meeting, "Reply to an Appeal of President Carter about the Issue of Afghanistan through the Direct Communications Channel"', *History and Public Policy Program Digital Archive*, Bukovsky archive, http://bukovsky-archives.net/. RGANI (formerly TsKhSD), f. 89, op. 14, d. 34, ll. 1-5, 29 December. Available online: http://digitala rchive.wilsoncenter.org/document/113080 (accessed 30 September 2018).

CPSU CC Politburo (1979c), 'Extract from CPSU CC Politburo Decision', *History and Public Policy Program Digital Archive*, as cited in Lyakhovsky, A. A., The Tragedy and Valour of the Afghani (Moscow: GPI 'Iskon', 1995), 107, 6 December. Available online: http://digitalarchive.wilsoncenter.org/document/111579 (accessed 30 September 2018).

CPSU CC Politburo (1979d), 'Transcript of CPSU CC Politburo Discussions on Afghanistan', *History and Public Policy Program Digital Archive*, TsKhSD, f. 89, per. 25 dok.1, ll. 1, 12-25, 17 March. Available online: http://digitalarchive.wilsoncenter. org/document/113260 (accessed 30 September 2018).

CPSU CC Propaganda Department (1968), 'Recommendations from the CPSU CC Propaganda Department on Efforts to Establish Political Control in Czechoslovakia, September 6, 1968 (Excerpts)'. In: J. Navratil (ed), *The Prague Spring 1968: A National Security Archive Documents Reader*, 497, Budapest: Central European University Press.

Crowley, M. (2016), 'Putin's Revenge', *Politico*, 16 December. Available online: https:// www.politico.com/magazine/story/2016/12/russia-putin-hack-dnc-clinton-election -2016-cold-war-214532 (accessed 30 October 2020).

Csémi, K. (1968), 'Meeting Notes Taken by Chief of the Hungarian People's Army General Staff Károly Csémi on Talks with Soviet Generals in Budapest to Discuss Preparations for "Operation Danube", July 24, 1968'. In: J. Navratil (ed), *The Prague Spring 1968: A National Security Archive Documents Reader*, 277–8, Budapest: Central European University Press.

CSTO (2014), *The Dictionary-Handbook on Information Security from the Parliamentary Assembly of the Collective Security Treaty Organization* [in Russian], St. Petersburg: SPIIRAN.

CWIHP (2018), 'About'. Available online: https://www.wilsoncenter.org/about-18 (accessed 30 September 2020).

Cynkin, T. (1988), *Soviet and American Signalling in the Polish Crisis*, London: Macmillan.

Czuchnowski, M. and J. Wojciech (2016), 'ISA: Change Party Founded by Russians [in Polish]', *Gazeta Wyborcza*, 25 May. Available online: http://wyborcza.pl/1,75398,201 32090,abw-partie-zmiana-zalozyli-rosjanie.html (accessed 30 September 2020).

Dailey, B. D. and P. J. Parker (eds) (1987), *Soviet Strategic Deception*, Lexington: D.C. Heath and Company.

Darczewska, J. (2014), 'The Anatomy of Russian Information Warfare: The Crimean Operation, a Case Study', Point of View, 42, May. Available online: https://www .osw.waw.pl/sites/default/files/the_anatomy_of_russian_information_warfare.pdf (accessed 30 September 2018).

Davis, D. B. (1971), *The Fear of Conspiracy: Images of Un-American Subversion from the Revolution to the Present*, Ithaca: Cornell University Press.

Dawisha, K. (1984), *The Kremlin and the Prague Spring*, London: University of California Press.

de Carbonnel, A. (2014a), 'Armed Men Seize Two Airports in Ukraine's Crimea, Yanukovich Reappears', *Reuters*, 28 February. Available online: https://www.reuters. com/article/uk-ukraine-idUKBREA1H0EM20140228 (accessed 30 September 2018).

de Carbonnel, A. (2014b), 'How the Separatists Delivered Crimea to Moscow', *Reuters*, 12 March. Available online: https://uk.reuters.com/article/us-ukraine-crisis-russia -aksyonov-insigh-idUSBREA2B13M20140312 (accessed 30 September 2018).

de Carbonnel, A. (2014c), 'Russian Military Surround Ukrainian Border Guard Post in Crimea', *Reuters*, 28 February. Available online: https://www.reuters.com/article/us-ukraine-crisis-balaklava-idUSBREA1R11420140228 (accessed 30 September 2018).

de Haas, M. (2010), *Russia's Foreign Security Policy in the 21st Century: Putin, Medvedev and Beyond*, Abingdon: Routledge.

Deacon, R. (1972), *A History of the Russian Secret Service*, New York: Taplinger.

Demichev, P. N. (1968), 'Building of Communism and the Tasks of the Social Sciences. Kommunist, No. 10 (July 1968), pp. 14-35'. In: R. A. Remington (ed), *Winter in Prague: Documents on Czechoslovak Communism in Crisis*, 208–12, London: MIT Press.

Deyermond, R. (2008), *Security and Sovereignty in the Former Soviet Union*, London: Lynne Rienner.

Deyermond, R. (2015), 'Disputed Democracy: The Instrumentalisation of the Concept of Democracy in US-Russia Relations During the George W. Bush and Putin Presidencies', *Comillas Journal of International Relations*, 3: 28–43.

Dobrokhotova, A. and C. Bigg (2016), 'Pro-Russian Activist Falls on Hard Times in Annexed Crimea', RFE/RL, 12 January. Available online: https://www.rferl.org/a/pro -russian-activist-crimea-hard-times/27483975.html (accessed 30 September 2018).

Dolgov, A. (2014), 'Ukrainian TV Channels Blocked in Crimea for 'Moral and Legal' Reasons', *Moscow Times*, 10 March. Available online: https://themoscowtimes.com /articles/ukrainian-tv-channels-blocked-in-crimea-for-moral-and-legal-reasons-3 2808 (accessed 30 September 2018).

Douglass, J. D. (1980), *Soviet Military Strategy in Europe*, Oxford: Pergamon Press.

Dubček, A. (1991), 'Foreword'. In: J. Valenta (ed), *Soviet Intervention in Czechoslovakia, 1968: Anatomy of a Decision*, ix–xi, London: The Johns Hopkins University Press.

Dubček, A. (1993), *Hope Dies Last: The Autobiography of Alexander Dubček*, London: Harper Collins.

Dutkiewicz, P. and R. Jackson (eds) (1998), *NATO Looks East*, London: Praeger.

DW (2017), 'Russian "Novaya Gazeta" Newspaper Set to Arm Reporters after Stabbing', 26 October. Available online: http://p.dw.com/p/2maXi (accessed 30 September 2018).

Dzhankoets, V. (2016), 'How the Capture of Dzhankoy Happened [in Russian]', *Krym Realii*, 2 March. Available online: http://ru.krymr.com/a/27584948.html (accessed 30 September 2018).

Dziak, J. J. (1981), *Soviet Perceptions of Military Power: The Interaction of Theory and Practice*, New York: Crane, Russka & Company.

Dziak, J. J. (1988), *Chekisty: A History of the KGB, Lexington*, D.C. Heath and Company.

Dzúr, M. (1968), '"Status of the Sumava Allied Exercise": Report to Alexander Dubček by CSSR Defence Minister Martin Dzúr, June 17, 1968'. In: J. Navratil (ed), *The Prague Spring 1968: A National Security Archive Documents Reader*, 160–2, Budapest: Central European University Press.

Dzúr, M. (1970), 'Report by Defence Minister Dzúr, June 9, 1970, Regarding His Activities on the Night of August 20–21, 1968 (Excerpts)'. In: J. Navratil (ed), *The Prague Spring 1968: A National Security Archive Documents Reader*, 411–3, Budapest: Central European University Press.

Dzúr, M., A. Mucha, and K. Rusov (1968), 'Briefing on the Sumava Exercises for Alexander Dubček and Oldřich Černík by Commanders of the Czechoslovak People's Army, July 1, 1968, with Follow-Up Talks between Dubček and Marshal Yakubovsky'. In: J. Navratil (ed), *The Prague Spring 1968: A National Security Archive Documents Reader*, 191–3, Budapest: Central European University Press.

Dzyadko, T. (2014), 'Triumph of the Will: Putin's War against Russia's Last Independent TV Channel', *The Guardian*, 10 April. Available online: https://www.theguardian.c om/commentisfree/2014/apr/10/putin-war-dozhd-russias-last-independent-tv-ch annel (accessed 30 September 2018).

Economist (2007), 'The Making of a Neo-KGB State', 23 August. Available online: http:// www.economist.com/node/9682621 (accessed 30 September 2018).

Economist (2008), 'Whataboutism: Come Again, Comrade?', 31 January Available online: http://www.economist.com/node/10598774 (accessed 30 September 2018).

Economist (2013), 'Russia's Chief Propagandist', 10 December. Available online: http://www.economist.com/blogs/easternapproaches/2013/12/Ukraine (accessed 30 September 2018).

Economist (2014), 'Edging Closer to War', 1 March. Available online: https://www.economist.com/blogs/easternapproaches/2014/03/russia-and-ukraine (accessed 30 September 2018).

English, R. D. (2000), *Russia and the Idea of the West: Gorbachev, Intellectuals, and the End of the Cold War*, New York: Columbia University Press.

Ennis, S. (2013), 'Putin's RIA Novosti Revamp Prompts Propaganda Fears', *BBC*, 9 December. Available online: http://www.bbc.com/news/world-europe-25309139 (accessed 30 September 2018).

Ennis, S. (2014), 'Russian TV Ratchets up Rhetoric on Ukraine', *BBC*, 2 March. Available online: http://www.bbc.com/news/world-europe-26411396 (accessed 30 September 2018).

EODE (2014), 'The Non-Governmental Organization EODE in a Few Lines'. Available online: http://www.eode.org/contact/ (accessed 30 September 2018).

EODE Press Office (2014), 'Referendums in the Republic of Crimea and Sevastopol: Joint Statement by the Independent International Observers', 21 March. Available online: http://www.eode.org/eode-press-office-referendums-in-the-republic-of-c rimea-and-sevastopol-joint-statement-by-the-independent-international-observers/ (accessed 30 September 2018).

Epstein, E. J. (1989), *Deception: The Invisible War Between the KGB and the CIA*, New York: Simon and Schuster.

Euromaidan Press (2015), 'Chronology of the Annexation of Crimea', 5 March. Available online: http://euromaidanpress.com/2015/03/05/chronology-of-the-annex ation-of-crimea/ (accessed 30 September 2018).

Fadin, A. (1997), 'In Russia, Private Doesn't Mean Independent: Bankers and Oil Tycoons Use the Media as a Business Weapon'. In: M. E. Price, A. Richter, and P. K. Yu. (eds), *Russian Media Law and Policy in the Yeltsin Decade: Essays and Documents*, 257–9, London: Kluwer Law International.

Farmer, B. (2015), 'Putin Will Target the Baltic Next, Defence Secretary Warns', *The Telegraph*, 18 February. Available online: https://www.telegraph.co.uk/news/worldne ws/vladimir-putin/11421751/Putin-will-target-the-Baltic-next-Defence-Secretary-w arns.html (accessed 30 September 2018).

Farmer, B. (2016), 'Head of MI6: Britain Faces "Fundamental Threat to Sovereignty from Russian Meddling"', *The Telegraph*, 8 December. Available online: http://www.telegraph.co.uk/news/2016/12/08/britain-faces-fundamental-threat-sovereignty-ru ssian-meddling/ (accessed 30 September 2018).

Fedchenko, Y. (2016), 'Kremlin Propaganda: Soviet Active Measures by Other Means', *Sõjateadlane (Estonian Journal of Military Studies)*, 2: 140–69.

Feifer, G. (2010), *The Great Gamble: The Soviet War in Afghanistan*, London: Harper Perennial.

Le Figaro, Fr & Reuters (2014), 'French Journalist Arrested in Crimea [in French]', 13 March. Available online: http://www.lefigaro.fr/flash-actu/2014/03/13/97001 -20140313FILWWW00247-un-journaliste-francais-arrete-en-crimee.php (accessed 30 September 2018).

Files of Gustav Husak (1968), 'Discussions Involving Certain Members of the CPCz CC Presidium and Secretariat, at the Soviet Embassy in Prague and the CSSR President's Office, August 22, 1968 (Excerpts)'. In: J. Navratil (ed), *The Prague Spring 1968: A National Security Archive Documents Reader*, 460–4, Budapest: Central European University Press.

Finkel, S. (2007), *On the Ideological Front: The Russian Intelligentsia and the Making of the Soviet Public Sphere*, New Haven: Yale University Press.

Fischer-Galati, S., ed. (1979), *The Communist Parties of Eastern Europe*, New York: Columbia University Press.

Frankland, M. (1992), 'Neighbours Make Very Bad Enemies', *The Observer*, 26 April.

Freemantle, B. (1982), *KGB*, London: Michael Joseph.

Fridman, O. (2016), 'A "Hybrid War" of Terms', *Vestnik MGIMO-Universiteta*, 50(5): 79–85.

Frolik, J. (1975), *The Frolik Defection*, London: Leo Cooper.

Gahrton, P. (2010), *Georgia: Pawn in the New Political Game*, London: Pluto Press.

Galeotti, M. (1995a), *Afghanistan: The Soviet Union's Last War*, London: Frank Cass.

Galeotti, M. (1995b), *The Kremlin's Agenda: The New Russia and Its Armed Forces*, Coulsdon: Jane's Information Group Ltd.

Galeotti, M., ed. (2010), *The Politics of Security in Modern Russia*, Farnham: Ashgate.

Galeotti, M. (2014), 'The "Gerasimov Doctrine" and Russian Non-Linear War', *In Moscow's Shadows*, 16 July. Available online: https://inmoscowsshadows.wordpress. com/2014/07/06/the-gerasimov-doctrine-and-russian-non-linear-war/ (accessed 30 September 2018).

Galeotti, M. (2016), '"Hybrid War" and "Little Green Men": How It Works, and How It Doesn't'. In: A. Pikulicka-Wilczewska and R. Sakwa (eds), *Ukraine and Russia: People, Politics, Propaganda and Perspectives*, 149–56, Bristol: E-International Relations Publishing.

Galeotti, M. (2018a), 'I'm Sorry for Creating the "Gerasimov Doctrine"', *Foreign Policy*, 5 March. Available online: http://foreignpolicy.com/2018/03/05/im-sorry-for-creati ng-the-gerasimov-doctrine/ (accessed 30 September 2018).

Galeotti, M. (2018b), 'The Mythical "Gerasimov Doctrine" and the Language of Threat', *Critical Studies on Security*, 27 February. Available online: https://doi.org/10.1080/2 1624887.2018.1441623 (accessed 30 September 2018).

Galeotti, M. (2019), *Russian Political War: Moving Beyond the Hybrid*, Abingdon: Routledge.

Gatehouse, G. (2017), 'Marine Le Pen: Who's Funding France's Far Right?', *BBC*, 3 April. Available online: http://www.bbc.co.uk/news/world-europe-39478066 (accessed 30 September 2018).

Gazeta.ru (2014a), 'Chaly Elected Mayor of Sevastopol in the People's Assembly [in Russian]', 23 February. Available online: https://www.gazeta.ru/politics/news/2014/02/23/n_5969069.shtml (accessed 30 September 2018).

Gazeta.ru (2014b), 'Crimea Chooses Russia [in Russian]', 3 March. Available online: https://www.gazeta.ru/politics/2014/03/15_a_5951217.shtml (accessed 30 September 2018).

General Prosecutor's Office of the Russian Federation (2017), 'Letter No, 87-103-2017, Addressed to the General Prosecutor's Office of Ukraine [in Russian]', 7 March. Available online: https://www.facebook.com/LlutsenkoYuri/posts/662715100594335 (accessed 30 September 2018).

Gerasimenko, O. and A. Galustjan (2014), '"No One Has a Clear Plan of Action," Says Acting Head of Crimea Sergei Aksenov [in Russian]', *Kommersant*, 22 September. Available online: https://www.kommersant.ru/doc/2569810 (accessed 30 September 2018).

Gerasimov, V. (2013), 'The Value of Science Is in the Foresight [in Russian]', *Voenno-Promyshlennyi Kurier (Military-Industrial Courier)*, 26 February.

German, T. (2009), 'David and Goliath: Georgia and Russia's Coercive Diplomacy', *Defence Studies*, 9(2): 224–41.

German, T. (2016), 'Russia and South Ossetia: Conferring Statehood or Creeping Annexation?', *Southeast European and Black Sea Studies*, 16(1): 155–67.

Getty, J. A., C. Andrew, V. Mitrokhin (2001), 'Reviews of Books: The Sword and the Shield: The Mitrokhin Archive and the Secret History of the KGB by Christopher Andrew and Vasili Mitrokhin', *The American Historical Review*, 106(2): 684–5.

Giles, K. (2016a), *Handbook of Russian Information Warfare*, Rome: NATO Defence College & DeBooks Italia srl.

Giles, K. (2016b), *Russia's 'New' Tools for Confronting the West: Continuity and Innovation in Moscow's Exercise of Power*, London: The Royal Institute of International Affairs. Available online: https://www.chathamhouse.org/sites/files/chathamhouse/publications/2016-03-russia-new-tools-giles.pdf (accessed 30 September 2018).

Giles, K. (2016c), *The Next Phase of Russian Information Warfare*, Riga: NATO Strategic Communications Centre of Excellence. Available online: https://www.stratcomcoe.org/download/file/fid/5134 (accessed 30 September 2018).

Girardet, E. (1985), *Afghanistan: The Soviet War*, London: Croom Helm.

Glantz, D. (1988), 'Surprise and Maskirovka in Contemporary War', *Military Review*, 68(12): 50–7.

Glantz, D. (1992), *The Military Strategy of the Soviet Union: A History*, London: Frank Cass.

Glikin, M., N. Kostenko, A. Kornya, and Y. Pismennaya (2011), 'Surkov Leaves Politics', *Current Digest of the Russian Press*, 63(51): 15.

Glukhovsky, M. (2014), 'Vadim Kolesnichenko: It's Time to Bury the Party of Regions [in Russian]', *Glavcom*, 25 September. Available online: http://glavcom.ua/intervi

ews/126485-vadim-kolesnichenko-partiju-regionov-pora-pohoronit.html (accessed 30 September 2018).

Goldgeier, J. M. and M. McFaul (2003), *Power and Purpose: U.S. Policy Toward Russia After the Cold War*, Washington, DC: Brookings Institution Press.

Golos (2014), 'The Ballot Form for Voting at the General Referendum on March 16, 2014 [in Russian]', Twitter, 7 March. Available online: https://twitter.com/golosinfo/status/441935863967399936/photo/1 (accessed 30 September 2018).

Goodson, L. P. (2001), *Afghanistan's Endless War: State Failure, Regional Politics, and the Rise of the Taliban*, London: University of Washington Press.

Gorbachev, A. (2015), 'The State of Russian Independent Media: Exiles, Enlighteners and Activists', *Newsweek*, 28 June. Available online: http://www.newsweek.com/state-russian-independent-media-exiles-enlighteners-and-activists-344187 (accessed 30 September 2018).

Gorelov, L. (1979), 'Conversation of the Chief of the Soviet Military Advisory Group in Afghanistan, Lt. Gen. Gorelov, with H. Amin', *History and Public Policy Program Digital Archive*, as cited in Znamya, no. 4, 1991, from the Archives of the General Staff of the USSR Armed Forces, 11 August. Available online: http://digitalarchive.wilsoncenter.org/document/110028 (accessed 30 September 2018).

Gornin, A. (2013), 'Shock and Awe at RIA Novosti', *Transitions Online*, 16 December.

Gorodetsky, G. (2003), *Russia Between East and West: Russian Foreign Policy on the Threshold of the Twenty-First Century*, Portland: Frank Cass.

Goryashko, S. and M. Ivanov (2014), 'Deputies and Senators Are Ready to Help the Crimean Central Executive Committee [in Russian]', *Kommersant*, 14 March. Available online: https://www.kommersant.ru/doc/2428788 (accessed 30 September 2018).

Government of the Republic of Crimea (2015), 'Decree of the Head of the Republic of Crimea of April 22, 2015, 114-U "On the Public Crimean-Tatar TV and Radio Company" [in Russian]', 22 April. Available online: https://rk.gov.ru/ru/document/show/8846 (accessed 30 September 2018).

Govorit Moskva (2017), 'Zakharova Confirmed the Fact of Yanukovich's Appeal to Putin to Request the Entry of Troops [in Russian]', 17 March. Available online: https://govoritmoskva.ru/news/113373/ (accessed 30 September 2018).

Grau, L. W. (2003), 'The Takedown of Kabul: An Effective Coup De Main'. In: W. G. Robertson (ed), *Block by Block: The Challenges of Urban Operations*, 291–324, Ft Leavenworth: U.S. Army Command and General Staff College Press.

Grau, L. W. and M. A. Gress (2002), *The Soviet-Afghan War: How a Superpower Fought and Lost*, Lawrence: University Press of Kansas.

Gregory, P. R. (2014), 'Putin's "Human Rights Council" Accidentally Posts Real Crimean Election Results', *Forbes*, 5 May. Available online: https://www.forbes.com/sites/paulroderickgregory/2014/05/05/putins-human-rights-council-accidentally-posts-real-crimean-election-results-only-15-voted-for-annexation/#67adf2b8f172 (accessed 30 September 2018).

Gregory, P. R. (2015), 'Army of Trolls', *Hoover Digest*, 2: 127–34.

Grieder, P. (1999), *The East German Leadership, 1946–1973*, Manchester: Manchester University Press.

Gusakova, E. (2015), 'Temirgaliev Dismissed after Stealing 70 Kilograms of Gold [in Russian]', *Rossiskaya Gazeta*, 19 February. Available online: https://rg.ru/2015/02/19/reg-kfo/temirgaliev-anons.html (accessed 30 September 2018).

Hammond, T. T. (1984), *Red Flag over Afghanistan*, Boulder: Westview Press.

Hans, J. (2014), 'Putin's Trolls [in German]', *Süddeutsche Zeitung*, 13 June. Available online: http://www.sueddeutsche.de/politik/propaganda-aus-russland-putins-trolle-1.1997470 (accessed 30 September 2018).

Harasymiw, B. (2001), 'Book Reviews: The Sword and the Shield: The Mitrokhin Archive and the Secret History of the KGB by Christopher Andrew and Vasili Mitrokhin', *Canadian Slavonic Papers*, 43(1): 145–7.

Harding, L. (2014), 'Russian News Channel TV Rain May Close after Main Carrier Pulls Plug', *The Guardian*, 4 February. Available online: https://www.theguardian.com/world/2014/feb/04/russian-news-channel-tv-rain (accessed 30 September 2018).

Harding, L. and S. Walker (2014), 'Crimea Votes to Secede from Ukraine in "Illegal" Poll', *The Guardian*, 16 March. Available online: https://www.theguardian.com/world/2014/mar/16/ukraine-russia-truce-crimea-referendum (accessed 30 September 2018).

Harf, M. (2014), 'Reported Deaths in Ukraine Street Clashes', *Office of the Spokesperson, U.S. Department of State*, 22 January. Available online: https://2009-2017.state.gov/r/pa/prs/ps/2014/01/220510.htm (accessed 30 September 2018).

Healey, D. and M. Isserman (1990), *Dorothy Healey Remembers: A Life in the American Communist Party*, New York: Oxford University Press.

Herd, G. (2010), 'Security Strategy: Sovereign Democracy and Great Power Aspirations'. In: M. Galeotti (ed), *The Politics of Security in Modern Russia*, 7–28, Farnham: Ashgate.

Van Herpen, M. H. (2016), *Putin's Propaganda Machine: Soft Power and Russian Foreign Policy*, London: Rowman & Littlefield.

Herszenhorn, D. (2014), 'Crimea Votes to Secede From Ukraine as Russian Troops Keep Watch', *The New York Times*, 16 March. Available online: https://www.nytimes.com/2014/03/17/world/europe/crimea-ukraine-secession-vote-referendum.html (accessed 30 September 2018).

Herszenhorn, D. and E. Barry (2011), 'Putin Contends Clinton Incited Unrest Over Vote', *The New York Times*, 8 December. Available online: https://www.nytimes.com/2011/12/09/world/europe/putin-accuses-clinton-of-instigating-russian-protests.html (accessed 30 September 2018).

Heuer Jr., R. J. (1987), 'Soviet Organization and Doctrine for Strategic Deception'. In: B. D. Dailey and P. J. Parker (eds), *Soviet Strategic Deception*, 21–53, Lexington: D.C. Heath and Company.

Higgins, A. (2014), 'Far-Right Fever for a Europe Tied to Russia', *The New York Times*, 20 May. Available online: https://www.nytimes.com/2014/05/21/world/europe/eu

ropes-far-right-looks-to-russia-as-a-guiding-force.html (accessed 30 September 2018).

Hobson, P. (2016), 'Battle for Sevastopol: How a Crimean Romantic Fought the Kremlin's Bureaucrat', *The Moscow Times*, 8 April. Available online: https://themosc owtimes.com/articles/battle-for-sevastopol-how-a-crimean-romantic-fought-the-k remlins-bureaucrat-52439 (accessed 30 September 2018).

Hoffman, D. E. (2011), *The Oligarchs: Wealth and Power in the New Russia*, New York: PublicAffairs.

Horbyk, R. (2015), 'Little Patriotic War: Nationalist Narratives in the Russian Media Coverage of the Ukraine-Russia Crisis', *Asian Politics and Policy*, 7(3): 505–11.

Hughes-Wilson, J. (2000), 'The Mitrokhin Archive: The Spy as Hero, Dissident, or Traitor?', *The RUSI Journal*, 145(1): 57–8.

Hutchings, S. and N. Rulyova (2009), *Television and Culture in Putin's Russia: Remote Control*, London: Routledge.

IISS (2021), 'The Protest Movement in Belarus: Resistance and Repression', *Strategic Comments*, 27(2): i–iii.

Ilyichyov, N. M. (2014), 'It's Not Comprehension, It's Misrepresentation', *Voennaia mysl'*, (Military Thought), 23(3): 148–54.

Indra, A., D. Kolder, A. Kapek, O. Svestka, and V. Bil'ak (1968), 'The "Letter of Invitation" from the Anti-Reformist Faction of the CPCz Leadership, August 1968'. In: J. Navratil (ed), *The Prague Spring 1968: A National Security Archive Documents Reader*, 324, Budapest: Central European University Press.

Interfax (2014a), 'Leader of the Party "Russian Unity" Aksyonov Becomes Premier of Crimea [in Russian]', 27 February. Available online: http://www.interfax.ru/world /361702 (accessed 30 September 2018).

Interfax (2014b), 'Putin Will Appoint Menyailo Governor of Sevastopol [in Russian]', 14 April. Available online: http://www.interfax.ru/russia/371542 (accessed 30 September 2018).

Interfax (2014c), 'Speaker of the Crimean Parliament: Crimea Can Secede from Ukraine If "the Country Falls Apart" [in Russian]', 20 February. Available online: http://www .interfax.ru/world/359837 (accessed 30 September 2018).

Interfax (2014d), 'The Referendum on Changing the Status of the Crimea Will Be Held on May 25 [in Russian]', 27 February. Available online: http://www.interfax.ru/world /361626 (accessed 30 September 2018).

Interfax-Ukraine (2010), 'Regions Party Gets 80 of 100 Seats on Crimean Parliament', 6 November. Available online: http://en.interfax.com.ua/news/general/52929.html (accessed 30 September 2018).

Interfax-Ukraine (2014), 'Shoigu Appoints Ex-Ukrainian Navy Commander as Russian Black Sea Fleet Deputy Commander', *Kyiv Post*, 24 March. Available online: https:/ /www.kyivpost.com/article/content/ukraine-politics/shoigu-appoints-ex-ukrainia n-navy-commander-russian-black-sea-fleet-deputy-commander-340610.html (accessed 30 September 2018).

International Republican Institute (2009), *Public Opinion Survey: Residents of the Autonomous Republic of Crimea, November 5–December 4, 2009*, Baltic Surveys Ltd. & the Gallup Organization.

International Republican Institute (2011), *Public Opinion Survey: Residents of the Autonomous Republic of Crimea, September 20–October 2, 2011*, Baltic Surveys Ltd. & the Gallup Organization.

International Republican Institute (2013), *Public Opinion Survey Residents of the Autonomous Republic of Crimea, May 16–30, 2013*, Baltic Surveys Ltd. & the Gallup Organization.

Interview A (2017), Personal Interview with the Author, Kyiv, Ukraine, Former Ukrainian Defence Official, 24 April.

Interview B (2017), Personal Interview with the Author, Kyiv, Ukraine, Former Deputy Commander of a Ukrainian Naval Infantry Unit Based in Crimea, 7 April.

Interview C (2017), Personal interview with the Author, Kyiv, Ukraine, Senior Researcher, formerly at Taurida National V.I. Vernadsky University, Simferopol, 21 April.

Interview D (2017), Personal Interview with the Author, Kyiv, Ukraine, Retired Ukrainian Army Colonel from Crimea, 6 April.

Interview E (2016), Personal Interview with the Author, London, United Kingdom, Expert on Russian Military Policy, 14 December.

Interview F (2017), Personal Interview with the Author, Kyiv, Ukraine, Participant Involved in the Feb-Mar 2014 Events in Sevastopol, 10 April.

Interview G (2017), Personal Interview with the Author, Kyiv, Ukraine, Participant Involved in the Feb-Mar 2014 Events in Crimea, 10 April.

Interview H (2017), Personal Interview with the Author, Kyiv, Ukraine, Senior Ukrainian Navy Officer, 21 March.

Interview I (2017), Personal Interview with the Author, Odesa, Ukraine, Senior Ukrainian Navy Staff Officer, 14 April.

Interview J (2017), Personal Interview with Author, Kyiv, Ukraine, Ukrainian Political Analyst, 24 March.

Interview K (2017), Personal Interview with the Author, Kyiv, Ukraine, Human Rights Lawyer Working in Crimea Feb-Mar 2014, 29 March.

Interview with Yuri Petrovich Fedash (2017), Personal Interview with the Author, Odesa, Ukraine, Former Commander of the Minesweeper 'Cherkasy', Ukrainian Navy, 14 April.

Interview with Yevhen Fedchenko (2017), Personal Interview with the Author, Kyiv, Ukraine, Director of the Mohyla School of Journalism at the National University of Kyiv-Mohyla Academy and Co-founder and Chief Editor of StopFake.org, 25 April.

Interview with Yuri Valentinovich Golovashenko (2017), Personal Interview with the Author, Kyiv, Ukraine, Former Battalion Commander of the Mountain Infantry Battalion of the Ukrainian 36th Separate Coastal Defence Brigade, Pervalne, 8 April.

Interview with Mykhailo Gonchar (2017), Personal Interview with the Author, Kyiv, Ukraine, President of the Centre for Global Studies Strategy XXI, 25 April.

Interview with Petr Dmitrievich Goncharenko (2017), Personal Interview with the Author, Odesa, Ukraine, Commander of the Admiral Nakhimov Naval Academy in Sevastopol at the Time of the 2014 Crisis, 13 April.

Interview with Marina Kanaliuk (2017), Personal Interview with the Author, Odesa, Ukraine, Assistant to the Commander of the Ukrainian Navy for Cooperation with the Russian Black Sea Fleet at the Time of the 2014 Crisis, 14 April.

Interview with Oleksii Kirillov (2017), Personal Interview with the Author, Odesa, Ukraine, Former Deputy Commander of the Ukrainian Navy Corvette 'Ternopil', 14 April.

Interview with Volodymyr Prytula (2017), Personal Interview with the Author, Kyiv, Ukraine, Editor-in-chief of Krym Realii, RFE/RL, 19 April.

Ioffe, J. (2010), 'What Is Russia Today? The Kremlin's Propaganda Outlet Has an Identity Crisis', *Columbia Journalism Review*. Available online: http://archives.cjr.org/feature/what_is_russia_today.php (accessed 30 September 2018).

Ioffe, J. (2014), 'A Week Before the Olympics, the Kremlin Is Attacking Russia's Last Independent TV Channel', *New Republic*, 31 January. Available online: https://newrepublic.com/article/116434/putin-attacks-dozhdtv-russias-last-independent-tv-channel (accessed 30 September 2018).

ITAR-TASS (2014a), 'Lavrov: Russia Not Giving Orders to Crimean Self-Defense Forces', 5 March. Available online: http://tass.com/world/722174 (accessed 30 September 2018).

ITAR-TASS (2014b), 'Minister of Information of Crimea: Ukrainian TV Channels Have Been Disabled on Moral Principles [in Russian]', 9 March. Available online: http://tass.ru/mezhdunarodnaya-panorama/1033727 (accessed 30 September 2018).

ITAR-TASS (2014c), 'People in Military Uniform without Insignia in Crimea Not Linked with Russian Army', 5 March. Available online: http://tass.com/russia/722183 (accessed 30 September 2018).

ITAR-TASS (2014d), 'Shoigu: Media Photos of Military Hardware with Russian Numbers in Crimea a Provocation', 5 March. Available online: http://tass.com/russia/722188 (accessed 30 September 2018).

Izvestia (1989), 'The Invasion in Retrospect: The Recollections of General Ivan Pavlovskii'. In: J. Navratil (ed), The Prague Spring 1968: A National Security Archive Documents Reader, 431–2, Budapest: Central European University Press.

Jewkes, S. and O. Vukmanovic (2017), 'Suspected Russia-Backed Hackers Target Baltic Energy Networks', *Reuters*, 11 May. Available online: http://www.reuters.com/article/us-baltics-cyber-insight-idUSKBN1871W5 (accessed 30 September 2018).

Johnson, A. R. (2010), *Radio Free Europe and Radio Liberty: The CIA Years and Beyond*, Washington, DC: Woodrow Wilson Center Press.

Johnson, L. K. (1989), *America's Secret Power: The CIA in Democratic Society*, Oxford: Oxford University Press.

Johnston, G. (1999), 'What Is the History of Samizdat?', *Social History*, 24(2): 115–33.

Jones, C. D. (2003), 'Soviet Military Doctrine as Strategic Deception: An Offensive Military Strategy for Defense of the Socialist Fatherland', *The Journal of Slavic Military Studies*, 16(3): 24–65.

Jonsson, O. and R. Seely (2015), 'Russian Full-Spectrum Conflict: An Appraisal After Ukraine', *The Journal of Slavic Military Studies*, 28(1): 1–22.

Kakar, M. H. (1995), *Afghanistan: The Soviet Invasion and the Afghan Response, 1979–1982*, London: University of California Press.

Kamyshev, D. and K. Bolletskaya (2014), 'For the Capture of Crimea [in Russian]', *Vedemosti*, 5 May. Available online: https://www.vedomosti.ru/newspaper/articles/2014/05/05/za-vzyatie-kryma (accessed 30 September 2018).

Karon, T. (1999), 'Yeltsin Threats Reflect Russian Anger Over Kosovo', *Time*, 9 April. Available online: https://content.time.com/time/magazine/article/0,9171,22885,00.html (accessed 30 September 2018).

Karpovich, O. and A. Manoilo (2015), *Color Revolutions: Techniques in Breaking Down Modern Political Regimes*, Bloomington: AuthorHouse.

Kashevarova, A. (2014), 'Stanislav Apetian: "Russia Should Learn to Provide Content" [in Russian]', *Izvestia*, 21 March. Available online: http://izvestia.ru/news/567947 (accessed 30 September 2018).

Kazlov, S. N. (ed) (1971), *The Officer's Handbook: A Soviet View [1977 U.S. Air Force Translation]*, Moscow: Soviet Ministry of Defence.

Kenez, P. (1985), *The Birth of the Propaganda State: Soviet Methods of Mass Mobilization, 1917–1929*, Cambridge: Cambridge University Press.

Kennan, G. (1946), 'Long Telegram/Moscow 511: The Charge in the Soviet Union [Kennan] to the Secretary of State'. Available online: http://www.gwu.edu/~nsarchiv/coldwar/documents/episode-1/kennan.htm (accessed 30 September 2018).

Kennan, G. (1948), 'U.S. Department of State Policy Planning Staff Memorandum: The Inauguration of Organized Political Warfare'. Available online: https://digitalarchive.wilsoncenter.org/document/114320.pdf?v=941dc9ee5c6e51333ea9ebbbc9104e8c (accessed 30 September 2018).

KGB (1963), 'KGB Handbook, "Ukrainian Bourgeois Nationalists" (excerpt)', *History and Public Policy Program Digital Archive*, Chapter selected from Ukrainian Bourgeois Nationalists (Moscow, Advanced School of the KGB under the Council of Ministers of the USSR, 1963), Authors: Col. B.S Shul'zhenko, leader; Col. I.V. Khamaziuk. Available online: http://digitalarchive.wilsoncenter.org/document/119632 (accessed 30 September 2018).

KGB (1980), 'Memorandum from the KGB Regarding the Planning of a Demonstration in Memory of John Lennon', *History and Public Policy Program Digital Archive*, TsKhSD, f.5, op.77, d.994, l.164 obtained by Gael Moullec and translated by Christa Sheehan Matthew, 20 December. Available online: http://digitalarchive.wilsoncenter.org/document/113935 (accessed 30 September 2018).

Khimshiashvili, P. and N. Raybman (2014), 'Crimean Rada Votes to Join Russia, Referendum Will Be Held March 16 [in Russian]', *Vedemosti*, 6 March. Available online: http://www.vedomosti.ru/politics/articles/2014/03/06/krymskij-referendum -perenesli-na-16-marta (accessed 30 September 2018).

Khitakhunov, A., B. Mukhamediyev, and R. Pomfret (2017), 'Eurasian Economic Union: Present and Future Perspectives', *Economic Change and Restructuring*, 50(1): 59–77.

Khvostunova, O. (2013), 'A Brief History of the Russian Media', *The Interpreter*, 6 December. Available online: http://www.interpretermag.com/a-brief-history-of-t he-russian-media/ (accessed 30 September 2018).

Kind-Kovács, F. and J. Labov, eds. (2013), *Samizdat, Tamizdat, and Beyond: Transnational Media During and After Socialism*, New York: Berghahn Books.

Kinter, W. R. and J. Z. Kornfeder (1962), *The New Frontier of War: Political Warfare, Present and Future*, Chicago: Henry Regnery Company.

Kiselyov, V. A. and I. N. Vorobyov (2015), 'Hybrid Operations: A New Type of Warfare', *Voennaia mysl', (Military Thought)*, 24(2): 28–36.

Kliatskin, K. (2016), *Crimea as It Was [Documentary Film]*, Babylon'13. Available online: https://youtu.be/tXGET1-fzmI (accessed 30 September 2018).

Klymenko, A. (2015a), *Human Rights Abuses in Russian-Occupied Crimea*, Washington, DC: The Atlantic Council of the United States and Freedom House.

Klymenko, A. (2015b), *The Militarization of Crimea under Russian Occupation*, Washington, DC: The Atlantic Council of the United States and Freedom House.

Knobel, A. (2017), 'The Eurasian Economic Union: Development Prospects and Possible Obstacles', *Problems of Economic Transition*, 59(5): 335–60.

Knott, E. (2017), 'Quasi-Citizenship as a Category of Practice: Analyzing Engagement with Russia's Compatriot Policy in Crimea', *Citizenship Studies*, 21(1): 116–35.

Kofman, M. (2016), 'Russian Hybrid Warfare and Other Dark Arts', *War on the Rocks*, 11 March. Available online: https://warontherocks.com/2016/03/russian-hybrid-w arfare-and-other-dark-arts/ (accessed 30 September 2018).

Kokoshin, A. A. (1998), *Soviet Strategic Thought*, London: MIT Press, 1917–91.

Komaromi, A. (2004), 'The Material Existence of Soviet Samizdat', *Slavic Review*, 63(3): 597–618.

Komaromi, A. (2012), 'Samizdat and Soviet Dissident Publics', *Slavic Review*, 71(1): 70–90.

Komsomolskaya Pravda (2014), 'The Leader of the "Right Sector" Yarosh Appealed for Help to Doku Umarov [in Russian]', 2 March. Available online: https://www.kp.ru/ daily/26201.7/3087600/ (accessed 30 September 2018).

Kondrashov, A. (2015), 'Crimea: The Way Home [Documentary Film, in Russian]', *Rossiya 1*, 15 March. Available online: https://www.youtube.com/watch?v=t42-71Rp RgI (accessed 30 September 2018).

Korrespondent (2014), 'The Decision on Crimea Was Made by Putin Alone–Peskov [in Russian]', 20 April. Available online: http://korrespondent.net/world/russia/3352058

-reshenye-po-krymu-prynymal-edynolychno-putyn-peskov (accessed 30 September 2018).

Kosygin, A. N. and N. M. Taraki (1979), 'Telephone Conversation between Soviet Premier Alexei N. Kosygin and Afghan Premier Nur Mohammed Taraki', *History and Public Policy Program Digital Archive*, Boris Gromov, 'Ogranichennyy Kontingent ("Limited Contingent")', Progress, Moscow, 1994, 18 March. Available online: http://digitalarchive.wilsoncenter.org/document/113141 (accessed 30 September 2018).

Kozlov, P. (2015), '"If it Had a Certain Director, the Director Needs to Get a Five Plus": Rustam Temirgaliev on the Development of Events Leading to the Referendum in Crimea [in Russian]', *Vedemosti*, 16 March. Available online: https://www.vedomost i.ru/politics/characters/2015/03/16/esli-eto-imelo-opredelennuyu-rezhissuru---re zhisseru-nuzhno-postavit-pyat-s-plyusom (accessed 30 September 2018).

Kramer, M. (1993), 'The Prague Spring and the Soviet Invasion of Czechoslovakia: New Interpretations', *Cold War International History Project Bulletin, (3)*: 2–13.

Kramer, M. (2010), 'The Prague Spring and the Soviet Invasion in Historical Perspective'. In: G. Bischof, S. Karner, and P. Ruggenthaler (eds), *The Prague Spring and the Warsaw Pact Invasion of Czechoslovakia in 1968*, 35–58, Plymouth: Lexington Books.

Kravtsova, Y. (2014), 'Observers Say Russia Had Crimea Plan for Years', *Moscow Times*, 26 March. Available online: https://themoscowtimes.com/articles/observers-say-russia-had-crimea-plan-for-years-33371 (accessed 30 September 2018).

Kremlin (1968), 'Soviet Government Diplomatic Note to the Czechoslovak Government, July 20, 1968'. In: J. Navratil (ed), *The Prague Spring 1968: A National Security Archive Documents Reader*, 265–7, Budapest: Central European University Press.

Kremlin (1998), 'Decree of the President of the Russian Federation from 25 July 1998, No. 886 [in Russian]', 25 July. Available online: http://www.kremlin.ru/acts/bank /12716 (accessed 30 September 2018).

Kremlin (2012), 'Staffing in the Presidential Administration: Vladimir Putin by His Decree Appointed Sergey Glazyev Advisor to the President [in Russian]', 30 July. Available online: http://kremlin.ru/events/president/news/16070 (accessed 30 September 2018).

Kremlin (2014a), 'Address by President of the Russian Federation', 18 March. Available online: http://en.kremlin.ru/events/president/news/20603 (accessed 30 September 2018).

Kremlin (2014b), 'Comments Regarding US Sanctions against Russia, Effective from March 20, 2014', 21 March. Available online: http://en.kremlin.ru/events/president/ transcripts/20627 (accessed 30 September 2018).

Kremlin (2014c), 'Direct Line with Vladimir Putin', 17 April. Available online: http://en. kremlin.ru/events/president/news/20796 (accessed 30 September 2018).

Kremlin (2014d), 'Executive Order on Recognising Crimean Military Service Members' Ranks, Documents on Education and Military Service', 20 March. Available online: http://en.kremlin.ru/events/president/news/20621 (accessed 30 September 2018).

Kremlin (2014e), 'Executive Order on Recognising Republic of Crimea', 14 March. Available online: http://en.kremlin.ru/events/president/news/20596 (accessed 30 September 2018).

Kremlin (2014f), 'Executive Order on Social Guarantees for Military Personnel in Crimea and Sevastopol', 31 March. Available online: http://en.kremlin.ru/events/president/news/20662 (accessed 30 September 2018).

Kremlin (2014g), 'Military Doctrine of the Russian Federation [English Translation]', 25 December. Available online: http://rusemb.org.uk/press/2029.

Kremlin (2014h), 'Vladimir Putin Answered Journalists' Questions on the Situation in Ukraine', 4 March. Available online: http://en.kremlin.ru/events/president/transcripts/20366 (accessed 30 September 2018).

Kremlin (2014i), 'Vladimir Putin Observed Western and Central Military District Forces Exercises', 3 March. Available online: http://en.kremlin.ru/events/president/news/20362 (accessed 30 September 2018) (accessed 30 September 2018).

Kremlin (2015), 'Direct Line with Vladimir Putin', 16 April. Available online: http://en.kremlin.ru/events/president/news/49261 (accessed 30 September 2018).

Kremlin (2017), 'Major Staff and Key Officials', 25 December. Available online: http://en.kremlin.ru/structure/administration/members (accessed 30 September 2018).

Krym.Kommentarii (2014a), 'Deputies of the Verkhovna Rada of Crimea Are Ready to Give Crimea to Russia [in Russian]', 19 February. Available online: http://crimea.comments.ua/news/2014/02/19/110004.html (accessed 30 September 2018).

Krym.Kommentarii (2014b), 'Mohyliov Advised the Speaker of Crimea to Think about What to Say [in Russian]', 20 February. Available online: http://crimea.comments.ua/news/2014/02/20/174340.html (accessed 30 September 2018).

Krym Realii (2015), 'Public Crimean Tatar TV and Radio Company Will Be Named 'Millet' [in Russian]', 25 April. Available online: https://ru.krymr.com/a/news/26977773.html (accessed 30 September 2018).

Kudors, A., M. Kaprāns, and M. Cepurītis (2014), *Russian Information Campaign against Ukraine – The 'Vilnius Summit' to the 'Crimean Referendum': Analysis of Messages [in Latvian]*, Riga: Centre for East European Policy Studies. Available online: http://appc.lv/wp-content/uploads/2014/06/Krievijas-info-kampaņa-pret-Ukrainu.pdf (accessed 30 September 2018).

Kugler, R. L. and M. V. Kozintseva (1996), *Enlarging NATO: The Russia Factor*, Santa Monica, CA: RAND Corporation.

Kuleshov, Y. E., B. B. Zhutdiev, and D. A. Fedorov (2014), 'Information-Psychological Warfare in Modern Conditions: Theory and Practice [in Russian]', *Bulletin of the Academy of Military Sciences of the Russian Federation*: 104–10.

Kux, D. (1985), 'Soviet Active Measures and Disinformation: Overview and Assessment', *Parameters*, XV(4): 19–28.

Kuzio, T. (2010), *The Crimea: Europe's Next Flashpoint?*, Washington, DC: The Jamestown Foundation.

Kuzio, T. (2015), 'The Origins of Peace, Non-Violence, and Conflict in Ukraine'. In: A. Pikulicka-Wilczewska and R. Sakwa (eds), *Ukraine and Russia: People, Politics, Propaganda and Perspectives*, 109–22, Bristol: E-International Relations Publishing.

Kuzio, T. (2016), 'Soviet and Russian Anti-(Ukrainian) Nationalism and Re-Stalinization', *Communist and Post-Communist Studies*: 4987–99.

Landler, M. and M. Gordon (2014), 'NATO Chief Warns of Duplicity by Putin on Ukraine', *The New York Times*, 8 July, A11.

Laruelle, M. (2009), *In the Name of the Nation: Nationalism and Politics in Contemporary Russia*, New York: Palgrave Macmillan.

Laruelle, M., ed. (2010), *Russian Nationalism and the National Reassertion of Russia*, London: Routledge.

Laruelle, M. (2015), 'Russia as a "Divided Nation," from Compatriots to Crimea: A Contribution to the Discussion on Nationalism and Foreign Policy', *Problems of Post-Communism*, 62(2): 88–97.

Laruelle, M. (2016), 'France: Mainstreaming Russian Influence'. In: A. Polyakova, M. Laruelle, S. Meister, and N. Barnett (eds), *The Kremlin's Trojan Horses*, 7–12, Washington, DC: Atlantic Council.

Latawski, P. and M. A. Smith (2003), *The Kosovo Crisis and the Evolution of a Post-Cold War European Security*, Manchester: Manchester University Press.

Lavrov, A. (2014), 'Russian Again: The Military Operation for Crimea'. In: C. Howard and R. Pukhov (eds), *Brothers Armed: Military Aspects of the Crisis in Ukraine*, 157–84, Minneapolis: East View Press.

Lavrov, A. and A. Nikolsky (2014), 'Neglect and Rot: Degradation of Ukraine's Military in the Interim Period'. In: C. Howard and R. Pukhov (eds), *Brothers Armed: Military Aspects of the Crisis in Ukraine*, 57–73, Minneapolis: East View Press.

Law of Ukraine No. 4061-VI (2011), 'On Election of the People's Deputies of Ukraine', 17 November. Available online: http://www.cvk.gov.ua/vnd_2012_en/law/law.pdf (accessed 30 September 2018).

Le Monde (2015), 'FN Funding: Russian Hackers Unveil Kremlin Exchanges [in French]', 2 April. Available online: http://www.lemonde.fr/les-decodeurs/article/2 015/04/02/fn-des-hackers-russes-devoilent-des-echanges-au-kremlin_4608660_4 355770.html (accessed 30 September 2018).

Leebaert, D. (1981), 'The Context of Soviet Military Thinking'. In: D. Leebaert (ed), *Soviet Military Thinking*, 3–27, London: George Allen & Unwin.

Legvold, R., ed. (2007), *Russian Foreign Policy in the Twenty-First Century and the Shadow of the Past*, New York: Columbia University Press.

Lenin, V. (1917), 'Decree on the Press'. In: J. Murray (ed), *The Russian Press from Brezhnev to Yeltsin: Behind the Paper Curtain*, 2, Aldershot: Edward Elgar.

Lenta.ru (2014a), 'Dear Readers – From the Dear Editorial Staff [in Russian]', 12 March. Available online: https://lenta.ru/info/posts/statement/ (accessed 30 September 2018).

Lenta.ru (2014b), 'Lenta.ru Has Replaced its Chief Editor [in Russian]', 12 March. Available online: https://lenta.ru/news/2014/03/12/goreslavsky/ (accessed 30 September 2018).

Lenta.ru (2014c), 'Matviyenko Spoke of Russian Victims in Crimea [in Russian]', 1 March. Available online: https://lenta.ru/news/2014/03/01/victims/ (accessed 30 September 2018).

Leonard, P. (2014), 'Russian Propaganda War in Full Swing over Ukraine', *Associated Press*, 15 March. Available online: https://www.yahoo.com/news/russian-propaganda -war-full-swing-over-ukraine-085411498.html (accessed 30 September 2018).

Leonor, A. (2016), 'A Guide to Russian Propaganda. Part 2: Whataboutism', *Euromaidan Press*, 31 August. Available online: http://euromaidanpress.com/2016/08/31/a-guide -to-russian-propaganda-part-2-whataboutism/ (accessed 30 September 2018).

Levada Centre (2014), *Public Opinion – 2013 [in Russian]*, Moscow: Analytical Centre of Yuri Levada. Available online: http://www.levada.ru/sites/default/files/om13.pdf (accessed 30 September 2018).

Limny, A. and A. Gorkin (1980), 'The Effectiveness of *Maskirovka* [in Russian]', *Voennaya Vestnik*, 5: 83–5.

Lipman, M., A. Kachkaeva, and M. Poyker (2018), 'Media in Russia: Between Modernization and Monopoly'. In: D. Treisman (ed), *The New Autocracy*, 159–90, Washington, DC: Brookings Institution Press.

Lipman, M. and M. McFaul (2001), '"Managed Democracy" in Russia: Putin and the Press', *The International Journal of Press/Politics*, 6(3): 116–27.

Lipsky, A. (2015), 'It Seems Appropriate to Initiate the Accession of Eastern Regions of Ukraine to Russia [in Russian]', *Novaya Gazeta*, 24 February. Available online: https://www.novayagazeta.ru/articles/2015/02/24/63168-171-predstavlyaetsya-pravi lnym-initsiirovat-prisoedinenie-vostochnyh-oblastey-ukrainy-k-rossii-187 (accessed 30 September 2018).

Littell, R., ed. (1969), *The Czech Black Book*, London: Pall Mall Press.

Lo, B. (2003), *Vladimir Putin and the Evolution of Russian Foreign Policy*, London: Royal Institute of International Affairs.

LTV (2015), 'Kremlin Cash Flows Towards Pro-Putin MEP', *Latvian Public Broadcasting*, 13 April. Available online: https://eng.lsm.lv/article/politics/politics/kremlin-cash-fl ows-towards-pro-putin-mep.a125270/ (accessed 30 September 2018).

Luhn, A. (2014), 'Russia Toughens Up Punishment for Separatist Ideas – Despite Ukraine', *The Guardian*, 23 May. Available online: https://www.theguardian.com /world/2014/may/24/russia-toughens-punishment-separatist-ideas (accessed 30 September 2018).

Lutsenko, Y. (2017), 'Wall Post [in Ukrainian]', Facebook, 17 January. Available online: https://www.facebook.com/photo.php?fbid=625853430947169&set=a.13902156 9630360.1073741834.100005675529100&type=3&theater (accessed 30 September 2018).

Lyakhovsky, A. (1995), *The Tragedy and Valor of Afghanistan*, Moscow: GPI Iskon.

Makarenko, O. and A. Shandra (2016), 'Ukraine Publishes Video Proving Kremlin Directed Separatism in Eastern Ukraine and Crimea', *Euromaidan Press*, 23 August. Available online: http://euromaidanpress.com/2016/08/23/ukraine-publishes -video-proving-kremlin-directed-separatism-in-ukraine/#arvlbdata (accessed 30 September 2018).

Malcolm, N. (1989), 'The "Common European Home" and Soviet European Policy', *International Affairs*, 65(4): 659–76.

Maley, W. (2009), *The Afghanistan Wars*, 2nd edn, Houndmills: Palgrave Macmillan.

Malyshev, M. (2014), 'The Results of the Referendum in Crimea Read by Mikhail Malyshev [Online Video in Russian]', *112 Ukraina*, 17 March. Available online: https ://www.youtube.com/watch?v=MWxiCWoP9Qs (accessed 30 September 2018).

Mankoff, J. (2012), *Russian Foreign Policy: The Return of Great Power Politics*, Lanham: Rowman & Littlefield.

Markham, J. (1989), 'Gorbachev Spurns the Use of Force in Eastern Europe', *The New York Times*, 7 July.

Marples, D. (2006), 'Stepan Bandera: The Resurrection of a Ukrainian National Hero', *Europe–Asia Studies*, 58(4): 555–66.

Marson, J. (2017), 'Kremlin Envoy Played Central Role in Eastern Ukraine', *Wall Street Journal*, 20 August. Available online: https://www.wsj.com/articles/kremlin-envoy-pl ayed-central-role-in-eastern-ukraine-1503258417 (accessed 30 September 2018).

Matsuzato, K. (2016), 'Domestic Politics in Crimea, 2009–2015', *Demokratizatsiya: The Journal of Post-Soviet Democratization*, 24(2): 225–56.

Mayevskiy, V. (1968), 'The So-Called "Quiet Counterrevolution"', Pravda, 3 Nov 1968'. In: *Committee on Government Operations, Subcommittee on National Security International Operations: Czechoslovakia and the Brezhnev Doctrine*, 20–1, Washington, DC: U.S. Government Printing Office.

Mazurov, K. (1968), 'Initial On-Site Report by Kirill Mazurov to the CPSU CC Politburo, August 21, 1968'. In: J. Navratil (ed), *The Prague Spring 1968: A National Security Archive Documents Reader*, 452, Budapest: Central European University Press.

MccGwire, M. (1991), *Perestroika and Soviet National Security*, Washington, DC: Brookings Institution Press.

McGuinness, D. (2014), '"Russian Agent" Row Hits Latvia Election', *BBC*, 10 April. Available online: http://www.bbc.co.uk/news/blogs-eu-26972863 (accessed 30 September 2018).

McKew, M. (2017), 'The Gerasimov Doctrine', *Politico*, 5 September. Available online: https://www.politico.com/magazine/story/2017/09/05/gerasimov-doctrine-russia -foreign-policy-215538 (accessed 30 September 2018).

McMichael, S. R. (1991), *Stumbling Bear: Soviet Military Performance in Afghanistan*, London: Brassey's.

Meduza (2015), 'Polite People: Who Are They? Special Report [in Russian]'. Available online: https://meduza.io/special/polite/who (accessed 30 September 2018).

Mejias, U. A. and N. E. Vokuev (2017), 'Disinformation and the Media: The Case of Russia and Ukraine', *Media, Culture and Society*, 39(7): 1027–42.

Melikova, N. and I. Korotchenko (2002), 'Putin Doesn't Even Mention NATO Expansion', *Nezavisimaya Gazeta [from Current Digest of the Russian Press]*, 29 May.

Melville, F. (1982), 'Coups and Killings in Kabul', *Time*, 22 November.

Merenkov, D. A. (2017), 'Crimean Tatar Factor in Crimea: Current State and Prospects [in Russian]', *Post-Soviet Issues*, 4(1): 73–9.

MFA Russia (1999), 'On State Policy of the Russian Federation in Respect of Compatriots Abroad [in Russian]', 24 May. Available online: http://www.mid.ru/pe reselenie/-/asset_publisher/evI8J0czYac3/content/id/283970 (accessed 30 September 2018).

MFA USSR (1979), 'Message to Soviet Ambassadors on the Invasion of Afghanistan, Attachment to CPSU Politburo Decree #177', *History and Public Policy Program Digital Archive*, TsKhSD, F. 89, P. 14, D. 32, translated for CWIHP by Gary Goldberg, 27 December. Available online: http://digitalarchive.wilsoncenter.org/document/11 3048 (accessed 30 September 2018).

MFA USSR (1980), 'Meeting of Soviet Foreign Minister Gromyko and Afghan Foreign Minister Shad Mohammad Dost, 04 January 1980', *History and Public Policy Program Digital Archive*, RGANI (formerly TsKhSD), f. 89, per. 14, dok. 36, ll. 1-13 [cited by Archive-Information Bulletin, 1993 as RGANI, op. 14, d. 36, ll. 13, copy, CC], provided by M. Kramer; trans. by D. Rozas. Available online: http://digitalarchive.wil soncenter.org/document/111582 (accessed 30 September 2018).

Miazhevich, G. (2014), 'Russia Today's Coverage of Euromaidan', *Russian Journal of Communication*, 6(2): 186–91.

Michel, L. (2013), 'EODE: A Non-Aligned NGO!', *EODE*, 10 February. Available online: http://www.eode.org/eode-a-non-aligned-ngo/ (accessed 30 September 2018).

Mickiewicz, E. (2008), *Television, Power, and the Public in Russia*, Cambridge: Cambridge University Press.

Mikhailov, K. and A. Samarina (2012), 'Kremlin Agitprop [in Russian]', *Nezavisimaya Gazeta*, 22 October.

Ministry of Defence of the Russian Federation (2014), 'Forces Involved in the Verification of Combat Readiness Are Transferred to Designated Areas [in Russian]', 27 February. Available online: https://function.mil.ru/news_page/country/more.htm ?id=11905614@egNews (accessed 30 September 2018).

Ministry of Defence of the Russian Federation (2015), 'First Monument to "Polite People" Opened in Amur Region', 8 May. Available online: http://eng.mil.ru/en/news _page/country/more.htm?id=12030093@egNews (accessed 30 September 2018).

Ministry of Defence of Ukraine (2014), 'Warrant Officer Sergey Viktorovich Kokurin Died during the Storming of the 13th Photogrammetric Operational Center of the Main Directorate of the Armed Forces of Ukraine in Simferopol [in Ukrainian]', 20 March. Available online: http://www.mil.gov.ua/news/2014/03/20/pid-chas-sht urmu-13-go-fotogrammetrichnogo-czentru-golovnogo-upravlinnya-operativnogo-z

abezpechennya-zbrojnih-sil-ukraini-u-simferopoli-zaginuv-na-postu-praporshhik
-sergij-viktorovich-kokurin/ (accessed 30 September 2018).

Miranda, J. (1985), 'Political Warfare: Can the West Survive?', *The Journal of Social, Political, and Economic Studies*, 10(1): 3–24.

Mitrokhin, V. (2007), 'The Nationalism Case. Folder 57. The Chekist Anthology'. In: *History and Public Policy Program Digital Archive*. Available online: http://digitala rchive.wilsoncenter.org/document/110788 (accessed 30 September 2018).

Mlynář, Z. (1980), *Night Frost in Prague: The End of Humane Socialism*, London: C. Hurst & Company.

Mohiuddin, Y. (2007), 'Boris Berezovsky', *International Journal*, 62(3): 681–8.

Morice, F. (2014), 'French Far-Right Politician Endorses Crimea Vote', *EUobserver*, 21 March. Available online: https://euobserver.com/eu-elections/123556 (accessed 30 September 2018).

Moscow Times (2012), 'Putin Appoints Outspoken Critic as Aide', 31 July. Available online: https://themoscowtimes.com/articles/putin-appoints-outspoken-critic-as -aide-16634 (accessed 30 September 2018).

Moskovskiy Komsomolets (2014), 'Daughter of the Permanent Representative to the UN at the Centre of an International Scandal [in Russian]', 22 March. Available online: http://www.mk.ru/politics/article/2014/03/22/1002271-doch-postpreda -v-oon-vitaliya-churkina-okazalas-v-tsentre-mezhdunarodnogo-skandala.html (accessed 30 September 2018).

Murray, J. (1994), *The Russian Press from Brezhnev to Yeltsin: Behind the Paper Curtain*, Aldershot: Edward Elgar.

Myagkov, A. (1976), *Inside the KGB: An Exposé by an Officer of the Third Directorate*, Richmond: The Foreign Affairs Publishing Co.

Navari, C. (2014), 'Territoriality, Self-Determination and Crimea after Badinter', *International Affairs*, 90(6): 1299–318.

Navratil, J. (ed) (1998), *The Prague Spring 1968: A National Security Archive Documents Reader*, Budapest: Central European University Press.

Nechepurenko, I. (2014), 'Putin Awards Journalists for "Objective" Crimea Coverage', *Moscow Times*. Available online: https://themoscowtimes.com/articles/putin-awa rds-journalists-for-objective-crimea-coverage-34996 (accessed 30 September 2018), 5 May.

Neef, C. and M. Schepp (2013), 'How Putin Outfoxed the West', *Spiegel*, 16 December. Available online: http://www.spiegel.de/international/europe/how-vladimir -putin-ruthlessly-maintains-russia-s-grip-on-the-east-a-939286.html (accessed 30 September 2018).

Neuromir TV (2015), *Polit Ring: Strelkov vs. Starikov [Television Show in Russian]*. Available online: https://vimeo.com/118459664 (accessed 30 September 2018).

Nezavisimaya Gazeta (1998), *The Law Will Guide US [in Russian]*, 18 November.

Niva, Nasha (2014), 'Soldiers of the GRU Spetsnaz Turned off the Electricity to the Naval Staff in Sevastopol, One Forgot to Remove a Tag [in Russian]', 3 March.

Available online: http://nn.by/?c=ar&i=123992&lang=ru (accessed 30 September 2018).

Nix, S. B. (2014), 'Responding to the Russian Invasion of Crimea: Policy Recommendations for US and European Leaders', *European View*, 13(1): 143–52.

NSC (1968), 'Notes on Emergency Meeting of the National Security Council', 20 August. Available online: https://www.cia.gov/library/readingroom/docs/1968-08-20a.pdf (accessed 30 September 2018).

NSDC (2014), 'Verbatim Report of the Meeting of the National Security and Defence Council of Ukraine under the Chairmanship of the Acting President of Ukraine, Chairman of the Verkhovna Rada of Ukraine O. V. Turchynov [in Ukrainian]', 28 February. Available online: http://www.rnbo.gov.ua/files/2016/stenogr.pdf (accessed 30 September 2018).

NTV (2014), *Common Fascism: Ukrainian Variant [Television Film in Russian]*. Available online: http://www.ntv.ru/video/964481/ (accessed 30 September 2018).

O'Brien, K. A. (2004), 'Interfering with Civil Society: CIA and KGB Covert Political Action During the Cold War'. In: L. K. Johnson and J. J. Wirtz (eds), *Strategic Intelligence: Windows into a Secret World*, 260–73, Los Angeles: Roxbury.

Oates, S. and G. McCormack (2010), 'The Media and Political Communication'. In: S. White, R. Sakwa, and H. E. Hale (eds), *Developments in Russian Politics 7*, 118–34, Durham: Duke University Press.

OGO (2010), 'Party 'Vanguard' Changes Its Name and Leader [in Ukrainian]', 17 September. Available online: http://ogo.ua/articles/view/2010-09-17/22782.html (accessed 30 September 2018).

Olah, I. and F. Szucs (1968), 'Report on the Sumava Exercises by Generals I. Olah and F. Szucs of the Hungarian People's Army to the HSWP Politburo, July 5, 1968 (Excerpts)'. In: J. Navratil (ed), *The Prague Spring 1968: A National Security Archive Documents Reader*, 199–201, Budapest: Central European University Press.

ORF (2012), '"Peace and Quiet" in Grozny [in German]', 2 February. Available online: http://news.orf.at/stories/2103993/2103995/ (accessed 30 September 2018).

Orlyansky, V. I. and N. F. Kuznetsov (2013), 'Operational Masking: Problems to Solve', *Voennaia mysl', (Military Thought)*, 22(1): 10–17.

Osborn, A. (2014), 'Merkel Raps Putin as Russian Forces Tighten Grip on Crimea', *Reuters*, 9 March. Available online: https://www.reuters.com/article/us-ukraine-crisis-idUSBREA1Q1E820140309 (accessed 30 September 2018).

Österreich (2014), 'Stadler Does Not Know Who Paid for the Crimean Trip [in German]', 18 March. Available online: http://www.oe24.at/oesterreich/politik/Stadler-weiss-nicht-wer-Krim-Reise-zahlte/136456012 (accessed 30 September 2018).

Pacepa, I. M. (2007), 'Moscow's Assault on the Vatican', *National Review*, 25 January. Available online: https://www.nationalreview.com/2007/01/moscows-assault-vatican-ion-mihai-pacepa/ (accessed 30 September 2018).

Patrushev, N. P. (2014), 'From the Interview of N. P. Patrushev on the Television Channel "Rossiya 24" [in Russian]', *Security Council of the Russian Federation*,

7 June. Available online: http://www.scrf.gov.ru/news/allnews/820/ (accessed 30 September 2018).

Pavlov, D. A., A. N. Belsky, and O. V. Klimenko (2015), 'Military Security of the Russian Federation: How It Can Be Maintained Today', *Voennaia mysl', (Military Thought)*, 24(1): 17–25.

Pavlushko, A. (2015), 'How "Ukrainian Berkut Officer" from Russian Ulyanovsk Assaulted Crimean Parliament Back in 2014', *Inform Napalm*, 9 July. Available online: https://informnapalm.org/en/how-ukrainian-berkut-officer-from-russian-ulyanovsk-assaulted-crimean-parliament-back-in-2014/ (accessed 30 September 2018).

Penkovsky, O. (1965), *The Penkovsky Papers*, Los Angeles: Collins.

Petrov, N. (2010), 'The KGB and the Czechoslovak Crisis of 1968: Preconditions for the Soviet Invasion and Occupation in Czechoslovakia'. In: G. Bischof, S. Karner, and P. Ruggenthaler (eds), *The Prague Spring and the Warsaw Pact Invasion of Czechoslovakia in 1968*, 145–63, Plymouth: Lexington Books.

Phelps-Fetherston, I. (1965), *Soviet International Front Organizations: A Concise Handbook*, London: Praeger.

PIK (2016), 'Who Was Pavel Chernev? [in Bulgarian]', 19 March. Available online: http://pik.bg/кой-бе-павел-чернев-от-бодигард-до-депутат-от-политик-до-кино актьор-и-риалити-герой-news504562.html (accessed 30 September 2018).

Poddubny, E. (2014), 'In Simferopol, Unknown Persons in Masks Attacked the Operator VGTRK [in Russian]', Vesti.ru, 1 March. Available online: https://www.vesti.ru/doc.html?id=1336405# (accessed 30 September 2018).

Polish Modern Records Archive (1968), 'Transcript of the Warsaw Meeting, July 14-15, 1968 (Excerpts)'. In: J. Navratil (ed), *The Prague Spring 1968: A National Security Archive Documents Reader*, 212–33, Budapest: Central European University Press.

Politonline.ru (2014), 'Anti-Russian Media Outlets Have Been Put in Their Place [in Russian]', 31 March. Available online: http://www.politonline.ru/comments/15966.html (accessed 30 September 2018).

Polityuk, P. and J. Finkle (2014), 'Ukraine Says Communications Hit, MPs Phones Blocked', *Reuters*, 4 March. Available online: https://www.reuters.com/article/us-ukraine-crisis-cybersecurity-idUSBREA231R220140304 (accessed 30 September 2018).

Pomerantsev, P. (2014), 'The Hidden Author of Putinism: How Vladislav Surkov Invented the New Russia', *The Atlantic*, 7 November. Available online: https://www.theatlantic.com/international/archive/2014/11/hidden-author-putinism-russia-vladislav-surkov/382489/ (accessed 30 September 2018).

Ponsard, L. (2007), *Russia: NATO, and Cooperative Security: Bridging the Gap*, London: Routledge.

Popenker, M. and N. R. Jenzen-Jones (2015), *The Russian GM-94 Grenade Launcher*, ARES. Available online: http://armamentresearch.com/wp-content/uploads/2015/09/The-Russian-GM-94-Grenade-Launcher.pdf (accessed 30 September 2018).

Powell, B. (2014), 'Pushing the Kremlin Line', *Newsweek*. Available online: http://
www.newsweek.com/2014/05/30/pushing-kremlin-line-251587.html (accessed
30 September 2018), 20 May.

Pravda (1968), 'Defence of Socialism Is the Highest Internationalist Duty, 22 August
1968'. In: *Committee on Government Operations, Subcommittee on National Security
International Operations: Czechoslovakia and the Brezhnev Doctrine*, 14, Washington,
DC: U.S. Government Printing Office.

Pravda (1989), 'Soviet and Warsaw Pact Apologies to Czechoslovakia, December
5, 1989'. In: J. Navratil (ed), *The Prague Spring 1968: A National Security Archive
Documents Reader*, 576, Budapest: Central European University Press.

Prchlík, V. (1968), 'Press Conference with Lt General Václav Prchlík, July 15, 1968'. In:
J. Navratil (ed), *The Prague Spring 1968: A National Security Archive Documents
Reader*, 239–42, Budapest: Central European University Press.

Price, M. E., A. Richter, and P. K. Yu, (eds) (2002), *Russian Media Law and Policy in the
Yeltsin Decade: Essays and Documents*, London: Kluwer Law International.

Prosecutor General's Office of Ukraine (2016a), 'The Court Has Granted Permission
to the Chief Military Prosecutor's Office to Conduct a Preliminary Investigation
Concerning the Special Adviser to the President of the Russian Federation [in
Ukrainian]', 3 October. Available online: http://www.gp.gov.ua/ua/news.html?_m
=publications&_c=view&_t=rec&id=193680 (accessed 30 September 2018).

Prosecutor General's Office of Ukraine (2016b), 'The Evidence of Complicity of the
RF Authorities in Waging an Aggressive War against Ukraine [in Russian and
Ukrainian]', 31 August. Available online: https://www.youtube.com/watch?v=l6K
1_vHrJPU (accessed 30 September 2018).

Prozumenshchikov, M. (2010), 'Politburo Decision-Making on the Czechoslovak Crisis
in 1968'. In: G. Bischof, S. Karner, and P. Ruggenthaler (eds), *The Prague Spring and the
Warsaw Pact Invasion of Czechoslovakia in 1968*, 103–44, Plymouth: Lexington Books.

Puddington, A. (2000), *Broadcasting Freedom: The Cold War Triumph of Radio Free
Europe and Radio Liberty*, Lexington: University Press of Kentucky.

Putin, V. (2014), 'Vladimir Putin Meets with Members of the Valdai Discussion Club;
Transcript of the Final Plenary Session', *Valdai Club*, 25 October. Available online:
http://valdaiclub.com/a/highlights/vladimir_putin_meets_with_members_of_the
_valdai_discussion_club_transcript_of_the_final_plenary_sess/?sphrase_id=36613
(accessed 30 September 2018).

Puzenkin, I. V. and V. V. Mikhailov (2015), 'Informational and Psychological
Capabilities in State Defence', *Voennaia mysl'*, *(Military Thought)*, 24(3): 1–6.

QHA (2014), 'State Broadcaster 'Crimea' Seized by Armed Men [in Russian]',
28 February. Available online: http://qha.com.ua/ru/politika/gtrk-krim-zahvatili-
voorujennie-lyudi/133688/ (accessed 30 September 2018).

Quotidiano Piemontese (2012), 'The City Council of Rivarolo Canevese Dissolved by
the Government Because of the Mafia [in Italian]', 22 May. Available online: http://

www.quotidianopiemontese.it/2012/05/22/il-comune-di-rivarolo-canavese-sciolto-dal-governo-per-mafia/# (accessed 30 September 2018).

Rachwald, A. R. (2011), 'A "Reset" of NATO–Russia Relations: Real or Imaginary?', *European Security*, 20(1): 117–26.

Radio Svoboda (2014), 'In Crimea, the Largest Private TV Channel Has Been Cut from the Airwaves [in Ukrainian]', 3 March. Available online: http://www.radiosvoboda.org/a/25283527.html (accessed 30 September 2018).

Razumkov Centre (2011), 'Attitudes of the Residents of Crimea on Likely Threats and to Questions of Significant Conflict Potentials [in Ukrainian]', *Natsional'na Bezpeka i Oborona*, 4–5(122–123): 27–39.

RBK (2016), 'Glazyev and Zatulin Responded to the Publication of Wiretaps of Their Conversations about Crimea [in Russian]', 23 August. Available online: http://www.rbc.ru/rbcfreenews/57bc262b9a7947855ab36bf2 (accessed 30 September 2018).

RBTH (2013), 'Gifts of the Magi Relic from Mount Athos to Visit Russia, Belarus and Ukraine', 13 December. Available online: https://www.rbth.com/news/2013/12/13/gifts_of_the_magi_relic_from_mount_athos_to_visit_russia_belarus_and_ukr_32572.html (accessed 30 September 2018).

Reid, C. (1987), 'Reflexive Control in Soviet Military Planning'. In: B. D. Dailey and P. J. Parker (eds), *Soviet Strategic Deception*, 293–311, Lexington: D.C. Heath and Company.

Renz, B. and H. Smith (eds) (2016), *Russia and Hybrid Warfare: Going Beyond the Label*, Helsinki: Kikimora Publications.

Reuters (2014), 'Russia Seizes Ukraine's Last Crimean Ship', 26 March. Available online: https://www.reuters.com/article/us-ukraine-crisis-minesweeper/russia-seizes-ukraines-last-crimean-ship-idUSBREA2P17H20140326 (accessed 30 September 2018).

RFE/RL (2013), 'Ukraine's Cabinet Backs EU Association Agreement', 18 September. Available online: https://www.rferl.org/a/ukraine-eu-membership-association-agreement-government-approve/25109791.html (accessed 30 September 2018).

RFE/RL (2014a), 'Russian TV Announces Right Sector Leader Led Ukraine Polls', 26 May. Available online: https://www.rferl.org/a/russian-tv-announces-right-sector-leader-yarosh-led-ukraine-polls/25398882.html (accessed 30 September 2018).

RFE/RL (2014b), '"There Was No Quorum": Crimean Lawmaker Calls Vote to Join Russia Flawed', 6 March. Available online: https://www.rferl.org/a/interview-crimea-vote-ukraine-russia/25288146.html (accessed 30 September 2018).

RFE/RL (2019), Kazakh President Nazarbaev Abruptly Resigns, but Will Retain Key Roles', 19 March. Available online: https://www.rferl.org/a/kazakh-president-nursultan-nazarbaev-says-he-is-resigning-/29830123.html (accessed 18 April 2021).

RIA Novosti (2014a), 'In Simferopol, Farewell to a Soldier and a Cossack Killed by a Sniper [in Russian]', 22 March. Available online: https://ria.ru/incidents/20140322/1000633150.html (accessed 30 September 2018).

RIA Novosti (2014b), '"Polite People" as a New Image of the Russian Army [in Russian]', 16 May. Available online: https://ria.ru/defense_safety/20140516/1007988002.html (accessed 30 September 2018).

RIA Novosti (2015), 'Admiral Kasatonov: Sevastopol Is Preparing for the Basing of 'Mistral' [in Russian]', 13 March. Available online: https://ria.ru/interview/20150313 /1052368767.html (accessed 30 September 2018).

RIA Novosti (2016), 'Analyst: The Conflict with Chaly Has Affected the Rating of Sergey Fedorovich Menyailo [in Russian]', 22 March. Available online: https://ria.ru/politics /20160322/1394497390.html (accessed 30 September 2018).

Richelson, J. T. (1986), *Sword and Shield: The Soviet Intelligence and Security Apparatus*, Cambridge: Ballinger.

Richter, A. (1995), 'The Russian Press After Perestroika'. In: M. E. Price, A. Richter, and P. K. Yu. (eds), *Russian Media Law and Policy in the Yeltsin Decade: Essays and Documents*, 5–17, London: Kluwer Law International.

Robbins, K. G. (1969), 'Konrad Henlein, the Sudeten Question and British Foreign Policy', *The Historical Journal*, 12(4): 674–97.

Roberts, K. (2014), 'Détente 2.0? The Meaning of Russia's "Reset" with the United States', *International Studies Perspectives*, 15(1): 1–18.

Robinson, N., ed. (2000), *Institutions and Political Change in Russia*, London: Macmillan.

Ronzheimer, P. and A. Thelen (2014), 'The Mission Is Secret! Bild Speaks with Russian Soldiers in Crimea [in German]', *Bild*, 3 March. Available online: http://www.bild.de/ politik/ausland/ukraine/geheim-soldaten-lueften-ihr-geheimnis-34916520.bild.html (accessed 30 September 2018).

Rose, C. (1988), *The Soviet Propaganda Network: A Directory of Organisations Serving Soviet Foreign Policy*, London: Pinter Publishers.

Roskomnadzor (2014), 'Roskomnadzor Warns 'Novaya Gazeta' [in Russian]', 10 October. Available online: http://rkn.gov.ru/news/rsoc/news27494.htm (accessed 30 September 2018).

Rossiskaya Gazeta (2012), 'Federal Law of November 12, 2012 N 190-FZ "On Amendments to the Criminal Code of the Russian Federation and Article 151 of the Code of Criminal Procedure of the Russian Federation" [in Russian]', 14 November. Available online: https://rg.ru/2012/11/14/izmenenia-dok.html (accessed 30 September 2018).

Rossolinski-Liebe, G. (2014), *Stepan Bandera: The Life and Afterlife of a Ukrainian Nationalist*, Stuttgart: ibidem-Verlag.

Rozhin, B. (2014), 'Polite People Have Captured Two Airports in Crimea [in Russian]', LiveJournal: 'Colonel Cassad', 28 February. Available online: https://colonelcassad.liv ejournal.com/1440088.html (accessed 30 September 2018).

RSFR (1934), 'Article 58, Criminal Code of the RSFSR'. Available online: http://www .cyberussr.com/rus/uk58-e.html#58-4 (accessed 30 September 2018).

RT (2014a), 'Crimean "Referendum at Gunpoint" Is a Myth – Intl Observers', 16 March. Available online: https://on.rt.com/sv7518.

RT (2014b), 'Putin Defends Annexation of Crimea: America Took Texas From Mexico [Online Video]', YouTube, 18 December. Available online: https://www.youtube.com/watch?v=Wyp7zzPPqQs (accessed 30 September 2018).

RT (2014c), 'Radio Voice of America Stops Airing in Russia Due to Contract Expiration', 9 April. Available online: https://on.rt.com/2khp2j (accessed 30 September 2018).

RT America (2014), 'US Shows Hypocrisy in Telling Russia to Stay Out of Ukraine [Video Online]', YouTube, 3 March. Available online: https://youtu.be/uRH6oagF-yY (accessed 30 September 2018).

Rubin, B. R. (1995), *The Fragmentation of Afghanistan: State Formation and Collapse in the International System*, London: Yale University Press.

Ruggenthaler, P. and H. Knoll (2010), 'The Moscow "Negotiations": "Normalizing Relations" between the Soviet Leadership and the Czechoslovak Delegation after the Invasion'. In: G. Bischof, S. Karner, and P. Ruggenthaler (eds), *The Prague Spring and the Warsaw Pact Invasion of Czechoslovakia in 1968*, 165–89, Plymouth: Lexington Books.

Russian Federation (1991), 'Law of the Russian Federation No. 2124-1 of December 27, 1991, on Mass Media (as Amended up to Federal Law No. 239-FZ of July 29, 2017)', 27 December. Available online: http://www.wipo.int/wipolex/en/details.jsp?id=17777 (accessed 30 September 2018).

Russian General Staff (2002), *The Soviet-Afghan War: How a Superpower Fought and Lost*, L. W. Grau and M. A. Gress (eds), Lawrence: University Press of Kansas.

Russian Unity (2009), 'Manifesto of the All-Crimean Social and Political Movement 'Russian UNITY' [in Russian]', 15 December. Available online: http://old.kozenko.ru/node/175 (accessed 30 September 2018).

Russian Unity (2015), 'Stages of the Formation of the Russian Community of Crimea [in Russian]', *Portal Russkogo Naroda Kryma*. Available online: http://www.ruscrimea.ru/cms/?go=mon&in=view&id=18 (accessed 30 September 2018).

Rustov, K. and F. Bedřich (1968), 'Testimony by the Chief of the CzPA General Staff and the Head of the CzPA's Main Political Directorate at a Meeting of the Presidium of the National Assembly, August 26, 1968 (Excerpts)'. In: J. Navratil (ed), *The Prague Spring 1968: A National Security Archive Documents Reader*, 484–6, Budapest: Central European University Press.

Ryumin, A. (2014), 'Photograph of Soldier in Crimea', TASS, March. Available online: https://gdb.rferl.org/EAA6907C-71A2-42C8-BFA1-38C60711416F.jpg (accessed 15 April 2021).

Sakwa, R. (1990), *Gorbachev and His Reforms, 1985–1990*, New York: Prentice-Hall.

Sakwa, R. (1998), *Soviet Politics in Perspective*, London: Routledge.

Sakwa, R. (2016), *Frontline Ukraine: Crisis in the Borderlands*, New York: I.B Tauris & Co Ltd.

Salem, H. (2014), 'Ukraine: Night Wolves and Unidentified Military Men Seize Key Crimea Sites', *The Guardian*, 28 February. Available online: https://www.theguard ian.com/world/2014/feb/28/ukraine-night-wolves-military-seize-crimea (accessed 30 September 2018).

Sallnow, J. (1989), *Reform in the Soviet Union: Glasnost and the Future*, London: Pinter.

Sanders, K. (2014), 'The United States Spent $5 Billion on Ukraine Anti-Government Riots', *Politifact*, 19 March. Available online: http://www.politifact.com/punditfact/ statements/2014/mar/19/facebook-posts/united-states-spent-5-billion-ukraine-anti -governm/ (accessed 30 September 2018).

Sanovich, S. (2017), 'Computational Propaganda in Russia: The Origins of Digital Misinformation', *Computational Propaganda Research Project, Oxford Internet Institute, University of Oxford*, June. Available online: http://comprop.oii.ox.ac.uk/ wp-content/uploads/sites/89/2017/06/Comprop-Russia.pdf (accessed 30 September 2018).

Sasse, G. (2007), *The Crimea Question: Identity, Transition, and Conflict*, Cambridge: Harvard University Press.

Schoepflin, G. (1993), *Politics in Eastern Europe 1945–1992*, Oxford: Blackwell.

Schudel, M. (2005), 'John Barron Dies; Espionage Reporter', *Washington Post*. Available online: http://www.washingtonpost.com/wp-dyn/articles/A18766-2005Mar8.html (accessed 30 September 2018), 9 March.

Schultz, R. H. (1988), *The Soviet Union and Revolutionary Warfare: Principles, Practices and Regional Comparisons*, Stanford: Hoover Institution Press.

Schultz, R. H. and R. Godson (1984), *Dezinformatsia: Active Measures in Soviet Strategy*, Oxford: Pergamon Press.

Scott, H. F. and W. F. Scott (1988), *Soviet Military Doctrine: Continuity, Formulation, and Dissemination*, London: Westview Press.

Secrieru, S. (2014), 'Turmoil in Ukraine: A Sign of the Coming Disorder in the Post-Soviet World?', *The Polish Quarterly of International Affairs*, 23(4): 75–98.

Sejna, J. (1982), *We Will Bury You*, London: Sidgwick & Jackson.

Sevastopol City Council (2014), 'The Session of the City Council Approved the Results of the General Referendum on March 16, 2014 [in Russian]', 17 March. Available online: https://web.archive.org/web/20140722133147/http://sevsovet.com.ua/index. php/2011-06-30-23-44-03/12395-na-sessii-gorodskogo-soveta-utverzhdeny-rezul taty-obshchekrymskogo-referenduma-16-marta-2014-goda (accessed 30 September 2018).

Sharkov, D. (2016), 'Pro-Russian Crimeans Unveil Monument to Annexation Troops', *Newsweek*, 16 March. Available online: http://www.newsweek.com/pro-russian-crim eans-unveil-monument-annexation-troops-437522 (accessed 30 September 2018).

Shekhovtsov, A. (2015a), 'Far-Right Election Observation Monitors in the Service of the Kremlin's Foreign Policy'. In: M. Laruelle (ed), *Eurasianism and the European Far Right*, 223–43, London: Lexington Books.

Shekhovtsov, A. (2015b), 'Russia and Front National: Following the Money', *The Interpreter*, 3 May. Available online: http://www.interpretermag.com/russia-and-fron t-national-following-the-money/ (accessed 30 September 2018).

Shekhovtsov, A. and A. Umland (2014), 'Ukraine's Radical Right', *Journal of Democracy*, 25(3): 58–63.

Shevardnadze, E. (1991), *A New World Vision: Soviet Foreign Policy in the Age of Perestroika*, New York: Pantheon.

Shevchenko, V. (2015), 'Crimean Tatar Media "Silenced by Russia"', *BBC*, 1 April. Available online: http://www.bbc.co.uk/news/world-europe-32145218 (accessed 30 September 2018).

Shevel, O. (2011), 'Russian Nation-Building from Yel'tsin to Medvedev: Ethnic, Civic or Purposefully Ambiguous?', *Europe–Asia Studies*, 63(2): 179–202.

Shinar, C. (2015), 'The Russian Oligarchs, from Yeltsin to Putin', *European Review*, 23(4): 583–96.

Shkandrij, M. (2015), *Ukrainian Nationalism: Politics, Ideology, and Literature, 1929– 1956*, New Haven: Yale University Press.

Shmatko, N. (1968), 'Occupation Order from the Soviet Commander in Trencin [Colonel Nikolai Shmatko], August 21, 1968'. In: J. Navratil (ed), *The Prague Spring 1968: A National Security Archive Documents Reader*, 450–1, Budapest: Central European University Press.

Shoigu, S. (2015), 'Speech at the National Centre of the Management of Defence, Awards Ceremony of a Professional Journalist Contest Media Ace 2015 [in Russian]', 27 March. Available online: https://www.youtube.com/watch?v=HAjPd6ZpQVk (accessed 30 September 2018).

Shuster, S. (2013), 'Western Diplomats Are Going to Disappoint Ukraine's Protesters', *Time*, 13 December. Available online: http://world.time.com/2013/12/13/western -diplomats-are-going-to-dissapoint-ukraines-protesters/ (accessed 30 September 2018).

Shuster, S. (2014), 'Exclusive: Leader of Far-Right Ukrainian Militant Group Talks Revolution With TIME', *Time*, 4 February. Available online: http://time.com/4493/ ukraine-dmitri-yarosh-kiev/ (accessed 30 September 2018).

Sidorov, D. and A. Orlov (2015), 'How TV Propaganda Is Done: Four Testimonies [in Russian]', *Colta.ru*, 6 August. Available online: https://www.colta.ru/articles/society /8163 (accessed 30 September 2018).

Simes, D. K. (2014), 'An Interview with Sergey Glazyev', *The National Interest*, 24 March. Available online: http://nationalinterest.org/commentary/interview-sergey-glazyev-1 0106 (accessed 30 September 2018).

Sindelar, D. (2014), 'The 20 Russian News Outlets You Need to Read Before They Get the Ax', *RFE/RL*, 1 April. Available online: https://www.rferl.org/a/twenty-russian -news-outlets-you-need-to-read-before-they-get-the-axe/25317371.html (accessed 30 September 2018).

Skilling, H. G. (1989), *Samizdat and an Independent Society in Central and East*, London: Macmillan.

Skilling, H. G. (1998), 'Foreword'. In: J. Navratil (ed), *The Prague Spring 1968: A National Security Archive Documents Reader*, xvii–xxi, Budapest: Central European University Press.

Skrypnyk, O. and T. Pechonchyk, (eds) (2016), *The Peninsula of Fear: Chronicle of Occupation and Violation of Human Rights in Crimea*, 2nd edn, Kyiv: KBC.

Slobodyan, E. (2017), 'What Does the Service for the Protection of the Constitutional System of the FSB Do? [in Russian]', *Argumenty i Fakty*, 29 August. Available online: http://www.aif.ru/dontknows/actual/chem_zanimaetsya_sluzhba_zashchity_konst itucionnogo_stroya_fsb (accessed 30 September 2018).

Slusser, R. M., J. Barron, and E. P. Dutton (1974), 'Book Reviews: KGB: The Secret Work of Soviet Agents by John Barron', *Russian Review*, 33(4): 437–8.

Smrkovský, J. (1968), 'Josef Smrkovský's Address to the People after His Return from Moscow, August 29, 1968 (Excerpts)'. In: J. Navratil (ed), *The Prague Spring 1968: A National Security Archive Documents Reader*, 489, Budapest: Central European University Press.

Snegovaya, M. (2015), *Putin's Information Warfare in Ukraine*, Washington, DC: Institute for the Study of War.

Sokolovskiy, V. D. (1975), *Soviet Military Strategy*, 3rd edn, H. F. Scott (ed), New York: Crane, Russak & Company, Inc.

Soldatov, A. and I. Borogan (2010), *The New Nobility: The Restoration of Russia's Security State and the Enduring Legacy of the KGB*, New York: PublicAffairs.

Solomina, O. N., V. F. Vdovin, and A. M. Vershik (2014), 'On Inadmissible Statements by the Presenter of "*Vesti Nedeli*" D. Kiselyov [in Russian]', *Society of Scientific Workers*, 18 March. Available online: http://onr-russia.ru/content/сбор-подписей-о-недопустимых-высказываниях-ведущего-вестей-недели-дкиселева-закрыт (accessed 30 September 2018).

Soshnikov, A. (2015), 'The Capital of Political Trolling [in Russian]', *MR7.ru*, 11 March. Available online: http://mr7.ru/articles/112478/.

Soviet Ministry of Defence (1965), *Dictionary of Basic Military Terms: A Soviet View [English Translation]*, Washington, DC: U.S. Government Printing Office.

Spillius, A. (2013), 'Russia Threatens Ukraine with Bankruptcy over Plans to Sign EU Agreement', *The Telegraph*, 22 September. Available online: https://www.telegraph.co.uk/news/worldnews/europe/ukraine/10327027/Russia-threatens-Ukraine-with-bankruptcy-over-plans-to-sign-EU-agreement.html (accessed 30 September 2018).

Sputnik News (2015), 'Lavrov Says Obama's Remarks Prove Direct US Involvement in Ukraine Coup', 2 February. Available online: https://sputniknews.com/politics/20 1502021017657515/ (accessed 30 September 2018).

Stent, A. E. (2014), *The Limits of Partnership: U. S.-Russian Relations in the Twenty-First Century*, Oxford: Princeton University Press.

Steury, D. P. (2010), 'Strategic Warning: The CIA and the Soviet Invasion of Czechoslovakia'. In: G. Bischof, S. Karner, and P. Ruggenthaler (eds), *The Prague Spring and the Warsaw Pact Invasion of Czechoslovakia in 1968*, 237–48, Plymouth: Lexington Books.

Stevens, J. A. and H. S. Marsh (1982), 'Surprise and Deception in Soviet Military Thought: Part II', *Military Review*, 62(7): 24–35.

StopFake.org (2014a), 'FAKE: Right Sector (Pravyu Sector) Appeal to Doku Umarov', 3 March. Available online: http://www.stopfake.org/en/right-sector-pravyu-sector-a ppeal-to-doku-umarov-fake/ (accessed 30 September 2018).

StopFake.org (2014b), 'Russian Blogger Exposed the Staging of a Shootout in Simferopol [in Russian]', 3 March. Available online: http://www.stopfake.org/r ossijskij-bloger-razoblachil-instsenirovku-perestrelki-v-simferopole/ (accessed 30 September 2018).

Sukhov, O. (2014), 'The Media War Behind the Ukraine Crisis', *Moscow Times*, 11 March. Available online: https://themoscowtimes.com/news/the-media-war-behi nd-the-ukraine-crisis-32837 (accessed 30 September 2018).

Sullivan, C. J. (2021), 'The Crumbling Kyrgyz Republic', *Asian Affairs*, 52(1): 44–61.

Suvorov, V. (1984a), *Inside Soviet Military Intelligence*, New York: Macmillan.

Suvorov, V. (1984b), *Inside the Soviet Army*, London: Grafton Books.

Suvorov, V. (1989), *Spetsnaz: The Story of the Soviet SAS*, London: Grafton Books.

Tandstad, B., S. A. Pettersen, and A. Svalbjørg (2014), 'NRK Journalists Deprived of Their Equipment in Crimea [in Norwegian]', *NRK*, 11 March. Available online: https://www.nrk.no/urix/nrk-journalister-anholdt-pa-krim-1.11598449 (accessed 30 September 2018).

TASS (1968), 'Statement, 21 Aug 1968'. In: *Committee on Government Operations, Subcommittee on National Security International Operations: Czechoslovakia and the Brezhnev Doctrine*, 13, Washington, DC: U.S. Government Printing Office.

TASS (1979), 'Telegraph Agency of the Soviet Union Announcement, Attachment to CPSU Politburo Protocol #177', *History and Public Policy Program Digital Archive*, TsKhSD, F. 89, P. 14, D. 32, translated for CWIHP by Gary Goldberg, 27 December. Available online: http://digitalarchive.wilsoncenter.org/document/111548 (accessed 30 September 2018).

TASS (2014), 'Malyshev: 96.77% of Crimean Voters Voted for Reunification with Russia [in Russian]', 3 March. Available online: http://tass.ru/mezhdunarodnaya-panorama/ 1052196 (accessed 30 September 2018).

TASS (2017a), 'Kremlin Got No Letter from Yanukovich Requesting to Send Forces to Ukraine', 16 March. Available online: http://tass.com/politics/935880 (accessed 30 September 2018).

TASS (2017b), 'Putin: Russia Does Not Threaten Sweden, but If It Joins NATO, Moscow Will React to the Threat [in Russian]', 1 June. Available online: http://tass.ru/pmef-2017/articles/4302587 (accessed 30 September 2018).

TASS (2017c), 'Yanukovych Said That He Did Not Ask to Introduce Troops of the Russian Federation to Ukraine in 2014 [in Russian]', 22 February. Available online: http://tass.ru/mezhdunarodnaya-panorama/4044021 (accessed 30 September 2018).

Taylor, A. (2014), 'Russia on Iraq: "We Told You So"', *Washington Post*, 12 June. Available online: https://www.washingtonpost.com/news/worldviews/wp/2014/06/12/russia-on-iraq-we-told-you-so/ (accessed 30 September 2018).

Telekritika (2014a), 'Digital Broadcasts of Ukrainian Channels Turned off in Crimea [in Ukrainian]', 10 March. Available online: http://ru.telekritika.ua/rinok/2014-03-10/91305 (accessed 30 September 2018).

Telekritika (2014b), 'In Crimea, Virtually All Ukrainian TV Channels Are Cut off [in Ukrainian]', 9 March. Available online: http://ru.telekritika.ua/kontekst/2014-03-09/91284 (accessed 30 September 2018).

Telekritika (2014c), 'Unidentified Persons, Who Have Captured the Crimean Parliament, Throw Stun Grenades at Journalists [in Ukrainian]', 27 February. Available online: http://ru.telekritika.ua/profesija/2014-02-27/90866 (accessed 30 September 2018).

Television Industry Committee (2013), 'Top Channels'. Available online: http://tampanel.com.ua/en/rubrics/canals/ (accessed 30 September 2018).

Teper, Y. (2016), 'Official Russian Identity Discourse in Light of the Annexation of Crimea: National or Imperial?', *Post-Soviet Affairs*, 32(4): 378–96.

The Guardian (2014), 'Am I a Terrorist?, Are We Causing a Threat to the Black Sea Fleet?', 3 March. Available online: https://www.theguardian.com/world/2014/mar/03/ukraine-recording-russia-officers-marines (accessed 30 September 2018).

The Institute of Mass Information (2014), 'Crimea: Pressure on Journalists', 15 March. Available online: http://imi.org.ua/en/articles/crimea-pressure-on-journalists-updated/ (accessed 30 September 2018).

The Ukrainian Helsinki Human Rights Union (2017), *26 February Criminal Case: Reconstruction and Legal Analysis of the Events of 26 February 2014 outside the Building of the Supreme Council of the Autonomous Republic of Crimea in Simferopol*. Available online: https://helsinki.org.ua/wp-content/uploads/2017/03/sprava_eng_print.pdf (accessed 30 September 2018).

Thomas, T. L. (2004), 'Russia's Reflexive Control Theory and the Military', *Journal of Slavic Military Studies*, 17(2): 237–56.

Thomas, T. L. (2015), *Russia Military Strategy: Impacting 21st Century Reform and Geopolitics*, Ft Leavenworth, KS: Foreign Military Studies Office.

Tigrid, P. (1971), *Why Dubček Fell*, London: Macdonald and Co.

Toal, G. (2017), *Near Abroad: Putin, the West and the Contest over Ukraine and the Caucasus*, Oxford: Oxford University Press.

Traynor, I. and O. Grytsenko (2013), 'Ukraine Suspends Talks on EU Trade Pact as Putin Wins Tug of War', *The Guardian*, 21 November. Available online: https://www.theguardian.com/world/2013/nov/21/ukraine-suspends-preparations-eu-trade-pact (accessed 30 September 2018).

Trenin, D. (2011), *Post-Imperium: A Eurasian Story*, Washington, DC: Carnegie Endowment for International Peace.

Trulock III, N. (1987), 'The Role of Deception in Soviet Military Planning'. In: B. D. Dailey and P. J. Parker (eds), *Soviet Strategic Deception*, 275–92, Lexington: D.C. Heath and Company.

TSN (2015), 'Putin vs. Ukraine: How the Kremlin Organized Propaganda [in Russian]'. Available online: https://tsn.ua/special-projects/liar/ (accessed 30 September 2018).

Tsygankov, A. (2015), '"Hybrid War": Political Discourse and the International Practice', *Vestnik Moskovskogo Universiteta*, 18(4): 253–8.

Tsygankov, A. (2016), *Russia's Foreign Policy: Change and Continuity in National Identity*, 4th edn, London: Rowman & Littlefield.

Turovsky, D. (2015), '"A Man Who's Seen Society's Black Underbelly": Meduza Meets "Anonymous International"', *Meduza*, 2 February. Available online: https://meduza.io/en/feature/2015/02/02/a-man-who-s-seen-society-s-black-underbelly (accessed 30 September 2018).

Ukrainian Central Election Commission (2004), 'Election of the President of Ukraine, Second Round: Results of Voting in the Regions of Ukraine [in Ukrainian]', 26 December. Available online: http://www.cvk.gov.ua/pls/vp2004/wp0011 (accessed 30 September 2018).

Ukrainian Central Election Commission (2012a), 'Election of People's Deputies of Ukraine: Nationwide Multi-Mandate Constituency [in Ukrainian]', 28 October. Available online: http://www.cvk.gov.ua/pls/vnd2012/wp300?PT001F01=900 (accessed 30 September 2018).

Ukrainian Central Election Commission (2012b), 'Election of People's Deputies of Ukraine: Single-Mandate Constituencies [in Ukrainian]', 28 October. Available online: http://www.cvk.gov.ua/pls/vnd2012/wp039?PT001F01=900 (accessed 30 September 2018).

Ukrainian Central Election Commission (2012c), 'Election of People's Deputies of Ukraine October 28, 2012: Single-Mandate Constituency No. 1 [in Ukrainian]', 28 October. Available online: http://www.cvk.gov.ua/pls/vnd2012/WP040?PT001F01=900&pf7331=1 (accessed 30 September 2018).

Ukrainian Central Election Commission (2012d), 'Election of People's Deputies of Ukraine October 28, 2012: Single-Mandate Constituency No. 10 [in Ukrainian]', 28 October. Available online: http://www.cvk.gov.ua/pls/vnd2012/WP040?PT001F01=900&pf7331=10 (accessed 30 September 2018).

Ukrainian Central Election Commission (2012e), 'Election of People's Deputies of Ukraine October 28, 2012: Single-Mandate Constituency No. 2 [in Ukrainian]', 28 October. Available online: http://www.cvk.gov.ua/pls/vnd2012/WP040?PT001F01=900&pf7331=2 (accessed 30 September 2018).

Ukrainian Central Election Commission (2012f), 'Election of People's Deputies of Ukraine October 28, 2012: Single-Mandate Constituency No. 6 [in Ukrainian]',

28 October. Available online: http://www.cvk.gov.ua/pls/vnd2012/WP040?PT001F01 =900&pf7331=6 (accessed 30 September 2018).

Ukrainian Central Election Commission (2014a), 'Extraordinary Election of People's Deputies of Ukraine, Single-Mandate Constituency: Dnipropetrovsk Oblast [in Ukrainian]', 26 October. Available online: http://www.cvk.gov.ua/pls/vnd2014/W P040?PT001F01=910&pf7331=39 (accessed 30 September 2018).

Ukrainian Central Election Commission (2014b), 'On the Results of the Elections of the People's Deputies of Ukraine: Nationwide Multi-Mandate Constituency [in Ukrainian]', 26 October. Available online: http://www.cvk.gov.ua/info/protokol _bmvo_ndu_26102014.pdf (accessed 30 September 2018).

Ukrainian Central Election Commission (2014c), 'On the Results on the Election of the President of Ukraine [in Ukrainian]', 2 June. Available online: http://www.cvk.gov.ua /info/protokol_cvk_25052014.pdf (accessed 30 September 2018).

Ukrainskaya Pravda (2014), 'The Court Banned the Activities of the Russian Bloc Party in Ukraine [in Ukrainian]', 13 May. Available online: https://www.pravda.com.ua/ news/2014/05/13/7025250/ (accessed 30 September 2018).

UKRINFORM (2012), 'Zatulin Griping Again at Ukrainian Sovereignty over Crimea, Sevastopol', 26 October. Available online: https://www.ukrinform.net/rubric-polytic s/1413212-zatulin_griping_again_at_ukrainian_sovereignty_over_crimea_sevast opol_291633.html (accessed 30 September 2018).

Ulc, O. (1979), 'Czechoslovakia'. In: T. Rakowska-Harmstone and A. Gyorgy (eds), *Communism in Eastern Europe*, 100–20, London: Indiana University Press.

UN Security Council (2014a), 'S/2014/146: Letter Dated 3 March 2014 from the Permanent Representative of the Russian Federation to the United Nations Addressed to the Secretary-General', 3 March. Available online: https://documents -dds-ny.un.org/doc/UNDOC/GEN/N14/252/61/PDF/N1425261.pdf?OpenElement (accessed 30 September 2018).

UN Security Council (2014b), 'S/PV.7125: Meeting Record of the 7,125th Meeting', 3 March. Available online: http://www.un.org/en/ga/search/view:doc.asp?symbol=S/PV.7125.

UNIAN (2008), 'Ukraine Forbids Moscow Mayor to Enter Its Territory', 12 May. Available online: https://www.unian.info/world/115240-ukraine-forbids-moscow-m ayor-to-enter-its-territory.html (accessed 30 September 2018).

UNIAN (2014a), 'The Command of the Military Unit in Yevpatoria Was Given an Ultimatum [in Russian]', 10 March. Available online: https://www.unian.net/pol itics/894749-komandovaniyu-voinskoy-chasti-v-evpatorii-peredali-ultimatum.html (accessed 30 September 2018).

UNIAN (2014b), 'The State Television and Radio Company "Crimea" Is Working under the Supervision of Armed Men [in Ukrainian]'. Available online: https://www.unian .ua/politics/891322-derjavna-teleradiokompaniya-krim-pratsyue-pid-naglyadom-oz broenih-lyudey.html (accessed 30 September 2018).

Urban, M. (1990), *War in Afghanistan*, 2nd edn, London: Macmillan.

US-Ukraine Foundation (2013), 'Victoria Nuland: Ukrainians Deserve Respect From Their Government [Video Online]', YouTube, 13 December. Available online: https://www.youtube.com/watch?v=2y0y-JUsPTU (accessed 30 September 2018).

USAID (2012), 'USAID/Russia Program, Closure, and Opportunities for Reengaging' [Internal Report].

USSR and ČSSR (1968), 'Protocol on Negotiations between Delegations from the Union of Soviet Socialist Republics and the Czechoslovak Socialist Republic'. In: J. Navratil (ed), *The Prague Spring 1968: A National Security Archive Documents Reader*, 477–80, Budapest: Central European University Press.

Ustinov, D. (1979), 'Soviet Defense Minister Ustinov, Report to CPSU CC on Mission to Afghanistan of Deputy Defense Minister Army-Gen. I. G. Pavlovskii', *History and Public Policy Program Digital Archive*, APRF, f. 3, op. 82, d. 149, ll. 120-122; translated by Mark Kramer; first publication in Russian in Novaya i Noveishaya Istoriia 3 (May–June) 1996, pp. 91–9 (document on 97–98), intro. by G.N. Sevastiono, 5 November. Available online: http://digitalarchive.wilsoncenter.org/document/111578 (accessed 30 September 2018).

Valenta, J. (1980), 'From Prague to Kabul: The Soviet Style of Invasion', *International Security*, 5(2): 114–41.

Valenta, J. (1991), *Soviet Intervention in Czechoslovakia, 1968: Anatomy of a Decision*, London: The Johns Hopkins University Press.

Vandiver, J. (2014), 'SACEUR: Allies Must Prepare for Russia "Hybrid War"', *Stars And Stripes*, 4 September. Available online: https://www.stripes.com/news/saceur-allies-must-prepare-for-russia-hybrid-war-1.301464 (accessed 30 September 2018).

Vaughan, D. (2012), 'Words, Words, Words...The United Nations and the 1968 Invasion', *Radio Praha*, 3 March. Available online: http://www.radio.cz/en/section/archives/words-words-words-the-united-nations-and-the-1968-invasion-1 (accessed 30 September 2018).

Verkhovna Rada of Crimea (2014a), 'No, 1630-6/14, The Decree of the Verkhovna Rada of the Autonomous Republic of Crimea "on Organization of the Republican (Local) Referendum on Improvement of the Status and Powers of the Autonomous Republic of Crimea" [in Russian]', 27 February. Available online: http://crimea.gov.ru/act/11610 (accessed 30 September 2018).

Verkhovna Rada of Crimea (2014b), 'No, 1691-6/14, The Resolution of the Presidium of the Verkhovna Rada of the Autonomous Republic of Crimea "on Certain Issues Involving the Organization and Holding of the Republican (Local) Referendum in the Autonomous Republic of Crimea" [in Russian]', 3 March. Available online: http://crimea.gov.ru/act/11607 (accessed 30 September 2018).

Verkhovna Rada of Crimea (2014c), 'No, 1702-6/14, The Decree of the Verkhovna Rada of the Autonomous Republic of Crimea "on Holding a General Referendum" [in Russian]', 6 March. Available online: http://crimea.gov.ru/act/11689 (accessed 30 September 2018).

Verkhovna Rada of Crimea (2014d), 'No, 1745-6/14, Resolution of the State Council of the Republic of Crimea on the Independence of Crimea [in Russian]', 17 March. Available online: http://crimea.gov.ru/act/11748 (accessed 30 September 2018).

Verkhovna Rada of Ukraine (2014), 'No, 757–18, On the Abolition of the President of Ukraine from the Exercise of Constitutional Powers and the Appointment of Extraordinary Elections of the President of Ukraine [in Ukrainian]', 22 February. Available online: http://zakon1.rada.gov.ua/laws/show/757-18 (accessed 30 September 2018).

Voice of Russia (2014), 'Russian Media Should Increase Presence in Crimea, Sevastopol - Slutsky', 25 February. Available online: https://www.sott.net/article/274558-Russian-media-should-increase-presence-in-Crimea-including-Sevastopol (accessed 30 September 2018). Original article removed from https://sputniknews.com/voiceofrussia/news/2014_02_25/Russian-media-should-increase-presence-in-Crimea-Sevastopol-Slut.

Vzglyad Business Newspaper (2014), 'Ex-Head of the SBU: Crimean Rada Was Captured by Military Special Forces from Sevastopol [in Russian]', 27 February. Available online: https://vz.ru/news/2014/2/27/674726.html (accessed 30 September 2018).

Walker, D. (2003), 'Just How Intelligent?', *The Guardian*, 18 February. Available online: https://www.theguardian.com/education/2003/feb/18/highereducation.academicexperts (accessed 30 September 2018).

Walker, S. (2014a), 'Crimean Leaders Get Red Carpet Treatment on Visit to Moscow', *The Guardian*. Available online: https://www.theguardian.com/world/2014/mar/07/crimean-leaders-red-carpet-visit-moscow (accessed 30 September 2018), 7 March.

Walker, S. (2014b), 'Russian Propaganda and Ukrainian Rumour Fuel Anger and Hate in Crimea', *The Guardian*, 4 March. Available online: https://www.theguardian.com/world/2014/mar/04/russian-propaganda-ukrainian-rumours-anger-hate-crimea (accessed 30 September 2018).

Walker, S. (2014c), 'Russians Pressure Ukrainian Forces in Crimea to Disarm', *The Guardian*, 3 March. Available online: https://www.theguardian.com/world/2014/mar/03/russia-pressure-ukraine-troops-disarm (accessed 30 September 2018).

Walker, S. (2015a), 'Putin Admits Russian Military Presence in Ukraine for First Time', *The Guardian*, 17 December. Available online: https://www.theguardian.com/world/2015/dec/17/vladimir-putin-admits-russian-military-presence-ukraine (accessed 30 September 2018).

Walker, S. (2015b), 'Salutin' Putin: Inside a Russian Troll House', *The Guardian*, 2 April. Available online: https://www.theguardian.com/world/2015/apr/02/putin-kremlin-inside-russian-troll-house (accessed 30 September 2018).

'Warsaw Letter' (1968), 'Letter from Five Communist and Worker Parties, united in Warsaw, to the Central Committee of the Communist Party of Czechoslovakia, 15 July 1968'. In: P. Windsor and A. Roberts (eds), *Czechoslovakia 1968: Reform, Repression and Resistance*, 150–6, Chatto & Windus.

Webster, A., C. Andrew, and V. Mitrokhin (2000), 'The Sword and the Shield: The Mitrokhin Archive and the Secret History of the KGB', by Christopher Andrew and Vasili Mitrokhin (Book Review)', *The Journal of Military History*, 64(3): 914–5.

'White Book' (1968), *On Events in Czechoslovakia: Facts, Documents, Press Reports and Eye-Witness Accounts*, Moscow: Press Group of Soviet Journalists.

Wilson, A. (2014), *Ukraine Crisis: What It Means for the West*, London: Yale University Press.

Windsor, P. and A. Roberts (1969), *Czechoslovakia 1968: Reform, Repression and Resistance*, London: Chatto & Windus.

Wise, D. and T. B. Ross (1964), *The Invisible Government*, London: Jonathan Cape.

Withnall, A. (2014), 'Crimeans Overwhelmingly Vote to Leave Ukraine and Join Russia in Contentious Referendum', *Independent*, 16 March. Available online: https://www.independent.co.uk/news/world/europe/crimea-referendum-how-why-and-where-next-for-soon-to-be-divided-ukraine-9195310.html (accessed 30 September 2018).

Yaffa, J. (2014), 'Dmitry Kiselev Is Redefining the Art of Russian Propaganda', *The New Republic*, 2 July. Available online: https://newrepublic.com/article/118438/dmitry-kiselev-putins-favorite-tv-host-russias-top-propogandist (accessed 30 September 2018).

Yakubovsky, I. (1968), 'Letter from Marshal Yakubovskii to Alexander Dubček on Gen. Prchlik's News Conference, July 18, 1968'. In: J. Navratil (ed), *The Prague Spring 1968: A National Security Archive Documents Reader*, 259–60, Budapest: Central European University Press.

Yanukovych, V. (2011), 'Decree No. 1209/2011: Declaration of the President of Ukraine: On the Celebration in Ukraine of Some Memorable Dates and Professional Holidays [in Ukrainian]', 30 December. Available online: http://zakon1.rada.gov.ua/laws/show/1209/2011 (accessed 30 September 2018).

Yost, D. S. (1987), 'The Soviet Campaign against INF in West Germany'. In: B. D. Dailey and P. J. Parker (eds), *Soviet Strategic Deception*, 343–74, Lexington: D.C. Heath and Company.

Zaks, D. (2016), 'Ukraine Bans Books Promoting Russia', *Agence France-Presse*, 30 December. Available online: http://m.france24.com/en/20161230-ukraine-bans-books-promoting-russia?ref=tw:i (accessed 30 September 2018).

Zannettou, S., T. Caulfield, E. De Cristofaro, M. Sirivianos, G. Stringhini, and J. Blackburn (2018), 'Disinformation Warfare: Understanding State-Sponsored Trolls on Twitter and Their Influence on the Web', *arXiv*. Available online: https://arxiv.org/pdf/1801.09288.pdf (accessed 30 September 2018).

Zawodny, J. K. (1971), *Death in the Forest: The Story of the Katyn Forest Massacre*, London: Macmillan.

Zevelev, I. (2008), 'Russia's Policy Toward Compatriots in the Former Soviet Union', *Russia in Global Affairs*, 6(1): 49–62.

Zhegulyov, I. (2017), '"If Patrushev Did Not Support us, There Would Be an American Fleet in Crimea": Interview with the Crimean Politician Leonid Grach about How the FSB Has Been Helping Crimea since 2005 [in Russian]', *Meduza*, 21 March. Available online: https://meduza.io/feature/2017/03/21/esli-by-nas-ne-podderzhal -patrushev-v-krymu-stoyal-by-amerikanskiy-flot (accessed 30 September 2018).

Zhegulyov, I., A. Sivtsova, and J. Skibitskaya (2017), '"No one Believed That This Was Serious": How Crimea Was Annexed: The Spring of 2014 through the Eyes of Moscow, Kyiv, and Sevastopol [in Russian]', *Meduza*, 21 March. Available online: https://meduza.io/feature/2017/03/21/nikto-ne-veril-chto-eto-vseriez (accessed 30 September 2018).

Zickel, R. E. and E. K. Keefe (1991), *Soviet Union: A Country Study*, Washington, DC: Federal Research Division, Library of Congress.

Zolotov, S. (1994), 'General Semyon Zolotov's Account of the Final Military Preparations for the Invasion, April 1994'. In: J. Navratil (ed), *The Prague Spring 1968: A National Security Archive Documents Reader*, 373–5, Budapest: Central European University Press.

Zygar, M. (2016), *All the Kremlin's Men: Inside the Court of Vladimir Putin*, New York: PublicAffairs.

# Index

Note: some page numbers are in **bold** to annotate the most significant content of the specific entry.

www.ingramcontent.com/pod-product-compliance
Lightning Source LLC
Chambersburg PA
CBHW050409280326
41932CB00013BA/1797